ॐ

Sri Ramaaya Namaha!

Sri Hanuman Lila

Veera Hanuman

ॐ

Sri Ramaaya Namaha!

Sri Hanuman Lila

as given in the

Valmiki Ramayana

Ramacharitamanas of Tulsidas

and

various other sources

interpreted in English and embellished by oral tradition

Narrated by

Vanamali

Aryan Books International

New Delhi

ॐ

Sri Ganeshaya Namaha!

Salutations to Lord Ganesha
May He remove all obstacles on the path of this scribe
And enable her to write this book on

The Lilas of Sri Hanuman

SRI HANUMAN LILA

ISBN: 978-81-7305-387-0

First Published: 2010

Reprinted: 2021

Published by:
Aryan Books International
Pooja Apartments, 4B, Ansari Road, New Delhi-110 002 (India)
Tel.: 23287589, 23255799; Fax: 91-11-23270385
E-mail: aryanbooks@gmail.com
www.aryanbooks.com

Printed in India

DEDICATION

ॐ *Anjaneyaaya vidmahe,*
Vayu putraaya deemahi,
Tanno Hanumath prachodayaath

I contemplate on Anjaneya,
I meditate on the son of Vayu,
May He give me enlightenment.

Dedicated to my dearest friend,
NILLI
One of the greatest *bhaktas* of
Sri Hanuman

Benediction given by
Sri Baba Neeb Karori ji Maharaj
as conveyed by his chief disciple
Sri Siddhi Ma

Hanuman sama nahi bad bhagi
Nahi kou Ram charana anuraagi,
Pavana tanaya bala pavana samana
Buddhi viveka vijnana nidhana
Kavana so kaaj katthin jaga maahi
Jo nahi chod tatha thum pahi.

There is no one as fortunate as Hanuman,
No one who has as much love for the feet of Rama,
Son of the wind god, who equals him (the wind) in strength,
Repository of intelligence, discrimination and understanding
O Dear One! If you shower your grace
No task is difficult in this world.

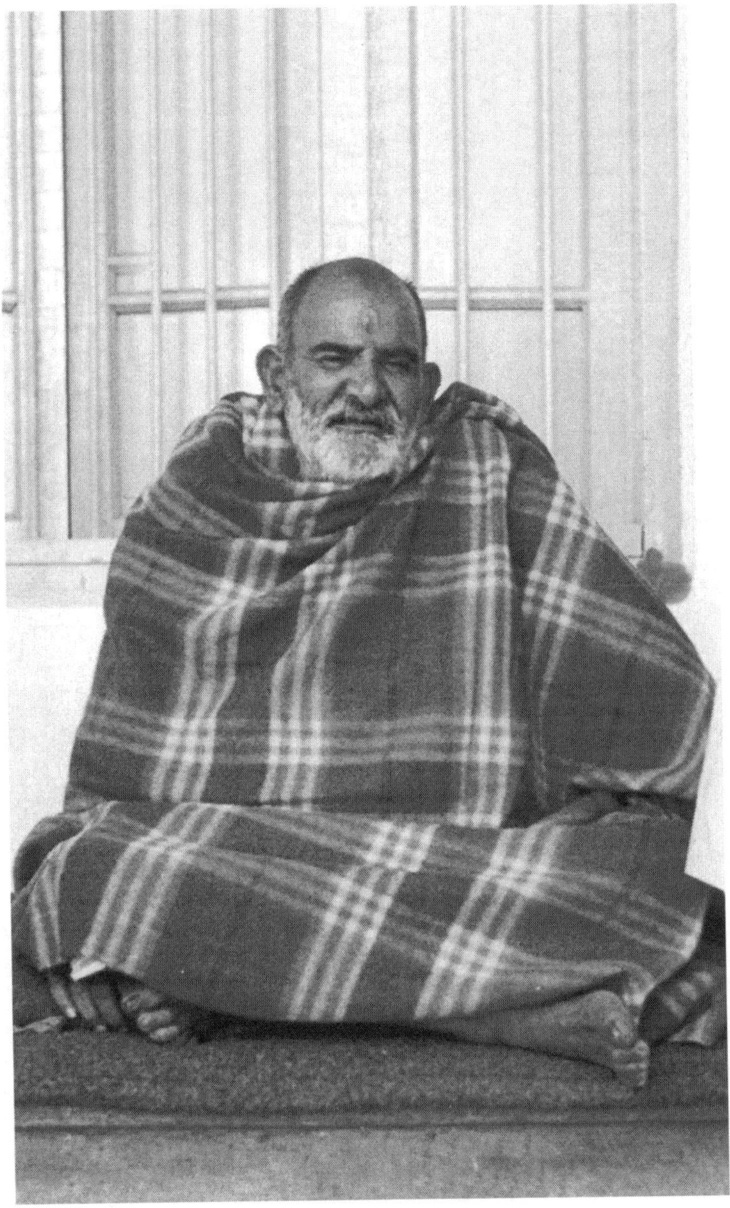

Sri Baba Neeb Karori ji Maharaj

Baby Hanuman jumping for the sun

FOREWORD

By Sri Krishna Das

Sri Vanamali is a rare being. She is a Devotee of the Lord in all His forms who has been blessed with the compassionate desire to communicate His *Lilas* to the English-speaking world.

In the West, there are many new devotees who desperately need access to the revered ancient scriptures of India. Sri Vanamali comes as the cool breeze of grace, filling the hearts and minds of the thirsty devotees with the stories of the Lord's joyous play. In this book on Sri Hanumanji, as in all her other books, she gives us access to the inner worlds of our beloved's *Lilas*.

Sri Hanuman is the greatest of all devotees of the Lord. He is a *Jnani* in the fullest sense of the word. He has merged with his Lord, Sri Rama, in his own being and He sees his Lord in everything and everyone. His realization of the truth does not end there.

As Sri Krishna says,

"And when he sees me in all and sees all in me,
Then I never leave him and he never leaves me.
And he, who in this oneness of love
Loves me in whatever he sees,
Wherever this man may live,
In truth, he lives in me..."

– *Bhagavad Gita*, Chap 6

This is the key to understanding Sri Hanuman. He serves Sri Rama in all beings, by removing the obstacles for those beings who realize the truth in themselves. He sees that, in fact, there ARE no "other" beings, but only Rama. Motivated by love born of truth, which manifests as compassion for beings who believe themselves to be separate, he works tirelessly to remove their suffering.

Another mystery of Sri Hanuman was revealed by Sri Neeb Karori Baba to one of his great old devotees, Dada Mukerjee. A small party of devotees had, along with Maharaj ji, climbed to the top of Hanuman Dhara in Chitrakut. They rested by the spring that comes out from the rock at the top of the hill.

Maharaj ji said to Dada, "This is where Hanumanji came to become calm and to cool himself off, after burning Lanka."

Then after a few seconds he said very softly, as if to himself, "Of course Hanumanji was always at peace."

No matter what he was doing, burning Lanka, destroying the demons, singing Ram Naam or serving the devotees, Hanuman was never outside of Sri Rama's being.

May the Lord be gracious to all.

Sri Krishna Das

Sri Krishna Das is well known to all lovers of music especially in the West, for his numerous recordings of heart-rending devotional lyrics. Even though he is known as Krishna Das, yet he can as easily be called Ram Das or Hanuman Das since he is a devotee of both.

ॐ *Sri Hanumathe Namaha!*

CONTENTS

ॐ *Sri Hanumathe Namaha!*

ॐ

Sri Ramachandraaya Namaha!

INTRODUCTION

Yatra Yatra Raghunatha Kirtanam
Tatra Tatra Krita Mastaka anjalim
Bashpavari pari purna lochanam
Marutim nammascha raakshasantakam

"I bow to Maruti, the destroyer of demons,
Who stands with folded palms,
In all the places where the glories of Sri Rama are sung,
Shedding tears of devotion and joy".

— *Ramacharitamanas* by Tulsidas

Modern science may claim to have traced the mechanical laws of evolution, but the ancient *rishis* of India discovered the spiritual laws of eternal values called the Sanatana Dharma, which is the divine thrust inherent in the human psyche enabling it to attain greater heights of evolution. This is the great contribution which India has made to the world, inspiring in the human being a strong desire to shake off his humanity and bring to light the divinity which is inherent in him. This is what is known as enlightenment. Age after age, India has produced enlightened souls who have continuously renewed and refreshed this great *dharma* – the Sanatana Dharma – and made it available to the whole of the human race. The sages desired that our country should progress not just materially but through a constant inner renewal of the cosmic law of righteousness, guided by the wisdom embedded in our heritage.

The epics and *Puranas* of this country are thus store-houses of wisdom and by reading them our spiritual evolution will be hastened. Truth is a matter of direct realization by our own individual efforts but the sages gave us many different methods to attain it. These saints were great souls who were far above the vulgar herd who want to see their names emblazoned in anything they write. Thus, their names remain a mystery. We can only show our gratitude to them by trying out the many paths which they gave us.

We find a great urge on their part to share their vital experiences with all those who have the hearts to understand. This experience is the highest available to the human psyche and is known as *brahmajnana*. The knowledge by itself is not the aim of life. It has to become a living understanding in which we actually experience the unity of life underlying all living beings – in fact the entire cosmos. From this is born an overwhelming love for the whole of creation and a burning desire to see human beings free themselves from the strangling limitations and illusions of this waking world of our common experience. This type of love is totally unselfish, characterized by a deep desire to share their most cherished possession with the whole of humanity and thus we see that the *rishis* tried every means in their power to enable our tragic and ignorant human race to acquire that which was the sumum bonum of human life. Every human being is nothing but a reflection of the divine. Involvement in the illusions of this world alone stops us from realizing our divinity.

The Upanishads give the path of *jnana* or wisdom, which is difficult for many to follow. They appeal only to those who are already endowed with great spiritual leanings. However, it is said that the Absolute, timeless and formless presence descends to this mortal plane in the form of the gods for certain mysterious purposes of its own. This is known as the *lila* or the play of god. The sages who came after the age of the Upanishads were determined to cater to the majority of human beings who might not have any spiritual leanings at all. They resorted to bringing the truths of the Upanishads forcibly to the minds of the average human being in the form of stories. The sage Vyasa, the author of the *Mahabharata*, was the greatest of these story-tellers. He said that if we listen carefully to a story, we will never be the same again. The story, especially if it has some spiritual basis will worm its way into our heart and break down our self-constructed barriers to the divine. Even if we start off by reading these stories as an entertainment, one or two of them will eventually slip through our defences and explode the hard shell of our humanity and disclose our divinity. These stories have an inexhaustible vitality in them so that people are never tired of listening to them. They can be listened to or read and pondered over and thus they are capable of promoting in the listener a deep understanding of life, death and destiny. Every story had implicit in it a moral value, which is likened to the fragrance of a beautiful flower. The *rishis* taught us that all forms are the letters of a form-word-power alphabet of a language which can help us to realise our spiritual reality, which is unconditioned by any form and yet is the supreme source of all forms.

The path of *bhakti*, or devotion to a personal God, is forcibly brought out in the Puranas or epics which tell stories of the great incarnations and of all the numerous gods of the Hindu pantheon, which are completely in tune with the truth of life. The culture of the Indian sub-continent was developed in the climate of these great epics. Every child was taught to emulate the classic examples given therein and thus bring his or her own life to perfection. The Hindu mind had no difficulty in picturing the Supreme in the form of an animal or of a human. Thus, we find Ganesha, depicted as a human being with the head of an elephant, and Hanuman, who was a monkey.

Hanuman is one of the most beloved figures in the Hindu pantheon of gods called Kimpurushas, who are actually animals but behave like humans. He is the symbol of utter and selfless devotion to his supreme deity, Sri Rama, the seventh incarnation of Lord Vishnu, scion of the solar race, the pinnacle of human perfection. Hanuman's entire strength came through the repetition of the name of Rama, the greatest *mantra* for this age of Kali, which if chanted with devotion, is said to give liberation from the coils of mortal life. Every temple of Rama has a figure of Hanuman seated at his feet bowing to him. Wherever the *Ramayana* is read or recited, a seat is left vacant for Hanuman since it is believed that he is always present at the reading of the story of his beloved master.

The Sanskrit word *sadhana* means any method by following which the aspirant or *sadhaka* can establish contact with the inner realms of her being. One of the easiest methods of *sadhana* is known as *japa* or the repetition of the name of God in whatever form we picture him. Hanuman gives us the picture of an animal that attained perfection solely by chanting the name of Rama, his personal deity and of utter and complete self-abnegation of his interests to that of his Lord and god – Rama. Humility and selflessness is a measure of our knowledge. The more we know the more we realise how little we know and how little we can do by ourselves.

According to legend, Hanuman is the son of the Wind God. Air sustains all living beings. One can exist without food, spend days without water; but it is impossible to exist even for a short time without air. Air is life. Therefore, Hanuman is also called 'Pranadeva' or the God of breath or Life.

Vaishnavites believe that the Wind God Vayu underwent three incarnations to help Lord Vishnu. As Hanuman he helped Rama, as Bhima he assisted Krishna, and as Madhavacharya (1197-76) he founded the Vaishnava sect known as Dwaita.

In Hindu symbolism, a monkey signifies the human mind, which is ever restless and never still. This monkey-mind happens to be the only thing over which man can have absolute control. We cannot control the world around us but we can control and tame our mind by ardent discipline. We cannot choose our life but we can choose the way we respond to it. Truly Hanuman is symbolic of the perfect mind, and embodies the highest potential it can achieve. He is the true picture of the *sthitha prajna* (man of steady intellect) of the *Bhagavad-Gita* and had perfect control over his mind. The name "Hanuman" gives a clue to his character. It is a combination of two Sanskrit words, *hanan* (annihilation) and *man* (mind), thus indicating one who has conquered his ego. According to *yoga*, the body is only an extension of the mind. Hence, Hanuman who had perfect mastery over his mind had the most developed body. He is Bajrangabali (one whose body is like a thunderbolt and whose movements are like lightning). He is so strong that he can lift mountains, and so agile that he can leap across the sea.

His strength is proverbial and thus he is the patron of physical culture. His image is enshrined in gymnasiums all over India and wrestlers worship him before commencing their practice. The *yogasana* known as *surya namaskara*, or salutation to the Sun God, is a mixture of all the main *yogic* postures combined with devotion and was composed by Hanuman in honour of his celestial *guru,* Surya.

Vayu, his divine father taught him *pranayama* or the science of breath control, which he in turn taught to human beings.

The scriptures refer to several events where Hanuman exhibited his power over the celestial bodies including the sun and Saturn. Hence, he gained power over the *navagrahas* or nine planets. These planets are Ravi, the sun; Soma, the moon; Mangal, Mars; Buddha, Mercury; Brihaspati, Jupiter; Shukra, Venus; Shani, Saturn; the bodiless, Rahu and the headless, Ketu. Their alignment in the astrological chart of a human being is supposed to decide a person's destiny. In many of his images, Hanuman is shown trampling a woman and holding her by her braid. This woman embodies 'Panavati' or baneful astrological influences.

Sorcerers manipulate cosmic powers to invoke malevolent spirits. People normally call upon Hanuman to protect them from such people. When Ravana invoked two such sorcerers, Ahiravana and Mahiravana, Hanuman turned the tables on them and invoked the power of Kaali to subdue them. Many Tantrics worship him because he has many *siddhis*, or supernatural powers, like the ability to change his size and ability to fly, etc. which he gained through his strict *brahmacharya* and *tapasya.* Thus, he displays the dual characteristics of *bhakti* and *shakti.* Either one or the other is given prominence in his shrines.

He is also the patron of Ayurvedic healers since he played a vital role in saving Lakshmana's life by bringing the magic herb from the Himalayas. He later saved Shatrugna's life also with the same herb.

As a warrior, Hanuman has no parallel. He uses both strength and guile to overpower the enemy. This was exhibited many times during the war with Ravana. He used both brawn and brain to achieve victory over his enemies.

Hanuman was also a master diplomat. He knew how to speak sweetly and make others see his side of the matter, without the use of force. Hence, he was Sugriva's spokesman when he approached Rama to find out his intentions. Again Sugriva sent him to try and subdue Lakshmana's anger at his own lapse. Rama sent him as his envoy to Sita twice, once to Lanka carrying his signet ring and again to fetch her after the war. He also sent him to Bharata to find out his intentions before setting foot in Ayodhya. All those who came into contact with him were most impressed by his diplomatic method of talking and beguiling ways.

Hanuman impressed both Rama and Ravana by his mastery over language, his grammar and his ability to use the right word at the right moment and in the right context as well as his perfect diction.

Strangely enough, he was also a great musician. He had been blessed by the goddess Saraswati and was thus able to play on the lute and sing lyrics in praise of Rama. He was the first to sing *bhajans,* songs of adoration and *kirtans,* songs of praise. His music was an outpouring of his great love for his beloved master and hence had the power to even melt rocks.

Hanuman is the perfect example of a student. He was totally focused, hard-working, humble, determined and brilliant. He flew to the solar orb in his determination to have the Sun God, Surya as his *guru.* However, he never flaunted his brilliance and scholarship but always sat at the feet of Rama – ever the humble servant.

Hanuman had no desire for name or fame. He preferred to live in mountains and caves. He practised total *brahmacharya*, which was very strange in a simian. Even when he lived in the palace he lived like a hermit, never indulging his senses. This was what gave him so much spiritual power.

He was also a *hatha yogi* since he practised *yogasanas* and *pranayama.* He was a *laya yogi* since he knew how to control his mind with *mantras* and *yantras.* Thus he acquired many *siddhis* or supernatural powers.

If *yoga* is the ability to control one's mind, then Hanuman was the perfect *yogi*, having perfect mastery over his senses, achieved through a disciplined lifestyle and by a strict adherence to celibacy, *brahmacharya* and selfless devotion, *bhakti*. He controlled his mind through absolute faith in the divine. Every event in his life was a gift from his master to be accepted without question. His life is a classic example to be followed by all devotees of God in any form. He shows us how a devotee should spend his or her life so as to reach the Supreme. He symbolises the pinnacle of *bhakti* and Hindus consider him to be the eleventh *avatara* of Rudra or Lord Shiva. Once it is said that Narada asked Brahma who he considered to be the greatest devotee of Vishnu. No doubt the sage was hoping that his name would be suggested. However, Brahma directed him to Prahlada, the king of *asuras* for whose sake Vishnu had taken a special *avatara* as Narasimha (the man-lion). Prahlada, with his characteristic humility, told him to go to Hanuman who he thought to be the greatest devotee of Vishnu since he chanted the name of Rama constantly.

Hanuman was a perfect *karma yogi* since he performed his actions with detachment, dedicating everything to Rama, his God. He was totally free from any desire for personal aggrandizement. In the whole of the *Ramayana* there is no incident in which he did anything for himself. All his feats were for the sake of others. When he described the war to his mother, she chided him for not killing Ravana and rescuing Sita by himself for that would have made him more famous than Rama. Hanuman replied that his life was not given to him to gain fame for himself but for serving Rama. His utter selflessness comes into great prominence when he saw how dejected Valmiki was by his work and without hesitation threw his own immortal classic into the sea.

Hanuman spent his entire life in the service of others. First he served Sugriva, then Rama. He personifies *bhakti* through *dasya bhava* or the attitude of the servant. This type of devotion is the perfect instrument to destroy the ego. He performed his duties humbly and modestly and with great devotion. He chose not to marry and have a family of his own so that he could devote himself entirely to the service of others. He never exceeded his orders even when he was capable of doing so. For instance, he could easily have killed Ravana and conquered Lanka on his own, as his mother said, but he refrained from doing so since he wanted to be the true servant and obey his master's orders.

He is one of the seven *chiranjeevis* (those who live till the end of this cycle of creation). He is noted for his mighty intellect and is supposed to be the only scholar who knows all the nine *vyakaranas* (explanation of the Vedas). He is supposed to have learnt the Vedas from the sun god himself. He is the wisest of the wise, strongest of the strong and bravest of the brave. He had the power to assume any form he liked, to swell his body to the size of a mountain as well as to reduce it to a thumb nail. One who meditates on him will attain power, strength, glory, prosperity and success in life.

Hanuman is the epitome of wisdom, continence, *bhakti* (devotion/faith), valour, righteousness and strength. His indispensable role in reuniting Rama with Sita is likened by some to that of a teacher helping an individual soul realise the divine.

Rama himself describes Hanuman thus: "Heroism, cleverness, strength, firmness, sagacity, prudence and prowess and power have taken up their abode in Hanuman."

Sage Agastya endorsed this view when he said to Rama, "What you say regarding Hanuman is true O Raghava! None else is equal to him in might, speed or intelligence."

He is easily reachable – just by chanting the *mantra* 'Rama'. Conversely, it is also held that the easiest way to attain Lord Rama is to worship Hanuman.

He is worshipped on Saturdays and Tuesdays, which are associated with Shani and Mangal, Saturn and Mars. Both these planets are associated with death and war and known to disrupt human life by their malefic influence. His offerings are simple. *Sindoor* (red lead), *til* oil (sesame), husked black gram and garlands of a certain tree (calotropis gigantica), in the north and garlands of betel leaves in the south. In the south his idols are often pasted with butter, which strangely enough never melts even during the hottest summer. He is also adorned with garlands of rice and *dal* doughnuts (*vadas*).

The reason for the vermilion paste will be given in the chapters that follow. But esoterically speaking, red is the colour of strength and virility. *Til* oil is used by wrestlers and gymnastics to massage their body. Butter and *dal* are sources of protein and generate energy, stamina and muscle.

The two scriptures which are read by all Hanuman devotees are the 'Sundara Kanda' of the *Ramayana*, where he discovered Sita in Lanka and the forty verses of the *Hanuman Chalisa* by Tulsidas. Wherever the *Ramayana* is read, a special seat is always reserved for Hanuman since the belief is that he will always be present at such a reading.

What are his physical characteristics? Is he the black-faced *langur* or the red-faced *bandar*? Sometimes he is described as a golden monkey with a red face. His face is supposed to have turned black when he wiped his face with his tail after destroying Lanka.

His tail is arched upwards and is the symbol of strength, agility and virility. He wears earrings made of five metals, gold, silver, copper, iron and tin. He came to the world adorned with these. Normally he wears only a loin-cloth in the manner of wrestlers and body builders. His images usually show him saluting Rama or standing guard and displaying his strength as he holds the mountain in one hand and his mace in the other.

The *Hanuman Chalisa* declares categorically that there is no blessing that he cannot bestow. Sita granted him the power to bestow the eight *siddhis* and nine types of wealth on others. However, the greatest boon one can ask of Hanuman is the uplifting of the spiritual qualities that he himself is known for.

Having polished with the dust of my master's feet, the mirror of my heart,
I narrate the pure fame of Raghupati (Rama), which bestows life's four desires.
Considering myself to be devoid of intellectual merits,
I invoke Sri Hanuman, the son of the wind god.
Bestow on me strength, intelligence and knowledge.
Remove my bodily ailments and vicious qualities.
(And allow me to write this book)

— *Hanuman Chalisa* by Tulsidas

ॐ *Sri Hanumathe Namaha!*

Destruction of Lanka

ॐ

Mahaviraaya Namaha!

CHAPTER ONE

MAHAVIRA

Historic Hanuman

More man prabhu biswasa,
Ram the adhik Ram kar dasa.

My heart, Lord, holds this conviction,
Greater than Rama is Rama's servant.

— *Ramacharitamanas* by Tulsidas

Our first meeting with Hanuman, the Monkey God, is in the great epic of Valmiki, *The Ramayana.* It occupies a unique place in the Hindu culture because of the representation of Rama as the ideal man and Sita as the ideal woman. Of all the Puranas it is one which has gripped the imagination of not only the Indian continent but has had far-reaching effects on the cultures of many other countries of the Far East. In fact out of all the numerous Puranas of the Hindu literature, the *Ramayana* is perhaps the only one which is known to every Hindu. There are many saints in India who have attained self-realization only by the chanting of the name of Rama. Hanuman is the classic example of this. He was the chosen messenger, warrior and servant of Rama. He lived only to serve Rama. In fact he is such an integral part of the epic that the saying, "Where Rama's story is, there is Hanuman", is commonly repeated.

However, it is a matter of conjecture as to how this remarkable "being" suddenly appeared in Valmiki's epic without any previous precedent either in the Vedas or the Puranas. These extraordinary beings that came to help Rama in the *Ramayana*, made their first appearance in the book of Kishkinda, which is a part of the *Ramayana* and they were called *vanaras* or monkeys.

But most obviously these creatures were not ordinary monkeys. They had immense strength and some had supernatural powers and ability to change their forms at will. Though Valmiki's *rakshasas* have precursors in Vedic literature, his *vanaras* do not. Ravana had asked for the boon that he should not be killed by the gods or any other superhuman beings but he did not mention humans and monkeys in this list since he thought they were far below his consideration. So it appears that the *vanaras* were created to fulfil this particular necessity. Many of their leaders were begotten on *vanara* women by the gods in order to assist Rama.

Thus, Hanuman was a *vanara* or monkey. He represents a stage of evolution which is lower than the *chandala* or outcaste. He rose to the stature of a god through sheer strength of character and one-pointed devotion.

In the story, we see that Hanuman combines simian agility and energy with human sagacity, eloquence and devotion, and eventually emerges as one of the epic's most complex and fascinating characters. Was he a creation of Valmiki's genius or is there any mention of him in any of the other Puranas or in the Vedas which have always been held to be the storehouse of all lore concerning the gods.

Some people might say that he owed his greatness to the fact that he was the son of the Wind God. If this is true then in the *Mahabharata*, all the Pandavas who were sons of the gods should have been deified but none rose to Hanuman's heights. We consider the Pandavas to be mortals but no one thinks of Hanuman as a monkey or even a human. He is a god! Actually Valmiki does not give us a portrait of his early life which might have led to his deification. We are left to conjecture this from his perfected portrait. Hanuman himself explains the secret of attaining spiritual perfection.

na mantradikritastata,
Na cha naisarngiko mama,
Prabhava esha samanyo,
Yasya yasyachutho hridi.

Hanuman states very clearly that his greatness was due to his constant effort and not due to his inborn character, which was that of an ordinary monkey. *Brahmajnana* is possible for all. *Moksha*, or liberation, is everybody's birth right. In his case, Hanuman declares that his entire spiritual development was attained by single-pointed devotion to god. He who thinks of the Supreme constantly becomes Supreme. Absolute surrender to god is the secret of spiritual perfection. Spiritual transformation cannot be brought about by the mere chanting of *mantras* or offerings in temples and other superficial rituals. It is also not something which can be inherited. An infant, whether begotten by a god or a man, is still an animal. Evolution only aids its physical growth. Spiritual growth is impossible without effort. Learning and discipline must be there for this higher form of evolution. An imperfect body is made perfect when it is made into an instrument of god. Then even our shortcomings will turn into advantages. When the entire personality is moulded into the Supreme, even shortcomings become helpful. So we find that it was his monkey nature that helped him to cross the ocean, reach Lanka, discover Sita and bring the message back to Rama. He had no private enjoyments. The good results of his actions always went to other people. Thus, Valmiki portrayed a remarkable character in Hanuman, a model for all those who aspire for liberation.

In his technique of creating real, down to earth beings, capable of deification, Valmiki excels Vyasa. The characters of the *Ramayana* are a happy combination of historic realism and religious symbolism which appeals both to the religious-minded as well as to the secular. With the sole exception of Krishna none of the other characters in the *Mahabharata* lend themselves to deification. In order to prove his divinity, Vyasa allows Krishna to perform miracles and exhibit his cosmic form many times. However, Valmiki's portrait of Rama is in black and white with no embellishments. He never allowed his poetry to become the hand-maid of mysticism. Rama is the "Maryada Purusha", the perfect human being who by his exemplary adherence to the cosmic *dharma* became a god and Hanuman an ordinary simian who by dint of his unflinching devotion to Rama and extraordinary attention to his duty also became a god.

According to the Hindu point of view, there is no objective world 'out there'. The whole manifested world is a subjective phenomenon created by our own selves. We – as humans – have the unique ability to condition our minds. In other words, we have the power to change the way we perceive life. And by changing our perception of life, we have the power to change our world. When Hanuman entered Rama's life, he changed Rama's world. He transformed a crisis (the loss of Sita) into an opportunity to rid the world of Ravana. He transformed a victim into a hero.

Even though Hanuman does not appear in the Vedas, yet the two gods to whom he claims paternity are both from the Vedas – Vayu, the god of wind and Rudra, the god of destruction. Rudra is both one and many and is the prototype of the later *puranic* Shiva. Hanuman's association with Vayu is shown in his swiftness. In *Ayurveda*, or the *Vedic* science of healing, illness is declared to be the imbalance between the three humours of the body – *vata, pitta* and *kapha.* Of the three, *vata* or wind plays a crucial role in the upkeep of the body. Many diseases including rheumatism, gout, epilepsy and paralysis, are attributed to an excess of the wind factor. Hanuman is closely linked with this essential humour as depicted in the delineation of his characteristics later on. Some of his important names are Vayuputra, the son of Vayu and Vatamaja, born of Vayu. All bodily functions are controlled by the five winds or *vayus.* These are *prana, apana, vyana, samana* and *udana.* They take care of the different automatic functions of the body like, breathing, digestion, excretion and so on which we are not aware of. There is one figure of Hanuman with five heads, which correspond to these five winds. Thus, it is said that he is in charge of our involuntary functions and devotion to him will give us health.

Of course apart from this, the present day picture of Hanuman came only after the advent of the Valmiki *Ramayana*, so his debut to the Hindu pantheon of gods is very recent. He belongs to the category of the "second generation" deities. However, as his devotees point out, in most regions of India, there are far more shrines to Hanuman than to his exalted master. Actually out of the trinity of Brahma, Vishnu and Shiva, it is only Shiva whose offspring seem to have sprung into prominence and in some cases even usurped their parent's high status. The three well known sons of Shiva are Ganesha, Kartikeya and Dharma Shasta or Ayyappa. Hanuman also claims to be the son of Shiva. In fact, he is supposed to be the eleventh Rudra as has been mentioned before. Ravana was a great devotee of Shiva and thus it appears strange that his son could have become his enemy. The story which circumvents this particular dilemma has it that Ravana had once sacrificed his ten heads to Shiva but had not appeased the eleventh Rudra, no doubt because he didn't have another head!

All the sons of Shiva seem to have exerted a great fascination on the Indian mind. Ganesha is universally acclaimed and worshipped by all sects of Hindus. He has even gone across the seas and you see many devotees of Ganesha even in the West. Kartikeya used to be very popular in the north at one time but now his temples are almost exclusively found in the south and in Sri Lanka. He is known as Skanda, Murugan and Swaminathan in the south. Ayyappa is a fairly modern advent. His main temple used to be in Kerala alone, in the place known as the Shabari Hills. He is the god for this age of Kali since he is supposed to have been born from both Shiva and Vishnu and has both their powers. His popularity is increasing in many other states in the South and now you can even find temples in Delhi. Hanuman, on the other hand, used to be more popular in the North since he is almost the hero of Tulsidas' *Ramacharitamanas*, which is perused daily by most Hindi-speaking people. But now we find that his worship is becoming more and more popular in the South. At one time there were no separate temples to him but now some of his biggest temples are found in the South like the one at Namakkal and Suchindram. He displays a versatility that is greater than that of the other second-generation deities. Ganesha has certain specialities but he is not an embodiment of boundless mercy and self-sacrifice or ascetic rigour like Hanuman.

Hanuman has a leg in both camps – Shiva and Vishnu. His father is Shiva and he is the greatest devotee of Vishnu in his *avatara* as Rama. Therefore, he became very popular with both Shaivites and Vaishnavites. Like the other sons of Shiva, he has a plethora of birth stories. Ganesha, as has been mentioned, is universally adored in both North and South India and is perhaps the most popular. However, Hanuman seems to be a close competitor in the popularity polls, though possibly Ganesha has a slight advantage over him since it has been declared in the Puranas that he has to be worshipped first before starting any venture. Of course, Hanuman is a "specialist" to whom people turn for the specific services in which he excels. He is capable of warding off all evil portents and planetary disturbances so he is slowly creeping into prominence. In fact in Maharashtra, which is predominantly a state devoted to Ganesha worship, we find that Ganesha's shrines are outnumbered almost four-to-one by those to Maruti.

Many scholars are of the opinion that Hanuman worship is an outgrowth of *yaksha* worship. The *yakshas* are the guardians of the wealth of the earth and are known for their great strength and swiftness. Their figures were often carved outside temples and villages, as *dwarapalas* or guardians of the gate, and also as *kshetrapalas* or guardians of the villages. Now we find that Hanuman's figure has replaced the early figures of *yakshas* and is always found outside temples and villages. Kubera, the king of the *yakshas*, is always depicted with a mace *(gada)* in his hands and of course this is the only weapon that Hanuman carries. After Rama left the earth, Hanuman retired to the Himalayas to a place which was close to a lake owned by the *yakshas*, thus showing his affinity to them. This is where he met his half-brother – Bhima.

A number of monkey idols have been unearthed in the excavations of the Indus civilization, which might suppose the worship of such a Monkey God from those times but the clues are very slight. The *Rigveda* is supposed to contain numerous allusions to Hanuman in the *Samhitas* as well as in the *Satapatha Brahmanas.* Some of the hymns are supposed to contain allusion to the events of the *Ramayana.* There is one specific *Rigvedic* passage in which some mention is made to a tawny, yellow bull-monkey called Vrishakapi. Indra's wife complains that this monkey has usurped her husband's portion of the *Vedic* offerings. The name Vrishakapi occurs in the Purana known as Harivamsa, in which he is identified with the eleventh form of Rudra. This name is also found in the *Mahabharata* in the *Vishnu Sahasranama* (thousand names of Vishnu), as one of the names of Vishnu. Documentation on Hanuman worship dates back only to about a thousand years and thus he is considered to be only a baby as far as Indologists are concerned. In fact some of his most significant manifestations have appeared only in the last few centuries.

The largest amount of material on Hanuman is however found in the Puranas. Mention of him is made in the *Agni, Vishnu, Kurma, Garuda, Brahmavaivarta, Narasimha, Kalki* and *Bhagavata Puranas.* The *Agni Purana* gives instructions for constructing an image of Hanuman with two feet pressing down an *asura* and with two hands, one of which holds a *vajra* or thunderbolt. The elaborate story of Ahiravana, which is not found in Valmiki's epic, is found in the *Shiva Purana.* This Purana also includes another variant of his birth in which his mother is impregnated with Shiva's seed and thus makes him an *amsa* or portion of Shiva himself. In another passage he is called an *avatara* of Rudra. This link with Shiva is mentioned in the *Skanda, Padma* and *Naradiya Puranas.* The last Purana also offers a *mantra* for Hanuman's worship and describes the *yantra* to be used in lieu of an icon. It also says that water, which has been potentised with the use of this *mantra*, will have the power to drive away ghosts and cure maladies like fever and epilepsy. The text also identifies Hanuman as the founder of classical music and musicians are advised to pray to him in order to attain perfection. The Purana also describes Hanuman as the embodiment of the combined power of Shiva and Vishnu. However, it is a fact that the majority of the earlier Puranas do not mention Hanuman and even if they do, it is only in the context of retelling of the *Ramayana.*

Another important fact is that mention of him is made more in the Puranas which are considered as Shaivite or pertaining to Shiva. From early times his worship has been upheld by the Shaivite ascetics. Like Shiva he displays ascetic tendencies and does not care for fame or fortune. Shaivites believe that both Shiva and Vishnu descended on earth as Hanuman and Rama to destroy the unrighteous Ravana who had misused the power that Shiva had bestowed on him. Without Hanuman, Rama would have been helpless. It was Maruti who found Sita, built the bridge to Lanka, and helped Rama to fight and kill Ravana. However, he never claimed any honour for himself and always remained in Rama's shadow. His attributes are most appealing to *yogis.* He is physically immortal and is linked with many herbs, and has many *siddhis* which are sought after by *yogis.* He was also held to be a strict *brahmachari* (celibate). Due to his supernormal powers of strength and fleetness, he is also worshipped by wrestlers and athletes.

Vaishnavites or the devotees of Vishnu naturally worship Hanuman as the embodiment of *bhakti* to Rama, the sixth incarnation of Vishnu.

Shaktas or the worshippers of the Divine Mother, worship him since the *Devi* is supposed to have been very pleased with him when he helped to unite Sita with Rama. Kaali was very pleased with him when he killed the sorcerer Mahiravana and offered his blood to her. He is supposed to be the guardian of a woman's chastity since he never looked on any woman with lecherous eyes.

In the Tantric tradition, Hanuman is seen as the perfect *Tantric* who has acquired all the eight *siddhis* (supernormal powers). After he rescued Rama from the great sorcerer, Mahiravana, he is also considered to be a master of sorcery and also one who can protect people from black magic.

Vedanta views Hanuman as the personification of *bhakti*, which is instrumental in uniting Sita (the *jivatma)* with Rama (the *Paramatma*) after destroying Ravana (*ahamkara* or ego).

Tales of Hanuman reached South East Asia through the merchant ships sailing from the east coast of India. Hanuman and Rama are very popular characters in the art of ancient Cambodia, Vietnam, Thailand, Burma, Bali and Malaysia.

Buddhist monks took the story of the monkey-hero to China where he became extremely popular as the Golden Monkey. However, his character in these countries is totally different from the Indian Maruti. There he lived a hedonistic life and terrorised everyone, including the gods and was eventually tamed by the Buddha himself.

Hanuman is supposed to be the original narrator of the story of Rama. Not only was he was an eye witness to the events he describes, but his motive in telling the tale was purely to extol his Lord, Rama. However, tradition has it that this tale survives only in fragments, filtered through the lenses of human story-tellers like Valmiki, Kampan, Tulsidas and so on.

Victory to thee, O Hanuman,
Ocean of wisdom and virtue,
Hail to thee O Lord of monkeys,
Illuminator of the three worlds.

— *Hanuman Chalisa* by Tulsidas

ॐ *Sri Hanumathe Namaha!*

ॐ

Anjaneyaaya Namaha!

CHAPTER TWO

ANJANEYA

Son of Anjana

Hanuman Anjana sunu,
Vayuputro mahabala,
Rameshta Phalguna sakha,
Pingaksha amitavikrama,
Utathikarmanaschaiva,
Sita – shoka vinashaka,
Lakshmana prana datha cha,
Dasagreevashcha darpaha,
Evam dwadasa naamani,
Kapindrascha mahatmana,
Swapakale pateth nityam,
Yatrakale visheshata,
Tasya mrityu bhayam nasti,
Saravatra vijayi bhaveth

Hanuman, the son of Anjana,
The powerful son of Vayu,
Friend of Rama and Arjuna,
The fiery-eyed doer of impossible deeds,
The dispeller of Sita's sorrow,
Giver of Lakshmana's life,
Foe of the ten-headed one,
One who meditates on this noble monkey with the twelve names,
In the morning,
And at the time of travel,

Will never be frightened of death,
And will ever be victorious.

— *Hanumath dhyanam*

The ancient *rishis* placed great importance to the choice of names. There is a mysterious connection between the word and the meaning and this is the foundation of the *yoga* known as *japa* or continuous repetition of the names of any deity. Hanuman is supposed to have gained all his powers from the continuous *japa* of the *mantra,* "Rama". The name that he is most commonly known by is Hanuman and this has two meanings. One meaning is that he has (*man*) a prominent or disfigured jaw (*hanu*). This came about as a result of his jumping for the sun as a child. Another meaning is one whose ego or mind (*man)* has been destroyed (*han*). His second most common name is Anjaneya or the son of Anjana as well as Anjaniputra. He has many names derived from his father Vayu. He is known as Vayuputra, Pavanaputra and Pavakatmaja as well as Maruti, all of which denote him as the son of Vayu, the Vedic Wind God. He is also known as Kesarisutha, the son of Kesari and Kesarinandana, Kesari's darling, in which he is linked with his simian father, Kesari. Strangely enough, he has no names which link him with Rudra. When calling on him in order to protect, he is known as Bajrangabali, which is actually a corruption of the Sanskrit word, *vajra* (thunderbolt) and *anga* (limbs), denoting one whose limbs are as hard as the thunderbolt. Another popular name is Sankata Mochana or the one who releases us from sorrows and dangers. He is also known as Veera and Mahavira denoting his great powers. Sometimes he is referred to as Panchavaktra or the five-faced one and Kapiswara or lord of monkeys.

There are many stories connected with the birth of Hanuman. He claims paternity to two gods and a simian father also but there has never been any argument about his mother. Many of his epithets, as we have seen, identify him as the "son" of someone but he has only one name which connects him with his mother. She has always been accepted as Anjana.

Even though he is normally considered as the son of the Wind God – Vayu, one story goes that he was actually the son of Shiva and Parvati and was born from Shiva's seed.

Shiva was not present when Vishnu took on the form of Mohini in order to outwit the demons. When he heard of Mohini's exquisite beauty, he was eager to see her. He went to Vaikunta, the abode of Vishnu and asked him to reveal his form to him. When he saw Mohini's world-enchanting form, it is said that even Shiva, the supreme ascetic, fell in love with her. He chased her and embraced her. At that time his seed, which was formed out of his great *tapasya*, slipped out. His semen which was gleaming on a leaf was caught by the seven sages, *sapta rishis*. When the propitious time came, they gave the seed to Vayu who took it to the forest where Anjana was doing *tapas*. She was seated on a hill worshipping Shiva and asking him to bless her with a son. The Wind God approached her as a gentle breeze and slipped the celestial seed through her ear into her womb. In due course, the baby monkey who was called Hanumat (in Sanskrit) was born out of Shiva's seed.

In the *Ananda Ramayana*, Hanuman is said to be Rama's brother, born of the same sacred potion that made Dasaratha's wives pregnant. Anjana had been worshipping Shiva for many years in order to get an exemplary son. Shiva told her that he was pleased with her *tapasya* and would be born to her as the eleventh Rudra. He told her to raise her cupped palms to heaven and wait patiently. Meanwhile, Dasaratha, the king of Ayodhya, was performing the *Putrakamesti Yaga* in order to have children. As a result, he received a celestial pudding to be distributed amongst his three wives. Having partaken of the sweet, they gave birth to Rama, Lakshmana, Bharata and Shatrugna. By divine ordinance, Vayu, in the form of a hawk, is said to have swooped and pecked a bit of the pudding from the hands of the youngest wife, Sumitra. He dropped it into Anjana's outstretched palms while flying over the hill where she was engaged in worship. She consumed the sweet morsel and Hanuman was born to her as a result. This actually made him Rama's half-brother.

Another story goes that Anjana was the daughter of Sage Gautama and his wife, Ahalya. The latter was seduced by Indra, the king of gods, who approached her in the form of her husband. When Gautama returned, he cursed both of them. Ahalya believed that her daughter had told on her to Gautama and cursed her to become a monkey. Anjana decided to perform austerities in order to overcome the effects of the curse. She was so absorbed in her *tapas* that an ant-hill started to grow over her. The Wind God Vayu took pity on her and fed her regularly through a hole in the anthill. Meanwhile, Shiva and Parvati used to sport in the forest, taking on the form of various animals. Once when they were in a monkey form, Shiva's seed was ejaculated and Parvati could not bear the intensity of his seed. So Vayu picked it up and carried it to Anjana. Three months later, Hanuman emerged from her mouth in the form of a baby monkey. (This story will be elaborated in another chapter).

The *Valmiki Ramayana* gives a different version of the birth of Hanuman. The celestial maid Punchikasthala was cursed by a sage and had to be born on earth as a monkey but she had the power to assume a human form at will. Once, when she was wandering along the mountain side in her beautiful human form, her garments were lifted up by the wind. Vayu was enamoured by her lovely limbs and ruffled her clothes and entered into her. Anjana sensed this violation and was all prepared to curse her unseen paramour when the god appeared before her and promised her that not only would there be no loss to her chastity but she would also get a powerful son equal in strength to himself.

The story as given in the *Shiva Purana* is a little different. Once Parvati heard her husband repeating the *mantra*, "Rama" and asked him the reason. Shiva replied that the *mantra*, Rama, was very potent since it designated the ultimate reality which had taken the form of an earthly prince and was an *avatara* of Vishnu.

"Parvati! Rama is very dear to me and I am going to incarnate myself on earth in order to serve him." Parvati protested at this but Shiva said that he would send only a portion or *amsa* of himself. Shiva decided to take on the form of a monkey since it is humble and has simple needs and a simple lifestyle and needed no observance of the rules of caste and stages of life. This would give him maximum scope for service. Initially Parvati was shocked at this but Shiva convinced her that the monkey form was the ideal one for avoiding the lure of *maya*. Parvati asked to accompany him and volunteered to become his tail, for the wife is an ornament of her husband as the tail is of a monkey. Shiva agreed to this and that is why Hanuman's tail is so beautiful and imbued with *shakti,* the power of the goddess.

Another story goes that Ravana and Kumbhakarna were incarnations of two of Shiva's attendants; hence he was obliged to protect them. However, they became arrogant due to the boons they had received from Brahma and started to harass the gods who appealed to Shiva to protect them. Shiva's anger was fully roused when Ravana imprisoned Mahakala, the lord of death and Shani, the planet Saturn. This is another reason why he decided to incarnate as Hanuman.

In the time of the *Manu Swayambhu*, a sage called Shilada did penance to please Shiva and requested that he would like to have a son like him. Shiva agreed to this and in his eleventh manifestation was born as his son, Nandi. The son performed penance and obtained the boon that he would be born as Shiva's devotee in the form of a bull. While Ravana was rampaging across the earth, he had the temerity to go to Kailasa. Nandi stopped him from entering and Ravana ridiculed him and taunted him and told him that his face resembled that of a monkey! Nandi cursed him that he would meet his end through a monkey's intervention. Later he requested Shiva to be allowed to be born on earth as Hanuman, "the bull" among monkeys.

One more story in the *Shiva Purana* says that the Wind God, Vayu assisted Shiva in slaying the demon called Jalandhara. Shiva offered him a boon and Vayu requested that Shiva be born on earth as his own son and Shiva agreed.

Vishnu wanted Shiva's help in order to slay Ravana so he prayed to Shiva and performed a *puja* to him by offering red lotuses, each having a thousand petals. Shiva appeared and informed him that he had already given the boon to Anjana that he would be born as her son and would certainly help him in his *avatara* as Rama.

Since Hanuman has been credited with a great number of birth stories, naturally many texts also set different dates on which he is said to have been born. Actually eight different dates have been given, which will be enumerated below. All birth dates are gauged according to the Hindu lunar calendar.

1. *Chitra Purnima* or the full moon of the month of *Chaitra* (March/April).
2. *Chitra shukla ekadasi* or the eleventh day of the bright fortnight of *Chaitra.*
3. *Kartika Purnima* or the full moon of the month of *Kartika* (October/November).
4. *Kartika Amavasya* or the new moon of the month of *Kartika.*
5. *Shravana shukla ekadasi* or the eleventh day of the bright fortnight of the month of *Shravana* (July/August).
6. *Shravan Purnima* or the full moon of the month of *Shravana.*
7. *Margashirsha shukla trayodasi* or the thirteenth day of the bright fortnight of the month of *Margashirsha* (November/December).
8. *Ashvin amavasya* or the new moon of the month of *Ashvin* (September/October).

Out of these, two have come to enjoy wide prominence. The most popular is the full moon in the month of *Chitra,* which heralds spring. This sets Hanuman's birthday five days after that of Rama who was born on *Chitra navami* or the ninth day of the bright fortnight of *Chitra.* This also places his birthday in *uttarayanam* or the waxing sun when it is moving northward, towards the Himalayas and the world of the gods.

However, in Ayodhya, the birth place of Rama, his birthday is celebrated six months later on the new moon of the autumn month of *Kartika.* This is also known as *yaksha amavasya,* which again points to his connection with the *yakshas,* which has been pointed out before. This date comes in *dakshinayana* or the night of the gods when the sun heads south, toward the realm of the dead and hence it is considered to be waning. These two birth dates give Hanuman a foothold in both halves of the ritual year, one which is associated with the bright forces or *devas* and the other with the world of the dead and elemental forces.

It is claimed that he was born either on a Tuesday or a Saturday and thus these two days are kept aside for his worship. According to Indian astrology, these two days are most inauspicious since they are governed by the malignant planets, *Mangala* or Mars which is the presiding planet of Tuesday and *Shani* or Saturn which presides over Saturday. Worshippers of Hanuman are automatically protected from the evil effects of these planets.

You are the incomparable emissary of Rama and the abode of might,
You are also known as Anjaniputra (Anjana's son) and Pavanaputra (son of the wind).

— *Hanuman Chalisa* by Tulsidas

ॐ *Sri Hanumathe Namaha!*

ॐ

Kesari Suthaaya Namaha!

CHAPTER THREE

KESARI PUTRA

Son of Kesari

Sarvarishtanivaarakam, Shubhakaram,
Pingakshamakshapaham,
Sitanweshana tat param, kapivaram,
Kodindusurya prabham

Greatest amongst monkeys,
With the effulgence of a hundred thousand suns,
Capable of removing all troubles,
With red-tinged eyes,
Who is renowned for having discovered Sita.

— *Hanuman Stotra*

The Puranas give graphic pictures of the many *lokas* or astral realms where dwell different types of beings. The *apsaras* were celestial dancers and normally lived in Indra's court. Punchikasthala was one such *apsara.* As a child she was adopted by Brihaspati, the *guru* of the gods who took her to his own *ashrama* and brought her up as his daughter. She had a highly spiritual nature and was sweet and kind to all. Even as a child she busied herself collecting flowers for his *puja* (rituals) and making herself generally useful to all. Thus, she grew up in this background of spirituality where she hardly ever saw any young men and certainly none who were not spiritually inclined. She was as sweet and untouched as one of the flowers which blossomed in the *ashrama* gardens. She never wandered beyond the precincts of the *ashrama* so she had no idea of the normal behaviour of young people. Thus, she grew up totally untouched and unaware of human nature. At the age of seventeen she was a raving beauty but had no idea of her own charms. One day as chance would have it, she wandered beyond the boundaries of the *ashrama* into the forest in order to pick better flowers and thus please her father. Just then her gaze was transfixed by the sight of some *gandharvas* (celestial singers) who were sporting in the lake and jousting with each other. Never had she seen such handsome, bare bodies. Her whole body flamed with desire when she beheld these beings. Her upbringing was totally forgotten. The flowers she had collected fell unheeded from her hands and she sat spellbound, watching the play of these celestial beings. She yearned with all her heart to get such a being as her husband.

In the evening Brihaspati noticed her absence and went in search of her. He was shocked to see her standing mesmerised by the erotic scenes which were being enacted in front of her eyes. So absorbed was she that she was totally unaware of his arrival.

"Punchikasthala!" He thundered. "What are you staring at? Have you forgotten that you are an *ashramite*? These types of scenes should not be viewed by you. Come back my child and promise never to come to this place again or else I may have to ask you to leave this *ashrama*.

For the first time she did not meekly agree with her father. In fact she was even bold enough to retort.

"What have I done that you should scold me so harshly? All I did was to gaze at these beings. They are so glorious to behold. I have never seen anyone like them!"

Brihaspati understood her feelings and gazed sadly at her.

"My child!" He said, "We are *ashram* dwellers. Our only aim in life is to get self-realization. The life of the normal ego-centred individual is shunned by us. But I realise your weakness. You are young and perhaps unable to overcome your feelings for a family life. Let it be. I will send you to the mortal world where you will be born as a monkey. In the short span of the life of a monkey, you will be able to assuage your desire for sex. After that you will be able to renew your original form and return to this world."

Punchikasthala fell at his feet and begged him to retract his curse. Brihaspati looked fondly at her and said.

"The curse of a saint is always a blessing. It is always meant to fulfil a deep divine purpose and my curse is no exception to this rule. You will be the mother of a male monkey who will be glorified in the whole world as the greatest of *bhaktas*. He will be renowned for his valour, intelligence and his adherence to *dharma*. He will be the supreme devotee of Lord Vishnu in his *avatara* as Rama, king of Ayodhya. The moment he is born you will regain your former body and be able to return to these heavenly regions."

Seeing her pleading look, he continued, "It is better for you to get rid of these lower desires now in the form of a monkey where they will be totally exhausted in the shortest possible time and then return to this *ashrama* where you can continue your former practices and gain liberation. You will be known as Anjana and will be able to assuage your thirst for sex with a handsome monkey of your choice. At the appointed time when you are united with your husband, the Wind God – Vayu will deposit the seed of Lord Shiva in your womb and thus you will get a baby who will have all the qualities of Lord Shiva and the speed and strength of the Wind God."

Everything happened as the sage had predicted. Punchikasthala was born in a tribe of monkeys as the daughter of the chief called Kunjara. She was named Anjana. However, she remembered her past life perfectly and was not happy leading the life of a normal monkey. As soon as she was able to, she left the tribe and penetrated deep into the forest. She wandered hungry and thirsty without finding anything to eat. At last she came upon a huge tree filled with luscious fruit. She jumped up the tree but just a she stretched her hand to pluck the fruit, she heard an ethereal voice.

"Anjana! You should not eat anything until you have bathed and said your prayers. You have come to this forest with a purpose. In order to fulfil this you should live the life of an anchorite. Do *tapasya* to Lord Shiva and Parvati to give you a wondrous son and deliver you from your curse."

Anjana was glad to follow this advice from a divine source. From that day onwards she strictly adhered to the life of an anchorite. She would get up early in the morning and take her bath and sit meditating on the divine couple, Shiva and Parvati. It was only after this routine, that she would pluck the fruits and leaves of trees and assuage her hunger.

One day she was rudely awakened from her austerities by a hideous noise. The whole forest seemed to be in a state of unrest. Birds were screaming and flying around in fear and even the animals seemed to be running for their lives. Suddenly she saw the enormous figure of a *rakshasa* (cannibal) standing in front of her. Trembling with fear she started to get up and run. But the creature accosted her.

"O beautiful one!" He roared. "Why are you running away from me? I will not harm you. My name is Shambasaadan and I'm the king of this forest. However, I am prepared to marry you and give you everything you desire. Come close to me and let us make love. Life is too short to waste time doing useless austerities!"

With this profound pronouncement, he made a lunge at her. Anjana escaped his clutches and ran for her life. Since she was a monkey she could swing from branch to branch but her sinister suitor was not to be put off so easily. He was so huge that he trampled over trees and bushes in hot pursuit. Half crazed with fear, Anjana cried out to her guardian deities to save her from this new calamity. To her amazement, just as he made a lunge to catch her, he was felled to the spot. She was astonished at this miraculous reprieve and went to investigate if he was really dead. She saw a huge cobra slithering off.

Just then a voice warned her that Shambasaadan was only unconscious and might recover soon. She bent and peered at his face and saw signs of life. Not waiting to investigate further, she ran deeper into the forest. At last, tired and desperate she came upon an *ashrama*. She threw herself at the mercy of the anchorites there and begged them to save her from this predicament.

Seeing her distress, they gave her water to drink and told her to take refuge there. When she mentioned the name Shambasaadan, they quivered with fear and told her that he was a cruel *rakshasa* who terrorised the whole forest. They could not practice their fire rituals without fear of his coming and despoiling everything.

"The only one who is capable of vanquishing him is a heroic monkey called Kesari." Hearing this Anjana prayed to her favourite deities to send Kesari and enable him to kill the *rakshasa* who was harassing all the *ashramites* and holding the forest in thrall. She spent the night in prayer.

It is said that Kesari had once killed a mighty elephant that was troubling the sages and hermits. That is how he got the name "Kesari", which means elephant. He was also called *Kunjara südana*, the elephant killer.

The next morning, the whole *ashrama* came to life and all of them felt some new hope in their hearts. They started to prepare their morning rituals – their *yajnas* and *yagas*. These were *Vedic* rites in which offerings were made into the blazing fire accompanied by *mantras* and secret incantations for the well being of the world and for their own spiritual progress. They were a bit worried about starting it since Shambasaadan came very often to put an end to their rites. They were waiting anxiously not knowing whether to start or not, when a mighty monkey came into their midst. He was tall and handsome and looked as if he was capable of routing anyone. He told them not to fear but to start their rituals and he would guard them as he had done of yore. He looked enquiringly at the new-comer in their midst and the *rishis* introduced Anjana to him. This was the hero, Kesari about whom they had told her. She took an instant liking to him and felt that he was truly capable of saving all of them from the scourge of the *rakshasa.* Without further ado, he jumped on to one of the trees and stayed hidden behind the leaves.

Just then there was a tremendous uproar and the whole forest became petrified. The birds squawked and flew hither and thither; the deer ran off in different directions not knowing where to flee. Suddenly the hideous form of the *rakshasa* appeared. Immediately he spied Anjana shaking with fear and trying to hide in a corner of the compound.

Putting out a huge, hairy hand he caught her and pulled her towards him and said in a disgustingly intimate voice as if to seduce her. He was reeking of stale blood and sweat and she shivered with disgust as he drew her towards him.

"Ah! My little dove!" He said beguilingly, "Why do you try to flee from me? Don't you know that I'm crazy about you? You can never escape me. I'll follow you to the end of the world if necessary. Come! Let us run away and we will live in luxury and happiness. These cowards don't have the power to save you but I'll protect and guard you always."

The terrified Anjana shrieked and cried out. "Save me! Save me! Is there no one who can save me from this beast?"

"God himself is helpless before me! So who can save you now?"

Just at that moment, the mighty Kesari jumped out of the tree with a loud roar and landed right in front of the *rakshasa.*

"O Shambasaadana!" He roared. "If you value your life, let go of the girl!"

Hearing this Shambasaadana put Anjana to the ground and said,

"O! Are you the one who has you come as her protector! I'll make mincemeat of you first and then deal with her later."

Taking this opportunity, Anjana ran into the hermitage and closed the door.

The *rakshasa* laughed long and loud as he saw Kesari standing before him with arrow fixed to his bow ready to let fly at him.

"O you stupid monkey!" He said. "Are you so presumptuous as to suppose that you can save this girl and the *ashramites*? I'll make short work of you and the *ashrama* and then make off with the girl."

So saying the *rakshasa* plucked a huge tree from the forest and threw it at Kesari. The latter immediately split the tree in mid-air with his arrow and felled it to the ground before it could cause any damage. This infuriated the *rakshasa* who uprooted a small mound near by and hurled it at Kesari. Once again Kesari shattered the mound with his arrow. The *rakshasa* couldn't believe his eyes. He flew at the monkey as if he would throttle him with his bare arms. Kesari rained a whole host of arrows at him.

The latter knew that he had met his match so he resorted to his magic tricks and took on the form of a maddened elephant. He caught the fleeing *rishis* and threw them around and destroyed their *ashrama* and defiled their *yajna kund.* Anjana saved herself by hiding in the hollow of a huge tree.

In the meanwhile, Kesari had been raining arrows at the mad elephant all the time but they merely grazed the skin of the animal and fell to the ground. The enraged pachyderm now turned his full fury on him and plucked the bow from him and stamped on it. Kesari immediately took the form of a small little monkey and flew into the air. He landed with great force on the forehead of the elephant. This is supposed to be an elephant's weakest point. He then proceeded to pound this tender spot with adamantine fists. Try as he might the elephant could not shake off the little monkey who was hammering on his weak point with such force. So he immediately changed his form back to that of a *rakshasa* and plucked off the monkey and dashed him to the ground.

Kesari regained his normal stature and started pelting the demon with his arrows. Even though blood was oozing from the wounds, he seemed to be completely unaffected and laughed in scorn. Anjana felt desperate and mentally begged Lord Shiva to save Kesari. Immediately she felt a response.

Shiva told her that the *rakshasa* could not be killed with anything but his own blood. She asked how this could be managed. The reply was that she should think of a ruse herself.

She cogitated deeply on the matter. Suddenly she spied an arrow which had fallen a little apart from the place where the two heroes were engaged in a desperate battle, which they both knew would be a fight to the finish. She could see that Kesari's strength was flagging. Spurred by this she crept forward and rescued the arrow and smeared it with the blood which had fallen from the *rakshasa.* Now she was on the look-out for an opportune moment to pass this to Kesari.

The demon now assumed the form of a gigantic buffalo and came with lowered horns to gore Kesari. The latter immediately fixed two arrows on his bow and aimed them at the buffalo's eyes. It was a real bull's eye and the buffalo reeled and bellowed in pain.

Anjana took this opportunity to rush to Kesari's side. She whispered Shambasaadana's secret to him, gave him the blood-smeared arrow and told him to shoot the arrow at the earliest opportunity. By this time the demon had realised that his best bet would be to discard the buffalo form and with it the fatal injury to its eyes. Anjana hardly had time to run off when Shambasaadana rushed at Kesari, shouting imprecations all the while.

He raised his huge iron mace above his head and flourished it.

"This will make an end of you once and for all, you puny, little monkey!" he shouted.

Before he could hurl the fatal weapon, Kesari prayed to Lord Shiva and let fly the arrow which Anjana had given him. The arrow poisoned with his own blood flew unerringly towards its mark and buried itself in the demon's heart. Shambasaadana gave a mighty roar and started reeling with pain. At last he fell with a tremendous thud, which made the whole earth shudder.

The relieved *rishis* now rushed out with shouts of joy, praised Kesari and thanked him for having rescued them from this constant pestilence. Once more they could conduct their rituals without fear of being molested by the demon. Kesari told them to thank Anjana for she was the one who had disclosed the secret of the demon's weak point and had he not been told of it, he would never have managed to kill him. The *rishis* now turned to Anjana and thanked her also.

"How can we show our gratitude to you both?" The *rishis* asked. They discussed the matter between themselves and then came and asked Anjana.

"My child! Will you be prepared to do our bidding? It is something for your own good?"

Anjana promised to obey the *rishis* no matter what they said.

The *rishis* then smilingly asked her, "Will you consent to marry Kesari?"

Anjana bent her head shyly. They took this as a sign of consent. Kesari also professed his willingness to this happy alliance and the wedding was conducted on a modest scale by the joyful *ashramites.*

O valorous one! With body like a thunderbolt,
Exterminator of evil thoughts and companion to the good.

— *Hanuman Chalisa* by Tulsidas

ॐ *Sri Hanumathe Namaha!*

ॐ

Vayuputraaya Namaha!

CHAPTER FOUR

VAYU PUTRA

The Son of Vayu

Lankadwipa bhayankaram, sakaladam,
Sugrivasammanitam,
Devendradi samastha devavinutam,
Kakasthadutam bhaje.

I worship the emissary of Rama,
Who is worshipped by all the gods starting with Indra.
Who subdued the terrible island of Lanka to Sugriva's great delight.
— *Hanuman Stotra*

Some years passed before their passion for each other was fully abated. Swinging from tree to tree, Kesari would pluck the sweetest and most luscious fruits for his beloved and thus they spent many happy years. However, their love did not produce any fruit. This again was her Guru's blessing for he had told her that the moment she held her first born in her arms she would be free from the curse and be able to return to her heavenly abode. He wanted to give her a chance to exhaust all her desires for physical pleasures before granting her a child. A time came when Anjana started to feel unhappy at the thought that though she had spent so many years as a wife, she still had not become a mother. Kesari knew the cause of her unhappiness and he told her that it was best that they should undergo some penance in order to be blessed with a son. Anjana told him that the only way was to do *tapas* to Shiva and Parvati and they would surely grant their wish for a noble son. Thus, the couple prayed intensely to the divine couple to grant their desire. They had only one meal during the day. They no longer slept with each other. The whole day was passed in deep prayer and *puja* to the divine couple. Summer came and then the rainy season, followed by autumn and finally winter. But the couple continued their *tapasya* unabated.

At last the divine pair decided to bless this couple who were so engrossed in their worship. They took on the form of monkeys and came and ate up all the fruits and food, which had been spread out for the morning ritual. Kesari was annoyed when he saw the mischievous antics of the two monkeys and was all set to drive them off when Anjana stopped him. "My Lord!" She said. "I don't think these are ordinary monkeys. I believe they are Shiva and Parvati who have come to bless us. So let us start worshipping them." Kesari agreed with her and they started to worship the monkeys as Shiva and Parvati. They were seated deep in meditation when they heard a voice saying. "O Anjana! O Kesari! We are pleased with your prayers and austerities and will certainly grant your desire. Deep in the forest there is a huge mango tree. Go there daily and circumambulate this tree and pray to Shiva to grant your desire. Within a week you will find a wondrous mango on the tree. Let Anjana eat this fruit and she will be blessed with a baby boy who will be equal in strength to the wind god – Vayu."

The couple was delighted to hear this and prostrated and thanked Shiva and Parvati for their blessing. Immediately they started to search the forest for this wondrous tree and very soon found it in the middle of a grove. Next morning they did their ablutions and proceeded to worship the tree and circumambulated it three times and did *puja* as prescribed by the divine pair. This went on for seven days. On the eighth day morning when they reached the tree, they were told by a divine voice to prepare themselves for the emergence of the celestial fruit. At that moment the whole tree was lit up by a heavenly radiance which slowly started to descend. The radiance proved to be a majestic celestial being that was holding the fruit in his hands. He came to a halt in front of the couple. They stood wonderstruck by the vision before them.

The Being now spoke, "O Kesari! Have no fear! Accept the fruit which I have brought you and give it to your wife Anjana. Let her eat it and she will surely conceive a child."

In a tremulous voice Kesari asked, "We are indeed most grateful to you. Pray deign to tell us your identity."

The Being replied, "I'm Vayu. I have come here at the behest of Lord Shiva. This mango contains his seed as well as my powers. Have no fear. Accept this fruit in your hands and invest it with your own prowess and give it to Anjana to eat. You will get a son who will be renowned in all the three worlds as the strongest, bravest as well as the foremost in devotion." Thus, Hanuman was endowed with the best of divine and simian qualities.

Kesari accepted the fruit, held it to his heart and prayed that all his strength would go into the fruit. He then handed it over to his wife who accepted it with great devotion. She took the mango in her hands and prayed to Lord Shiva and to Vayu. Then she fell at her husband's feet and asked for his blessings also. Only then did she eat the divine fruit. Immediately she was impregnated. The foetus soon started to grow within her womb. It was filled with all three qualities – divine, mortal and animal. Kesari looked after her with great love and care. As the foetus within her started to grow, Anjana was filled with a heavenly radiance. At last she knew her time had come. It was Tuesday – the full moon day of the month of *Chaitra.* She bathed in the stream and prayed to her favourite deities and lay down on a bed of freshly plucked leaves and flowers which Kesari had lovingly arranged for her inside a bower. Very soon she gave birth to a beautiful baby monkey. As soon as he was born he let out a loud roar. Kesari was anxiously waiting outside and as soon as he heard the roar he came inside to take in the beautiful scene of his son being nursed by his wife.

Many exceptional traits marked his birth. He did not come into the world as a naked little monkey. His golden coloured, furry body was adorned with supernatural ornaments. He had a tight red loincloth, a sacred thread of twisted *munja* grass and a pair of heavy, elaborately carved earrings. The normal sacred thread worn by humans is made of cotton thread but the one worn by Anjana's son was made of a wild, coarse grass or *munja*, which resembled a rope made of hemp. This was a kind of omen of his future life as a celibate and an ascetic. It was also suggestive of his animal origin as well as his humility.

His earrings were said to be invisible to the eyes of most mortals. His mother told him that only the one who would be his Master would be able to perceive the earrings. Rama of course was the only one who did see them. These earrings have an interesting legend connected with them.

At the time of Hanuman's birth, the undisputed leader of the monkey-world was Vaali, a strong and powerful ape. When Vaali came to know that Anjana was pregnant with a child who was bound to develop into a dominant rival, he decided to put an end to all competition while the child was still in its mother's womb. He created a dart using five metals – gold, silver, copper, iron and tin. When the unsuspecting mother was asleep, he sent the missile into her womb. A normal child may have succumbed to this dastardly attack, but not one born of Shiva's fiery seed. As soon as it touched the baby's body the dart melted, and transformed itself into a pair of beautiful earrings. Thus, wearing the trophies of his first battle, fought while still in his mother's womb, Hanuman entered this world.

At that moment, Shiva and Parvati took the form of monkeys and arrived to bless Anjana's son. Vayu also arrived to gaze at his son. Thus, all those who had contrived to produce the child arrived to bless him. Vayu told the parents to call him Maruti.

How Shiva's seed came into the mango is another story. Shiva was the eternal ascetic who had conquered lust. He had reduced Kama, the God of Love to ashes. However, in order to please his wife, Parvati, and fulfil her desire for sexual pleasures, Shiva took on the form of a male monkey and Parvati of a female monkey and thus they sported in the woods, hanging from the branches and swinging and making love in a wild and abandoned manner as monkeys are wont to do. At that time Parvati discovered to her dismay that she was expecting a child. Her first born had an elephant's head so she was not at all anxious to have another in the form of a monkey. She confided her fears to her Lord. Shiva, thus, teased her about this and told her that all creatures were one with him and a child born of his seed would indeed be perfect in every way, whatever his form. She was not convinced and begged him to remove the seed from her womb and transfer it to a more fitting receptacle. Shiva called Vayu to come to his aid and told him to take the seed and place it in a suitable womb. Vayu took the seed and impregnated the mango and further endowed it with his own powers and bestowed it to the pious couple who were praying for a son.

Golden-hued and splendidly adorned,
With heavy earrings and curly locks.

— *Hanuman Chalisa* by Tulsidas

ॐ *Sri Hanumathe Namaha!*

ॐ

ॐ

Marutaatmajaaya Namaha!

CHAPTER FIVE

MARUTI

Flight to the Sun

Kyatha Sri Rama duta, pavanatanubhava,
Pingalakshashikhavan,
Sitashokapahari Dashamukha vijayi,
Lakshmana pranadata.

You are known as the son of the wind and messenger of Rama,
With red eyes,
Dispeller of the sorrows of Sita and vanquisher of the ten-headed one,
And the giver of life to Lakshmana.

— *Hanuman Stotra*

Indeed, having both Shiva and Vayu as his illustrious fathers, Maruti was no ordinary child. He was restless, spirited, energetic and inquisitive. He was obviously endowed with awesome strength and the scriptures abound in tales expounding his remarkable feats. One of his most remarkable feats which is recounted in all his tales has to do with his jump to the sun. In fact this amazing achievement is the one which gave him his most popular name – Hanuman.

The baby was a voracious eater. His appetite could never be totally appeased. The poor parents did their best to satisfy him but he was never completely satisfied and was always demanding more food. By the time he was a year old, he started climbing and eating all the fruit in the surrounding area. One day Anjana took him with her to the river and allowed him to do whatever mischief he wanted on the banks while she had her bath. After having eaten as many fruits and shoots from the trees as he could get, he was still hungry. Suddenly he spied the huge, orange orb of the sun which was rising in the sky and thought to himself that this must be an exceptionally big type of fruit. He called out to his mother to come and have a look at this new fruit. She thought that it must be some fruit on a tree and told him to go for it. Nothing loathe, the child gave a magnificent leap and soared up to the sky, towards the orb of the sun. When Anjana came out of the river after her bath, she couldn't see her son and looked anxiously for him. At last she spied him flying towards the sun. She shouted to Kesari to come and see what their son was up to. He jumped towards the little fellow to try and catch him but was unable to do so and fell back dejected. The parents didn't know what they should do now.

The celestials watched his progress with wonder. "Neither the Wind God nor Garuda or even the mind can move as swiftly as this son of Vayu. If this is his speed as a mere baby, what will be his speed when he becomes a youth?"

The Wind God was also closely following him to protect him from the danger of getting scorched. The Sun God realized that he was an innocent child. He also knew of the great purpose that Lord Vishnu in his form as Rama, would accomplish through him and thus he did not harm him.

Unfortunately that day happened to coincide with the day of the solar eclipse when the planet Rahu was supposed to swallow the sun. Suddenly Maruti saw Rahu (a malefic planet) shaped like a serpent making his way towards the sun in order to devour him. Mistaking him to be a huge worm, the inquisitive monkey dashed towards him and attempted to catch hold of his tail. Rahu fled for his life, and sought shelter at the feet of Indra, the lord of the gods. He spoke angrily to Indra, "You have allotted the sun and the moon to me for appeasing my hunger on certain days and now I find that my share has been given over to some other creature. Today is the night of the new moon and this is the day on which I have been told to devour the sun. Now look what's happened! Here comes another creature to thwart me."

Indra picked up his deadly thunderbolt, mounted his white elephant named Airavata and went towards the impudent monkey. The clouds rumbled and lightning thundered across the vast skies in an expression of Indra's wrath. But neither this scary scenario, nor the mighty armed Indra on his high mount, was sufficient to induce even a trace of fear in the heart of the little monkey. On the contrary, the spectacle only added fuel to his excitement. He decided that an elephant was just what he needed as a vehicle and tried to grab it. He caught hold of its trunk and leapt on its back. Taken aback by the sudden appearance of a baby monkey behind his back, Indra was all set to strike him with his thunderbolt. Vayu arrived on the scene at the opportune moment and tried to stop him but Indra was not to be deterred.

"He is only a child! What sort of a god are you that you are prepared to wage war against a small child?"

Indra retorted, "He may be a child but he tried to swallow Surya and catch hold of Rahu. I merely came to their aid."

Vayu did his best to dissuade him but Indra hit Maruti on the chin with his bolt and left a mark on it forever. Hence Anjana's child got the name Hanuman. *Hanu* means "chin" in Sanskrit. However, even Indra's thunderbolt was unable to kill him. But the impact threw him off the back of the elephant. As he hurtled through the air unconscious, his father Vayu sprang to his rescue and caught him in mid air.

The sight of his beloved son lying helpless in his arms infuriated the Wind God. He drew in a mighty breath and sucked away all the air from the cosmos. "Let all those who have harmed Anjana's son choke to death," he thought out aloud. Vayu went into seclusion, taking the atmosphere with him. All living beings began to get asphyxiated. There was panic in the cosmos. Without air, life on every level was threatened. Nothing stirred in the universe and the recitation of the Vedas by the Brahmins ceased and the stomachs of the gods began to shrink.

Anjana and Kesari waited in vain for their child to return to them from the sky. When there was no sign of him, they started to weep and beat their breasts in sorrow.

"Ha Shiva! Ha Parvati! We had to go through so much of trouble to get a son and now he has been cruelly parted from us. What have we done to deserve this?"

Seeing their sorrow, Vayu appeared before them and comforted them.

"Your son is safe with me. I'm keeping him with me for some time in order to teach Indra and the other gods a lesson. Don't worry; I'll bring him back to you safely."

Hearing this assurance, the parents were pacified.

However since Vayu, the Wind God refused to blow any more, the whole earth started to suffer. Unable to breathe, all creatures started to suffocate and die. Very soon it looked as if the whole world would perish. Indra felt very sorry for his impetuous deed. He knew that he alone was responsible for the whole thing. He should have desisted from using his thunderbolt even though he had been egged on by Rahu. All the gods now ran around desperately trying to find out the whereabouts of Vayu. He could be found nowhere. They ran to Shiva and Vishnu and begged for their help. They were aware of everything and knew exactly where Vayu was hiding the child. They went to the nether world along with Brahma. Vayu was very happy to see them and prostrated and told them the whole story of how his son had been ill-treated by Indra and Surya.

Brahma, Shiva and Vishnu pacified him and all the gods gave him many blessings. As soon as Brahma touched him, Maruti revived. Now all the gods vied with each other to give him boons.

Indra took off his garland of lotus flowers and placed it round the baby's neck and said, "Since this infant's chin has been broken by my thunderbolt, he shall in future be known as Hanuman (one who has a disfigured chin). He will also be invulnerable to my thunderbolt."

The Sun God now said, "I bestow on him a hundredth part of my brilliance. Moreover when the time comes for him to study, I myself shall impart the knowledge of all the Vedas and *shastras* to him. There will be none superior to him in the knowledge of the *shastras.*

Varuna, the god of waters, gave him the boon that he would never need to have any fear from water.

Agni, the god of fire, promised never to harm him.

Yama, the god of death, now said that he would be immune to all diseases and would never come under his sway and have the ability to choose the time of his death.

Kubera, the king of the *yakshas*, said that his mace would never be able to kill him in war and that he would always remain unwearied during battle.

Shiva gave him the supreme boon that he would be a *chiranjeevi* (one who lives forever) and would never be able to be killed by any of his weapons.

Viswakarma, the divine architect, now pronounced that he would be impervious to any weapon made by him.

Brahma gave him another boon that he could never be killed by the *brahmastra*, the weapon that bore his name and also gave him physical immortality for the duration of a cosmic eon. Turning to the Wind God he said, "Your son will be invincible. He will be the terror of his foes, and give freedom from fear to his friends. He will be able to change his form at will and go wherever he pleases with the speed of his choice. Whatever he does will turn out to be glorious."

Vishnu now turned to the Wind God and said, "This son of yours will become a great Vishnu *bhakta* (devotee). No one will be able to vanquish him. He will be like a brother to my *avatara* as Rama and his wife Sita, who is Lakshmi incarnate."

All the gods now said that there would be no one on earth or heaven that could equal Maruti in strength and speed.

Brahma concluded the session by bestowing on Hanuman a strength greater than even Vayu and Garuda, and endowed him with a speed faster than even the mightiest wind.

Thus, after getting the blessings of all the gods, Vayu returned in triumph to the earthly regions whence all creatures revived and started to breathe normally once again. Vayu took Hanuman to his earthly parents and related the whole story to them. They were delighted to hear of the wondrous boons which their dear son had acquired. They were also happy to hear his new name though not so happy to see the mark on his chin. However, they decided that it suited him.

Another version of the same story as given in the *Valmiki Ramayana* describes how Vayu saw Anjana on the hill in Kishkinda and fell in love with her. He gently stole away her clothes and embraced her. Naturally she objected violently to the loss of her chastity so he assured her that there would be no loss in her chastity and blessed her with a wonderful son who would be endowed with his own strength and vigour. She felt the babe within her move so she went to a cave and gave birth to a lovely baby monkey. He had white fur, a red face and brownish-yellow eyes. Reluctantly she left him in the cave and returned to her husband.

The baby was hungry. Dawn was approaching and still no one came to feed him. The sky grew lighter and lighter and at last he saw the glorious sun rise into the air like a big ripe mango fruit. Instinctively he knew that monkeys were frugarians and this was food for him. He crawled out of the cave and crouched down and leapt towards the sun. Vayu came from the north and blew cool fresh air over him so that he would not be scorched by the heat of the sun. This was the day of the solar eclipse and as the baby monkey approached the sun, the disembodied head of the *asura* Rahu advanced to swallow the sun. Closer and closer he came with wide open mouth and was astounded to see this strange creature approaching the sun. Hanuman decided that Rahu was another fruit and lunged towards him. Rahu ran to Indra for protection and both of them returned, mounted on the Airavata, Indra's elephant. Hanuman was delighted to see them and wondered at the amount of strange creatures in the sky! He dashed towards the elephant despite Indra's shouts to keep off. Indra was furious at the audacity of the creature and struck him with the flat side of his thunderbolt and he fell unconscious to the earth. The rest of the story is similar to the one recounted above.

After this incident Hanuman was overflowing with vigour due to all the boons he had received from the gods and he was up to all types of mischief. Sometimes he teased the meditating sages in the forests by snatching their personal belongings and disturbing their well-arranged articles of worship. He broke their sacrificial ladles and vessels and interrupted their oblations and tore up their bark cloths. He stole their water pots and sandals and pulled their beards when they were meditating and tossed their sacred stones into the ponds. Since no one dared to stop him, he became bolder and smashed their vessels and tore up their scriptures and dropped huge boulders on the hermitages. Time and time again both Kesari and Anjana forbade him from doing such mischief but knowing himself to be invulnerable from the curses of Brahmins, Hanuman continued his pranks. The sages knew of the boons which had been given to him, and they put up with his behaviour as long as they could. At last finding his antics unbearable, they placed a curse on him. They declared that Hanuman would forget his own prowess, and would be able to recollect it only when others reminded him of it. Immediately Hanuman forgot his divine powers and began to behave like an ordinary monkey.

At one time it is said that he even harassed the children of the gods. When they appealed to Indra, he advised them to seek instruction from Hanuman himself about the art of wrestling so that they would be able to fight with him when necessary. So in this story, he became the *guru* and they learnt from him the esoteric secret of wrestling of which he was a master.

In the 'Sundarakanda', Jambavan, the big bear had to remind Hanuman of his abilities and encourage him to go and find Sita. It was only then that Hanuman remembered his unusual talents and accomplished the impossible and made the amazing leap to Lanka. During the course of the war he demonstrated some of his phenomenal abilities but each time it was Jambavan who reminded him and prompted him. This story also goes to show that Hanuman is a deity whose dormant *shakti* can be activated through hymns. The motif of forgetting and remembering is suggestive of the journey of the *jivatma* back to self-knowledge.

The sun is two thousand leagues away,
Yet you swallowed him, taking him to be a sweet fruit.

— *Hanuman Chalisa* by Tulsidas

ॐ *Sri Hanumathe Namaha!*

ॐ

Tatwajnanapradaaya Namaha!

CHAPTER SIX

KESARI-NANDANA

Hanuman's Education

Anetho bheshajatre,
Lavanajalanidhe,
Laghane deekshito ya,
Veera Sreeman Hanuman,
Mama manasi vasath,
Karyasiddhim tanotu.

O powerful Hanuman!
Who crossed the ocean so easily,
Do thou remain in my mind,
And allow me to accomplish everything.

— *Hanuman Stotra*

When he attained five years of age, Kesari decided that it was high time his son got a formal education. The sage Agastya told them to send him to the Sun God, Surya.

"The sun is the source of all light and knowledge and has already blessed Hanuman. He will surely accept him as a pupil."

Anjana was not too happy at sending her son so far off. However, Kesari urged her that this was the best thing for their child and thus Hanuman was sent to the Sun God for instruction on the Vedas and all allied subjects. Kesari's choice of Surya as his teacher was because the sun is the sole *karma sakshi* or the eternal witness of all the deeds of human beings.

Hanuman did not remember his great powers and innocently asked his mother how he would reach the solar orb. She reminded him that he was the son of the Wind God and immediately he soared into the sky.

Hanuman respectfully approached the chariot of the solar deity. Aruna was the name of his charioteer and he allowed Hanuman to approach his master and prostrate to him.

"You see everything there is to see in the universe and therefore you know everything there is to know. Please accept me as your pupil."

Surya hesitated for he remembered only too well what had happened the last time Hanuman came near him and felt quite nervous about accepting him.

"I don't have the time," he said. "You see I move across the sky in this chariot night and day, always facing forward and never slackening my pace. How can I possibly give you instruction?"

Hanuman cheerfully replied that he did not see any problem in this. "You can teach me as you ride across the sky. I will face you and move backwards matching my pace with yours so that I can get instruction straight from your lips."

The Sun God agreed reluctantly for he was well aware of Hanuman's divine nature and exceptional abilities. He also knew that he was born knowing everything and all he needed to do was to stimulate his memory.

Happy at being accepted, Hanuman placed his body into orbit around the sun. He enlarged his body and placed one leg on the eastern ranges and the other on the western ranges and turned his face toward the sun. Pleased with his persistence, Surya started to teach him all he knew. Hanuman kept moving backwards in order to remain facing Surya continuously. Impressed by the zeal and determination of his student, Surya taught him all he knew. Thus, Hanuman rotated like a planet before the chariot of the Sun God, withstanding the awesome glare, until he became well versed in the four books of knowledge (the Vedas), the six systems of philosophies (*darshanas*), the sixty-four arts or *kalas* and the one hundred and eight occult mysteries of the *tantras*. He flawlessly memorised each *mantra* and verse in the shortest possible time. It is said that Hanuman rivals the sage Brihaspati, the *guru* of the gods in all the branches of learning as well as in the practice of austerities. Having become a master of all that he had set out to learn, it was now time for him to pay for his education and give the fee known as *guru-dakshina*. Surya demurred and said that having such a devoted pupil was payment enough for him but when Hanuman insisted on giving something to express his gratitude, the Sun God asked him to look after the welfare of his son Sugriva, who was the step-brother of Vaali, the king of monkeys. Thus, Surya gave a most precious gift to his son Sugriva for without Hanuman, Sugriva would not have been able to accomplish anything.

There is another version to the same story. When Hanuman reached the Sun God's chariot, he found that he already had a great number of other pupils. These were the tiny sages known as the Valakhilyas who were a thousand in number. When Hanuman humbly requested the sun to accept him also as one of his pupils, these hot-tempered sages informed their *guru* that they would not study the Vedas in the company of a monkey! Surya did not know what to do for he feared the curse of these irascible sages. This was when Hanuman devised the ruse of running backward in front of the sun so that he could learn everything without being compelled to join the company of the narrow-minded sages! As a result of facing the solar orb for so long, his face became black.

Another version relates how Hanuman was so intelligent that he was able to learn the whole wisdom of the Vedas in a mere fortnight. The sun god, however, was loath to part with his exceptional pupil, who was a part of Shiva himself. So he repeatedly caused Hanuman to forget what he had learned so that the lessons were dragged on for many months. However, Hanuman pleased him so much by his docility and devotion that he released him and gave him the boon that henceforth those who invoked Hanuman's name would never forget their lessons!

Another story goes that when he was asked by his parents to seek the sun as his *guru*, he merely seated himself in meditation and continuously repeated the *gayatri mantra*, which is the great *mantra* to invoke the supreme intelligence as reflected in the sun. He sat in meditation the whole day, following the course of the sun across the sky until it set in the west. At the end of the day he was perfectly blessed with all knowledge. Actually the ancient *rishis* had the ability to absorb whatever information they wanted from the ether. Knowledge of Veda exists in space in the form of sonic vibrations. The *rishis* had inner antennas, which were capable of picking up these vibrations. These vibrations are very subtle and always exist in space and can be compared to the television and radio signals with which we are familiar. The *rishis* did not need any external aids like the ones we use, to pick up signals. Hanuman practised the same technique.

The parents were still eager to find an earthly *guru* for him and didn't know whom to approach. One day when Hanuman was playing in the forest, he saw a ferocious tiger approaching him. The tiger pounced on him with a menacing growl but Hanuman was undeterred. He jumped ten feet into the air and landed on the tiger's back and caught him in a merciless hold. He tore open the gaping jaws and tore them apart. The tiger was pretty exhausted by now and Hanuman rode on his back effortlessly. However, before he could go far, the tiger collapsed.

Just then there appeared before Hanuman a hunter wearing a tiger skin and adorned with a necklace of tiger claws. A bow and quiver were slung across his broad shoulders. Seeing his form Hanuman felt a great love well up in his heart. He fixed his admiring gaze on him without blinking.

The hunter laughed and asked, "Aren't you frightened of me? I might be a monkey hunter and might catch you and take you back with me!"

Hanuman gazed fearlessly at him and replied, "I have no fear of anyone but I would like to know who you are. I haven't seen anyone like you around here."

The hunter replied, "I'm a hunter and I live far away in the Snow Mountains. If you are not frightened of me, I am willing to teach you many interesting things."

"My parents are on the look-out for a tutor for me," said Hanuman. "Come with me and I'll take you to them."

Anjana and Kesari were shocked to see their darling son coming hand in hand with such a rough looking fellow. They were even more shocked when Hanuman told them that he wanted to go with his new-found friend to learn the arts.

"Are you out of your mind? Just looking at him one can see that he is an uncultured and uneducated boor. How can such a fellow teach you anything?" asked Kesari.

"Father, how can you make such statements about someone you don't know? I want him as my *guru.*"

"Doesn't the pupil have any say in the choice of a *guru*?" asked the hunter.

"Maybe he has," Kesari replied, "But he's only a child and I'm not interested in keeping you as his *guru!*"

"Shouldn't you test my prowess before branding me as an uncultured brute?" Persisted the hunter.

Anjana and Kesari were amazed at these words of the hunter. They looked at each other and Kesari said, "I don't think this is an ordinary hunter. I think we should give him a chance to prove his mettle."

So saying he challenged the hunter to a duel with his weapons. The hunter was nothing loath but said that they would need an umpire to decide who the winner was. Kesari suggested Anjana. The hunter laughed and said that she was hardly a good choice since obviously a wife would always choose her husband as the winner even if he was defeated. Kesari admitted the truth of this and mentally called upon Vayu to help him. Immediately Vayu appeared in a gust of wind and agreed to do the umpiring.

Now Kesari girded up his loins and charged at the hunter with upraised fists and pounded his chest and threw him a few lengths away. Anjana was delighted to see her husband's feat and applauded him. However, her happiness was short-lived. The hunter coolly rose up and came up to the huge figure of Kesari and caught hold of him and threw him easily into the air. Kesari landed with a thud, which totally knocked him out. Anjana ran to his aid and massaged his body till he slowly regained consciousness. He managed to rise up painfully and was all set for another bout but Anjana begged him not to have another encounter with the hunter. Kesari could not bear to admit defeat and shot a glance at the hunter who seemed to be having a quiet laugh at his expense.

"Let us try our prowess with weapons now", Kesari said.

The hunter immediately stood ready with his bow and arrow. Kesari also took up his bow and shot arrow after arrow at the hunter who parried them all with ease and eventually shot down Kesari's bow so that he stood defenceless.

Anjana realised that this was no ordinary hunter. Mentally she closed her eyes and brought her favourite deity to mind. When she opened them she saw that the hunter was none other than Shiva himself. Hastily she plucked some flowers and ran forward and placed them at the hunter's feet. Hanuman also brought some flowers and placed them at his chosen *guru's* feet. The hunter placed his palms on the boy's head and blessed him. Turning to Kesari he asked with a laugh, "Now do you have any more objections to my becoming your son's tutor?"

Kesari fell at his feet and begged him to pardon him. "It is our great good fortune that you have come here in person and agreed to become our son's *guru*. Because of this we have had the good fortune to see you with our own eyes. Pray forgive my transgressions and take our son as your pupil."

Shiva agreed and touched the boy's tongue with his ring and lo and behold, the child started to sing a paean of praise to the Lord. He then whispered the sacred syllable (*pranava mantra*) in the child's right ear by which Hanuman became a fully enlightened being. He then told Hanuman that Saraswati, the goddess of arts, would grant him proficiency in music when the time came and when he so desired it.

The parents were delighted to hear all this and prostrated again and again to the Lord.

Thus, Lord Shiva taught Maruti all the esoteric knowledge of *mantras* and *yantras* and various other spiritual secrets. It is said that Vishnu taught him *bhakti yoga*, *samkhya yoga* and *hatha yoga*. Parasurama, the sixth incarnation of Vishnu, is supposed to have taught him the secrets of wrestling.

Now his father Vayu took over his teaching. First of all he taught him the esoteric secrets of *pranayama* or the science of breath control. He then taught him to fly like birds and jump vast distances. One day he presented him with a beautiful lute and told him to sing and praise the Lord with this accompaniment. Hanuman was delighted and spent the evening hours known as *sandhya*, singing to God. Once, while he was bathing in a forest pool, he heard the dulcet sounds of a nightingale and thought to himself that he would really love to sing like that. Just then he remembered the words of Shiva who had encouraged him to pray to the goddess Saraswati if he wanted to be a master of the fine arts. As soon as this idea came to his mind, he jumped into the pool and stood waist deep in water and prayed to the goddess to grant him a boon.

Hearing his fervent plea, the goddess appeared and shook him slightly so that he opened his eyes. She then told him to ask for any boon.

He bowed low before her and asked her to grant him knowledge of all the fine arts as well as the ability to sing. Smilingly she agreed to his request and told him to take up the lute and start singing. Having prostrated before her, he took the lute and sat under a tree and started to sing. Hearing his melodious voice accompanied by the lucid notes of the lute even the wild animals came near to listen. Celestial beings passing in the sky also stopped to enjoy the music.

Just at that time Narada, the divine sage, who was a famous singer and a great devotee of Lord Vishnu happened to pass by and was struck by this sight. He thought he was the only one who played on the lute and sang for the Lord and he was not too pleased at this intruder into his particular field. He came down hurriedly to the ground to find out what was so special about Hanuman's voice that made the whole forest go into a state of ecstasy. He approached the young devotee and tapped him on his shoulder. Hanuman opened his eyes and saw the sage standing with his lute in front of him. Narada told him who he was and Hanuman bowed with all humility before him. Narada then asked him to sing another song for him. Hanuman agreed and began to sing. When he heard his dulcet notes, Narada was totally immersed in the music and when he stopped he felt truly humbled and said,

"O Hanuman! I came to test your ability and now I'm convinced that you are a great master of music. I see that the goddess Saraswati has indeed blessed you with all her gifts. Let me add my blessings to hers. You are certainly superior to me."

Hearing this Hanuman fell at the feet of the divine sage and said, "O noble one! Surely none can compare with you in devotional singing. Your fame has spread over all the three worlds. I'm nothing compared to you."

Narada was pleased both by Hanuman's humility as well as by his divine voice. Having blessed him he rose up to go and was dismayed to find that the lute which he had placed on a rock had become stuck to the boulder that had melted at the sound of Hanuman's music!

Turning to Hanuman he begged him to sing once again so that the rock would melt once more and free his lute. Hanuman did so and the celestial sage was able to retrieve his lute. In the age of Dwapara, all solid things like rocks were supposed to have melted when they heard the ravishing notes of the flute which Lord Krishna played in the forest of Vrindavana. The same was the case here. Having realised Hanuman's greatness, Narada blessed him once again and went on his way.

Some years passed in this delightful fashion. However, the time was fast approaching when this idyllic time would come to an end. One day when Anjana was immersed in meditation, she heard a voice from within her calling, "Punchikasthala! Punchikasthala! Your time for reprieve has come. You may now return to your celestial abode!"

When she heard this a flood of memories arose in her and her past life became vivid in her mind. "I'm not a monkey called Anjana. I'm the celestial maiden known as Punchikasthala. I am the adopted daughter of Brihaspati, the *guru* of the gods. I am now freed from my curse and can return to my father's *ashrama.*"

But somehow this thought did not bring her any joy. Her eyes filled with tears.

Her husband Kesari came near her and asked her the reason for her tears. Baby Hanuman came close and hugged her and promised never to get into any mischief. At this Anjana burst into tears and hugged him close.

"My darling son! It's time for me to return to my abode and leave you. But I cannot bear the thought of leaving you and going back."

Neither Anjaneya nor Kesari could figure out her meaning.

"What are you saying? I don't understand. Where do you have to go? This is your home."

"My Lord!" She said, "In reality I'm not Anjana but an *apsara* called Punchikasthala. I belong to the *ashrama* of Brihaspati. I took the form of a monkey due to a curse but now I have been reprieved from it and given permission to return home. But the thought of parting from you and my beloved son is tearing me apart."

"O Anjana! I cannot live without you. I will definitely not allow you to go anywhere," cried Kesari.

"My beloved husband! None can change the course of destiny. You will not be able to stop me. So please give me leave to go."

Baby Maruti now spoke true words of wisdom. "O Mother!" He said, "Go in peace. You are absolutely right in saying that none can stop the wheel of destiny."

The Wind God, Vayu now appeared and comforted her and said, "Don't grieve about your son. We are all here to see to his welfare. If you have to go, go in peace."

The heroic Kesari could not bear this parting. "I cannot live without you beloved! Wherever you go I will follow."

Hearing her husband's oath, Anjana closed her eyes for a few minutes and meditated on her *guru*. Mentally she begged him to allow her to go to the mountain of Kanchana, in the Himalayas along with her husband, in order to practise *tapasya*. She clasped Hanuman in her arms, kissed his forehead and gave him to Vayu. Then turning to Kesari she said, "My Lord! I feel the same way as you. If you want to accompany me, clasp me in your arms."

He did as bidden and to the amazement of her son, they both rose up into the sky and then turned into two balls of light. He watched in wonder as they slowly disappeared towards the north. Brihaspati granted her wish and they both went and stayed at the mountain known as Kanchana.

Thou art the son of Shiva and Kesari's joy,
Your glory is sung throughout the world.

— *Hanuman Chalisa* by Tulsidas

ॐ *Sri Hanumathe Namaha!*

ॐ

Manojavaaya Namaha!

CHAPTER SEVEN

JITENDRIYA

Conquering of the Senses

Manojavam Marutathulyavegam
Jitendriyam buddhimatam varishtam,
Vathatmajam vaanarayudhamukhyam,
Sri Rama dutam shirasa namami!

I bow to the messenger of Rama,
Who was the son of Vayu and the best amongst monkeys,
Who had his senses under perfect control and was highly intelligent,
Who was as fast as the mind and as swift as the wind.

— *Hanuman Stotra*

After his parents left, Hanuman was left solely in the care of his foster father – Vayu. After some years in the forest, Hanuman thought to himself that there must be more to life than just eating and playing in the forest. He mentally asked his father, Vayu to come to his aid and told him that he was anxious to see the world and meet great saints. Vayu agreed to his request and said,

"Indeed it is time for you to go from here. However, I'd like you to get married first before going anywhere. Then you can go to the kingdom of the monkeys known as Kishkinda. The king of that state is a great and powerful monkey known as Vaali. He has a brother called Sugriva. Befriend him and you will certainly gain fame and fortune."

Hanuman bowed low before his father and said firmly, "My Lord I am not in the least interested in a family life. I have taken on a vow of chastity and I hope I will never have to break it. However, I'm pleased by your other advice. I will certainly set out for the kingdom of Vaali without further ado."

He bade a fond farewell to his playmates in the forest and started out towards Kishkinda. He travelled through the trees as monkeys do. After some time he was very thirsty and hungry. He spied a stream below him and came down to drink the water. Hardly had he scooped some water in his palms than he heard a horrendous voice saying, "No one is allowed to drink this water without my permission!" Hearing this Hanuman let the water fall from his hands and looked around for the person. Seeing no one he said, "Who are you? Why are you hiding in the foliage like a coward? Why don't you reveal yourself?"

At these words the whole forest was shaken by the sound of a roar and the horrible figure of a *rakshasa* appeared before Hanuman. He was not to be deterred by this figure and asked him who he was.

The *rakshasa* replied, "Why should I introduce myself to you? You have trespassed on my land and now I will certainly make my mid-day meal out of you!" So saying he opened his cavernous mouth and prepared to swallow Hanuman whole. His mouth emitted the stench of blood. Before he could catch him, Hanuman made use of the powers given to him by his father, Vayu and enlarged himself so that he stood face to face with the *rakshasa.* The demon was a bit astonished to see this feat by this little monkey but he knew a few tricks himself so he also became larger and larger and made a lunge at Hanuman with these words.

"Now let me have my lunch!"

Immediately Hanuman magnified his body to double the size of the *rakshasa* and gave him one kick which felled him to the ground. But the demon rose up with re-doubled vigour and the two of them fought for a long time without either being vanquished. Hanuman now realised that this was not an ordinary *rakshasa* and begged Lord Shiva to come to his aid. He picked up a piece of *dhruva* grass and breathed the *mantra* of the great weapon of Shiva known as *paasupatha.* This he hurled with all his might at the demon who was hurled a few yards away. His body fell on a rock and was smashed to smithereens. Out of the pieces there rose a divine form which came towards Hanuman and bowed low before him.

"My Lord!" He said, "I was a *gandharva* in my previous life and became a *rakshasa* due to a curse. Thanks to you I have been redeemed from this!"

Hanuman wanted to know how he was cursed and the *gandharva* replied.

"Once I tried to kidnap the daughter of a *rishi* and he cursed me that I would become a *rakshasa.* When I begged him to release me from this curse he told me that I would meet my end at the hands of one who was born from Shiva's seed. At that time I would be released from my curse. So now I see that you are the one who was foretold by the *rishi.*"

The *gandharva* now blessed Hanuman and proceeded on his way. Hanuman also was able to quench his thirst in the clear waters of the stream and take his fill of the fruits before progressing on his journey.

Maruti now continued his journey through the sub-continent of Bharatavarsha. He met many great sages on the way and got their blessings. He also encountered fierce beasts and strange birds and saw many lovely trees and flowers. At last he reached a huge forest known as Vidarshana, which was so dark and menacing that none dared to go through it even during the day. It was supposed to be the haunt of *rakshasas* and other night wanderers and was also inhabited by many wild beasts.

Hanuman contemplated on Lord Shiva and fearlessly entered the forest. As he walked on he was beset with stinging mosquitoes and other poisonous insects. Vines and tendrils wound round his feet and tried to stop him from proceeding. As evening approached he could hear the menacing growls of wild beasts all around him. He decided to spend the night on a tree but all through the night he could hear the heart-rending roars of an elephant in pain. With the break of dawn he hurried to the site of the cries and discovered a magnificent elephant half in and half out of the river. His rear legs were firmly planted in the water and try as he might he seemed unable to get out of the water and drag himself to the bank. Hanuman felt very sorry for the royal beast and went close and peered into the water to find out what was preventing the elephant from getting out of the water. He was shocked to see that one of the creature's legs was cruelly gripped in the strong jaws of an alligator. The huge alligator was slowly but surely dragging the elephant down into the water. Blood was oozing from the elephant's feet and flowed like a red stream in the river. The elephant lifted up its trunk and cried piteously. Feeling sorry for the noble animal, the fearless son of the Wind God leapt into the water.

He grasped the tail of the reptile and pulled it. However, the alligator refused to let go and dragged him along with the elephant further into the water. Hanuman immediately realised that this was the wrong thing to do. He let go of the tail and jumped nimbly on its back and grasped its jaws which were locked in the elephant's legs. Using his enormous strength he tore open the jaws and thus freed the elephant from its agony. The crocodile went crazy with the pain and the thought of its lost prey. It thrashed its tail violently in the water and turned with gaping, bloody jaws at its new enemy. Anjaneya immediately swam to its rear and grasped its tail and dragged it to the banks. Before the creature could gather its wits, he once again grasped the tail and swung it above his head and whirled it round and hurled it a hundred yards away. It crashed to the ground and died immediately.

Suddenly, to his amazement, a beautiful maiden rose out of the crocodile body and came near him and bowed low.

"Who are you and how did you come to take on a crocodile's form?" He asked.

"O Anjaneya!" She said, "I am an *apsara* called Ambalika. I belong to the court of Indra, the king of gods. Once as I was bathing with a group of my friends in the pellucid waters of a Himalayan lake, we happened to see a group of young ascetics meditating on the banks. We were smitten by their looks and approached them and tried to entice them with our songs and dances. At last they opened their eyes and cast their compassionate glance on us and advised us strongly to leave them alone if we did not want to be cursed. My friends hurriedly left the place but I lingered on, smitten by the beauty of one of the ascetics. Again and again he warned me not to try him further but I refused. At last he cursed me that I would become a cruel crocodile and live in a mud pool in the forest of Vidarshana. I begged him for reprieve and he relented and told me that I would be saved by the son of the Wind God, born of the seed of Shiva! I see now that you are the one predicted by the ascetic. I would like to give you a boon for having saved me. You will never have to fear from drowning. Water will not be able to harm you. Now please give me leave to go!"

Hanuman was amazed to hear her story and told her to go on her way.

After this episode he continued his journey. After passing through many forests and crossing many mountains and river, he arrived in a forest at the outskirts of the kingdom of Kishkinda. From afar he could hear the roars of wild beasts and trumpets of elephants. He jumped on to a tree in order to have a look at what was happening and found that a noble looking monkey was surrounded by wild elephants and other beasts and was slowly losing ground. Nothing loathe Hanuman jumped into the fray and routed the elephants.

The monkey asked him, "Who are you, who appeared at the right moment to save me?"

"I am Anjaneya, the son of Anjana but people also call me Hanuman. But tell me who you are. You seem to be pretty exhausted. How did you get into this predicament?"

"My name is Sugriva and I am the younger brother of Vaali, the king of this land. This forest is the hide-out of a fierce *rakshasa* called Mayavi. My brother and I had decided to get rid of him once and for all. My brother told me and my friends to come by this trail while he went by another. Though we managed to locate Mayavi, we were unable to kill him. After a fierce fight he killed all my friends. Turning to me he said, "I will let you off since I have no quarrel with you. It's your brother Vaali whom I'm after!" However, as soon as I escaped from him, I was attacked by beasts as you saw. I was too tired by then to defend myself and had you not come I would have been in a bad state!"

Hanuman smiled and said, "O Sugriva! You and I are meant to be friends. We have a long history before us!"

"I don't understand what you mean," said Sugriva.

"Time will reveal my meaning to you. I have given a promise to your father, Surya to be your friend. However, tell me about Mayavi. Who is he? Is he such a terrible creature?"

"What a question!" said Sugriva. "He's indeed a mighty warrior. Only my brother will be able to vanquish him."

Hanuman smiled when he heard this and said, "There is nothing and no one that one cannot conquer in this world if one controls the mind. However, we will talk of all this later. We were fated to meet and our friendship is only starting. You need some rest and after that we will continue on our way."

Sugriva embraced him and begged him to be his friend forever and invited him to his kingdom of Kishkinda.

Seeing him to be in no fit state for travel, Hanuman carried him with ease on his back until they came to a river where they bathed and refreshed themselves. Then Hanuman brought some fruits from the forest and after partaking of that they rested for the night in the trees.

During the night they talked of many things. Hanuman asked Sugriva to tell him the story of his birth and that of his brother, Vaali.

Once there was a very chaste woman called Shilavati. Her husband, Ugratapas caught leprosy but she continued to look after him very lovingly. Once he told her that he wanted to have intercourse with a courtesan. Nothing daunted Shilavati decided that it was a wife's duty to fulfil her husband's desires, however unreasonable. Since he was in a pitiful state and unable to walk she proceeded to carry him in a basket on her head to the courtesan's house. On the way she passed the field where a great sage called Mandavya had been impaled on a stake, by the king's orders through false charges. The sage could not bear to see how this noble woman was being exploited by her vile husband. He cursed him that he would die before the break of dawn! Shilavati immediately countered the curse by praying that the sun would not appear the next morning. Such was the power of her chastity that it happened as she wished.

Next morning the sun did not appear at his normal time. His charioteer called Aruna came to collect him and found him to be immobile. He decided to visit the world of Indra till the Sun God was ready to start on his daily round. When he reached Indra's heaven, he found the gate barred to all men. Indra was holding court with his *apsaras* (heavenly dancers) and they were enacting a drama for him. He gave orders that only women were to enter. Aruna came just at this time and was disappointed to hear this edict. He was determined to see the celestial show and thought of a ruse to get in. He changed himself into a woman and slipped in unnoticed and mingled with the flock of dancers. But Indra, who was noted for his eye for beauty, immediately spied the glamorous new maiden in their midst. He dismissed the other dancers and stopped Aruna at the door when he tried to slip out with the rest of the dancers.

Indra was used to getting any woman he wanted and he tried to beguile poor Aruna who didn't know what to do. Finally she had to disclose her secret. Indra was mad when he heard this and said that she would have to pay the price for having deceived the whole court like this. Aruna was forced to agree and Indra forcibly took her. A lovely baby boy was born out of this union. Since Aruna couldn't possibly take the child with her, Indra gave her to Ahalya, the wife of the sage, Gautama to bring up.

In the meantime, due to Shilavati's great austerity, the sun could not rise. The whole world was in darkness. At last the gods found out the reason for this strange state of affairs. They approached the sage, Atri, the father of Ugratapas and urged his wife Anasuya to go and beg Shilavati to withdraw her will. The latter stopped her prayers and allowed the sun to come out.

When the sun looked about for his charioteer, he was nowhere to be found. He was quite cross with him for being so late. Aruna tried to slip in unnoticed but Surya accosted him and asked him the reason for his tardiness. Aruna was forced to tell him the whole story. Surya pardoned him but was struck with a desire to see the form which had enchanted Indra. Aruna tried his best to dissuade him but Surya insisted and at last he had to give in to his wishes. The inevitable happened and Surya fell for her charms and made love to her. Another beautiful baby boy was born of the union who was also given to Ahalya to look after. One day when Ahalya was playing with the children, both of them insisted that they should be carried on either hip. She became quite cross and said, "You little monkeys! How can you torment me like this?"

Her husband came in just in time to hear her say this. He became quite angry at her behaviour and said, "If that is your wish, let both of them turn into monkeys!"

A sage's word must always come true and so the two boys turned into monkeys. Ahalya was very unhappy at the fate of her two lovely boys. However, a sage's anger is always short-lived and her husband prophesied that the two would become mighty beings.

Indra heard about the fate of the two boys and had them brought to his court and gave them shelter. The child born to him was named Vaali because he had a very long and powerful tail and the son of Surya – Sugriva since he had a beautiful neck.

There is another story connected with the birth of the two brothers, Vaali and Sugriva. Once upon a time the creator, Brahma came down to the earth and rested on the mountain called Meru, which is the axis on which the earth revolves. At that time a tear fell from his eye and when it touched the ground, the very first monkey (*vanara*) was born. Brahma named him Riksha and stayed with him for a while. The little monkey played on the hill and ate all the fruit he wanted. Every evening he returned to Brahma and laid some flowers at his feet. One day Riksha saw his reflection when he bent to drink from a lake. He thought it was the face of an enemy trying to grab him and pull him into the water. He jumped into the lake to attack the adversary. He didn't know that it was a magic lake and when he came out of the water, he found that he had been changed into a female. He was a most entrancing female monkey and as she stood on the hillside of Meru, both Indra and Surya fell in love with her. That same morning, first Indra and then Surya came down and made love to her.

Children of the gods are born very quickly. The monkey girl had two golden coloured babies and that afternoon as she washed them in the lake, they splashed water all over her and by the time they were clean she found that she had changed sex once again and become Riksha.

He took his sons to Brahma. They named Indra's son Vaali and Surya's son, Sugriva.

Brahma gave the kingdom of Kishkinda to Riksha. Kishkinda was a dense forest rich in fruit trees and inhabited by various wild animals. Brahma created many other monkeys or *vanaras* with the power of flight and speech and asked them to make friends with the bears. The two brothers were inseparable and as they grew older, the father taught them all the arts at his command. When Riksha died, many other contenders to the throne arrived but Vaali killed or maimed every other challenger and became the undisputed ruler of the monkey world. He declared himself to be the sole Lord of all the trees and the female monkeys of Kishkinda. His authority was unquestioned and as one who had successfully earned his dominant place among the apes, Vaali was not obliged to share the spoils of power with anyone, but being of a magnanimous nature he shared everything with his younger brother, Sugriva who was his second-in-command and who in turn served his elder brother faithfully. Indra gave his son a victory garland of little golden, lotus flowers which would make him invincible.

Once Vaali heard of the churning of the milky ocean by the gods and the demons and decided to go and see this event for himself. All of them reached the banks of the ocean of milk. When he saw that his father Indra and the other gods were flagging, it is said that Vaali took over the churning himself. Such was his strength that he could single-handedly accomplish what the two protagonists were unable to do. Indra was mighty pleased with his son's prowess. For having helped them, the gods blessed him with immeasurable strength. Another boon they gave him was that anyone who approached him for a fight would lose half their strength which would come to him.

Many precious things appeared out of the ocean. Two beautiful damsels also appeared. They were known as Tara and Rumi. Vaali accepted Tara as his chief wife and Sugriva chose Rumi. The brothers returned joyfully to their kingdom and reigned in peace for a long time. In course of time Vaali got a son called Angada.

Vaali was a great devotee of Shiva and everyday he went to all the eight directions and bathed in the oceans and worshipped Shiva in all his aspects. At one stride he could cross the seven seas and reach the mountain known as Charuvala, which lay beyond the seas. When he moved it was with the force of a typhoon. No lance could pierce his chest. When he strode across the earth the mountains shook and the storm clouds scattered in all directions, afraid to precipitate rain. All nature feared him and even Yama, the God of Death, was afraid to approach him. Thunder softened its voice and even lions refrained from roaring in his presence. Once it is said that he picked up the ten-headed Ravana and tucked him inside his tail!

Supremely wise, virtuous and clever.
You are always eager to fulfil any mission of Rama's.

— *Hanuman Chalisa* by Tulsidas

ॐ *Sri Hanumathe Namaha!*

ॐ

Brahmachaarine Namaha!

CHAPTER EIGHT

SUGRIVA MITRAM

The Friend of Sugriva

Buddhirbalam Yasho dhayryam,
Nirbhayatwam arogata,
Ajadyam vaak padutwam cha,
Hanumatha smaranaath bhaveth

One who meditates on Hanuman will become famous and get,
Great intelligence, strength, courage,
Freedom from fear and disease,
As well as expertise in talking.

— *Hanuman Stotram*

Hanuman now accompanied Sugriva to Kishkinda and was introduced to Vaali. Sugriva described how Hanuman was solely responsible for having saved him from the wild beasts. He also told him about his greatness. Vaali was at first rather suspicious of Hanuman who he had tried to kill as a baby since he feared that he might possibly be a usurper to his throne but when he heard that Hanuman was a good singer, he insisted on hearing him sing. Hanuman took up the lute and started strumming it. When he began to sing the whole court went into a state of ecstasy. As the music wafted out, all the monkeys left their respective work and crept in, mesmerised by his voice. Vaali was charmed and told him that he could remain in his land forever.

Sugriva took Hanuman on a tour of their land. When they reached a mountain called Rishyamukha, Hanuman was struck by the serenity of the place and told Sugriva that this mount was indeed very holy. Sugriva agreed but sadly said that it was out of bounds for his brother Vaali. Hanuman enquired the reason for this so Sugriva told him the whole story.

Once there was a demon called Dundubhi who managed to get many boons from the creator Brahma. One of these boons was that he could never be killed by any weapon. Having got these boons he proceeded to vanquish the gods and disturb the sages and kings of the land. His hands were always itching for a fight and he could never find a worthy opponent. Unable to bear his urgent desire to try out his strength, he rose from the nether world and thrashed through the ocean and swam ashore. He thrust his horns into the sand and bellowed to the waves, "Fight me!" But the waves just kept coming on and on. They didn't care whether he was there or not.

The long, watery arms of the sea hissed and swelled round Dundubhi's feet and appeared to be warning him to go back or else drown. A huge wave now rose up foaming and frothing, steadily coming closer and closer. Dundubhi thought it better to retreat.

Then he went to the snowy Himalayas, white as Shiva. He rushed up the snow-clad slopes and battered the sides with his horns. The mountain king, Himavan turned his rocky face and looked glassy-eyed at the irate buffalo. He was clothed in a white robe of snow and falling water, with a belt of ice. In a booming voice he said, "Don't bring war to this untouched country. Why harm my men of peace? The strong will never get angry because we know that our serenity is our armour. Now go and leave me in peace."

Hardly had he said this than a huge cloud of mist and snow covered him and he disappeared from view. The mountain seemed to disappear along with Himavan. The ice and sleet cut into Dundubhi, biting and crushing him so that he ran screaming and never stopped till he reached the cave fortress of Kishkinda.

He desecrated all the fruit trees in the forest surrounding the fortress. He then stuck his enormous head into the cave city and roared. Vaali came out on his balcony and told him to go while he still had life to do so. Dundubhi challenged him to fight. Vaali put on his golden garland and came charging out of the gates and both of them had a duel in which neither was able to vanquish the other. At last Vaali used his superhuman strength and caught hold of the buffalo's horns as he came charging at him with lowered horns. He whirled him above his head and flung him as far as he could. Dundubhi could hardly stand up but Vaali followed him and kept picking him up and whirling him round and round. At last he dashed him on the ground. The demon started vomiting blood and finally died in agony. Vaali's rage was still unabated. He lifted up the carcass and threw it many leagues away, where it fell with a tremendous thud on this mount on which stood the *ashrama* of the sage Matanga. As the carcass passed over the head of the sage, it splattered blood all over him. Rudely disturbed in his meditation, the irate sage rushed out and was met by the gory sight of the huge carcass of the buffalo demon.

He made a dire pronouncement. "If the one who has done this despicable deed ever comes within four miles of this hallowed place, his head will burst into a thousand pieces! Let all the monkeys who are camping in this place who belong to his tribe also depart instantly or they will all be turned into rocks!"

"That is why my brother never dares to come to this beautiful place." Hanuman thought a while and told Sugriva that one day this very mount would be a sanctuary for him. Beyond that he refused to reveal anything even though Sugriva pressed him.

Dundubhi had a friend called Mayavi who was the son of the architect of the demons called Mayan. He was furious at the fate of his friend and swore to avenge his death. He had come to Kishkinda and challenged Vaali for a fight. At that time Vaali had chased him off. Sugriva had also accompanied him but Vaali had told him to go off and that is how Sugriva came to meet Hanuman. Vaali was sure that he had got rid of the nuisance once and for all but the demon was not to be deterred so easily. Once again he came to the gates of the cave fortress of Kishkinda and woke everyone with his blood-curdling roars at midnight. The monkeys tried to drive him off but he shooed them off like flies. At last they appealed to their king. Vaali took up his arms and went out of the gates but the demon was nowhere to be seen. Well versed in the magic arts of his father, he had simply disappeared from the scene. Vaali shouted to him to reveal himself. "Coward that you are, why don't you come and fight with me like a hero. What is the use of hiding yourself?"

Hearing this, Mayavi came out of his hiding place. He saw that Vaali was flanked by Sugriva and Hanuman and laughed in scorn. "Are you such a hero that you can't fight by yourself and have to ask for help from two others?"

Turning to his brother and Hanuman, Vaali asked them to return to the palace since this duel was to be between him and Mayavi alone. Hanuman complied but Sugriva refused to leave.

Turning to Mayavi, Vaali said, "This will be a fight to the finish between us. I will not let you return alive from this place."

Mayavi laughed in derision when he heard this and said scornfully, "I will finish you off first and then kill your brother and son and become the king of Kishkinda!"

Without wasting time in a useless verbal combat, Vaali lunged at Mayavi with his bare fists. Then ensued a mighty battle between the two. At last Mayavi realised that once again he had misjudged the powers of his opponent. He ran off into the forest with Vaali in hot pursuit. Sugriva also followed since he feared for his brother. Vaali caught up with Mayavi and they had another fierce battle in the middle of the forest. To Sugriva's amazement the two heroes fought on without showing any signs of fatigue, for one whole day and night. As dawn appeared, Vaali saw that Mayavi showed signs of fatigue so he pressed on, determined to kill him at all cost. The demon knew he was beaten and fled beyond the edge of the world, into a subterranean passage. Vaali followed but before entering he turned to Sugriva and said,

"Please wait for me here. I will surely kill him and return. But if for some reason he kills me, then don't wait, seal the mouth of the cave with a stone and return to the kingdom, or else he will come out and kill you. Remember if he is killed, milk will flow out of the cave and if I am killed, it will be blood, so if you see blood, close the cave with a stone and save yourself. You are certainly no match for him!"

Sugriva stayed at the mouth of the cave waiting anxiously for his brother for one whole year. At last one day he heard a thunderous sound coming from the cave and soon after that a stream of blood started to flow. Sugriva was sure that the sound was his brother's death-cry and that the demon had killed him. The stream of blood confirmed his suspicions. Crying bitterly for the fate of his brother, he sealed the mouth of the cave with a huge boulder and made his way to the kingdom where everyone was awaiting their victorious return. The monkeys wept when they heard the whole story. Sugriva was sunk in gloom and the *vanaras* feared that the kingdom was going to be ruined. The ministers urged him to take over the kingdom and at last he was forced to agree.

However, the truth of the matter was that Vaali had actually killed Mayavi but a traitor to the last, the demon had wrought his magic and changed the milk which was oozing from him into blood so that he could create dissension between the brothers. When Vaali came to the mouth of the cave he found to his consternation that it had been firmly sealed. He couldn't believe that his brother had betrayed him in this cruel fashion. He concluded that his greed for the throne must have prompted him to act in this pitiless manner. Using his mighty strength he kicked the boulder aside and came out like a tornado. He was filled with an uncontrollable rage against his brother. He went outside the gate and roared with anger. The citizens shuddered when they heard this roar. They ran to Sugriva and informed him that Vaali had arrived at the gate! Sugriva couldn't believe his ears. Surely he had seen blood flowing out of the cave! Could this have been a trick of the malicious demon? Before he could go to the gate, Vaali had rushed into the court foaming at the mouth. Without much ado he picked up Sugriva like a bit of straw from the throne on which he was sitting and threw him a hundred yards away.

"Ungrateful wretch!" He shouted. "You thought you could kill me and steal the throne for yourself. You are a hundred times worse than Mayavi. If you fear for your life then make yourself scarce. If I ever find you hanging around here again, that will be the end of you!"

So saying he ran after Sugriva and before he could raise himself up, he pounced on him and boxed and pounded him in the presence of all the courtiers and officials. Sugriva tried to explain that he was innocent but Vaali gave him no chance to say anything. No one dared to stop Vaali in his terrible rage. He seized Sugriva by the scruff of his neck and tried to smash his head against a rock. Sugriva managed to slip out of his hands and flee but was hotly pursued by his brother. At last he was inspired to go to the mountain of Rishyamukha, which he had shown to Hanuman long ago. Vaali was filled with rage at the fact that he couldn't follow him. He pulled out a few trees in his fury and threw them at his brother. Sugriva was prostrate with grief and anger and hid inside a cave to lick his wounds and try to figure out what he should do next.

Vaali returned to Kishkinda and took up the reins of the kingdom once again. Frustrated in his attempts to punish Sugriva, he killed his brother's children and forcibly acquired Sugriva's wife, Rumi. So Sugriva lost both his kingdom and his wife!

When Sugriva followed his brother to the cave, Hanuman decided to leave Kishkinda and went to the forest to meditate. Very soon he found that his mind was peaceful and under control. He started to look like a veritable sage.

This was the time when Vaali was chasing Sugriva who ran and took shelter in Rishyamukha which was forbidden territory for his brother. Vaali was so incensed at the fact that he couldn't catch hold of him that he started uprooting trees and hurling them after Sugriva. One of these trees fell in front of Hanuman when he was meditating and made him open his eyes. He thought for a while and realised that everything had come to pass as he had foreseen. His friend had been thrown out of Kishkinda and had taken refuge in Rishyamukha. Without wasting another moment he went and met Sugriva and comforted him.

"Don't worry Sugriva! Truth shall prevail. Even though you are down now, good times are ahead of you. Meditate on god and don't harbour ill-will towards your brother and all will go well."

Sugriva followed his advice and the two of them spent their time on the mountain and soon some of his other friends joined them.

However, Vaali could never forgive his brother and everyday he would climb the hill opposite Rishyamukha and terrorise his brother with abuses, threats and displays of strength. He would scream and shout, beat his chest; gnash his teeth and hurl abuses at his brother. As mentioned before, Vaali had the habit of bathing in all the oceans of the world. Effortlessly he would jump from ocean to ocean and take his bath every morning. Every time he flew over Rishyamukha, he would give a mighty kick on the head of the hapless Sugriva if he happened to be standing below him. One day Hanuman decided to stop this vile practice once and for all. As Vaali passed overhead, he jumped and caught hold of his long tail and tried to drag him down. His idea was to make him fall on the mountain and thus destroy himself as per the curse of the sage. However, Vaali was noted for his amazing strength and was a good match for Hanuman who had infinite powers but had to be prompted by someone before he could use them fully. Vaali realised that the person who had caught him must be Hanuman since Sugriva would not dare to do this, so he thought that the best thing would be to carry Hanuman back to Kishkinda and there kill him. However, they were equally matched and neither could make their plot work. At last they decided to make a pact with each other. Hanuman told Vaali that he would release him if he promised not to keep harassing Sugriva. Vaali agreed provided Sugriva would promise never return to Kishkinda or make claims on the throne. It was only then that Hanuman let him go. Vaali was pleased with this pledge since he had feared that Hanuman would be another contender to his throne.

In Valmiki's *Ramayana*, Hanuman makes his debut in the 'Kishkinda Kanda'. He played a very subdued role in the beginning of the 'Kanda', in which took place his momentous meeting with Rama. Sugriva never knew that Hanuman's strength was superior to his brother's. Had he known of it, he would have asked Hanuman to fight with Vaali instead of approaching Rama. But both of them were ignorant of Hanuman's exceptional powers and thus Sugriva appealed to Rama. In fact without the curse of the *rishis,* the entire course of the *Ramayana* war might have been different, for Maruti could have fought the war single-handed.

Rama, Lakshmana and Sita eternally abide in your heart,
Nothing delights you so much as to listen to the Lord's stories.
— *Hanuman Chalisa* by Tulsidas

ॐ *Sri Hanumathe Namaha!*

ॐ

Ramabhaktaaya Namaha!

CHAPTER NINE

RAMADASA

Famous Encounter

ॐ *Namo Hanumathe,*
Rudravataaraaya,
Vishwarupaaya,
Amitha-vikramaaya,
Prakataparaakramaaya,
Mahaabalaaya,
Suryakoti samaprabhaaya,
Ramaduthaaya namo Namaha!

Prostrations to Hanuman, the messenger of Rama,
The avatara of Rudra,
Who could take on the form of the whole universe,
Who had amazing powers,
Who performed incredible feats,
Whose strength was unbelievable,
And who was as brilliant as a thousand suns.

— *Hymn to Hanuman*

Months passed in this way. Sugriva was always bewailing his loss but Hanuman always gave him good counsel. In the meantime destiny was already weaving her inextricable strands and the time was slowly but surely approaching when Sugriva's fortunes were going to turn for the good. Once when Sugriva and Hanuman and some of the other monkeys were sitting on a rock, they saw a chariot flying over the mountain towards the south. A beautiful woman and an enormous man were in the chariot.

The woman was crying piteously and as soon as she saw them, she tore off a piece of her upper garment and tied her ornaments in a bundle and threw it down. The monkeys picked up the little bundle which she had thrown and kept it safely in their cave.

Far away in Ayodhya, which was the capital of their land, many strange things had happened. The king of the land was Dasaratha and he had four sons called Rama, Lakshmana, Bharata and Shatrugna. Rama was the incarnation of Vishnu and was an exemplary person. He had married Sita, the daughter of the king of Videha who was noted both for her beauty and her conduct. It so happened that Dasaratha decided to crown Rama as the king since he was getting old. However, before the event took place, due to a series of strange misunderstandings, the king was forced to give in to his favourite queen – Kaikeyi's pleas to send Rama to exile in the forest for fourteen years and install her own son Bharata in his stead. The poor king had given her two boons long ago and the queen took this opportune moment to ask him to fulfil his promises. The king was most reluctant to give in to her demands but she threatened to kill herself if he refused. When Rama heard of this, he decided to carry out his father's promise even if it meant giving up his kingdom. His wife Sita and his brother Lakshmana insisted on accompanying him to the forest and the three of them set out without further ado. The king could not bear this parting and died soon after.

Kaikeyi's son Bharata was away when all this happened. When he returned he was furious with his mother and refused to accept the throne. He went after his brother, whom he loved dearly and begged him to return. However, Rama refused to comply with his wishes and told him it was his duty to go and do as his father had wished. Bharata reluctantly returned but refused to sit on the throne, meant for his brother. He kept Rama's sandals on the throne and lived the life of a sage outside the city, in a hut like his brother.

In the meantime Rama, Lakshmana and Sita spent an idyllic time in the forest roaming around and meeting many sages. Unfortunately in the last year of their exile, Ravana, the wicked *rakshasa* king of the island of

Lanka saw Sita and fell in love with her and abducted her and took her off to his island retreat. Sita had thrown her bundle of jewels when they passed over the hill of Rishyamukha where Sugriva and Hanuman were sitting.

Rama was desperate and did not know how to get her back. Lakshmana tried to comfort him and they went from place to place trying to locate her whereabouts. They met an old woman saint called Shabari, who advised him to go and meet a monkey called Sugriva who would help him. With this in view the brothers were on their way to the hill of Rishyamukha.

Before proceeding to the famous encounter between Rama and Hanuman as given in the Valmiki *Ramayana*, we will see another very sweet story in which it is said that Rama met Hanuman when they were both very young children.

Knowing that Vishnu had taken an incarnation as Rama, Shiva longed to have a glimpse of him and watch his childhood pranks. He took on various disguises in order to gain entrance to the palace. He pretended to be an astrologer, a mendicant and a bard in order to have a look at the child but he was unsuccessful in all his attempts. A last he decided to take on the guise of a monkey trainer and go with a monkey. So he went to Anjana's cave and requested her to send her son with him. Anjana recognised him as her favourite god and bowed low to him and brought Hanuman before him. Maruti also thought that he looked very familiar. In fact the thought flashed across his mind, "He and I are one!"

Shiva put a leash round the baby monkey's neck and apologised to him for the discomfort. They went to Ayodhya and drew crowds wherever they went. Maruti held everyone spellbound with his clever tricks. They reached the palace gates where the gate keeper scornfully told them to clear off. Shiva in his guise as a *madari* (monkey trainer) just stood there playing on his drum. Inside the palace, Rama, who was just four years old, heard the sound of the drum and started to throw a tantrum and Dasaratha commanded that the *madari* be admitted. In the palace courtyard, the two of them performed for the royal princes. This was no ordinary show for the drummer was Nataraja, Lord of dancers, now dancing in the form of an ordinary monkey trainer. Vishnu who makes the entire universe dance to his tune clapped his hands in delight, oblivious to all but the monkey's antics. He gazed wide-eyed at the drummer and the dancing monkey. No one in the court except the royal *guru*, Vasishta guessed the secret and he bowed his head in reverence to Shiva.

When the dance was over the entertainers were given rich gifts but when they prepared to leave, Rama began to cry and insisted that the monkey be left behind. The mother felt embarrassed to ask the *madari* to give up his source of livelihood. All at once the drummer vanished and the monkey jumped into Rama's arms. After that Hanuman became Rama's constant companion. During the day he served the princes and joined in all their games. He would fetch balls for them and disentangle kite strings and fan them while they played board games. He would row for them when they went on the river and guard them when they went swimming in the Sarayu River. He would retrieve arrows when they practised archery and climb trees to pluck fruits for them. As a reward for all this he was allowed to sleep in Rama's bed and eat the left-overs on his plate and was even allowed to ride on his shoulder. He remained with him as the royal pet until the time when Vishwamitra came to take Rama to save his *yaga*. At that time Rama secretly instructed Hanuman to go to Kishkinda and enter Sugriva's service and await his coming.

The story as given by Valmiki follows the course of Rama's and Lakshmana's journey through the sub-continent and their meeting with the tribal woman Shabari who instructed Rama to approach Sugriva. Sugriva was sitting with Hanuman and his other ministers under a tree when they spied Rama and Lakshmana coming up the hill. Sugriva as usual was filled with misgivings and feared that Vaali had sent them to kill him. Hanuman climbed on top of a peak and observed the two who were approaching. At the very first sight of Rama, he was filled with an ecstasy, the reason for which he was unable to say. He felt as if he was seeing god. He cupped his palms together above his head and bowed to him. Turning to Sugriva he told him that he was sure that these people had not been sent by Vaali and that they were not coming with bad intentions. However, Sugriva was not convinced of this and told Hanuman to go down in disguise and find out their intentions. Hanuman took on the form of a young Brahmin and went down to the brothers. This was indeed an encounter which was to have far-reaching consequences not just for Hanuman but for the whole world of devotees for all time to come.

As he approached them an unaccountable feeling of joy overcame him. His mind was clear and pure and none of the suspicions of his chief darkened his thoughts. The birds seemed to be chirping more musically than usual. The soft and gentle breeze from the south wafted a divine fragrance towards his nostrils which he thought was a benediction from his father. The creepers which were entwining the trees seemed to shed their flowers in his path. Never for a moment did he realise that this was to be the turning point of his life and that he was about to meet his master whom he would serve faithfully for the rest of his life!

With one jump Hanuman came close to where the two were coming and changing his identity he went near and bowed to them.

Of the many facets of Hanuman's personality, the outstanding quality that attracted and endeared him to his master, Rama was his power of eloquence. As he approached the brothers for the first time, Hanuman felt a thrill of joy and all his faculties of intelligence, discretion, observation and power of speech surfaced. Paying homage to both the brothers he addressed them in a soft and pleasing manner. Valmiki has given a beautiful description of this in his *Ramayana.*

"How have you two ascetics of remarkable vigour, unfailing prowess, most austere vows and excellent appearance come to this region? Your looks are that of some royal sages or of gods. You seem to be searching for something. Your presence adds charm to this lake of sparkling waters. Having eyes resembling the petals of a lotus and wearing a rounded mass of matted hair, you two gallant men resemble each other! You seem to be heroes come down to this earth from heaven!"

Seeing that the brothers still remained silent Hanuman decided to disclose his identity. "I am a monkey named Hanuman and have been sent by the virtuous king of monkeys called Sugriva. He seeks your friendship and has asked me to negotiate for him." Actually the astute Hanuman added that last bit himself for he realised that these people were capable of helping Sugriva.

Valmiki portrays Hanuman as a model speaker who by the magic of his words and their skilful presentation was able to win the heart of Rama who was a stranger.

Rama was struck by the Brahmin's demeanour and totally captivated by his sweet speech. He told Lakshmana that no one could speak in this way unless he had mastered the Vedas. He noted that there was no defect in his countenance, eyes, forehead, brows or limbs.

"O Lakshmana! He has delivered a wholesome, distinct and remarkable speech, grammatically correct, fluent and delightful to hear. Even the mind of an enemy with uplifted sword, will be moved by his speech."

The first impression that both had about each other developed into a mutual attraction, binding them together for life, in a saga of selfless service, sacrifice and devotion. All the subsequent events in the epic only served to bring them closer, deepening their love, admiration and understanding of each other.

From this moment onwards, Hanuman enshrined Rama as the Lord of his heart. He accepted him alone as the Supreme Lord. His mind and intellect were totally surrendered to him.

This life of selfless service and single-pointed devotion to his Master hastened his spiritual unfoldment. In the devotional literature of the world Hanuman's *bhakti* to Rama has no parallel. He will ever remain the purest and most exalted *bhakta* the world has ever known. Valmiki says that even a very casual mention of the name of Rama was enough for his eyes to well up with tears of profound joy and to fold his palms before him.

Lakshmana now said to Hanuman, "Know us to be the sons of the great king, Dasaratha of the land of Kosala. This, my brother is his eldest son, Rama and I'm his brother Lakshmana. Just at the time when he was going to be anointed king of the land, he was disinherited of his sovereignty by some unpardonable trick of destiny and came to live in the forest with me and his consort, Sita. She is a veritable Lakshmi and deserves to live in a palace adorned with all jewels and comforts. However, she chose to follow him to the forest. Unfortunately a *rakshasa* whose name is not known has abducted her and taken her to his stronghold. We have come here in search of her. We were told by the great sage, Shabari that we should enlist the support of a monkey chief called Sugriva who would be able to help us in our search."

He added that Sugriva's name had also been told to them by a giant called Kabandha whom they had released from a curse.

"We are indeed happy to hear that you are Sugriva's minister. By the pleading of such an envoy, all the objects of the sovereign in whose service he happens to be employed will be accomplished. My noble brother is the ruler of this land but by a cruel fate he has been forced to take to the life of a mendicant and we will be happy to accept help from your master Sugriva in order to find his consort."

Hanuman said, "The noble Sugriva is in the same predicament as your brother. He has been deprived of both his throne and his spouse by his brother and exiled by him and forced to take refuge on this hill. He will certainly help you to find Sita."

Lakshmana now turned to his brother and said, "Brother it looks like we have arrived here at the right time to the right place to meet the right person. Let us go with him and meet Sugriva."

Hearing the story of Rama's selfless renunciation of the throne, Hanuman's initial admiration turned into great respect and love. He realised that Rama was no ordinary person but a great being, worthy of veneration.

Rama willingly agreed to meet Sugriva but Hanuman knew that the brothers would be unable to scale the impossible slopes of Rishyamukha so he resumed his monkey form and took the two brothers on either shoulder and jumped with them up the hill to the peak where Sugriva was sitting with his other ministers.

Placing Rama and Lakshmana down before Sugriva, he said, "I would like to present to you Rama, the scion of the race of Ikshvaku, and his brother, Lakshmana who are both sons of the emperor, Dasaratha. In order to keep his word to his wife, Kaikeyi, the king was forced to banish Rama to this forest. He came accompanied by his brother and his wife. Unfortunately his wife was abducted by some *rakshasa* and he has come here seeking your aid in finding her."

Sugriva, who had been suspiciously watching their approach, now came forward with outstretched arms and clasped Rama's hands in his own and said sweetly, "I'm indeed honoured that you have come to me to seek my aid. Let us clasp our hands in friendship and take an oath to help each other. If you promise to help me kill my brother, Vaali and restore my wife and throne, I shall surely swear to help you to find your wife!"

After hearing Sugriva's story which resembled his, Rama said, "*Dharma* is the law of civilisation, based on duty not desire, which ensures social stability. He who upholds *dharma* is an *Arya* and he who does not is a *rakshasa.* Vaali is an animal, a barbarian who is no different from Ravana. Both believe that might is right. Both have become kings by force and they do not respect the sanctity of marriage. If civilisation has to be established, people like Vaali and Ravana need to be destroyed."

Hanuman immediately lighted a fire and made Rama and Sugriva stand on either side and forge a pact of friendship with the blazing fire as witness. They worshipped the fire with flowers and went round it three times and swore to help each other. After this they clasped each other in their arms and swore eternal friendship.

Sugriva broke off a flower-laden bough and placed it on the ground as a seat for Rama and Hanuman did the same for Lakshmana.

Now that they were comfortably seated, Sugriva narrated his pitiful tale to Rama and begged him to kill Vaali who had insulted him and treated him so unfairly.

Rama smiled and said, "My arrows, sharp like the fangs of a serpent will descend on your brother and finish him off in no time. So have no fear."

Sugriva now told Rama, "I have heard from Hanuman how the *rakshasa* has abducted your beloved spouse. Rest assured that wherever he might have hidden her, in the bowels of the earth or the vaults of heaven, I shall deliver her to you. Therefore cast away your grief for you shall surely get your beloved back! I think she must have been abducted by Ravana. In fact I feel that it was she who was being dragged away in his aerial vehicle."

Rama was amazed to hear this and eagerly asked him to narrate the tale.

Sugriva said, "While I and Hanuman were sitting on this mountain with four others, we saw an aerial vehicle passing overhead. I think it was Ravana who was inside. He was carrying a most beautiful woman in his arms. She was wriggling and crying out loudly, "Rama! Lakshmana! Save me! Save me!"

Seeing us standing below she tore off a piece of her upper garment and tied her jewels in it and dropped it down without Ravana noticing. We have kept it safely and I will show them to you and you will be able to know if they belong to your wife."

Rama was greatly excited when he heard this and asked Sugriva to show it to him immediately. Sugriva went into the cave where they lived and brought out the bit of cloth and gave it to Rama. Rama opened the scarf and saw his beloved wife's jewels inside. He pressed them to his bosom and tears started to flow from his eyes and he could no longer speak. At last he controlled himself and turning to Lakshmana he showed the jewels to him and said, "Lakshmana don't you recognise these jewels as belonging to the princess of Videha?"

Lakshmana replied, "I do recognise her anklets which I used to see every time I bowed at her feet but my eyes never went beyond that to her neck."

"O Sugriva! said Rama, "Do you know where that wretch has carried away my queen? His end is approaching fast for I shall surely follow him and kill him."

Sugriva said, "I'm not sure where his abode is situated even though I know that he is the mighty king of Lanka but I swear to you that my monkeys will discover his whereabouts and recover Sita. It ill befits a noble soul like you to give way to your grief like this."

At that moment far away in Lanka, Sita felt her left eye tremble by itself and the same thing happened to Vaali in Kishkinda and Ravana's ten left eyes also trembled. This is considered to be a good sign for females and a bad omen for males.

Hearing this Rama checked his grief and listened to the sad tale told by Sugriva about the injustice which had been done to him by his brother and assured him that he would kill Vaali. However, Sugriva was not quite convinced for he knew his brother's amazing powers and feared that the slender Rama would not be a match for him.

Falteringly he spoke, "I realise that you have great strength but constant harassment has made me timorous. I'm not sure if you can beat the mighty Vaali in combat. Actually he is so powerful that once he even subdued the mighty Ravana." He went on to tell Rama about this feat.

Once the mighty night wanderer, Ravana desired to conquer the heavens and bring Indra, the king of the gods, to heel. He called his eldest son Meghanatha and told him his wish.

Meghanatha said, "O Father! Why do you hesitate to ask me such a thing? You have only to say one word and you know that I shall obey you. Come, let us go to Indra's heaven and capture him."

Thus, the two of them went to Indra and challenged him to a fight. Indra was a bit reluctant since he was not sure of the outcome, however since he could not refuse he agreed. Very soon it became apparent that Ravana was going to be defeated. His son Meghanatha immediately stepped into the fray and effortlessly subdued Indra and tied him and threw him before his exultant father. It was after this feat that Meghanatha got the new name of Indrajit (conqueror of Indra). Ravana took Indra back to his stronghold and tied him to a pole in the middle of the courtyard for all to see. He then looted the heavens and revelled in his greatness. Indra's pitiable state was reported to Brahma by the sage Narada. It was Brahma who had given many boons to Ravana and made him invincible so he felt a bit guilty and went to Lanka and made Ravana release Indra. The latter was most ashamed of the whole affair and crept back to heaven hoping that the other gods had not heard of this shameful episode. However, Narada came there soon after and told him of a way by which he could get even with Ravana.

"Your son Vaali is the one person who can humble Ravana's pride," he said.

"Leave it all to me. I'll see that justice is done!" So saying Narada departed to Lanka where he was welcomed by Ravana. There he fanned the flames of Ravana's pride by telling him that there was a monkey called Vaali, who was Indra's son who went about telling everyone that he would get even with the person who had humiliated his father! Ravana was indignant at this and swore to kill this impertinent monkey. He was all set to go to Vaali armed with all his weapons and accompanied by an army. Narada laughed to see these preparations and said,

"He is only a monkey. You don't need all these weapons and army to subdue him. All you need is a rope. You can creep up behind him and tie him up before he knows what's happening!"

So Ravana desisted from taking his army and weapons and went in search of Vaali. Narada, who didn't want to miss the fun, offered to accompany him. They crossed the southern sea and found Vaali deep in meditation on the shore. He was in the habit of jumping from sea to sea every morning to do his morning ablutions and prayers.

Seeing his enormous frame Ravana was a bit daunted but Narada egged him on and told him to creep up behind and catch his tail and then bind him without difficulty. Now a monkey's tail is his greatest strength and Vaali's tail was very special. In fact he had been named Vaali because of the extraordinary length and strength of his tail. *Vaal* is the Sanskrit name for "tail".

Ravana crept up from behind and caught his tail. Vaali did not stir from his prayers but simply caught hold of Ravana's hand in his tail. Then Ravana put out his other hand and that also met with the same fate. Very soon Vaali had bound Ravana's whole body in his tail and continued uninterruptedly with his prayers! Narada thought it expedient to leave the place as fast as he could.

Vaali's tail had wound tightly round Ravana's whole body, holding him in a fierce grip so that only his face was to be seen. Keeping Ravana thus bound in his tail, Vaali went from ocean to ocean and each time he had a dip, Ravana was submerged again and again in the salty water! This went on for many months. At last his son Indrajit became anxious about his father's whereabouts and was all set to go and fight with Vaali. Again Narada arrived on the scene and told him not to confront Vaali since the latter had really no enmity with Ravana but was waiting for Indrajit to present himself since he was the one who had bound his father. Narada told Indrajit that Vaali would definitely kill him if he went. He advised him to wait patiently till Vaali released Ravana of his own accord.

As foretold Vaali grew tired of having Ravana hanging on his tail and released him. Ravana was completely subdued and begged his pardon. Vaali agreed on condition that he and his son would not go and make a nuisance of themselves to his father, Indra in heaven. In return Vaali promised that he would never make war against Ravana nor side with those who wanted to conquer him.

This was the story told to Rama by Sugriva since he wanted to make Rama understand Vaali's great strength. He also added that Vaali had a boon that he would automatically get half the strength of anyone who confronted him. This is one of the reasons that Rama chose to kill him from behind a tree.

Every arduous task in the world,
Becomes easy thanks to your grace.

— *Hanuman Chalisa* by Tulsidas

ॐ *Sri Hanumathe Namaha!*

ॐ

Shooraaya Namaha!

CHAPTER TEN

PRANADEVA

Killing of Vaali

ॐ *Hanumathe Rudravataraaya,*
Ramasevakaaya,
Ramabhakti tatparaaya,
Ramahridyaaya,
Lakshmana shakti nivaranaaya,
Lakshmanarakshakaaya,
Dushta nigrahanaaya,
Ramadutaaya, namo Namah!

I bow to Hanuman, the messenger of Rama,
The avatara of Rudra, in the service of Rama,
Totally engrossed in devotion to Rama,
Ever keeping Rama in his heart,
Who saved Lakshmana and gave him back his powers,
And who is the destroyer of the wicked.

Hanuman whispered to Lakshmana that Sugriva had told them this story only because he doubted Rama's ability to kill him. He did not dare to ask him for a show of strength but he would be happy if Rama showed some of his prowess. Lakshmana told Rama of Sugriva's fears. Rama laughingly went up to the enormous skeleton of the demon, Dundubhi and lifted it up with his toe and flung it to a distance of about eighty miles! Sugriva was a little appeased by this feat but he still spoke doubtfully.

"This carcass was filled with blood and flesh and ten times as heavy as it is now when Vaali lifted it and flung it here. Now it's only a bare skeleton. I wonder if I could ask you to perform one more feat and thus assure me of your might. Vaali's arrow could pierce a *sal* tree which has a huge circumference, without any difficulty. Here are seven *sal* trees growing in a row. If you can pierce one of them and split it into two, my fears will be laid to rest once and for all."

Rama smiled and without a word he fitted his arrow to his mighty bow, known as the Kodanda. The arrow was gold plated, thicker than a finger, half as long as a staff, marked with his name and decorated with the feathers of the fastest birds and tipped with iron. The *sal* (ironwood) trees were as thick as turrets. The arrow flew from the bow and split not one tree but all seven trees and then pierced the earth and is said to have gone to the subterranean world and then returned to its own quiver!!

Sugriva couldn't believe his eyes. He felt most ashamed at having tested Rama's powers like this and he prostrated at his feet and begged his pardon for having doubted him.

Standing with folded palms before Rama, Sugriva said, I am now fully convinced that you can kill even Indra, the king of the gods if you so choose, so why not his son, Vaali. Let us proceed straight away to Kishkinda and you can meet him face to face."

They went through forests and mountains, fragrant with sandalwood and came to a grove of most beautiful trees from which arose a fragrance of oblations being offered into the fire and Rama questioned Sugriva as to what that grove was and to whom it belonged.

Sugriva said, "This hermitage belonged to seven sages known as Saptajanas. They used to practise severe penance here for many years. They slept on water and subsisted on air alone. They never stepped out beyond this grove. When the time came for them to depart from this world, they were given bodily liberation. However, this grove is still sacrosanct. None dare enter it. One can hear music and ethereal voices singing from within. The perfume rising from sacred wood fires lighted during *yajnas* permeates the air as you can see. Let us all bow to those glorious sages from here and get their blessings before proceeding."

All of them bowed low in front of the holy place and then walked on. When they reached the outskirts of Kishkinda, Rama and the others concealed themselves behind the trees of the thick forest which surrounded Kishkinda.

Rama now told Sugriva to go forward alone and challenge Vaali for a duel. "I will stand aside unseen and shoot my arrow into him at the right moment."

In lieu of the fact that Sugriva had told him about Vaali being able to take over half the strength of his opponent, Rama decided to shoot him from behind a tree. Another reason for this strange act was that Rama feared that if he confronted Vaali, he might refuse to fight with him since he had no quarrel with Rama and then he would not be able to keep his pledge to his friend, Sugriva. So Rama told Sugriva to go and challenge his brother and he and Lakshmana would follow close behind him. Sugriva mentally prepared himself and boldly went to the gates of Kishkinda and bellowed loudly and challenged his brother to a duel. Enraged at hearing his brother's roars, Vaali got up with such force that the base of the cave sank and his eyes spat fire. Grinding his teeth in anger, he slapped his thigh and clapped his hands so that the sound echoed through the valleys. He charged out with such speed that the ornaments round his neck snapped and scattered their gems all around. Vaali came out of the cave looking like the morning sun rising over the horizon. He grabbed Sugriva who was certainly no match for him and bashed him to a pulp. With great difficulty he managed to extricate himself from his iron grip and take to his heels. He ran all the way back to Rishyamukha before Vaali could finish him off.

Rama in the meantime had been keenly watching the fight and found to his dismay that he couldn't distinguish between the two brothers who looked like two peas in a pod. Fearing to discharge his arrow in case he killed Sugriva instead of Vaali, he desisted. He followed Sugriva who was in a very poor state.

Sugriva could hardly speak yet he whispered, "If you didn't want to kill my brother why did you not refuse at the very outset instead of letting me get battered like this? Fully believing your word I challenged him and see what has happened!"

Rama tried to pacify him. "My dear friend," he said, "how can you think that I have betrayed you? Your brother and you resemble each other in stature, costume and embellishments. Even your roars sound similar. Both of you were clasped in each other's arms trying to strangle each other. How could I shoot my deadly arrow when I knew that I might kill you instead of him! Please do return to Kishkinda and challenge him once again but this time you must wear a garland by which I will be able to distinguish you."

He told Lakshmana to take a liana from the mountainside which was covered with flowers and looked like a beautiful garland and put it round Sugriva's neck. Battered and bleeding though he was, Sugriva licked his wounds and proceeded towards Kishkinda, followed by Rama, Lakshmana, Hanuman and a few of his other friends.

Rama urged Sugriva to go and challenge Vaali fearlessly once again as now he was sure that his arrow would find its mark.

Sugriva went and roared outside the gates. Vaali was in his seraglio lolling about with his wives when he heard the roar. He couldn't believe his ears. His amorous mood gave way to one of violent loathing. How could Sugriva who he had just reduced to pulp a few hours ago dare to come and challenge him again! He was filled with a blind rage. He was determined to finish off his brother once and for all. He had been a real thorn in his side for a long time and once he was dead he could enjoy the company of his wife, Rumi without feeling any guilt. He was well aware of his crime in consorting with his younger brother's wife while her husband was still alive. He had somehow stifled his conscience for he was infatuated with Rumi even though his own wife Tara was very beautiful and wise. With Sugriva out of the way he could have Rumi without any pangs of shame for the law allowed a man to marry a deceased brother's wife in order to protect her! Thinking thus, Vaali gave a big bellow of disgust and rage and rushed out.

The beautiful Tara stopped him as he was going and gave his some sage counsel.

"My Lord! She said, "This brother of yours was beaten by you and ran off with his life just a short while ago. How is he emboldened to return and roar like this without the assurance of help by some powerful ally? The crown prince Angada, your son gave me the following report. He said that two young and expert warriors, known as Rama and Lakshmana, the sons of the emperor Dasaratha, have entered this forest and formed an alliance with Sugriva. I'm sure Sugriva has been emboldened by their protection or else he would never have dared to accost you like this. Please don't go now. Tell him to return tomorrow morning and then you can fight with him if it pleases you. Better still you can make friends with him and allow him to return to the court. Be kind to him. Return his wife to him. She is very unhappy here. Somehow my heart sinks within me and I see only bad omens. I beg of you not to go now."

Vaali's time had come and he just would not listen to reason. Moreover, he was anxious to appropriate Rumi all for himself. Brushing off Tara's detaining hand he ordered her to return to the other women. She placed Indra's golden garland round his neck and embraced him sadly for she had a premonition that she would never see him alive again.

Vaali brushed her aside and rushed out. He glared angrily at Sugriva and charged at him like an infuriated bull. They started to grapple in deadly earnest. Sugriva's strength was flagging and he looked round desperately for Rama, wondering why he was not coming to his aid. Vaali lifted him above his head in order to dash him on a rock and thus end his career! The golden necklace was shining round Vaali's neck. Rama had no trouble in recognising him. He saw Sugriva's agonised look. He stretched his powerful arrow on his bow and let it fly with a tremendous twang. It found its mark on Vaali's breast and felled him as easily as it had felled the *sal* trees. The full moon shone with all splendour and lighted up the huge fallen body of Vaali, which was now bleeding and weak. Vaali had never thought even for a moment that there was any weapon or power on heaven or earth that could conquer him in a fight. He was invulnerable according to the promise of the gods yet here he was, laid low on the bare ground of his own kingdom with just one arrow. He was really anxious to know who this exceptional warrior was who was able to kill him with one arrow. His name must be on the arrow. With his last remaining strength he pulled the arrow out of his chest. Blood gushed out of his heart like a spring which had been dammed for a long time. Everything was blurring before his dying eyes and he had to hold the arrow close to his eyes before he could spell the name "Rama" on it. For a moment gratitude filled his heart. All creatures had to die at one time or other and far better for him to die at the hands of Rama who was supposed to be an *avatara* of Vishnu than by the weapon of a *rakshasa* or *asura* or a wild animal. This feeling was swiftly replaced by anger at the way he had been killed. He looked up feebly as Rama and Lakshmana approached him. Summoning his waning strength he upbraided Rama for his act.

"You are supposed to be the scion of the line of Ikshavku and noted for your adherence to *dharma.* How could you have killed me from behind a tree when I was fighting with my brother? When Sugriva challenged me for the second time, my wife Tara warned me not to go for she feared that he was being helped by you but I told her that I had no fear of you since I knew you would not stoop to any type of unrighteous act. What have I done that you should have killed me from behind? I hear you are looking for your wife. I could have killed that wretch Ravana and brought her back to you single-handed. I have already defeated him once and spared his life but this time I would not have done so. Why did you have to ally yourself with this worthless Sugriva?"

Vaali had exhausted himself by this speech and he fell back gasping for breath. Rama waited patiently for Vaali to have his say for he knew that on the face of it, he had every right to berate him. At last when Vaali had stopped, he spoke to him with compassion in his eyes.

"O Vaali! How dare you speak to me about *dharma* and *adharma* when you are living a life steeped in sin? Your younger brother, who is full of good qualities and loves you very much, should have been treated by you as a son. Without giving him a chance to clear his name you beat him up and banished him to Rishyamukha in order to keep his wife. According to the law of this land, anyone who is guilty of sleeping with his brother's wife when he is still alive is punishable by death! You have continued your enmity with your brother only to fan your own lust. Sugriva is as dear to me as my brother, Lakshmana. I have sworn friendship with him and publicly made a pact to kill you and restore his kingdom and his wife. What sort of a friend would I be if I did not keep my promise?"

Vaali considered Rama's words and realised that he spoke the truth. He bitterly regretted his cruelty to his younger brother whom he should have treated as a son. He also knew that his action in having stolen his wife was despicable.

"O Rama!" He said, "You have spoken rightly. I'm not worried about myself. Death is inevitable for all but I'm worried about my son, Angada. Please consider him as your own son and see that he is looked after properly. Please don't let my beloved wife Tara be insulted by Sugriva. She is wise and good. I realise that I'm fated to meet death at your hands and that is why I refused to listen to her when she urged me to desist from fighting."

With his last breath Vaali took off his gold chain which had miraculous powers and put it over Sugriva's neck. He begged him to forgive him for all he had done to him and told him to look after Angada as his own son as well as his beloved wife Tara. Sugriva felt such remorse for his act that he couldn't say a word.

Rama promised to see that Sugriva gave the best treatment to Angada and Tara. Hearing of the tragic end of her husband, Tara now ran to his side along with her son Angada. Casting herself over his body, she bewailed his fate. Rama urged her to get up and see to the obsequies but she refused to budge from the place. Taking up the fatal arrow which had killed her husband, she threatened to plunge it into her own heart and had to be forcibly stopped by her attendants.

Hearing her cries and his brother's kind words, Sugriva lost whatever courage he had and told Rama that he would also immolate himself on his brother's pyre. Let Angada help him to find Sita. Neither Rama nor anyone else could console him.

At last Hanuman approached Tara and told her in gentle tones, "An embodied soul always reaps the good and evil fruit of his actions done in the past. The body is like a bubble on the water. It might burst at any time and is not worth grieving for. Your duty now is to look after your son, Angada who is solely dependent on you. It is your responsibility to see that the last rites are done for your husband in the proper way. That's the only thing you can now do for him."

Rama spoke sternly to Sugriva and told him that he had done this only at his request and for him to wash his hands of the whole matter was not a manly thing to do. It was his duty to see to the obsequies of his dear brother rather than opt to perish in the flames. He commanded Sugriva to bring a palanquin and take his brother's body to the river side. At last Sugriva did as he was bidden. The monkeys brought out the royal hearse which was like a chariot without wheels. They dressed their dead king in jewelled clothes and placed his body on a bier covered with flowers and placed it on the pyre which had been prepared for him. Angada set fire to it and all of them offered water and did all the usual rites which had to be done for a departed soul.

By the law of the jungle, after Vaali's death, his killer would automatically become king with the right to kill Vaali's children and to claim his wives.

However, Rama wanted to make the *vanaras* leave their old laws and adopt the law of *dharma.* So he told Sugriva to ask the monkeys whether they were agreeable to have him as king. When they agreed, Sugriva asked Tara if she was willing to be his queen. When she agreed, he adopted Vaali's son, Angada and made him the heir to the throne. Thus did Rama make the monkeys change their ways and follow the rule of righteousness.

Hanuman was determined to conquer his animal instincts and took a vow of celibacy and service. By the vow of celibacy he crushed the desire for sensual pleasures and by that of service he trampled the tendency to inflate his ego.

After this, Hanuman approached Rama and stood with folded palms and spoke these words to him.

"O Lord by thy grace this kingdom has now been acquired by Sugriva. Pray enter the palace and crown him king."

Rama refused to enter the city since he said that he had given his word to his father not to enter any city for the duration of fourteen years. However, he gave all instructions as to how Sugriva should be anointed as king and how Angada should be crowned as the Prince Regent. He advised Sugriva on the duties of a good king. "Whatever you do, let it be based on the sanctioned codes of good conduct. Never hurt anyone with your words, even if it be an enemy."

Sugriva said, "I want to serve you. Please command me."

Rama said, "The rainy season is coming. At the end of it bring your army and come and help me find Sita."

Hanuman begged to be allowed to accompany Rama and serve him during the four months of the rainy season. Again Rama had to decline his offer.

"Your presence is absolutely necessary for Sugriva. He will need your support and judgement. Come to me after four months and I'll tell you what you can do for me." He and Lakshmana decided to spend the approaching four months, of the monsoons in a cave nearby. At the end of the four months, Sugriva promised to get all the monkeys and start on the great quest to find Sita.

Sugriva duly entered the city in state and was crowned as king with Angada as the crown prince. Tara also drew what comfort she could from the fact that at least her son's well being was being looked after.

"You rendered great service to Sugriva,
Arranged his meeting with Rama and gave him kingship.

— *Hanuman Chalisa* by Tulsidas

ॐ *Sri Hanumathe Namaha!*

ॐ

Ramadutaaya Namaha!

CHAPTER ELEVEN

RAMADUTA

Messenger of Rama

Anjana garbha sambhuta,
Kapindra sachivottama,
Rama priya namastubhyam
Hanuman raksha sarvada

I bow to the beloved of Rama,
Born from Anjana's womb,
Greatest of simians,
Hanuman! May thou look after everyone.

Rama and Lakshmana now spent the four months of the monsoon season starting from July to October in a cave on the mountain called Prasravana. The sun now started to move south. Dark clouds heavily laden with water covered the skies so that the sun was not to be seen at all. The heavens burst and gushed down the mountainside and deluged the fields. The birds were silent. No animal stirred out while the waters poured and roared. Wild vegetation covered the landscape with monstrous creepers and vines. The sky was perpetually overcast. The persistent gloom and dampness were reflected in Rama's heart.

"The skies are weeping at the fate of my beloved, as indeed I am too," thought Rama. For four months the brothers were confined to the small cave with nothing to do but watch the continuous downpour going on outside. The four months were months of torment for Rama since he was always imagining his beloved Sita's state and how anxious she must be about his whereabouts and whether he would come to rescue her. But there was nothing he could do about it since the monsoon season was not suitable for any sort of travel.

The rains ended at last and the sky began to clear. Rama was waiting anxiously for Sugriva's arrival but almost a month passed and still there was no sign of him. Seeing his unhappiness Lakshmana said, "Brother I think that the ungrateful monkey has totally forgotten the promise he made to you. I will go and remind him forcibly of his duties!"

Lakshmana was not a calm person by nature and the four months of confinement inside the cave had not improved his temper in any way and now the sight of his brother's agitation made his blood boil. He strapped the quiver to his shoulder and took up his bow and strode towards Kishkinda looking like a thundercloud. Rama cautioned him not to get angry and try conciliatory methods with Sugriva.

In the meantime Hanuman was always conscious of his duty and couldn't bear this delay any longer. Sugriva was always closeted in the harem with his wives, drinking and cavorting and making merry. He had totally forgotten the passage of time. His bedroom was so gorgeous and comfortable that he had hardly left it for the past four months. He wasn't even aware of the storms raging outside. He was surrounded by his beautiful wives with long tresses and heavy breasts who provided him with all comforts and sang and danced for him. Having been denied all the pleasures of the senses for such a long time, Sugriva found it impossible to control his appetite for food and sex. He was lying in a euphoric daze when Hanuman entered the harem where he had never gone before.

"O Sugriva!" He said, "It ill befits you to forget the promise made by you to Rama. Because of him you are now enjoying all these luxuries. The rainy season has long past and you have not redeemed your promise. Therefore, issue orders immediately to the monkeys that they should assemble for the great endeavour of finding Sita."

Hearing these words of his able minister, Sugriva aroused himself a little and told Hanuman to send word to all the monkeys and bears in all the lands under his sway to come and assemble at Kishkinda in a week's time.

"Let my entire army be assembled under their generals without delay so that Rama may not think that I have been lagging in my duties." Having made this effort Sugriva sank back into the arms of his wife.

Lakshmana walked with purposeful strides to Kishkinda. The earth shook with the force of his angry steps. The entrance to the city was through a cave which was guarded by monkeys, so that no one could enter without permission. Seeing Lakshmana they took up trees in order to stop him from entering. When he saw this he became doubly incensed. Seeing his fury they fled in all directions. They ran to Sugriva and told him of Lakshmana's violent mood. The king was totally inebriated and lost to the world in the arms of his brother's wife. He hardly knew what they were saying. The monkeys now ran to Angada who hurriedly came out of the gate to meet Lakshmana to try to pacify him. Lakshmana ordered him to call his uncle immediately. He could hear the sweet strains of music and signs of revelry floating in the air and when he thought of the agony that his brother had endured these past four months, his blood boiled. Angada was scared out of his wits and ran and informed his uncle and mother of the situation.

Hanuman also went to him and apprised him of the gravity of the situation.

"Rama is a wonderful friend but he will be like a malefic comet if aroused to wrath. It is your tardiness that has made Lakshmana come here in search of you. You have to go and pacify him."

But Sugriva was totally intoxicated and in no condition to meet Lakshmana.

"What crime have I committed? Why should he be angry with me?" whined the tipsy monarch.

"You must admit that you have allowed time to elapse. You have lost track of the seasons in your ardour. Rama has been counting the days to go in search of his wife. Pained in heart and mind, he has sent Lakshmana to remind you of your promise. Please go and talk sweetly to him."

Sugriva did not dare to go and face him so he begged Tara to go and pacify him since he knew that Lakshmana would not display his anger before a woman. Tara was also in a state of inebriation. Her gait was unsteady and her hair and clothes dishevelled.

In the meantime Lakshmana had forced an entrance into the palace and noted the abundance of wealth and luxury. His heart burned with rage when he thought of his dear brother's plight and how this ungrateful monkey was enjoying himself, oblivious to the woes of his master.

He was loathe to force an entrance into the inner apartments.

Tara met him just outside the harem and pacified him with her sweet words.

"Why O Prince!" She said, "Are you so angry? Who has been foolish enough to kindle your wrath?"

Lakshmana replied, "Your husband seems to have forgotten all the rules of *dharma*. Lapped in lust, he has forgotten the promises he made to my brother. If you wish to do him some good, go and tell him to rouse himself from this orgy of lust and help Rama. Ingratitude leads to the destruction of the best of men. We have been betrayed by one whom we considered a friend!"

Tara replied in a sweet and gentle tone. "O Prince! Please don't be angry with Sugriva. You know that *kama* (lust) is a powerful emotion. Even *rishis* have fallen beneath its spell, what need be said about a mere monkey who is fickle by nature and who has been denied these pleasures for many years. Please pardon him for his apparent indifference which has been caused by weakness. Actually he has already ordered the army to be mobilised and soon thousands of monkeys from all over the country will assemble here to start out on their quest to discover Sita. Please return to your dear Lord and apprise him of the situation."

Lakshmana was slightly appeased by these words and turning to Hanuman he asked him if it was true that the monkey hordes had been commanded to come. Hanuman assured him that he himself had despatched messengers to all the great monkey strongholds in the sub-continent and very soon all of them would come.

By this time Sugriva had got himself under some sort of control and he accompanied Lakshmana and went to Rama, prostrated at his feet and begged his pardon for his seeming tardiness. Rama was always the soul of compassion and he immediately forgave Sugriva and embraced him. Just then Jambavan, the king of bears, arrived. He was an old, dark bear with a crown and earrings of gold, with smoky grey eyes, huge paws and long arms and stood on two feet. He pointed out to Rama, the monkey troops that had started to arrive from all over the world. The whole hillside was covered with tree folk. They came in millions, lion-tailed, dark-faced, red-bottomed, white-furred and golden-haired, ranging from all parts of the country from the Himalayas to the tip of the southern sea. The entire world's tree folk answered Sugriva's call and crowded round their king to await his commands.

Sugriva was delighted and pointed out the different types to Rama.

"Look over there at the white tree-dwelling monkeys who can change their forms at will. Note the tall blue coconut monkeys who are as strong as elephants, the yellow honey-wine monkeys with sharp teeth, the charcoal monkeys born to the daughters of the *gandharvas*, who worship the sun, the grey apes from the woods skirting the edge of the world who are handsome from eating only berries, the black ones with snaky tails from the caves on the banks of the Ganga, the red ones with lion manes and all the great bears of the earth, dark as gloom, brown, black and terrible in combat. They have all answered my call and are ready to do your slightest bidding."

Rama was very pleased to see them. Since Sugriva did not know the exact whereabouts of Lanka, Rama asked him to choose four leaders who could take their troops to the four quarters and begin the search for Sita without further ado. The general, called Vinata, was sent to scour the eastern regions.

"Dawn first appears bright with brilliant glory in the east and people living there also become golden coloured. Search everywhere but stay away no longer than one month from today." One quarter of the monkeys followed him. The ground trembled as they left.

Another batch led by Sushena, his father-in-law, was sent to the west.

"Explore the west for Sita. That is where the sun's light ends and the lady of the night has her home. Follow the cool forest streams that flow from the high cold lakes, search the kingdoms and empires, the plateaus and waste lands. There live the *gandharvas*. But don't let any creature see you. Do not go farther than where the sun goes. Return here within a month."

Satabali, the white-furred bear, was told to proceed north.

"Go to the enchanted lands of the Himalayas where the mountain of Kailasa raises pale and silver as the moon and go to the palace of Kubera, the Lord of wealth. Examine the icy slopes of the Himalayas and listen to the music of the Apsaras and the Nagas who live beneath the ground. Turn back from the dark and fearful northern border of the country and let not more than a full month pass before you return." With him went the third quarter of the monkey warriors.

At last he called Hanuman and Angada and told them to proceed to the south. Jambavan also lumbered in after them and all sat on rugs before Sugriva.

Sugriva said, "We saw Ravana fly south with the princess. I make Prince Angada the leader of the batch. Pavana Putra, the son of the wind, will surely find her." He then took out a scroll and gave it to Hanuman and said. "Memorise this and give this message to the demon king when you meet him."

Hanuman turned to Rama who was sitting beside Sugriva and prostrated at his feet and begged him to bless him. Rama placed his lotus palms on Hanuman's head and blessed him. He then took him aside and gave him a perfect description of Sita so that he would know her when he saw her.

"O Hanuman," he said, "I feel sure that you will be the one to find Sita. Look at her feet and you will find that her toe nails glow like rubies. Her heels have been compared to a quiver. As for her waist, it is delicate and unseen. However, it is enough for you to observe her feet. They are incomparable. When you see her, give this ring to her so that she will know that you are not a spy but have come as my messenger. It is the signet ring of the Ikshvakus and she will surely recognise it." Rama then gave a description of how she spoke, how she walked and how her voice would sound. He also narrated some anecdotes to him, which only he and she knew so that she would have no doubt that Maruti was indeed her husband's messenger.

Hanuman respectfully listened to every word that Rama spoke. He had a very good portrait of Sita in his mind now and he felt that when he saw her, she would look familiar to him. He took the ring and reverently placed it on his head and bowed low to Rama and departed to the south followed by a host of monkeys led by Angada and Nila.

Even before a month had passed, the generals who had been sent to the east, west and north returned despondently and declared their inability to find out anything concerning Sita. All of them felt sure that Hanuman alone would accomplish the impossible.

Hanuman proceeded to the south with his party and passed many forests and rivers. The stipulated time of one month was coming to a close and the monkeys were exhausted and hungry since they had just passed a forest which was totally denuded of fruits and roots due to the curse of a sage. They had crossed chasms and ravines and forests and thickets. They couldn't find even a drop of water to drink. Exhausted and dispirited, they collapsed on the hill side. Just then Hanuman noticed two birds with water dripping from their wings, coming out of a cave. He told the monkeys that there must be water and fruits inside and decided to follow the birds. It was pitch dark in the tunnel so they walked single file, one catching the tail of the other until they suddenly came to a wonderful grove with trees of gold under which was sitting a woman ascetic. At first they thought that this must be Sita but Hanuman observed her carefully and could not detect any of the signs given by Rama. He approached her in all humility and begged her to tell him the story of the cave and this wondrous place.

She told them that her name was Swayamprabha and that she was the guardian of this cave which belonged to her friend Hema, the *Apsara*. The demon king Ravana had married Mandodari, Hema's daughter. Swayamprabha now plied them with fruits and nuts to eat and delicious honey drinks until they were satiated. She was very lonely and did everything to charm the monkeys and make them stay on. Even Jambavan, the wise old bear, succumbed to her allure and forgot about their mission. Only Hanuman remembered and told her the whole story of their search and courteously asked her whether he could do anything for her in return for her hospitality. She begged him to marry her and stay on in the cave and she would give him anything he wished for. He sternly refused her offer and insisted that he would have to leave with or without his companions. Seeing his determination she promised to help them. She told him that this was a magic cave and no one who entered it ever got out alive. However, she took pity on them and told them to close their eyes and she would transport them out of the cave. When they opened their eyes they found that they were standing on the shore of the Southern Sea. The perfume of sandalwood from the Malaya Hills swept over them. Around them stretched the lifeless sands without a single fruit tree and before them, the ocean-emerald green stretching to the horizon. The island of Lanka was nowhere to be seen.

Angada looked at the sun and realised that much more than a month had passed since they had entered the cave. He was utterly dejected. None of them knew what they should do now. Hungry and helpless, the monkeys groaned in despair. Angada looked at the dejected monkeys and said, "I'd rather starve myself to death than return and face Sugriva's wrath!"

The rest of the monkeys and bears swung their arms up and down and cried, "We will die with you!"

Hanuman told Angada not to be a coward and that it was better to return and face Sugriva who was sure to be kind to them. Angada had painted a lurid picture of Sugriva to all the other monkeys and all of them agreed that it would be better to fast to death. Nothing Hanuman said could persuade them to change their minds.

They lay on the seashore with their heads facing south.

In the meantime a huge vulture by the name of Sampati heard their talk and came out of the cave where he was living. Seeing the monkeys lying in rows on the beach, he congratulated himself on finding that his food had been supplied to him by the kind gods.

"Today fortune has indeed favoured me. I have not eaten for days and here are some delicious monkeys, all laid out in neat rows, waiting for me to go and gobble them up!" With these words, the bird started to hop towards them, since he didn't have any wings.

When they saw this enormous bird hopping towards them with the sole purpose of devouring them, the monkeys started lamenting their fate. They who had decided to starve to death now appeared to be frightened of being eaten alive!

Angada started wailing, "Just look at our fate. This bird looks like Yama, the god of death himself coming to make an end of us. It is said that all birds and animals love Rama. Even the old eagle Jatayu was prepared to give up his life for Rama's sake! Then why should this bird try to kill us and stop us from helping Rama?"

Actually Sampati was the brother of Jatayu, who had helped Rama during his exile and had been killed by Ravana while trying to stop him from carrying away Sita. As soon as Sampati heard the word "Jatayu" he stopped in his tracks and enquired from Angada as to what he knew of Jatayu who was his younger brother. He requested him to help him down from the rock since his wings had been burnt. Angada now became a bit bolder and helped the old vulture to climb down the rock and then he narrated the whole story of Rama and of their own search for Sita.

Sampati's eyes filled with tears when he heard of his brother's fate and he wept bitterly. Angada asked him how he knew Jatayu and Sampati recounted his own story to them.

"Jatayu was my younger brother. When we were young we had a competition to see who could fly higher and we flew straight at the sun. When I saw that Jatayu was getting burnt due to the scorching heat, I flew over him and protected him so that he escaped but I fell to the ground with my wings totally burnt. I have not been able to fly ever afterwards and I have never met my dear brother since. My life has been one long suffering since then and I have kept myself alive because I have been told that my redemption would come when I hear the story of Rama."

As soon as he heard Angada's tale of Rama, the old eagle sprouted wings and soared into the sky like a young bird to the surprise of all the monkeys. They were astonished at the miraculous power of the story of Rama. Sampati swooped down once again and told them that he had seen Sita being abducted by Ravana. Angada begged him to tell them all he knew.

Sampati said, "One day while I was sitting on this rock, I saw a beauteous young lady being carried away by force by one of the night wanderers who was undoubtedly their king – Ravana. She was trying her best to wriggle out of his grasp but he held her in a fierce grip. She was crying out piteously for Rama and Lakshmana."

Hearing this, a flash of hope dawned in the hearts of the monkeys and they crowded round the old eagle and begged him to tell them all he knew.

He continued, "Ravana is the son of Vishravas who was the son of Pulastya, one of the seven sages. He had two wives. One was a *yakshi* who gave birth to Kubera and the other was a *rakshasi*, who gave birth to Ravana. This city of Lanka which I can see with my keen eagle's vision was built by Kubera. Ravana was jealous of his brother and did austerities to Shiva and was given a sword with which he defeated and drove out his brother and appropriated the island for himself. He also grabbed Kubera's aerial car, the Pushpaka. Riding on this flying chariot and wielding his divine sword, Ravana indulged in an orgy of rape and plunder. Once he had kicked a hermit and called him a monkey. The enraged hermit cursed Ravana that monkeys would indeed be the cause of his death.

Peering to the south Sampati assured the monkeys that with his keen eagle's vision he could see Sita sitting in a grove surrounded by *rakshasis.* Sampati blessed the monkeys and told them that they would surely be successful in their search and advised them to select one out of their clan who would be able to leap to Lanka and give them news of Sita.

Angada and the other monkeys now became hopeful once again that their mission would be successful and started making plans as to who could jump further and who would be able to go to Lanka and get news of Sita.

Angada now asked each of the monkeys as to how far he was capable of jumping. One said he could jump ten miles, another twenty, and another thirty and so on. But they all proclaimed their incapacity to jump a hundred *yojanas* or eight hundred miles! Angada himself said that he felt sure he could jump all the way to Lanka but feared that he would not be able to make it back.

Jambavan, the great old bear, was noted for his sagacity and strength. The incarnation of Rama was taken to annihilate Ravana and before he took birth as Rama, Vishnu asked the creator Brahma to create a number of monkeys who would be able to help him in his mission. The story goes that Brahma cogitated over this for a while and then he felt sleepy and yawned. Out of his mouth jumped a small creature that later became the wise old bear – Jambavan.

Another story about his birth goes as follows. Once when Brahma was reclining on his lotus seat, there suddenly appeared two huge demons before him called Madhu and Kaitabha. Seeing them, Brahma was frightened out of his wits and started to perspire. Jambavan is said to have been born out of those divine drops of perspiration. He was a great devotee of Vishnu and is supposed to have taken birth along with Vishnu in each of his incarnations. In this manifestation he had taken on the form of a bear in order to help Rama. Though he had possessed mighty powers before, he was old and weak now and confessed his inability to do this amazing deed.

All the while Hanuman was sitting apart, gazing at the sea and chanting the name of Rama. While all the other monkeys were bragging about their prowess, Hanuman alone sat silent, deep in some reverie of his own.

Jambavan now went to him and said, "O jewel amongst monkeys! Why are you remaining silent? Don't you know that you are the son of the Wind God? You have the ability to jump as far as you wish. In fact even as an infant you jumped over twenty thousand miles in order to catch the sun! You alone amongst us have the power to accomplish this impossible task. Rise up and soar into the air and leap over the vast sea, for you can easily do this."

Hanuman had been cursed by the *rishis* that he would never remember his extraordinary powers. In fact he would have to be reminded of his strength by someone before he could put it to use. Hanuman listened intently to Jambavan's words – "Only in you are found strength, good sense and valour. In you alone does one find perfect adaptability to the exigencies of place and time. Scholar in ethics, in you alone is there perfect morality." These are the words that Valmiki makes Jambavan say while he exhorted Maruti to undertake the impossible task of crossing the mighty ocean. Hanuman rose up and with his usual modesty, he bowed to the aged bear and told him that he was prepared to do as commanded.

"Your words give me so much courage that I feel that I can vanquish the entire race of *rakshasas* single handed if they will not hand over Rama's immaculate wife. The span of this ocean seems quite insignificant to me. The grace you have conferred on me and my Lord's command are like two wings which will carry me across this vast expanse of water with the greatest of ease. I will fly to Lanka as swiftly as the powerful arrow released by Raghava. If I fail to locate Sita in Lanka, with the same speed will I fly to the abode of the *devas*. If I fail again, I will bind and bring Ravana and hand him over to my Lord." His supreme confidence in his ability to achieve what he had been told to do came from his total dedication to his Master.

Hearing his vow, the gods extolled him thus, "One in whom undaunted courage, foresight, balance of mind and skill are found, as in you, will never feel any tediousness in any work which he undertakes."

Our mind needs to be constantly reminded of its divine potential and of the fact that it can achieve phenomenal heights provided it realizes its divine destiny. It needs to be reminded that nothing can be performed by itself and that everything is done by the divine power operating within us. Thus, Hanuman is symbolic of the perfect mind, and embodies the highest potential it can achieve.

Hanuman releases all afflictions of those,
Who concentrate on him, in thought, word and deed.

— *Hanuman Chalisa* by Tulsidas

ॐ *Sri Hanumathe Namaha!*

ॐ

Mahakayaaya Namaha!

CHAPTER TWELVE

SUNDARA

Sundara Kanda

"Atulita baladhamam,
Hemashylabha deham,
Bhanujavana Krishanyam,
Jnaninaamagraganyam,
Sakalaguna nidhanam,
Vanaraanaam-adhishtam,
Raghupathi priyabhaktam,
Vatajaatam namaami"

"I bow to the son of the Wind,
Whose strength is incomparable,
Whose body has a golden sheen,
Like the colour of the sun,
Foremost of the wise,
Filled with all noble qualities,
Greatest amongst simians,
The beloved devotee of Rama."

— *Sri Hanumath Stotram*

Reminded of his powers, Hanuman was suddenly filled with his own strength and expanded himself till his head almost reached the heavens. His face glowed like the rising sun, energy throbbed through his powerful limbs and his eyes blazed like planets. His breath rumbled like a volcano which was about to erupt. His tail was held above him like the banner of the war god, Kartikeya. All those who saw him trembled in fear. Birds squawked and scattered in all directions, wild animals hid in their caves and even the fish darted to the bottom of the ocean. The monkeys alone were unafraid and watched, spellbound by this feat. They cheered wildly and jumped up and down with joy.

From his gigantic height he spoke to them, "Fear not O Monkeys! I come from the loins of the Wind God who is mighty beyond measure. I can circumambulate the mountain Meru and can overtake the blazing sun. My form as I leap across will resemble that of Lord Vishnu in his incarnation as Trivikrama (the one who measured all the three worlds in three steps). I shall cross the sea in a matter of moments and see Rama's queen and bring her back if possible. I shall now go to the top of this mountain which alone will be able to sustain my weight as I jump."

In his exuberance he jumped from peak to peak and crushed their tops as easily as breaking off the stem of a flower! The other monkeys watched open-mouthed at this display of power. He then jumped to the top of Mount Mahendra, which was the highest spot on the beach, and prepared to make the leap across the sea. Under the force of his weight, the mountain shuddered and released its waters; animals ran around crying in terror. Hanuman composed himself and fixed his mind on Rama and repeated the magic *mantra* "Rama, Rama". He then folded his palms and looked to the east and received the blessings of his father, the Wind God. He flexed his muscles and slapped them in the way of wrestlers. He then squatted on the ground with hands on the ground and one foot stretched behind like a racer and gave a mighty roar as he leapt into the sky. Trees and bushes were uprooted by the force of his jump and scattered their flowers on him as if in benediction. His tail, which was curled above him, looked like a banner as he coursed through the sky. Clouds parted to make way for the amazing son of the Wind God. Sea creatures rose to the surface to watch in wonder at this astonishing feat. He could touch the sky above and see the glimmering sea below.

Midway between Jambudwipa (India) and Lanka, lies the mountain known as Mainaka. Varuna, the Lord of the sea, saw him passing and thought to himself that he should do something to help the messenger of Rama. So he told the mountain which was submerged in the ocean, to rise up and offer some rest to Anjaneya. Mainaka did as commanded and suddenly Hanuman saw the golden peaks of the mountain rising up from the ocean, blocking his passage. The mountain took a human form and begged him to accept his hospitality and that of the king of the ocean and rest a while before proceeding on his journey.

With his single-pointed devotion to duty, Hanuman refused to accept the mountain's appeal and told him firmly that the time allotted to him was very short and he was bound to accomplish his purpose and return as fast as possible, so he simply touched the mountain with his hand in acceptance of the welcome offered to him and sped on his way, anxious to reach Lanka before the sun touched the western horizon. The mountain now sank back and renewed its former position in the ocean.

The gods then decided to test Hanuman and told Surasa, the mother of the serpents, to intercept him so that they could ascertain his strength. She promptly took on a huge and hideous form and stood arms akimbo in front of Hanuman as he was skimming across the sea.

"The gods have ordained that no creature can cross the southern sea without entering into my mouth. Today they have given you to me as my food so I shall eat you up." This was one of the reasons that no creature ever made its way to Ravana's stronghold.

So saying she opened her cavernous mouth and prepared to swallow him. Hanuman spoke sweetly to her and begged her to allow him to pass since he was the messenger of Rama and had urgent business on hand. He promised to return to her after accomplishing his purpose. She was adamant and said that he would have to pass through her mouth before proceeding. Hanuman was angry at her lack of understanding and doubled his size. Surasa promptly opened her mouth even wider and Hanuman again doubled his size but Surasa kept opening her mouth even wider. The intelligent Hanuman then reduced his size to that of a thumb and entered her mouth and came out again through her nostrils!

"Now that I have fulfilled your vow that none can pass without entering your mouth, please allow me to pass," he said.

The gods were happy to see Hanuman's quick wit and intelligence and they told Surasa to give him way. She said, "Move forward O high-souled Hanuman, foremost of monkeys and proceed on your way and enable Rama to re-unite with Sita!"

Hanuman bowed and coursed along the sky with the speed of wind, trailing clouds of glory behind him.

At this time another demoness known as Simhika who lived in the sea and was able to catch her prey by catching their shadow on the water, saw Hanuman flying and thought to herself that the gods had blessed her with a good dinner that day. She seized his shadow and Hanuman felt himself being dragged down. He was wondering what had happened to him when the creature rose up from the water and prepared to devour him. Hanuman instantly grew to enormous proportions but the creature also widened her mouth and flew at him. He immediately reduced his size and fell into her mouth and tore out her vital parts with his sharp nails. He then expanded himself and split her apart so that she fell dead in the ocean. The fish rushed up to eat her carcass.

As Hanuman soared into the sky once again, all the gods and divine beings extolled him. "You have indeed performed a most meritorious deed in having killed this terrible creature. He, in whom firmness, true vision, understanding and skill exist, can never fail in any undertaking. May you accomplish your purpose and return soon, O Son of Vayu!"

Very soon after that Hanuman spied the island of Lanka looking like a jewel set in the heart of the ocean. He observed the forests and the rivers and cascades and flower gardens with which it was surrounded. The city was built on a level place just below the highest summit of the three-peaked hill known as Trikuta and looked as if it rested on clouds. Actually this peak was a piece of the fabled Mount Meru. Once upon a time it is said that Vaasuki, the holy serpent on which Vishnu reclined, had a contest with Vayu, the god of wind. In order to prove his prowess, the snake curled himself round Mount Meru and refused to budge. Vayu was furious and blew with all his might with the result that the whole world was thrown into chaos. The gods ran to Vishnu and begged him to intercede. Vishnu ordered Vaasuki to release his hold on the Mount. The snake uncoiled one of its twists and immediately Vayu tore off a piece of the Mount which was exposed and blew it far off into the ocean. He dropped it in the southern sea and in course of time it came to be called Trikuta. Soon after this incident, Kubera, the son of the sage Vishravas, wanted to build himself a city. His father told Vishvakarma, the architect of the gods, to build him a city on top of the peak of Trikuta. It was a beautiful city and was called Lanka. Ravana was another son of Vishravas. He gained many boons from Brahma and became puffed up with pride. He waged war against his brother Kubera and drove him out of the island and grabbed it for his own.

Hanuman descended on the summit of a hill and beheld the stunning city of Lanka with its rooftops gilded with gold by the setting sun. The splendour of Ravana's city left him breathless. If it was so beautiful from the outside how splendid would it be from inside, he wondered. He noticed that the city was fully protected by the sea which girt it on all sides. It had four gates facing the four directions and the walls surrounding it were made of gold. Lanka was strongly fortified and surrounded by moats and trenches crawling with poisonous serpents. The hill side was covered with trees and flowering bushes and the mansions were glittering in the evening light. He could also see the clean, white roads bordered by green, luscious looking grass. Situated as it was on top of the hill, Lanka looked as if it was floating on air as there were so many clouds surrounding it. The warm wind playing over his face smelt of pepper, cloves and fragrant spices.

Maruti nimbly jumped from rock to rock as he made his way towards the northern gate. The moat which ran round the walls was filled with man-eating fish.

Elephants stood under the stone gate arch and fierce looking *rakshasa* bowmen looked out from the roofs and turrets. Hanuman wondered if it would be possible for Rama to breach the ramparts of this city, even if he managed to cross the sea with his army of monkeys. "Even my father, the god of wind, would find it difficult to enter this city, undetected," he thought to himself. However, he decided that his immediate job was only to find out the whereabouts of Sita and give a full report to his master. He realised that he could never enter Lanka in his present form, guarded as it was by fierce *rakshasas.* He pondered a while as to how he was to accomplish his purpose of finding out the princess of Videha (Sita). He waited for darkness which fell like a mantle over the city. A pale moon floated across the sky accompanied by her attendant stars and Lanka loomed above him like a dream. He reduced his form so that he became as small as a cat and tried to creep through the northern gate. "A cat can go anywhere it wants to, in the night," he thought to himself.

Lankini was a warrior maiden who had once guarded the abode of Brahma. He had cursed her for her arrogance and told her that she would have to leave his celestial realm and guard the city of the demons until a monkey defeated her and released her from his curse. She kept a vigilant watch outside the gates of Lanka while all others slept soundly inside. She stood with arms akimbo before Maruti and obstructed his passage.

"Who are you, O denizen of the forest?" She asked. "Protected by the forces of Ravana and guarded on all sides, none may enter these portals without my permission."

Hanuman countered with another question. "Who are you O gentle goddess? Why are you so anxious to stop me?"

She was not pacified by his humble demeanour or his disguise and retorted, "I am the personification of the city of Lanka, O monkey, and it's my duty to guard it from all intrusion. Prepare to die for I will kill you now."

Unruffled by this declaration, Hanuman spoke meekly, "I have merely come to view this city of which I have heard many splendid accounts."

Lankini had blazing eyes and mighty arms bearing every type of weapon. She was not impressed by his sweet words and laughed in derision, "Without overcoming me you will not accomplish your purpose, O monkey!" With these words she boxed him on his cheeks.

Hanuman was incensed by this and without saying a word he closed his left fist and gave her a glancing blow which felled her to the ground.

Stunned by the blow as much as by the loss of her dignity, Lankini spoke,

"Spare me O jewel among monkeys! I shall leave this place and allow you to enter. The creator Brahma spoke the following words to me when he kept me here: 'One day you will be felled by a blow by a mere monkey. When that time comes know that the fate of the city is doomed as well as that of Ravana's!' I see now that the time foretold by Brahma has come. You may enter the city and go about your business. You will surely find the virtuous daughter of King Janaka." Saying this, Lankini left Lanka for good.

There is another story about the guardians of Lanka. Ravana was such a great devotee of Shiva that both he and Parvati had come to live in Lanka, thus making the island invulnerable. When the gods headed by Indra complained to Brahma about Ravana's tyranny, he went to Lanka and begged the divine pair to withdraw their protection. Shiva agreed to take birth as a monkey who would be instrumental in bringing about Ravana's destruction and Parvati took the form of Kaali and was installed in a temple at the gate. When Hanuman entered Lanka he saw the temple of the three-eyed goddess, holding divine weapons and flanked by eight *yoginis*. She challenged him and revealed herself as the cosmic mother in all her terrible manifestations. Hanuman responded by manifesting his own cosmic form, which contained the energies of all the gods. She recognised him as the son of her own Lord, Shiva and bowed to him. Maruti begged her to leave the island for no one would be able to conquer it as long as she protected it. The goddess agreed to leave and asked him to see to it that the nine nights of her worship (*Navaratri*) which usually occurred in autumn would also be performed in spring. Hanuman agreed to do this and she left the island for good.

What a wonder that you kept the signet ring of the Lord in your mouth,
And leapt across the sea.

— *Hanuman Chalisa* by Tulsidas

ॐ *Sri Hanumathe Namaha!*

ॐ

Kapishwaraaya Namaha!

CHAPTER THIRTEEN

PAVANA PUTRA

Search for Sita

"Ullankhya sindho, salilam, salilam,
Ya shokavahnim janakatmajaaya,
Adaaya tenaiva dadaha Lankaam,
Namaami tam pranjalir-anjaneyam."

I bow to Anjaneya,
Who leapt over the waters of the sea,
And removed the sorrow of Janaka's daughter (Sita),
And burnt the city of Lanka.

— *Sri Hanumath Stotram*

Having got rid of the guardian of the city, Hanuman leapt easily to the top of the ramparts and surveyed the sleeping city spread like a carpet beneath him. The town was planned with meticulous care and neatly laid out streets, flanked by superb mansions from which floated peals of laughter and sounds of various musical instruments. The latticed windows were studded with diamonds and shone in the moonlight. Palaces gleamed in the silvery sheen of the moon. Hanuman glided unnoticed along the well-swept roads scattered with rose petals and sprinkled with sandalwood oil and flanked on either side with magnificent buildings of various shapes and sizes. It was the last full moon of autumn and the moon rose in all its glory. Midnight is the time when the night wanderers go out to eat the flesh and drink the blood of their victims. In Lanka it was the time of enjoyment and revelry, the time to drink and make love and be merry. Hanuman heard the sounds of every type of indulgence, the music of lutes and horns and the low beat of drums – chattering voices and ogres clapping time. Along with this were the deep melodic chants from the Vedas by the Brahmins who were kept especially for this purpose. On the streets carrying lighted torches, he saw the night patrols of *rakshasa* warriors. Some were clad in rich and regal heraldry, some in feathers and quills and some wore rotting, raw, skins while others walked naked with shaven heads. They were armed with studded bludgeons and knives and spears and javelins. These were the warriors, who had conquered the heavens and the nether worlds along with Ravana's son, Indrajit.

In the course of his cosmic conquests, Ravana had subdued many of the Vedic gods and made them work as his servants. However, he had dealt really harshly with two of the most dangerous of these deities and imprisoned them at the southern edge of Lanka. The south is supposed to be the most inauspicious cardinal direction. In his inspection of the city, Hanuman came to the southern tip and found a grotesque black figure chained to a rock. Hanuman approached him and asked him who he was and why he had been chained.

"I am Kaala, Lord of Death. Ravana has chained me here with a belt which has been secured by Rudra's *mantra*."

Hanuman, who was Rudra's son, went close and touched the belt which instantly came apart and released Kaala who was so grateful that he gave him the boon that anyone who remembered Hanuman would have no fear of death.

Just then Hanuman heard a pathetic cry for help. He followed the sound and found Shani, the malefic planet, Saturn, who had also been imprisoned by Ravana. The deity had been chained by his feet to the ceiling of the cave and was hanging like a bat with his face to the wall so that his evil gaze could not fall on anyone. Maruti broke the chain and freed him.

The grateful Shani told him that even though the blue sapphire is believed to give protection against his evil influence, the blue coloured Lord Vishnu is the sapphire of sapphires and all Vishnu's devotees would be automatically protected. He then gave the boon to Hanuman that all those who worshipped him would not be troubled by Shani and gave him the title,

"Sankata Mochana" or the one who delivers from sorrow. However, later stories show the spiteful Shani attacking his benefactor who was forced to deal with him more firmly.

As he reached the centre of the city he saw a smaller wall which ran in a great circle made of sixteen colours of rose gold which enclosed the palaces and gardens of the Demon King. He jumped over the wall and landed in a garden. Bright lamps burned on golden posts and the gravel on the paths was made of jewel dust. There were small temples everywhere from which the perfume of incense flowed. The temples were surrounded by arbours and pavilions. In the centre of the park was the spired palace with golden domes and walls studded with gems and scattered with diamonds. Hanuman slipped past hooded watchmen and fierce night birds, trained to scream if they were disturbed. He went round the palace and there in a huge courtyard he saw the fabled aerial chariot known as the Pushpaka that Ravana had stolen from his brother, Kubera. It was breathtakingly beautiful, made entirely of flowers – the chariot of spring, driven by the mind and resting on air, two fingers above the ground. He got into it and gazed spellbound at the interior. It would take a whole month to explore it. There were hills and lawns and flowers and golden benches and everything which you could fancy. There was even a swimming pool with a splashing fountain!

At last Hanuman decided to get down and explore the palace grounds further since it was obvious that Sita was not in the chariot. He saw another huge courtyard where Ravana's garrison was housed. He peeped into all the palaces of Ravana's great generals. He noted the huge numbers of horses and elephants.

Then he decided to follow his nose since the smell of wonderful types of food and wine assailed his nostrils. Boldly he entered the hall from where the delicious aroma was flowing and noticed the golden walls studded with precious jewels. The palace thronged with ravishing princesses whom Ravana had abducted. The whole place was lighted up as if it were day, by lights burning inside golden lamps. The scene was one of total revelry and debauchery. Hundreds of voluptuous looking females sprawled about in various states of dishevelment. Some lay on the carpets with flowing hair and scattered jewels, some were dancing and some drinking. The red dots on their forehead were often smeared by their lover's hands, their girdles loosened, clothes crushed and garlands trampled. Pearls gleamed in the lamp light between their heavy breasts and heavy gold earrings hung from their ears. Some women were applying sandal paste on their bodies as well as those of their lovers. Others remained with their arms entwined round their beloved's necks. They were all in a half-intoxicated state and their breath smelt of the liquor made from cloves. They were all enchanting to look at, elegantly clad, fragrant with perfumes, with curved eyes and long lashes and sidelong glances, guaranteed to entice men. All the most beautiful women from various parts of the world had been captured and brought to Lanka by Ravana. It appeared as if his main job had been to course through the length and breadth of the worlds in his aerial vehicle grabbing the virgin daughters of the *nagas, gandharvas, daityas* and *rishis*. All of them had cried and struggled when they were captured and sworn to kill themselves, but in the end they had succumbed to his fatal charms, for his expertise in the art of love-making was proverbial. He had been cursed by their parents over and over again as well by the women whom he had brought forcibly. Hanuman looked at all of them and knew instinctively that none of these could be Sita. He imagined her to be pale and emaciated, pining for her husband, looking like the full moon seen through a cloud.

He stepped over alabaster floors and sprang up a stairway of lapis and burnished gold until he reached the end of a hall paved with silver which ended in a jade door with cut amethyst handles. This was the entrance to Ravana's bedroom. Softly he turned the handle and entered. The room was lit with flaming lamps of gold and covered with sleeping women. Each woman was lovelier than the next. They were sleeping deeply after an evening of drinking, dancing and music. Their fragrant hair was loose and their jewels scattered. Their girdles had come loose and their silken robes fell unheeded to either side.

Suddenly he spied Ravana, chief of the night wanderers, reclining on a cot made of crystal, ivory, sandalwood and gold. It was unbelievably beautiful and he stood for a while admiring it. The white umbrella of royalty was above it. The Demon King lay fast asleep on the bed. He was a magnificent figure of a man with huge, powerful arms and broad chest covered with white silk. He had ten devilishly handsome heads adorned with long, heavy gold earrings. He was clad in the purest of white garments and was sound asleep. On one side was a table with the leftovers of a magnificent repast of exotic foods. Hanuman went closer and helped himself to some delicious fruits. Being a monkey he did not care for cooked foods. After his tasty repast, he surveyed the rest of the room.

Four lovely women stood at the four corners of Ravana's bed and fanned him gently. Many charming women were sleeping in abandoned positions all round him. Some of them were clutching musical instruments which they must have been playing for Ravana. Suddenly Hanuman spied a most attractive woman sleeping on a couch set apart. She was so beautiful that for a moment he thought she must be Sita but he soon realised that Rama's wife would never adorn herself like this nor would she be able to sleep so deeply. He realised that the woman must be Mandodari – Queen of Lanka, daughter of Mayan, Ravana's chief wife, renowned for her beauty and chastity.

Long ago Ravana had heard that Shiva's wife, Parvati was the most beautiful woman in the world. Desirous of possessing her, he performed many austerities to please him. Shiva was pleased and granted him a boon. Ravana immediately asked for Parvati! Shiva was forced to allow him to take her to Lanka. When she saw him coming to get her, Parvati decided to teach him a lesson. She caught a *manduka* (female frog) and transformed it into a beautiful female and called her Mandodari. Ravana saw her and thought it was Parvati and took her off to Lanka and made her his chief queen. Like all female frogs, Mandodari came to consort with Ravana only at the start of the rainy season but she was a most faithful wife and always gave him unconditional support.

Another story concerning Mandodari makes her out to be Sita's mother. Once Ravana performed a grand *yaga,* using the blood of sages as a sacrificial offering. Thousands of sages were beheaded and their blood collected in a jar that Ravana gave Mandodari for safe keeping. During the night, Mandodari got up with a raging thirst and accidentally drank up the contents of the jar. The blood of the sages entered her body and made her pregnant. In due course she gave birth to a daughter. Oracles prophesied that the baby would be the cause of Ravana's destruction. Due to her love for her husband, Mandodari threw the baby into the ocean. The Sea God, Varuna saved the baby and gave it into the arms of the earth goddess. This was the baby that Janaka, the king of Videha found in one of the furrows while he was ploughing the field at the commencement of a sacrifice. He named the child Sita since she was found in a *sita* or furrow.

When he first came into the hall, Hanuman had felt slightly embarrassed at the thought of being forced to look at all these voluptuous females in seductive poses but then he realised that though he was moving amongst such extraordinary beauties his mind was totally unaffected and untouched by any of them. The *vanaras* as a race were not noted for their continence! But unlike other monkeys, Hanuman was a *brahmachari* and had never thought of consorting with any woman.

Not wanting to waste any more time, he pressed on through the portrait gallery and many other places but was unable to find Sita. He became totally despondent and did not know where to look for her and started to suspect that Ravana might have killed her. He thought he had completely exhausted all the places where he could possibly find her. It would be better to die rather than return to Rama with this tragic news. Tears rolled down his eyes at the thought. At last just at that moment when he decided that he would have to return with his mission unaccomplished, he saw a grove which he had not seen before. It was filled with many types of trees, prominent among which was the *ashoka.* He leapt on to the wall which enclosed the grove and surveyed the garden which was filled with all types of trees laden with fragrant blossoms. Many flower-laden creepers embraced the trees and everywhere there was a fresh and wonderful fragrance unlike the artificial perfumes found inside the palace. There was a charming pond with steps inlaid with gems and covered with lotuses. It was obviously a favourite haunt of the demon king, since it was so well tended. Hanuman jumped on to an *ashoka* tree and concealed himself amongst the thick foliage and surveyed the garden. The night was passing and he still had not discovered Sita. The birds were beginning to wake up and flew up in clouds, chirping angrily at being disturbed by Hanuman's frolics. The sun glided down the Trikuta peak and slipped into Lanka and set the golden walls afire. The temple bells started to ring and inside Ravana's bedroom, the bards sang songs of praise to waken the Lord of Lanka.

Rama had told Hanuman that Sita was extremely fond of flowers and he hoped that she might come to that enchanting grove for a walk. The garden seemed to be made for her, with its flowering shrubs and waterfalls and ponds. Looking around in the light of the setting moon, he saw a small temple with white pillars. The steps were of coral and the surface covered with gold. It gleamed in the moonlight. As he peered closer, he suddenly spied a woman and knew unmistakably that this was Sita – the beloved of Rama. She looked like the crescent moon, pale and wan. She was emaciated through fasting, and was clad in a soiled, yellow garment and devoid of all ornaments. Her lovely eyes were filled with tears which dropped unceasingly to the ground. Sorrow seemed to be her constant companion. Her long black hair was tied in a simple braid which fell to her thighs. She, who had been a stranger to sorrow, now knew only grief. Unwashed and unkempt as she was, she resembled a flame covered with smoke and Hanuman knew instantly that this was indeed Sita, the darling of Rama, the princess of Videha. She was surrounded by *rakshasis*. Hanuman was filled with sorrow to see the beautiful queen of Ayodhya in such a sad plight. She who had been protected by the lotus-eyed Rama was now being protected by *rakshasis* with crooked eyes and deformed bodies! She was surrounded by these horrendous monsters, some with one eye or one ear and some without ears and some with noses on their forehead, some hairy and some bald, some hunchbacked and some with faces resembling goats, foxes, camels and horses. Some had huge ears covering their bodies and some three eyes. Some had hanging bellies and flapping lips and voices like rasps. Some were leering, others grim. All of them without exception were misshapen and frightening to behold. Ravana had specially chosen them to frighten Sita into submission to his will. Surrounded by these hideous creatures, Sita was seated at the foot of one of the trees, the picture of despair with her head in her hands.

Hanuman thought to himself, "This is indeed Sita. Neither the lack of ornaments nor the fact that she is clothed in rags and is frail and emaciated can hide the fact that she is a raving beauty. She is as beautiful as Rama described her – exquisite eyebrows, graceful, rounded breasts, lips as red as a berry, peacock blue throat, slender waist, lotus petal eyes – all these are visible through her screen of sorrow."

She sat on the bare ground like a female ascetic, bound in a net of grief, the picture of shattered hope. Though parted cruelly from her husband, her mind was full of him alone. Her lips were constantly murmuring the *mantra*, "Rama, Rama". This was indeed the woman for whom Rama was pining. Hanuman could see that she belonged only to Rama, body, mind and soul.

"She is meant only for Rama and he for her. Their love for each other is so great that it is only because of it that they have managed to remain alive. All Heaven's stars may fall, and earth may break apart. Fire may burn cold, and waters run uphill, but Sita will never turn from Rama!" Hanuman prostrated mentally to Rama and whispered, "Lord I have found her!"

He was overcome with sorrow at the sight of the princess of Videha who had been parted so cruelly from her husband. "Fate is indeed all powerful," he thought to himself, "or else why should this innocent lady have to suffer like this. She was protected by no less a personage than her illustrious husband and Lakshmana. Her husband killed thousands of *rakshasas* at Janasthana for her sake, because Ravana's sister was threatening her and now she is held captive by that very Ravana, surrounded by these hideous women, with no privacy even to weep. She has no eyes for this beautiful garden. Her eyes are in her heart and her heart is with Rama."

Hanuman was just wondering how he could present himself to Sita when he heard the sound of music coming from the palace. It was the time known as Brahma Muhurtam. With the break of day, the bards began to chant the Vedas to wake up the demon king of Lanka. Drums started booming and lutes playing to welcome the dawn. The perfume of incense spread over the city from the fire sacrifices which were being performed everywhere. Ravana was greeted with many women waving *chourie* fans and *ghee* lamps. As soon as he woke up, his first thought was of Sita. Day and night he could think of nothing but Sita. Even though he had so many beauties from all the three worlds in his harem who were willing to gave in to his passion, his mind was always fixed on her who refused even to look at him and treated him with utter scorn. He had never met with such resistance from any woman in all his life and he certainly had a lot of experience with females of every type. Her resistance only served to whet his appetite. It was a challenge to him and he was determined to make the citadel fall at all cost. He was sure that no woman could resist him for long and that it could only be a matter of time before she succumbed like all the others. He would happily have forced her to comply with his desire but he had been cursed that if he took a woman without her consent, his head would burst, so he had to desist. Every morning as soon as he woke up, he was irresistibly drawn towards the grove and hurried there before he attended to any of his state matters.

Anjaneya looked up as the noise of bugles and cymbals came closer and then he saw Ravana approaching with a bevy of belles. Most of them looked sleepy due to the intoxication of the night but they hurried after their Lord, carrying *chourie* fans, golden lamps, cushions and pitchers of wine. When he came close to the tree on which Sita was leaning, he commanded the *rakshasis* surrounding her to push off and also told his entourage to stand apart so that they would not be a witness to his ardent wooing! Hanuman came down the tree a little in order to have a closer look at the king of Lanka. He concealed himself behind the leaves and peered through the gaps. He had only seen him when he was asleep. Now he looked even more magnificent. He was clad in the finest of white garments which billowed like a cloud behind him and was adorned with many fantastic ornaments, all meant to charm the heart of any female.

Hearing the tread of his feet as he approached, Sita quivered with fright and loathing. Despite her pitiable condition her beauty shone like the full moon seen through a cloud. One single braid fell over her left shoulder as she tried to cover herself with the pitiful remnants of her clothes and crossed her arms in front of her in a desperate attempt to cover her breasts from Ravana's piercing, lustful gaze.

Looking at her pitiable efforts to cover herself Ravana said, "O Princess of Mithila! Why do you try to hide your beauty from my eyes? I am sure there is no one in all the three worlds as exquisite as you. Why do you shun my gaze and turn away from me? You should be clad in the finest of silks and adorned with costly jewels, yet you sit on the ground, wearing only a soiled rag, eating nothing and trying to hide your beauty from me by crossing your arms. Even thus you put all the other ladies of my harem to shame. I would exchange all of them for one smile from you! I abducted you only because I fell a prey to your unbelievable beauty. Pray listen to my appeal. Your husband is a coward otherwise he would have come to rescue you long before this. Don't waste your youth and beauty in pining for him. Accept me and I will make you my foremost queen and give you the whole world if you so desire it! Your lovely hair is matted, your silk garment is soiled and torn and you are half-starved and emaciated, yet you continue to fascinate me. Night and day I am haunted by your face. Can't you see that I am crazy with love for you? After having met you, I cannot bear to look at my other wives. Youth and beauty are short-lived. Do not waste both in unnecessary sorrow. Come, shake off your grief and accept my love. Rise up, dress yourself in lovely silks and satins. Wear jewels and perfumes. This bare ground is not a fitting couch for your flaming beauty. You have seen me and my glory. What has Rama got to compare with this? He is only a mendicant, clad in bark with not even a kingdom to call his own. Take it from me that you will never see him again. You probably consider my action to be unrighteous. But in the code of the *rakshasas* it is quite acceptable to take another man's wife for his own. Why are you torturing yourself like this? I can easily force you to comply with my will but I have been patient because I want you to come to me of your own accord. I want your love and not just your body. I have never said this to any other woman. But your time and my patience are running short. I gave you one year in which to make up your mind and the time is almost up!"

Not once did Sita look at Ravana during this impassioned speech. Though she was terrified of Ravana and sickened by his sensual talk, she clutched at the remnants of her tattered pride along with her tattered clothes. Without raising her eyes, she picked up a straw from the ground and placed it before her and spoke to it as if addressing the king of Lanka! It was a graphic reminder to him of her attitude – that she cared two straws for him!

With utter scorn she said, "O you of poor intellect! Know me to be the beloved of Rama, scion of the race of Raghu. Do not keep your mind on me. Fix it on your own consorts. Having one of impure heart as its ruler, the city of Lanka as well as the whole *rakshasa* clan will perish in the flames of my husband's wrath. He is the repository of all virtues. How can I who am his wife bear to even look at another man? If you want to save yourself and your clan try to propitiate him. He is kind and compassionate to those that surrender. But he is as severe as he is compassionate and if you don't surrender to him, his arrows will descend like serpents on you and destroy you completely! Remember how he destroyed your whole garrison in Janasthana single handed. Why are you bent on destroying your race? An entire kingdom can perish, if its ruler becomes the slave of his passions. Lanka is doomed. What a fool you are to think that you can tempt me with gold and riches? Rama is to me what sunlight is to the sun. Restore me to him and thus earn my gratitude if you will but never hope to earn my love for that is irrevocably given to Rama! How will he not destroy you, who have dared to abduct his beloved wife? You boast of your courage, yet you crept into the hermitage in disguise and stole me away when my husband was not there! Was this the action of a brave man? Soon shall my Lord come and rescue me and shoot deadly arrows at you which will suck your life's blood. So beware! You and your clan will be totally wiped out!"

Ravana was furious at her words and retorted angrily, "The kinder I am to you, the more intolerable you become. It's only my love for you and the fact that you are a woman that makes me refrain from killing you straight away. I have given you twelve months to make up your mind. Out of that only two months remain. After that you either share my bed or become my breakfast. If you still refuse, death shall be your lot! My cooks will make mince meat of you for my breakfast!"

Despite the fact that she was quaking inside Sita retorted angrily, "O vile wretch! Your days are indeed numbered. Is there no good man here to advice you? I wonder why your tawny eyes do not drop off when you gaze at me lustfully. Why does your tongue not drop off when you speak such words?"

Ravana looked at her with his amber eyes smouldering with anger. "O woman, you are devoted to a man who is beset with ill luck and devoid of resources. I shall get rid of you today itself. You do not deserve any compassion!"

Then turning to the *rakshasis* who were stationed there to guard Sita, he spoke harshly. "It's your duty to see that this woman submits to my will before the day is over. Threaten her, cajole her and if all fails, use force or whatever you think is necessary but see to it that she submits to my will!" With these words Ravana angrily strode off to his own palace to be fawned over and waited upon by his numerous wives, all of whom were distasteful to him now.

A few of the women who had followed Ravana felt sorry for Sita but none dared say anything. Some took the opportunity to ingratiate themselves in his favour and entwined their soft arms round his neck and offered themselves in lieu of Sita, but he shook them off angrily and strode off making the ground tremble with the force of his strides.

You possess the elixir of Rama *bhakti*,
And remain eternally his true servant.

— *Sri Hanuman Chalisa* by Tulsidas

ॐ *Sri Hanumathe Namaha!*

ॐ

Sita Shokavinaashakaaya Namaha!

CHAPTER FOURTEEN

SANKATA MOCHANA

Dispeller of Sorrow

"Markadeya mahotsaha,
Sarvashoka vinashaka,
Shatrun samhaara mam raksha,
Shriyam dapaya-me prabho."

O Lord! Pray give me all auspiciousness.
Thou art the greatest amongst simians,
One who can take away all sorrow,
Save me from being troubled by enemies.

— *Hanumath Sthuti*

The *rakshasis* who had been asleep when Ravana came were now wide awake and eager to do as he told them. All this time they had desisted from doing any harm to Sita since that had been his bidding but now that they had got orders from him to act as they wished, they rushed to her. All of them were deformed and ugly. Some had one ear or ears which came down to their waist, some had one eye or three eyes, and some had heads and feet of elephants, horses or cows. Some had huge heads or huge mouths, huge tongues and bent nails. All of them pounced on Sita gleefully and started to torment her with their sharp tongues.

"What a stupid woman you are that you will not listen to a great soul like Ravana. He is prepared to keep aside his own wife Mandodari and make you his favourite consort. Yet stupid fool that you are, you refuse his kind offer. At his command the trees scatter flowers and the clouds release rain. The sun and the moon would stop shining if he did not wish it. You are a brainless idiot not to agree to his wishes!"

Sita replied angrily, "You are giving me cheap and sinful advice. Destitute and deprived of his kingdom though he is, I will ever remain faithful to my husband. You may kill me and eat me if you will but I will not budge from my resolve!"

Another declared loudly, "Ever since I saw her, I have had an irresistible desire to feast on her luscious breasts and berry-like lips and delicious liver and spleen. Come let us have an orgy. Bring out the wine and we will chop her into little bits and feast on her!" So saying she licked her chops and drooled from her thick, black lips. Sita shrunk back in fear and disgust and started to weep uncontrollably.

Hanuman who was hiding in the foliage could not contain his anger and sorrow to hear the *rakshasis* upbraiding and torturing Sita like this. But he knew that this was not the right time to reveal himself.

Sita was now crying like a stricken deer. All the pent up feelings which she had repressed before Ravana now broke loose and she burst into heart-rending sobs. "O Rama! O Lakshmana! Where are you? When will you come for me? This heart of mine must surely be made of iron that it doesn't break even though I'm in agony. What a vile wretch I am to keep on living even though separated from my beloved and leading such a miserable existence. I realise now that death will not approach a person, till the appointed time has come or else how can I continue to live in the midst of these cruel creatures, in the palace of this lecherous man, parted from my beloved Rama?" So saying she sank to the ground and burst into uncontrollable sobs.

Again she raised herself for she was filled with doubts. "How will my Lord know that I am here and how will he cross the ocean and come here? My death draws near. But I'm not afraid. Far better for me to die than fall to the lures of this wicked Ravana! It looks as if I will see Yama before I see the lotus-eyed Rama!"

Hearing her laments and the cruel words of the *rakshasis,* an old ogress called Trijata now approached Sita and kept the others at bay and told all of them of the dream she had.

"Listen O *rakshasis*! I just had a dream in which I saw Rama coming in a golden palanquin, clad in white raiment and wearing celestial garlands.

Sita was then re-united with her beloved husband. I saw Ravana with shaven head, falling from his aerial car. He was dripping with oil, attired in black and had a red garland round his neck. Again I saw him being pulled by a woman on a chariot drawn by asses. He was totally intoxicated and out of his wits. The woman in black was drawing him in a southerly direction. His son, Indrajit and brother – Kumbhakarna were also following him. Only his youngest brother – Vibhishana was left here. I saw Lanka being burnt up by an agile monkey who was Rama's envoy."

"Therefore, I adjure you to take care of Sita. See that no harm befalls her or else you will also suffer the same fate as Ravana and his clan!"

Hearing this, the *rakshasis* disbanded and returned to their posts and Sita sat alone under the tree. She had reached the end of her tether. She felt she just could not go on any more. Physically and mentally she was at her lowest ebb and decided to make an end of her life before Ravana came again. Taking out the cloth which was wound round her waist she decided to hang herself with it before Ravana could torture her to death. However just at that very moment she felt some auspicious omens on her body. Her left eye, arm and thigh started to throb. These are considered to be extremely favourable omens for a woman, so Sita's heart took courage and she desisted from her desperate attempt.

Hanuman was watching everything from his vantage point and decided that the time had come for him to reveal himself and try and comfort Rama's wife.

"I have been told to find out her whereabouts and also ascertain the strength of the enemy but I would be failing in my duty if I did not give her some comfort before leaving or else the daughter of Janaka may well give up her life before Rama comes. I might frighten her if I jump down in my monkey form for she is already terrorised by these misshapen *rakshasis*."

Hanuman thought deeply over the matter and then decided on a plan to allay Sita's fears. In a very sweet voice he started singing the whole story of Rama's life, ending with his being sent as an envoy. Sita was thrilled to hear his tale and looked around anxiously to see where the voice came from. Brushing her dishevelled hair aside, she looked up at the tree and tried to find the person who was responsible for bringing this ray of hope into her stricken heart. The thick foliage hid him from her sight. Her eyes roved in all directions but she couldn't find him. The *rakshasis*, in the meanwhile, had given up their efforts to persuade her. Some had gone to tell Ravana and the rest were snoring under the trees in ungraceful postures.

Hanuman took this as an opportune moment and jumped lightly down to a branch where he could be seen. At last her anxious eyes spied him – the messenger of Rama, harbinger of hope and happiness. She beheld a small, cute monkey with white fur and red face closely watching her from amongst the leaves. His eyes were like liquid gold and he was smiling at her. He looked harmless but she still had her doubts. She had been cheated and tormented so many times in the past few months that she was always suspicious of everything and everyone. Sita was sure that she was dreaming and cried out to Rama to save her.

"What can be the cause of this apparition? Surely it must be another trick of the wicked Ravana."

Hanuman guessed what was going on in her mind and decided that it was high time for him to appear before her. He nimbly leapt down and stood with folded palms before her. He then raised his palms above his head and extolled her.

"Who are you, O fair lady of exquisite limbs? Are you a goddess or a celestial?

Tell me for whom are you grieving? If you are indeed Sita, the wife of Rama who was stolen by Ravana, please tell me."

Sita was elated when she heard these words and cried out, "Yes indeed, I am the daughter-in-law of the great Dasaratha and the wife of the noble Rama. My father is the king of Videha and I am called Sita. I accompanied my husband to the forest and was kidnapped by Ravana and brought here. He has given me two more months to succumb to his passion. If Rama does not come before that I will end my life. But tell me who you are, who has brought me the nectar of Rama's name which has put new life into me?"

Hanuman listened attentively to these words and then spoke humbly to her. "My lady!" He said, "I have come as an envoy of your husband. He is alive and well and is waiting for me to tell him of your whereabouts. He grieves for you night and day and has sent me, as his messenger to tell you that he will come for you very soon and kill Ravana and rescue you."

A thrill of pure joy shot through Sita when she heard these comforting words of Anjaneya. She had been living in the darkness of despair for so many months that she had almost given up all hope of rescue. However, when he tried to get closer to her, she who had been cheated so many times by Ravana began to suspect that he was Ravana again coming in another form to seduce her. Her mouth went dry and her limbs grew weak and she sank to the ground, unable to cling to the branch she was holding.

"O Ranger of the Night! I know you are capable of assuming many forms. Yet I feel that you are not he. Somehow I can't explain it but for once delight has sprung in my heart which makes me believe that you are actually what you claim to be. In which case may good befall you. Speak to me once again of Rama. Let me hear it even though it might be a dream. The very thought of Rama brings delight to the universe so what does it not do to me?"

In order to put her mind at rest Hanuman prostrated full length before her and refused to look up.

"My sweet lady! Have no fear. I have been sent by your noble husband to comfort you. He will come shortly, accompanied by the heroic Lakshmana. They are always thinking of you and talking about you. They have made a pact with the Sugriva, the king of monkeys and I am his minister, Hanuman."

At last she was convinced that he was indeed a messenger from Rama. Sita then asked him to describe the features of Rama and Lakshmana. When Hanuman gave these details she was highly gratified.

"Rama has broad shoulders, mighty arms, a charming countenance and lotus petal eyes. He has a voice, deep as thunder and a dark blue complexion.

He is full of splendour and is greatly adored by all who meet him and is steadfast in his vow of chastity. He is devoted to truth and righteousness. His brother Lakshmana is equal to Rama in strength, charm and has a golden colour. They had been ranging the earth searching for you before they came to the mount of Rishyamukha and met Sugriva. When Rama saw the jewels which had been dropped by you, he nearly swooned with joy. He had to be revived by me. My Lady! That scion of the race of Raghu burns for you as much as you burn for him. Have no fear, for that tiger among men will surely come and rescue you. Now tell me what may I do for you before I return?"

Sita was delighted to learn of her husband's grief at her loss even though she was upset that he had to pass through such tortures of the mind. She was thirsty for news of her husband and asked him to tell her everything that had happened to him after she was abducted. What did he do and where did he go and how long would it be before he reached Lanka and so on. Eagerly she lapped up every scrap of news that Hanuman gave her. He was only too happy to speak of Rama – his god. He told her of how the monkeys had seen her being carried off by Ravana and had picked up her jewels which she had thrown to them and all the other incidents ending with his finding her. At the end of the recital he stood respectfully with folded palms before her. Sita's joy knew no bounds. She was now convinced that he had indeed come from her beloved. Tears of happiness replaced the tears of sorrow which had been flowing in torrents down her cheeks. Hanuman now handed over to her the precious signet ring which Rama had given him to inspire confidence in her. She took the ring which had adorned her husband's finger and pressed it to her bosom. She was speechless with delight. Her whole demeanour now blossomed like a plant which had been watered after long months of no rain. With eyes filled with gratitude as she looked at this adorable little monkey who had brought new hope to her barren heart.

"You are indeed a jewel among monkeys. How did you cross this enormous sea and go round the city of Lanka without being discovered? You are no ordinary monkey? May you be blessed. Now tell me more about my Lord. Has he become indifferent to me due to the long separation or does he grieve as I grieve?"

Hanuman now told her the two stories which only she and Rama knew and which he had told him in secret so that she would know that he had been sent by her husband.

After their wedding when they were returning in the chariot, Rama had gently rubbed his feet over hers. To his horror he found that her lotus-like feet were so sensitive that even this gentle pressure made them red. Later on when they were in the forest he asked her.

"O My gentle princess! Remember the time when I stroked your feet with mine on our way back from our wedding and your feet became swollen and red. How is it that you have no problem now in placing those delicate feet on these hard stones and thorns?"

He also mentioned another incident which happened soon after their marriage. Rama had asked her to massage his feet. Before doing so she had removed her jewel-studded bangles. He had then questioned her as to why she did this and she had replied, "My Lord! I have heard it said that when Visvamitra took you to the hermitage of the sage Gautama, he asked you to place your foot on a stone which turned into a woman called Ahalya who had been cursed that she would remain a stone until you placed your divine feet on her. Think of the fate of my poor jewel studded bangles if you place your feet on them?"

Sita was overcome with emotion when she heard these stories known only to her and Rama and she was convinced that Maruti was indeed the messenger of Rama.

Hanuman felt himself to be deeply privileged to hear such intimate stories from both parties. Once again he comforted her, "The only reason your Lord has not come is because he did not know where you were. His mind is ever fixed on you so have no fears on that score. He lives in a cave and hardly eats or sleeps. He does not care for anything any more and is always lost in thought. Even when he falls into a fitful sleep, due to exhaustion, he wakes up crying, "Sita! Sita! Whenever he sees something which is pleasing to you, he sighs and is inconsolable. As soon as I return he will come with a huge army of monkeys and bears. Have no fear. Live in hope my Lady, your deliverance is nigh!"

Sita was thrilled to hear that Rama's desire for her was as great as hers for him. "Dear monkey! Your words bring both happiness and unhappiness to me. When I think of his unhappiness I become sorrowful too. Both happiness and sorrow are the outcome of one's actions in a past life. Please tell my Lord that my time is fast running out. I have only two more months to live. After that I will become the repast of that night wanderer. His brother Vibhishana and another *rakshasa* called Avindhya warned Ravana of the dire consequences of his action in having abducted me and told him to return me to my Lord but Ravana's time is drawing to a close and hence he cannot listen to reason. Please tell my Lord to come soon for life is unbearable without him."

Hearing this pitiful plea, Hanuman's heart melted with sorrow and he told her.

"O noble lady! Please don't give way to further grief. Climb on my back and I will transport you this minute back to Rama. Have no fear."

Sita was both touched and amused at hearing this offer of the little monkey. Thinking of him as only a baby monkey, she was quite unaware of his prowess.

"Dear little monkey," she said, "Your good nature has made you suggest the impossible. How can a tiny creature like you carry me across the sea?" Hanuman now decided to inspire confidence in her and started growing to an enormous size right in front of her eyes.

"I have the capacity to carry the entire city of Lanka over the sea if I want to, so have no fear for I will surely transport you without any difficulty!"

Sita was astonished to see his size and said, "Indeed I realise that you are no mean monkey but the true son of the Wind God. However, I don't think it's proper on my part to go with you. When they see me being borne away by you these evil *rakshasas* may pursue you and cause you to drop me into the raging sea. Moreover, I was abducted by the cruel Ravana and kept here in his domain for so many months. It is only right and proper that my husband should come and rescue me after killing him or else Rama's fame may suffer. Besides, I keep my Lord enshrined in my heart always and don't wish to touch any other man on my own accord. I was forced into contact with Ravana when I was helpless. Therefore, O gallant monkey! Bring him here with all speed for I don't think I should go with you."

Hanuman agreed with her and said that it was only his eagerness to see her re-united with her husband that had made him make such an improper suggestion. He could well understand her delicacy in touching another male. So he begged her to give him some token by which he could convince Rama that he had indeed seen her.

As proof of the fact that he had met her, Sita handed over to Hanuman her hair ornament, the *chudamani.* "Seeing this jewel my Lord will be reminded of the three most important people in his life, my father, his father and myself. This was given to me as part of my dowry by my father in his father's presence." With these words she handed over the precious ornament to him which she had carefully kept hidden in her clothes.

Then she recounted two incidents in their lives in the forest known only to her and Rama.

With sobs choking her throat she said, "Remind him of the time when we had bathed in the river near the mountain of Chitrakuta and he rested with his head on my lap. He went to sleep and a crow came and pecked my breast. I threw a clod of mud at him and shooed him off but he would not leave me alone and came and pecked me again and again. I started to cry and Rama woke up and teased me about my fears and comforted me and then we lay down in each other's arms and fell asleep. But that vile crow was biding his time and swooped down and clawed my breasts. The hot drops of blood fell on my Lord's face and woke him up. He was furious and looked around for the culprit who had dared to do this to me and saw the crow sitting on a branch. He recognised the crow to be Jayanta, the son of Indra. Rama immediately took up a blade of *kusa* grass and invoked it with the power of Brahma, and threw it at the crow. It flew off in fright but the *astra* followed him wherever he went. He found no asylum anywhere and at last returned to Rama and begged him to withdraw the missile. Rama said that the *brahmastra* once invoked had to do some damage and so he took away the crow's right eye and spared his life. How is it, O Hanuman, that he who invoked the might of the *brahmastra* against a crow who harmed me, now remains silent when this demon has dared to abduct me?"

Once again she said, "Remind him of the time when he smeared the red dot on my forehead and powdered a red stone and put a red dot on my cheek as a joke!"

Sita's eyes filled with tears when she recounted these two stories which were known only to her and Rama. With tears choking her voice she told Hanuman, "How can I reward you, who have given me back my life? I was ready to end my wretched life when you came and instilled confidence and hope in me. You are indeed a son to me. Tell my Lord, O noble monkey, that I will not live another month more. If he does not come by the end of the month I shall take my life before that ogre can touch me."

Hearing this impassioned appeal, Hanuman assured her that Rama's only thought was of her alone. "Fear not, O gentle Lady! Rama and his brother will soon come and kill the *rakshasas* and rescue you. I have seen with my own eyes how desolate Rama is without you so have no fear on that score. Before you know it, he will be here with the monkey army and totally exterminate these terrible night wanderers!"

He took the jewel which she handed over to him and pressed it to his heart. He then went round her thrice and bowed low to her and asked her permission to leave.

"Keep good cheer O gentle princess! I will soon return with Rama and the monkey hoards that will kill the *rakshasas* and rescue you. Do not give in to grief but remain full of hope for there is no one in the whole world whom Rama cannot overcome!" So saying, Hanuman bowed to Sita once again and took his leave.

As he fell at her feet, Sita blessed him with all her heart. "O Anjaneya! Your name and fame will be remembered in the world as long as the names of Rama and Sita remain. We will never accept any worship in which your name is not included." She placed her palms over his head in blessing and gave him leave to depart.

The goal of all mystical yearning is the union of the individual soul with the universal soul. In the *Adhyatma Ramayana*, a Sanskrit text dating from the fourteenth or fifteenth century, Sita is said to represent the individual soul (*jivatma*), which has been separated from the universal soul (*Paramatma*) symbolised by Rama. In this beautiful interpretation, Hanuman shows the ability of *bhakti* to annihilate the *ahamkara* or ego (Ravana), and re-unite the two.

Sheltered by you one gains all delight,
Protected by you, one fears no one.

— *Sri Hanuman Chalisa* by Tulsidas

ॐ *Sri Hanumathe Namaha!*

ॐ

Vajrakayaaya Namaha!

CHAPTER FIFTEEN

BAJARANGABALI

The Burning of Lanka

"Sri Rama bhaktakula moulim-achintya-veeryam,
Sri Rama sevaka janavana lola chittam
Sri Rama nama japalina hridam kumaram,
Vande Prabhanjana sutham Raghurama dasam"

Hail to thee, O son of Anjana! Servant of Rama,
Greatest of all Rama *bhaktas*, possessed of unbelievable powers,
Whose mind ever delights in doing service to Rama,
And chanting the names of Rama.

— *Hanumath Sthuti*

Hanuman was loathe to leave Sita and she on her part felt desolate at parting from him, who had given her hope and a reason to live after all these bitter months of anguish. He decided that though he had achieved his main purpose which was to find Sita, he would have to prove his worth to her so as to bolster up her courage. He was so angry with Ravana that he decided to ravage his favourite garden before he left. He set about this destruction in a most methodical manner.

Like a raging tempest, he uprooted every tree and trampled it with his enormous feet. He muddied the ponds and crushed the rocks and laid waste the entire garden which was so pleasing to Ravana. The creepers were torn from the trees, the temple smashed, the pools splattered with the copper coloured buds of the Ashoka trees and lakes churned and made muddy. The little hillocks were ground to powder and the beloved garden of Ravana was made into a desolate waste. Having desecrated the garden he climbed to the top of the archway to the garden and waited expectantly for things to happen. He did not have long to wait. There was a great commotion in the garden itself. The birds were screeching in terror and the deer and peacocks were running around crying and bleating piteously. The *rakshasis* were woken up from their sleep by a noise resembling a hurricane, created by Hanuman. They rushed to Sita and asked her who this gigantic monkey was, who was bent on destroying the garden. She pleaded ignorance of the whole matter. The women ran to Ravana and reported what had taken place. They said that they suspected that Sita knew who he was, but refused to divulge his identity. He had destroyed every part of the garden except the grove in which she sat.

Ravana was furious when he heard of the destruction of his pleasure gardens and ordered the palace body-guards to go and subdue the creature. The army approached Hanuman who had stationed himself on top of the archway to the garden. He was really pleased to see the approaching troops. He lashed his tail on the ground and filled the whole of Lanka with the horrendous sound. The troops rushed at him from all sides and attacked him with numerous weapons. He grew in size and clapped his hands on his shoulders in the manner of wrestlers and spoke in a thunderous voice, "I'm Hanuman, the servant of Lord Rama. Not a thousand Ravanas are capable of withstanding my powers. I will return only after devastating Lanka." He then proceeded to break off a bar which was protruding from the arch and thrashed the demons that had come to catch him and made them run for their lives.

Ravana couldn't believe that his troops had been defeated by a mere monkey. He ordered, Jambumali, the son of his chief general to go and flog the monkey. Jambumali got into his two-wheeled chariot drawn by three white mountain ponies. He held a red bow decorated with solid gold flowers. Hanuman made short work of his troops and then jumped nimbly on to the spire of the temple and started to destroy it. The guards tried to drive him off but Hanuman uplifted a pillar and thrashed them soundly. The he shouted loudly, "Hail to Rama, Hail to Rama!" in a resounding voice.

At this point Jambumali assaulted Hanuman with thousands of arrows, some of which were aimed at his mouth. Hanuman uprooted a tree and hurled it but it was cut to pieces by the demon's arrows. In great rage Hanuman took the iron bar which he had used previously and hurled it at his enemy's chest. It pierced him and he fell down dead.

The news made Ravana mad with rage and he commanded the seven sons of his chief minister to go and kill the monkey. Hanuman jumped into the air and avoided the arrows of the seven and rained rocks on their heads and killed them all. He then despatched another five generals who had been sent by Ravana. Streams of blood began to flow down the main highway of Lanka leading to the palace, carrying the mangled bodies, legs and arms of the slain. Ravana was quite bewildered by this unexpected turn of events and despite the remonstrations of his wife, Mandodari, he sent his youngest son Aksha Kumara to subdue the monkey. Mounted on a beautiful chariot drawn by eight horses, the young prince set off from the palace, eager to prove his prowess. He wore golden armour and looked like the rising sun. He let fly many arrows at Hanuman who resembled a blazing fire and was covered with blood. Hanuman couldn't help but admire the young man who seemed to be a replica of Ravana. But he had no recourse but to fight with him even though he was loathe doing so. He decided to frighten him off the field by destroying his chariot. He jumped into the air and pounced down on the horses and felled them with his fists and broke his chariot. The valiant prince now rose into the air and started discharging arrows at Hanuman. The latter was full of admiration for the boy but decided that he could not afford to show any leniency. He caught hold of his legs and swung him round many times and hurled him far off in the hope that he might survive and run away. However, the prince never rose up. Hanuman then jumped back to his stronghold on top of the arch to await the next person who would be sent by Ravana.

Ravana couldn't believe that his dear son had been killed by this dreadful monster. He was filled with remorse at having sent him to his death. He decided to summon his eldest son, the valiant Indrajit, to go and capture the monkey alive since he wanted to find out who he was and why he was causing such destruction. He feared that there was something unusual about him and that was the reason why his army could not handle the situation. He walked through a tunnel under the city wall which ended in a secret door leading to a hidden grove in the woods. There under a banyan tree sat his son, Indrajit immersed in his esoteric practices. Ravana stood for a while in silence until Indrajit got up and saluted him. Ravana said, "My son! You are the pride and hope of our race – invincible in battle. You are not only proficient in weapons but also have command of all types of magic powers. A gigantic monkey is on the rampage and has killed many of our best warriors. I don't think it is an ordinary monkey and it appears that it cannot be subdued with weapons so you must use your other tricks and capture him alive."

"Rest assured father! I shall capture him for you."

So saying Indrajit, the son of Mandodari, got into his celestial chariot and sallied forth with no fear in his heart. He was raven-haired, dressed in blue and yellow silk, his skin dark red and a yellow flower in his hair. His eyes were dark green with cat's pupils, and a golden chain was wound nine times round his waist. He held a round, blue, steel-shield in one hand and a bow backed with gold serpents in the other and a sword in a silver sheath on his belt. He who had subdued Indra felt pretty sure he could capture a monkey without much effort. However, he realised that this was no ordinary monkey and could not be killed with ordinary weapons. He climbed to another tower as tall as the one on which Hanuman had perched himself and sent an arrow with the *mantra* invoking the mystic noose known as *naga pasha.* These were actually ropes made of snakes. Hanuman fell to the ground tied invisibly hand and foot and unable to move.

Anjaneya realised the magic potency of the noose which was binding him and decided to remain silent. The stupid forces of Indrajit could not see the subtle ropes which were binding him and brought their own ropes and chains and bound him up. The moment the gross ropes touched his body, the subtle effects of the *mantra* were nullified. Indrajit was angry to see the folly which had been committed by his men but wondered why Hanuman made no effort to set himself free. He decided to wash his hands off the affair and returned to his lair in the forest to continue with his interrupted rituals. Hanuman wanted to be taken before Ravana so he allowed Ravana's henchmen to parade him along the streets of Lanka. Some people abused him and some threw stones at him while others jeered and made jokes. Hanuman took it all without turning a hair. They dragged him and teased him and tortured him but he put up with all these insults.

At last he was dragged before the ten-headed Ravana who looked dazzling in all his finery. He was clad in the softest of white silks which looked like billows of surf on the seashore. He sat on a throne covered with doeskin, set in the centre of a long indoor altar, made of a golden frame filled with earth. He wore ten crowns of flaming red flowers and gleaming gold. A gold chain hung from his neck forged of flat, heavy links from which were hanging, golden devil faces with diamond eyes and open ruby lips and long, shiny, ivory teeth. His green eyes were gleaming with strange lights and looked piercingly at Hanuman. For a few minutes Maruti was dazzled by his charisma and could not help feeling that had he not been so cruel, Ravana might well be competent to become the ruler of all the three worlds.

When Ravana looked deep into the tawny eyes of the monkey, some unknown fear gripped his heart. He remembered the incident long ago when he had tried to approach Shiva, his favourite deity. At that time, Shiva's bull vehicle had stopped him. This had infuriated him so much that he had shouted at Nandi, "O you monkey! How dare you try to stop me from entering?"

Nandi had cursed him in return. "Beware O Ravana! You have called me a monkey and one day a monkey will be the cause of your downfall!"

This had infuriated Ravana even further and in his arrogance, he had put one finger under the mountain of Kailasa, the abode of Shiva and tilted it perilously. Parvati had been frightened. In order to comfort her and to quell Ravana's pride, Shiva had simply pressed the mountain down with his big toe and crushed Ravana's finger! Ravana is supposed to have placated Shiva by composing the extraordinary hymn, known as the "Shiva Thandava Stotra."

Tulsidas describes Hanuman's entry into Ravana's court thus:

"The monkey observed the glory of Ravana's court. Even the gods and the regents of the quarters stood meekly with folded palms anxiously watching his changing expressions."

Hanuman, however, stood like a colossus and was totally unperturbed by the sight of the powerful demon king!

"He was no more disturbed by the sight of his power than Garuda by the sight of snakes!"

Ravana wanted to insult him and did not even offer him a seat that was due to him as a messenger. All the others were given seats. Hanuman decided that the insult was to his master and not to him. He thought of Garuda, the eagle vehicle of Vishnu who was the enemy of snakes and chanted his *mantra*. Immediately the snakes released him from their noose. Hanuman shook himself and lengthened his own tail and coiled it into a seat that was much higher than Ravana's throne. He seated himself with dignity on this self made seat and looked down on Ravana from this high position!

For a moment as he looked into the amber eyes of the monkey, Ravana thought that this was the time foretold by Nandi so long ago but he shrugged off the incident as being of no consequence and asked his minister to question the *vanara* about his reason for coming to Lanka. The minister asked, "You have nothing to fear O monkey, if you tell the truth. Have you been sent by Indra, king of the gods? What is your motive in penetrating this impenetrable fortress and destroying the garden? If you speak the truth, you will be let free."

Hanuman replied firmly and boldly to Ravana's questions. His only motivation was to change Ravana's heart so that he would release Sita and avoid war.

Maruti looked intently at Ravana and said, "I am the servant of Lord Rama, prince of Ayodhya and prince among men. I have come here to speak with you. You have abducted his beloved wife and he has asked me to ascertain her whereabouts. I devastated your garden only so that I would be brought face to face with you. I am incapable of being bound by nooses or killed by missiles. I allowed myself to be bound only to see you. You are well acquainted with the laws of *dharma* and know how injurious it is to steal another person's property. By your great austerities you have won many boons including the one that neither gods nor demons nor *yakshas* or any other celestial beings can kill you but you did not add human beings in your list since you thought no human being could kill you, but remember Rama is a human being and he is being helped by monkeys who again were not in your list! Therefore, I ask you to listen to reason and return Sita to her husband or else you as well as your whole clan will be mercilessly slaughtered by my Master! He is the equal of Vishnu in prowess and since you have wronged him so woefully, he will not spare you. Listen to me and let Sita go and save yourself and your country! Sita spells death for you and your clan. Let her go and save yourself when you can!"

In all his answers Hanuman wanted to stress the fact that by himself he was incapable of performing any of the acts attributed to him. His strength and inspiration was due to Rama and Rama alone!

Ravana's blood-shot eyes rolled with rage and shot flames of red and gold. He ordered the monkey to be executed forthwith. However, his younger brother, Vibhishana intervened and said, "Brother you know the dictates of *dharma* and you know that it is most improper to kill an envoy. You will surely lose your fame and your store of merit if you do this heinous act."

Ravana was even angrier at hearing this and insisted that this monkey who had done so much of harm to his city and killed his son, deserved to be put to death. Vibhishana begged him to re-consider his decision and said that the only way he could lay hands on the two princes and lure them to Lanka would be to let the monkey go.

Ravana thought about this and agreed that this was a point to be considered but he insisted that the monkey should be mutilated. "A monkey's tail is his prize possession so let his tail be set on fire at once and let him return with a burnt tail to be the butt and scorn of his friends and relations!"

Ravana issued a command that the monkey's tail should be lighted and that he be paraded round the entire city so as to provide some fun for the populace who loved the sight of anyone being tortured.

The demons were delighted at this order which was entirely to their liking. All the time when he had been dragged to the court, they had been shouting fiendishly, "Kill him! Roast him! Eat him!" And so on. Now they fell on his tail with glee and started to wrap it in oil- soaked rags before setting it on fire. While his tail was being swathed, Hanuman made it grow out of all proportion. It became longer and longer until it circled the entire city of Lanka ten times. The confused demons ran around in circles trying to wrap the tail in cloth and found that even though they collected all the scraps and bales of material in the whole of Lanka they could not cover this colossal tail which simply grew and grew! The citizens were forced to surrender their clothes and the women their *saris*. When they had exhausted the entire amount of cloth in Lanka, they were at a loss to know what to do. Hanuman laughed to himself and at last allowed his tail to be covered. Then they brought huge cauldrons of oil and soaked his tail in oil before setting it on fire. Hanuman was delighted and immediately lashed his blazing tail and killed all those surrounding him! Then he controlled himself and allowed them to bind him and sling him on a pole and take him round the city. He did this so that he could make a mental map of the entire city and take in those things which had not been obvious to him in the darkness of the night when he had wandered through the streets.

All the *rakshasas* lined the streets of Lanka with their womenfolk, all anxious to see this spectacle. Some of the *rakshasis* ran gleefully back to Sita and reported the whole matter to her. Sita was filled with sorrow when she heard this. She closed her eyes and prayed to the god of fire to reduce the heat on Hanuman's tail. Thereupon, to Hanuman's surprise, he found that the fire on his tail had no power to burn him!

After having made a mental map of the city, Hanuman flexed his muscles and easily broke the bonds which had been tied round him and jumped on to the city ramparts with his flaming tail and decided that it would be good to destroy Lanka and thus reduce Ravana's pride. "This fire which has been used to punish me has been denied its food so I will give it some sustenance."

In one of his most Rudra-like acts of destruction, he began to jump over the tops of the buildings like a flaming meteor. Bounding from house to house he set fire to each of them in a methodical manner until at last the whole of Lanka was a flaming conflagration. The only place he avoided was the mansion of Vibhishana and the *ashoka* grove in which Sita sat. Very soon the flames changed the beautiful city of Lanka into a cremation ground. There was pandemonium everywhere. People were screaming and running around, women and children were wailing, horses and elephants were stampeding. The wind began to spread the blazing fire through the length and breadth of Lanka. The flames shot up to the skies and appeared like the fire of universal destruction. The mansions made of pearls and gems with lattices of gold cracked with loud reports and toppled to the ground like card houses. The gold plating on the buildings melted and streams of molten gold trickled towards the sea. Houses along the streets collapsed and gates and grills snapped and smoked. Screams and shouts rent the air as the terrified citizens ran hither and thither in their effort to escape from the conflagration. The whole of Lanka was like a flaming torch. It was an awesome spectacle.

"Surely this is not a mere monkey but Rudra in disguise, in his form as Mahakala or the Time spirit of destruction!" cried the *rakshasas*. Hanuman sat on top of the ramparts and surveyed his work with glee. At last he was satisfied that he had completely destroyed Lanka so he jumped into the sea to cool himself off and put out the fire on his tail.

This is the only time that we find Hanuman resorting to his monkey nature and engaging in an act of wanton destruction. When his temper had cooled a little he was filled with remorse for what he had done.

"What have I done?" He thought to himself. "An angry man is capable of committing any crime. He alone can be called a sage who controls the anger in his mind and does not retaliate even when provoked. I am truly a sinner. If Sita has been destroyed along with this fire then I have killed my Lord also for he will not live a moment without her. My journey would have been in vain. The whole of Lanka has been reduced to ashes. Is it possible that Sita is still alive? By virtue of her asceticism and her exclusive devotion to her husband, it is possible that fire itself cannot touch her."

As he was thinking like this in deep remorse, he saw some astral beings, winging their way above him and talking amongst themselves.

"Strange indeed that the whole of Lanka is in flames and the only place left unscathed is the grove where Sita is sitting!" He was overjoyed to hear this and jumped to the grove in order to find out if this was indeed true and found her still sitting under the tree, exactly as he had left her. Both of them were delighted to see each other and Sita begged him to stay another day with her.

"Your very sight, O dear monkey brings consolation to my heart. If you go I'm tormented with doubt as to when you will return. Are the other monkeys capable of leaping across the sea as you have done? How will my Lord accomplish this feat?"

Again Hanuman comforted her and assured her that Sugriva was no mean monkey but was able to accomplish wonders and very soon she would see the monkey hordes cross the ocean and Rama coming to rescue her. Sita was full of hope when she heard this and reluctantly agreed to his departure.

"You showed your small, slight form to Sita,
Then assuming a terrible form you burnt the city of Lanka."

— *Hanuman Chalisa* by Tulsidas

ॐ *Sri Hanumathe Namaha!*

ॐ

Pingalakshaaya Namaha!

CHAPTER SIXTEEN

SHOORA

The Faithful Servant

"Yasyasthi Ramakarunamrita vaibhavena,
Lokaavasaana Samayavati dheergham-ayur,
Tam veera purusha kalagranimajaneyam,
Vande prabhanjanaasutham Raghurama daasam."

Hail to thee O son of the wind! Servant of Rama,
O Anjaneya! Thou art indeed a powerful person,
Who by the grace and blessings of Lord Rama,
Will continue to live till the end of the world.

— *Raghuramadasashtakam*

The gods were delighted at Hanuman's mighty deeds and the grandsire Brahma himself gave him a letter to give Rama, which contained a detailed account of his exploits in Lanka. In this account of his adventures it is said that Sita returned Rama's ring to him together with her hair ornament. So Maruti had three precious articles with him to give to Rama. After all the adulation he received from the gods and from Sita, it is only natural that Hanuman felt a twinge of pride at his accomplishments.

He was eager to get back to Rama. He turned round to have a last look at the city. The fabulous city of Lanka, which had appeared like a gleaming pearl pendant set in the heart of the sky, now lay in shambles at his feet. He felt a pang of compunction but decided that Ravana deserved it. He now sprang to the highest peak in Lanka and grew in size. He fixed his mind on Rama who he was longing to see and repeated the powerful *mantra* of Rama and took a flying leap from the peak towards the northern shore of the sea. Hanuman looked like a mountain with wings as he sailed across the sky. He saw the sea surging beneath him as he turned his face north and sped on his way. He passed with ease through the crimson tinted clouds and coursed through the sky like an arrow. By the time he reached the mainland he was feeling very thirsty. He looked down and saw an *ashrama* with a lake beside it. He went down and found a sage seated in meditation. Hanuman humbly approached the sage and requested to be allowed to drink from the lake. The *yogi* nodded his head. Hanuman placed his three treasures next to the sage and went to the lake to drink. While he was at the lake an ordinary *vanara* bounded out of the bushes, picked up Rama's ring and dropped it into the sage's water pot. When Maruti returned, he found that the ring was missing and questioned the sage as to what had happened. The *yogi* said not a word but pointed to his water pot. When Hanuman put his hand into the pot, he was stunned to find that it was filled with rings which were exact replicas of the one that Rama had given him. Hanuman asked the sage to kindly tell him which was the one which he had brought. At last the sage broke his silence and said that all of them belonged to Rama. When Hanuman looked bewildered, he went on to say that in each of the eons known as Treta, Hanuman would come and drink water from his lake and a monkey would come and pick up the ring and drop it in his water pot. Hanuman was naturally stunned and asked in a meek voice, "How many rings are there in the pot?"

The sage smiled and said, "Why don't you count?"

Hanuman began to count and soon found that it was countless! It was then that he realised that he was not unique. In the Lord's creation one age follows another. Many others had come before him and many others would follow. This was enough to obliterate whatever pride he had felt in his achievements. Later on when he met Rama, he found that the ring was already on his finger. Rama smilingly admitted to Hanuman that he himself had taken on the form of the sage in order to take away even the smallest trace of pride in his devotee. Hanuman fell at his feet and begged him never to let him fall a prey to pride again. Rama granted him this boon.

Hanuman now rose up into the air and continued with his interrupted journey. When he neared the spot where he had left his friends, he gave a massive roar to announce his approach.

"Ah! Hanuman has been successful in his mission as is obvious from his roar," said the other monkeys. Feeling overjoyed they sprang from tree top to tree top and peak to peak in the usual way of monkeys, eager to be the first to welcome the returning hero. Hanuman landed on the mount of Mahendra from which he had jumped. The other monkeys joyfully gathered round and placed their little gifts of roots and fruits in front of him as a token of their appreciation. They made him sit and encircled him and pelted him with questions. Hanuman bowed to Jambavan and Prince Angada and narrated his tale. The excited monkeys embraced him and sprang from rock to rock with upraised tails.

Angada praised him and said, "There is no one equal to you, O Hanuman! You have given us back our lives and only because of you Rama will be united with Sita."

Again and again he had to repeat his story to the excited monkeys who were all gathered round him and chattering with joy. Every detail was heard with great delight by the monkeys. The crown prince, Angada now said that it would be best if they all went to Lanka and rescued the princess of Videha and took her back to her Lord. Jambavan put him off this impetuous scheme by saying that it was Rama's duty to rescue her and they had only been told to find her. The faster they returned and gave the message, the better it would be for Rama.

They decided that Jambavan was right and the whole troop started on their return journey. Their enthusiasm lent wings to their feet and the monkeys made the return back to Kishkinda in half the time. They were all anxious to get there soon and be the first to break the pleasant tidings to Rama. At the entrance of the town there was an orchard called Madhuvana which was filled with fruit trees and flowers laden with nectar. It was a haven for bees who buzzed around collecting nectar and making hives. The garden belonged to Sugriva and was guarded by his uncle. The monkeys begged the prince to allow them to taste the fruits and honey and were given permission by him. That was all they needed. They devastated the orchard and got pleasantly drunk on the honey much to the disgust of the caretaker. Monkeys are normally difficult to control and these monkeys who were the colour of the honey which they had imbibed in vast quantities played havoc in the garden pelting each other with the combs and squashing the fruits and rioting wildly.

Sugriva's uncle was the guardian of the grove and he tried his best to stop them but they paid no heed to him. The whole garden was filled with intoxicated monkeys, reeling about in different states of inebriation. At last he threatened that he would go and report the matter to Sugriva. Sugriva was seated with Rama and Lakshmana and the guard narrated the whole story and insisted that the monkeys should be severely punished but contrary to his expectations, Sugriva told him not to worry about them. In fact, he seemed rather pleased.

Turning to Rama he said, "My Lord I feel sure that these monkeys have accomplished your purpose and that is why they are so bold as to desecrate the king's orchard. There is no doubt that Hanuman has discovered Sita!"

Rama and Lakshmana were filled with delight to hear this. Sugriva told his uncle to return to Madhuvana and send Hanuman and the other monkeys to him without delay.

He went immediately to Madhuvana and bowed humbly to Angada.

"You are the crown prince and I was told by Sugriva that you could have your fill of honey. Pray forgive me and the guards for having tried to stop you. You have been asked to return to Kishkinda straight away."

Like stones shot from a catapult, Angada immediately leapt into the air, followed by Hanuman and the others. Seeing them coming, Sugriva told Rama,

"I feel sure that Sita has been traced by Hanuman. None but he is capable of accomplishing this task. He is endowed with intelligence, valour and capability. Moreover Angada would not have dared to ransack the honey grove which was bequeathed to me by my grandfather, had he not accomplished their purpose."

Even before he reached Rama, Hanuman shouted, "Seen have I Sita!" He phrased his sentence in this way because he knew that Rama's heart was filled with expectation and until he heard the word, "seen" he would be in agony. Hanuman wanted to spare him even this one moment of pain if he could and thus he cried out, "Seen have I Sita!"

Hanuman now landed close to where Sugriva and Rama were sitting and bent low over his feet. He reported that Sita had been found and was in sound health and filled with devotion to her husband. By this time Angada and the other monkeys were also longing to have their say and jostled each other in their anxiety to tell the tale which they had heard second hand from Hanuman. Rama looked lovingly at them and said, "I'm sure you have all done very well but now I would like to know more about Sita. What did she say? Did she send any message or token for me?"

Hearing this, the monkeys turned sheepishly to Hanuman and begged him to continue with the story.

Hanuman bowed low before Rama and told him the whole story of his conquest of Lanka and his meeting with the lovely, lonely princess of Videha who was eating her heart out for her beloved husband.

"O valiant prince! Your consort has been detained in a grove by that night wanderer, Ravana. She is forlorn and remains absorbed in you alone. She sleeps on the bare ground and is pale and wan like a lotus flower at the approach of winter. She told me two incidents which are known only to you." He went close to Rama and whispered in his ear, "One is about the crow Jayanta, who pecked her breasts and the other about the red dot you playfully placed on her cheek. She also asked me to give you this jewel which she used to wear in her hair and which she had preserved carefully without it being noticed by the *rakshasis.* I offered to bring her to you on my back but she refused to leave in such a secretive manner. She said that she would wait till her husband came and rescued her after killing the one who had treated her so abominably. At the end she told me to tell you this, "O son of Dasaratha! Fallen as I am into the clutches of this ogre, I will not survive beyond a month!"

All the while when Hanuman was speaking, Rama's eyes were overflowing with tears. He clutched her jewel to his breast. A flood of memories swept over him and he said, "My heart melts at the sight of this jewel which was presented to her by my father-in-law, King Janaka at the time of our marriage and was fastened on her head by her mother. It is a precious jewel which was given to him by Indra, king of the gods. I remember very well how charming she looked with her hair adorned with this jewel. Repeat to me once again O Hanuman every incident of your meeting with her. I can't hear enough about her. She says she can't survive another month without me but I won't be able to survive even for a moment without my dark-eyed darling!"

"Who else but the son of the Wind God could have achieved such a stupendous task? Not only did you fly over the ocean and give solace to Sita but you also laid waste the whole of the city of Lanka! The best type of servitor is the one who not only accomplishes everything his master told him to do but uses his intelligence and does even more."

(In the words of Valmiki), "No one endowed with a body, whether a god, a human being or a sage, has put me under such obligation, as you have done O Hanuman! My mind shrinks from facing you for at the moment for I have nothing to repay you."

He continued, "Listen to me, my son! I have thought over the matter and I have concluded that the debt I owe you can never be repaid! At present I have nothing to reward you except this embrace."

So saying Rama clasped Hanuman to his chest and hugged him. Hanuman's eyes filled with tears at this mark of love from his master. He fell at his feet and said,

"O Lord! You have given me the supreme gift. What else do I need?"

Turning to Lakshmana, Rama said, "Let us not waste even a moment now that we know where she is."

He then looked at Sugriva and asked him if he had any idea on how to cross the ocean. Sugriva told him not to give way to despair and that his monkeys would easily construct a bridge across the sea by which all of them could cross without any difficulty. Rama now urged him to order the army to start on their march to Lanka since they had only one month!

Before starting their journey to the south, Rama questioned Hanuman once again about the fortifications of Lanka, the number of entrances and the type of missiles they possessed.

Hanuman answered, "My Lord! First of all, Lanka is surrounded by the sea which itself is a natural fortification. Then it is built on a hill encircled by a thick forest and a river. It also has artificial fortifications of moats and walls. A high protective wall of gold, inlaid with jewels surrounds the city. These walls are again encircled by fathomless moats infested with poisonous serpents and alligators. Each gateway has a drawbridge by which the moats can be crossed. The central drawbridge at the northern gate is strongly garrisoned and extremely strong. The city has four main gates with strong doors closed with massive bars. At the entrance to the gates are stationed enormous catapults, capable of discharging darts and huge boulders. Hundreds of huge sharp-edged steel clubs bristling with iron spikes are kept ready at every gate. Ravana himself reviews his forces now and again. Lanka is thus extremely difficult to get into.

"Inside, the city is packed with horses and elephants in rut. Thousands of *rakshasas* carrying poisoned darts and swords are stationed at the eastern gate, an army of foot soldiers along with horses, elephants and chariots are garrisoned at the southern gate. A million *rakshasas* carrying swords and shields are stationed at the western gate. A hundred million of Ravana's crack regiment coming from noble houses are at the northern gate. Finally hundreds and thousands of men are stationed in the central military barracks. These drawbridges, gates and walls were smashed and burnt by me as well as many of the stately mansions of the nobility. Actually there is no need to try and take the whole of the monkey army across to Lanka. Just a few of us can easily go and get Sita for you since most of the fortifications have already been broken by me. However, it is possible that they have all been repaired. If it's your wish that all the monkeys should be transported then that also can be done. We await your command!"

Rama immediately ordered Sugriva to start their march at the propitious time when the sun was at its zenith. This is an auspicious hour known as "*abhijit*" and spells victory for anything which is commenced at that time.

"Today is a very propitious day and now is the hour to start so let us not delay any further. The lid of my upper right eye is twitching and for a man this is a most favourable omen. Let the monkey known as Nila accompanied by a *lakh* of agile monkeys march at the head of the army and choose the best route. Let him lead the army through a route full of fruits and roots and honey and fresh water. Be vigilant since the enemy might try to poison our water sources. If there are any weak limbs in the army let them remain at Kishkinda for we have a formidable task ahead of us. Let some of the best generals guard the left and right flanks of the army. The mighty Jambavan and a few of the others shall guard the rear. I myself shall ride on Hanuman's back and Lakshmana on Angada's and remain in the centre so that we will be able to move faster."

Sugriva immediately gave orders according to Rama's instructions and the mighty contingent of assorted monkeys started to move forward with great enthusiasm. They set out in a southerly direction. Some were leaping in all directions in order to guard the army from all sides; others were breaking branches and clearing a passage. All of them were shouting and screaming in excitement and feasting on the fruits and fragrant honey. Nila was the commander-in-chief of the army and held the monkeys in check lest they should do any mischief while they passed villages en route as they pressed forward like the tide of the sea. The monkeys had to cross mountains, rivers and deserts as they advanced towards the southern sea.

There was great excitement amidst the *vanara* hoards that leapt from tree to tree, shouting and waving their tails in glee. They bounded and hopped and swung from branch to branch, plucking trees and waving banners of flowering creepers, sparring and playing pranks on each other and feasting on fruits and honey. They were all in high spirits. Mile after mile they covered effortlessly, camping beside lakes and traversing hills and forests until they reached the southern sea.

All the while Lakshmana pointed out to Rama many good and auspicious signs and thus kept up his brother's spirits. At last they reached the Mahendra Mountain. Rama and Lakshmana climbed the mountain and beheld the turbulent sea stretching before them as far as the eye could see.

Rama gave orders that the monkeys should camp on the beach while they made plans about the method of crossing the sea. The noise made by the monkeys drowned the roar of the sea! Thousands and thousands of monkeys arrived and camped on the shore. In fact they appeared like another ocean. They stared fascinated at the storm-lashed waves and wondered how they would cross it!

Looking at this formidable array of water, Rama said to his brother,

"O Lakshmana! They say that grief decreases with the passage of time but in my case it seems to be just the opposite. Every moment away from my beloved increases my agony. The time stipulated by her is passing away. Every moment is precious and I have no idea how to transport this army across the ocean. I only survive because I know that she is still alive." Lakshmana comforted him as best as he could and they spent the night on the beach.

Feeling the wind on his face he said, "O gentle breeze, please blow over my beloved's face and then return and caress me, while her touch is still warm upon you. She must have called for me, time and time again as she was being carried away, over the sea. I am tormented at the thought of her helplessness. Now that I know where she is I am on fire to see her. I long for her smile, her gentle glances and her caressing voice. She was always slim and now with this continuous fasting, she must be weak and emaciated. I am aching for the day when I can kill that fiend and clasp her to my bosom!"

"Sri Rama praised you highly and said,
"You are as dear to me as my brother Bharat".

— *Sri Hanuman Chalisa* by Tulsidas

ॐ *Sri Hanumathe Namaha!*

ॐ

Mahatmane Namah!

CHAPTER SEVENTEEN

MAHATMAN

Ravana's Council of War

"Shatruchedaika- mantram
Sakalamupanishadvaakya sampujya mantram
Samsarothara mantram
Samuchita samaye
Sanganiryana mantram."

"The only mantra for vanquishing foes,
The mantra which contains all the truths of the Upanishads,
The sole mantra by which we can cross the ocean of existence.
The mantra which will save us at the time of death."

— *Sri Hanumath Stotram*

Looking at the dreadful destruction done to his city by Hanuman, Ravana was stricken with sorrow. He called his councillors together and asked them for a plan of action. His spies had informed him of the approach of the monkey contingent. He felt sure that Rama would succeed in crossing the sea. Ravana called a council of war and said, "Our impregnable and glorious citadel has been laid waste by a mere monkey and some of our best men have been killed. How are we to proceed? We have to come to some fast decision before the enemy reaches the further shore as they are sure to do."

Unfortunately he did not realise that he was surrounded by sycophants and toadies. All they knew was to bolster up his already bloated ego. One of Ravana's generals now spoke confidently, "O mighty ruler! You have conquered everything from the heavens to the nether regions. There is no one in all the three worlds who doesn't tremble at the very mention of your name. Why should you fear Rama? His army is only composed of monkeys and bears. How can it be compared with yours? Your son, Indrajit is also said to be unconquerable. You don't have to stir from this stronghold? He will annihilate the enemy hordes single-handed even before they cross the ocean. That would be the best thing to do."

Now Prahasta, the commander-in-chief of his army, spoke, "You have only to command me Sire and I shall personally cross the ocean and destroy the army of monkeys."

"This assault of our city by a mere monkey is not to be tolerated," declared another *rakshasa.* "I shall dispose off Rama and his army in a trice and will return before night sets. You have only to give the command!"

Many of the valiant heroes of Ravana's army now made the same claim and insisted that they would go single-handed and destroy Rama's army.

These words of comfort by his ablest men made Ravana feel very confident. He cast his glance on all of them in approbation.

After listening to all their boasts, Vibhishana, Ravana's youngest brother now spoke, "Dear Brother! We should not be led away by vain boasts. It is not good to underestimate the power of the army. Ever since Sita arrived here, evil portents have been seen. You have many sycophants O King, who are ready to please you with evil advice. Send back Sita and save yourself and your people. We would all like to live in peace and harmony. Rama is no mean enemy as you might think! He is a dangerous opponent."

Ravana dismissed Vibhishana's advice scornfully. "I see no cause for fear from a mere mortal like Rama, supported by a motley crew of untrained monkeys. They will be helpless against our well-trained and powerful army." With these words he insultingly dismissed his younger brother.

All of them now thought of a plan that would make Rama turn back. Ravana ordered the sorceress Benjkaya to take on Sita's form and pretend to be dead. The corpse was cast adrift on the sea and washed ashore close to Rama's camp. When it was brought before Rama, he turned pale for he recognised the necklace as belonging to Sita.

"Ravana must have killed her and cast her body on the sea," he cried and fell to the ground in agony.

Hanuman, however, sensed that something was wrong. He ordered the monkeys to make a pyre and place the corpse on top and light it. As soon as the flames began to lick the body, it jumped up and ran towards the sea! Hanuman caught her and forced her to reveal the whole foul plot to Rama.

After having told Rama the whole story, she fell at Hanuman's feet and begged him to marry her, for she could no longer return to Lanka. Hanuman declined the offer but promised to give her shelter in Kishkinda. Thus, she spent the rest of her life in Kishkinda singing the praises of her saviour!

When he realised that his trick had been seen through, Ravana dismissed the council for the day. When he returned to his own palace, he brooded over his younger brother's words but due to his infatuation for Sita he could not accept it. In fact day and night he could think of nothing but Sita. The more he thought of her, the more determined he became to keep her with him at any cost.

He knew that war was imminent so he decided on another council of war. The ten-headed king of the *rakshasas* got into his golden chariot and drove to the assembly hall in state where he was met with a blare of trumpets. All his best troops lined the roads to the hall to honour their king. He ordered the foremost of his generals, including his younger brother, Kumbhakarna, who normally slept for ten months of the year to be woken up and brought to the hall forthwith. They came one by one and bowed at his feet.

Ravana ordered Prahasta, his commander-in-chief, to see to it that all four parts of the army – cavalry, elephant brigade, chariots and infantry – were stationed at all the four gates in readiness for any attack. He then spoke to that assembly of *rakshasas* who were eager to please him in whatever way they could.

"All of you must know that I have abducted Sita, the consort of Rama. It appears as if she is some enchanted being conjured by the demon Mayan who is full of magic tricks. Looking at her fair and lovely countenance I have become a slave of passion and am no longer my own master. Having been told of our stronghold by the monkey Hanuman, it appears that Rama and Lakshmana are already encamped on the other shore with their army of monkeys. I know that we have nothing to fear from these mere mortals leading a host of irresponsible monkeys. However, it is best to be prepared for whatever may come and thus we must immediately devise a plan to kill those two wretched brothers."

His brother Kumbhakarna was already annoyed at being woken up from his beautiful slumber and when he heard this declaration of passion by Ravana, he flew into a mighty rage and said in a thunderous voice.

"You did not choose to consult any of us before you abducted another man's wife! That was the time when you should have asked our opinion. Actions undertaken by a monarch, which run counter to the principles of *dharma* (righteousness), are sure to produce only misfortune! However, since I am your brother, I shall endeavour to set right what you have wrongly performed! Let them come and I'll make short work of them! After having killed Rama and Lakshmana, I shall devour his monkey hordes! With Rama out of the way, I'm sure Sita will succumb to your will! But remember that I do not approve of all this!"

Ravana was silent even though he did not care for the frank manner in which his brother spoke. However, he knew that he was indispensable to their army and so kept his peace. Then spoke another mighty general called Mahaparshwa.

"Who is it that can dare lord it over you, O thou mighty sovereign of all the three worlds? Who is it that will not drink a pot of honey after having procured it? Make Sita submit to your will even if you have to use force to do so. In the meantime all of us shall reduce your enemies to smithereens!"

Ravana now divulged his dire secret to them. "In days of yore, I ravished a celestial nymph called Punchikasthala. She ran to the creator, Brahma like a stricken deer. He knew what had happened and cursed me thus: "If you dare to violate any other woman without her consent, your head will be split into a hundred pieces." This is why I have not so far forced the charming princess of Videha to my bed. However, there is no doubt that Rama does not know my prowess and that is why he is marching into a death trap. I am not capable of being defeated even by the gods. What then to speak of a mere mortal helped by a pack of apes and monkeys!" With these words he roared uproariously with mirth. The rest of the court except for his two brothers joined him and the whole court dissolved into laughter at this ridiculous picture of the great Ravana being defeated by a pack of monkeys and bears! But Ravana had forgotten the boon he had received from Brahma. He had asked for immunity from death from all types of heavenly and demonic beings. In his arrogance he had refused to consider human beings and monkeys as worthy of being possible opponents and now they were the very ones who were advancing purposefully towards him.

It is said that Punchikasthala swore to take revenge on Ravana and that is why her son Hanuman destroyed his precious city and was instrumental in the destruction of not only Ravana but of his whole hierarchy.

Hearing the boastful words of Ravana and the others, Vibhishana made a last bid to save him from his doom. "I beg of you O brother to listen to me and give Sita back to Rama before the monkeys invade this island. You know what one monkey was able to do to your wonderful city. Think of our fate when thousands of them start pouring in. Sita is a deadly serpent which has wound itself round your heart. She will be the cause of your death! Give her back before you and your people are destroyed totally!"

Turning to the other ministers he said, "It is the duty of a minister to advise a king wisely and save him from the consequences of his own folly, if possible. Why are all of you determined to bring about his downfall and the destruction of your race?"

Ravana's eldest son, Indrajit now spoke hotly, "This younger uncle of mine seems to be the only one in the race of *rakshasas* who is not endowed with courage, virility, prowess and fortitude. His nature is quite different from ours. He is a coward and your name will be in the dust if you listen to him. Why should he try to frighten us? Even Indra, the wielder of the thunderbolt, was cast by me to the ground! I even dashed his elephant to the earth and set all the celestial hosts into panic! Do you think I am incapable of subduing two insignificant mortals?"

Vibhishana listened to his nephew's talk without rancour. "My dear boy, I am afraid you are not able to distinguish between right and wrong. You are a mere boy and your intelligence is not steady. Though you profess to love your father, you are actually doing great harm to him by encouraging him in his folly!"

Ravana was furious when he heard his brother's well-intentioned words.

"It is better to live with an avowed enemy than with a relation who is jealous and secretly works to bring about your ruin. Fire and weapons I do not fear, the dangerous ones are the near and dear. Bees fly away after sucking the last drop of honey from a flower, so the unworthy give up a relationship which has ceased to be profitable. You alone, my brother, do not like to see the whole world honouring me! Had you not been my brother you would not be alive now. A curse upon you! You are a disgrace to our race!"

Vibhishana did not like to stay to get any more curses and said, "You are my elder brother and thus command respect. Whatever I said was meant only for your good. It is always easy to find people who will try to please you with honeyed words, but there are very few who will dare to tell a king the unalloyed truth to his face. I'm afraid I cannot tolerate your inequities any more. You are surrounded by sycophants and fools. A man in the noose of death can never listen to the salutary advice given by well-wishers. However, I wish you well. May prosperity attend you. For my part I cannot stay any longer with one who is steeped in *adharma!*" So saying he rose up into the air along with his four ministers and went to the other shore and hovered over Rama's camp.

It is said that the three brothers, Ravana, Kumbhakarna and Vibhishana typify the threes types of *gunas* or modes of nature – *sattva, rajas* and *tamas.* Vibhishana was the example of *sattva* or the quality of harmony and goodness, Ravana of *rajas* or passion and Kumbhakarna of *tamas* or inertia, sloth and stupor.

Vibhishana heeded your council and became King of Lanka,
As the whole world knows.

— *Sri Hanuman Chalisa* by Tulsidas

ॐ *Sri Hanumathe Namaha!*

ॐ

Bhaktavatsalaaya Namaha!

CHAPTER EIGHTEEN

BHAKTAVATSALA

Rama Gives Sanctuary

"Anjananadanam veeram,
Janaki shokanashanam,
Kapishamaksha hantaram,
Vande, Lanka bhayankaram."

Salutations to the courageous darling of Anjana,
Who removed Sita's sorrows,
King of monkeys whose very look could kill hundreds,
And conquer the terrible city of Lanka.

— *Hymn to Hanuman*

Sugriva was filled with suspicion when he saw the five *rakshasas* looking like miniature mountains hovering in the sky. He suspected that they had been sent by their ten-headed king to kill them.

Vibhishana spoke from the air. "I'm Vibhishana, younger brother of Ravana. I advised him again and again to return Sita to Rama but he refused to see reason and thus I have sought refuge in Rama!"

Hearing this appeal, Sugriva ran to Rama with this news and warned him not to take him at face value since he was a *rakshasa.*

"It is wise never to trust these night wanderers. He is also Ravana's brother. He may be a spy sent by Ravana to find out our strong and weak points or he may even strike us himself in the middle of the night since he has four stalwarts at his command. Like an owl which waits for the opportune moment and then destroys the whole clan of crows, he will join us and wait for the right time and annihilate us. I think it best that he and his friends should be killed before they do harm to us."

All the other monkey heroes like Angada, Nila and others tended to view Vibhishana with suspicion and advised that he should be watched carefully and his movements noted and anything of a suspicious nature immediately reported to Rama.

Rama looked enquiringly at Hanuman who as usual had remained silent. When thus requested by Rama, Anjaneya said,

"Vibhishana does not have the looks of a deceitful person to me. His mien and voice are open and pleasing. I think he has decided that it would be going against the law of righteousness to stay with one as debased as his brother. Moreover, he must have heard of your glory and your adherence to *dharma*. Hence, he has defected. One who comes as a spy would not announce himself as he has done. He was the only one who pleaded my case with Ravana and begged him not to kill me when I devastated the garden. This is my humble opinion and now my Lord, you can take whatever decision you like to take."

Rama was delighted to hear Hanuman reflect his own views on the subject and said, "I fully endorse what the noble Hanuman has said about Vibhishana even though I know that the rest of you are fully devoted to me and that's why you have given me this advice. However, on my part I have taken a vow that I will never turn away a person who has surrendered to me or taken refuge in me. Whatever his intentions may be, if he appears to have come in a friendly spirit it is my duty to accept him."

Sugriva, the prudent, spoke once again and warned Rama of the dangers of accepting the brother of the ten-headed Ravana who was sure to prove perfidious and untrustworthy and deserved instant death.

With a slight smile Rama said, "A righteous man may be born even in a clan of *rakshasas*. The scriptures enjoin us to welcome even an enemy who comes to one's door asking for protection. Such a person should be protected even at the cost of one's own life. I would be guilty of a great crime if I did not give him asylum."

After saying this Rama made his oft-quoted vow, "I promise to give security to all living beings that come to me even once and seek my protection. I will do this even if Ravana himself comes! O Sugriva! Let

Vibhishana be brought before me at once and let him be treated on equal terms with me."

Sugriva spoke, "My Lord! You are too noble. I am sure he is a spy. It would be safer to kill him."

Rama replied with a smile, "I know that you speak out of your love but the code of *dharma* says that one who has taken refuge should never be abandoned. My principle is to give succour to anyone who comes and declares that he wants to join me. His character is immaterial. Go and bring him here."

Sugriva bowed to Rama and went and gave an assurance of safety to Vibhishana who immediately descended on the beach and fell at Rama's feet.

"I am Vibhishana, Ravana's youngest brother and have sought refuge at your feet for you are capable of giving shelter to all created beings. I have come to you after having abandoned my city, friends and relatives. Now you are my all. My life and welfare are in your hands. I have surrendered my joys and sorrows and my very life at your blessed feel. Please accept me as your devoted slave."

Rama was touched by his devotion. He smiled tenderly at him and bade him welcome and gave him permission to stay. Afterwards he asked him about Ravana's strength and weaknesses.

Vibhishana was only too happy to oblige. "I am capable of giving you many hints about Ravana and his generals. My eldest brother has a boon that he cannot be killed by the gods or demons or celestial beings or serpents or birds. My powerful second brother, Kumbhakarna is an exceptional warrior. The commander of the forces, Prahasta is an indomitable soldier. Ravana's eldest son, Indrajit has invincible armour and is clothed in iguana skin which cannot be pierced by arrows. Having propitiated the god of fire, Indrajit has the ability to remain invisible when fighting. The army consists of tens of thousands of ogres able to change their form at will, living on flesh and blood. As for Ravana, he has defeated even the gods in battle."

Rama listened carefully to this account and then said with a smile, "Indeed I am well aware of Ravana's exploits which have been recounted to me by various persons. However, I give you my word that I shall not return to Ayodhya without killing this monster who has abducted my wife. I will then crown you as king of Lanka! Though he may run and try to hide in all the worlds, Ravana will not be able to escape the fury of my arrows. Until I achieve this, I will not enter Ayodhya. I swear this in the name of my three brothers."

Vibhishana fell at his feet and assured him that he would give him all assistance in this noble endeavour. "I swear in the name of *dharma* that I will assist you in all ways, to the best of my ability but the one thing that I will not do is to kill my own people!"

Rama embraced Vibhishana and asked Lakshmana to bring water from the sea to anoint him as king of the *rakshasas*. Water was forthwith brought and poured over Vibhishana's head by Lakshmana in the formal ritual known as *abhisheka* in the presence of all the monkeys in order to proclaim him as king of the night rangers!

In the meantime, Ravana sent a spy to try and make friends with Sugriva and encourage him to return to Kishkinda and thus desert Rama. The spy took the form of a monkey and tried to ingratiate himself with Sugriva. When he felt that he had his confidence, he took him aside and told him that his master was Ravana who was really very anxious to make friends with him since he had been a friend of his brother, Vaali. He told him to take his army and return to Kishkinda and win Ravana's favour for all time. Sugriva was so angry to hear this that he jumped on him and nearly choked him to death. The other monkeys came running to find out what the commotion was about and when they heard of the spy in their midst they would have torn him to pieces but he shouted to Rama to save him since he was only an envoy. Rama immediately ordered the monkeys to release him and he flew away squawking in fear and reported the matter to Ravana.

Rama now asked Vibhishana for a stratagem to cross the ocean. Vibhishana told him that for this he would have to ask Sagara, the Lord of the ocean, to help him to make a bridge which would carry his army across.

"This ocean owes its very existence to the Sagara brothers who belong to the Ikshvaku clan and are your ancestors. Therefore, he is bound to help you."

When Rama heard this salutary advice he lay on the beach facing the east with his arm as a pillow, on a mat of *kusa* grass and started meditating on the Lord of the ocean. When Sagara did not appear after three days and nights of meditation, Rama lost his temper and told Lakshmana. "Do you see O Lakshmana? How this haughty ocean refuses to show himself even though solicited so politely by me. Forbearance and politeness are misconstrued for weakness in this world. But mark my words today I shall dry up this ocean with all its wealth. My arrows shall suck up the waters so that it will remain dry and my army can cross it without difficulty!"

So saying Rama let fly his potent arrow deep into the sea causing consternation amongst the aquatic creatures. The waves were as tall as mountains. The earth trembled and quivered in agony. The sky became pitch black and meteors flashed across the firmament even as lightning flashed. The ocean throbbed and moaned in pain. Lakshmana caught Rama's arm before he could release his second arrow. However, since it had already been mounted it had to be discharged.

"Shoot it in the opposite direction," said Hanuman. Rama shot it to the north and the place where it fell came to be known as the Thar Desert!

Seeing the confusion caused in his waters, the Sea God, Sagara rose out of the water clad in red robes and wearing a garland of pearls and red flowers. The darkness caused by Rama's anger lifted due to the radiance of the jewels round Sagara's neck. His hair was covered with sea-weed and water kept pouring down his long grey hair and beard. He rose up to the surface of the ocean on the crest of a wave. Slowly he came to the shore and approached Rama and stood humbly in front of him with folded palms kept above his head. He was decked with many jewels and ushered to the shore by waves. Coming near Rama, Sagara spoke.

"My Lord, you are known to be the abode of kindness and mercy. I did not appear before you earlier because I cannot go against my nature. As you know earth, fire, air and water have their own specific qualities.

I cannot go against these. I am fathomless and incapable of being swum across. However, I will allow your monkeys to make a bridge and keep the stones afloat and thus give them a safe passage so that they may not be harmed by crocodiles and other reptiles. Let the two brothers known as Nala and Nila be allowed to make a bridge across the sea. They have been given a boon that any stone they place on the water will be able to float." With these words the Sea God melted back into the ocean.

Nila and Nala now came forward and told Rama to order the monkeys to collect material for the construction of the causeway.

The monkeys were delighted to get orders from Rama and immediately ransacked the forest for trees and boulders which they dragged to the shore and threw into the sea. The two brothers, Nala and Nila were remarkable engineers and saw to it that the rocks and trees brought by the monkeys were kept in the right places. The enthusiastic monkeys uprooted trees and brought huge boulders. Rocks as large as hills were carried on their willing shoulders and thrown into the sea. However, they were dismayed to find that the rocks though floating quickly dispersed on the choppy waters. Hanuman quickly thought of the brilliant idea of writing the Sanskrit words *ra* and *ma* on alternate stones and allowing the crack between them to stand for the long vowel *aa*.

Maruti said, "The Lord's name is the greatest of all *mantras* and the bridge will be made in an unbroken line of Rama *mantras*!"

Work was progressing very satisfactorily with Hanuman supervising everything and working harder than any of the others. However their enthusiasm dampened when they found that once again the stones refused to stay together and drifted away in all directions! Hanuman decided to investigate the reason for this. He dived into the ocean and found that the fish were responsible for dismantling the bridge. He shook his tail vigorously and thrashed the waters thus paralysing the fish.

He then confronted Swarna-matsya, the golden mermaid, queen of fishes and demanded an explanation.

"I was ordered by Ravana to disperse the stones," she said. Then looking closely at Hanuman she said enticingly, "Who are you? You seem to be strong and handsome and intelligent. What have you got to do with this war between Rama and Ravana? Marry me and enjoy life as it is meant to be enjoyed. Together we will rule the sea, unconcerned with the worries of the world above!"

"Hanuman replied, "Of what use is my strength, beauty and wisdom if they are of no use to others? He who uses his abilities only for his own aggrandisement is a fool. As for me I live for my master – Rama. I have no life apart from him. So saying, Hanuman declined her offer and rose to the surface. The queen was impressed by Hanuman's selflessness and ordered all her creatures to help him in building the bridge. The fish, serpents, seals and sea monsters held the stones together and the bridge to Lanka started to take shape.

Hanuman worked twice as hard as any of the others, constantly repeating the magic *mantra* of Rama as every stone was placed and the work went on with great speed. The bridge was a hundred leagues long and ten leagues wide. On the very first day one fifth was completed. In this way, the monkeys guided by Nala and Nila managed to span the ocean and complete the bridge in five days! Even now parts of this amazing bridge can be seen in the ocean off the coast of Dhanushkodi, which is the modern town closest to Sri Lanka.

Rama was amazed to see the miracle of the floating stones and asked the monkeys how it was done. They replied that it was only due to the power of his own name which Hanuman was engraving on every stone. Rama was intrigued and thought to himself that if his name could produce such miracles then surely he himself should be able to do the same. So he quietly moved to another part of the beach and started to throw some stones in the water. Much to his disappointment none of them floated. When he turned round he found that Hanuman had been standing at a safe distance and watching the whole proceedings. Rama was a bit abashed and asked Hanuman the reason why he did not have as much power as his name.

Hanuman's interpretation was in accordance with his devotion.

"My Lord!" He said, "Anything which you choose to hold in your hands will be saved and anything which you let go will naturally fall. The stone which slips from your grasp will obviously have to sink!"

Rama now joined Lakshmana near the bridge and watched the work. It is said that a small squirrel that was anxious to help Rama used to jump into the water and roll on the sand and then go and shake off the dust on the bridge, since that was the only effort it was capable of making. Hanuman picked up the little fellow and asked him what he was doing. The little one reared itself up beside the mighty monkey and said, "The causeway is made with a lot of ragged rocks. My Lord's tender feet will get torn when he walks on it so I thought I would make a nice soft sandy surface for him to walk on!" Hanuman was amazed at the little creature's devotion which seemed to exceed his own. He took it to Rama who kept it on his lap so that it could nestle close to him. Rama comforted the little one by passing his three fingers over its back. The Indian squirrel bears the mark of Rama's fingers on its back to this day. It has three lines on its back. Rama calmed its fears and told it that its tiny efforts were as valuable to him as the gigantic achievements of the monkeys. The sand he had brought was as precious to him as the rocks of the *vanaras*. Thus, the little squirrel also found a place in Rama's heart.

Another interesting legend connects Hanuman with the baleful planet Saturn (*Shani*). It is believed that Saturn visits each individual at least once in his lifetime for a period of seven-and-a-half years. Just as the bridge was being built, it was time for Saturn to come into Hanuman's horoscope. He requested Shani to postpone his visit till he had successfully assisted Rama in regaining Sita. But despite the fact that Hanuman had freed him from Ravana's dungeon, Saturn, true to his nature, was adamant and Hanuman had to comply with the law of nature. He allowed Saturn to sit on his head as his hands were busy carrying stones and uprooting trees and his legs were too humble to seat such an exalted personage.

For a few minutes Saturn happily settled on Hanuman's head and watched the proceedings with glee. The mighty monkey continued with his work, piling heavy boulders and stones on his head in an apparently casual manner and carrying them to the construction site. After a while Saturn found it impossible to bear the load of the heaped boulders on top of him and wanted to climb down. Hanuman insisted that he complete his mandatory seven-and-a-half years. Saturn pleaded for release saying that the seven-and-a-half minutes that he had spent on Hanuman's head felt like seven-and-a-half years. Hanuman smiled and allowed him to go. Since then it is believed by all worshippers of the monkey god that those who are suffering from the ill effects of the seven-and-a-half year stay of the malefic planet will definitely get a remand from their sentence if they worship Hanuman.

By the fourth day of construction, the monkeys had uprooted all the mountains and stones in South India and started to fly north to uproot the peaks there. Hanuman also flew to the Himalayas where he was struck by the sight of a lofty mountain called Dronachala. However, he found it impossible to uproot and realized that it was made of a black stone called *saligrama*, which is used in the worship of Vishnu. Hanuman told the mountain that he wanted to use it to help the *avatara* of Vishnu called Rama and he would be touched by Rama's feet. At this the mountain allowed itself to be uprooted but en route Maruti was met by Nala and Nila who told him that the causeway was complete and Rama had ordered all monkeys to drop the mountains they were carrying and return immediately to camp. Many monkeys were on their way at that time carrying mountain peaks. On hearing Rama's order they dropped the peaks over the whole of South India and thus created the present day topography of the land. Hanuman, however, was still far to the north and when he heard Rama's order he set the mountain down in the forest of Vrindavana near the Yamuna River. The mountain was crest-fallen at being denied the chance to worship Rama and reminded Hanuman of his promise to take him to Rama.

Maruti was in a dilemma. Was he to break his promise to the mountain or disobey Rama's orders! He flew back to Rama and told him the whole story. Rama comforted him by saying, "Return to the mountain and tell him that the time for us to meet has not yet come. I will return to the earth in the next age of Dwapara as Krishna and will play with my friends on top of this mountain. I will even lift it up with my little finger and hold it aloft. It will be known as Govardhana and will be worshipped as an embodiment of myself."

Hanuman delivered this message and the mountain was satisfied and waited for the advent of the Lord as Krishna in the *Yuga* known as Dwapara.

Rama was anxious to install a *lingam* of Shiva and pray to him for success in his endeavour before crossing the bridge. In one day, the two brothers Nala and Nila made the small dais on which the *lingam* was to be installed. Rama entrusted Hanuman with the work of bringing a really auspicious *lingam*. Hanuman immediately set off for Kailasa from where he hoped to get a *lingam* from Shiva himself. However, he was unable to return at the appointed time. The priests warned Rama that the auspicious time was about to pass. So Rama himself made a beautiful *lingam* of Lord Shiva with sand and it was installed at the correct time. All the monkeys were thrilled to see this. Anjaneya arrived soon after with a beautiful stone *lingam* given by Shiva and was most disappointed to see that the function had taken place without him. Seeing his despondent look, Rama comforted him and told him to remove the *lingam* which he had kept and install his own instead. Anjaneya did his best to remove the *lingam* but was unable to do so. He even tried to wrap his tail round it and pull it up but his tail broke instead. Rama lovingly moved his hand over his tail and restored it to its original beauty and size.

He told him, "O son of Vayu! Do not be distressed. Our endeavour would have been unsuccessful had I not worshipped the *lingam* at the appointed time. Hence I was unable to wait for you. A *lingam* once installed by me cannot be moved; however I give you permission to install this *lingam,* which you have brought to the east of this dais. The main entrance will be kept there so that anyone who comes to worship at this place will have to offer worship at your *lingam* first. Hanuman was very happy to hear this. This place where Rama installed the *lingam* is known as Rameswaram (Rama's Lord Shiva) and is a famous place of pilgrimage to this very day.

There is another strange story about the installation of the *lingam* which shows the Indian ability to give credit even to an enemy if it's called for. It is said that at the time when Rama wanted to install a *lingam*, there was no priest to officiate. He asked Hanuman to fly to Lanka and request Ravana who was a great devotee of Shiva and a Brahmin to come and do this service. Ravana agreed but said that Sita would also have to be present since the sponsor of the ritual should have his wife beside him. So Sita was fetched from the garden and Hanuman accompanied by Ravana and Sita went in the Pushpaka Vimana, Ravana's flying chariot, to the mainland. Rama asked Ravana to suggest a source for the *lingam* and Ravana suggested Kailasa. Hanuman was sent to procure the required *lingam* but was unable to return in time. Ravana insisted that the ceremony had to be conducted at the auspicious hour and Sita moulded a *lingam* out of the sand. Ravana observed all the rites punctiliously and even intoned Rama's *sankalpa* or intention for which the ceremony was being conducted – the slaying of Ravana and the rescue of Sita! The rest of the story is the same as above.

The causeway was complete and the installation over. Even the gods came to survey it and from above it looked like the central parting of the hair of a woman, so elegant and beautiful was it! Now it was time to cross. Rama and Lakshmana blew their conches and saluted Durga, the goddess of war. Hanuman let out a war cry, filling the hearts of the monkeys with confidence. Sugriva now invited Rama to climb on Hanuman's back and cross the bridge while Lakshmana rode on Angada's back. They led the way followed by the rest of the *vanara* hordes who followed, dancing and bounding with joy. They would leap into the air and jump into the sea and swim for a while. They made such a clamour that the noise of the sea was successfully shut out. It was as if the sea held its breath, while the army crossed.

As they approached their destination, Ravana hurled two missiles and destroyed the two ends of the bridge. Rama and his troops were stranded in the middle unable to cross to Lanka or return to Jambudwipa. Hanuman immediately came up with a brilliant solution. He increased his size and stretched himself over the gap, placing his hands on the shore of Lanka and his feet on the edge of the bridge. The monkeys scrambled over his back and jumped on to Ravana's stronghold. As Rama walked over Maruti's back, he said, "I'm indeed blessed today for my Lord's feet have stepped on my back."

At last they set foot on enemy territory. Rama was touched by the enthusiasm and devotion of the monkeys and their innocent love. Sugriva was all set to put up camp on the other side in a place which abounded with fruits and roots and clear water. However, Rama saw many evil portents bidding dire consequences for the whole earth and told Sugriva that they should immediately march towards Lanka instead of dallying there at that pleasant spot. Thus, the monkey hordes continued to advance until they came in sight of the ramparts of Lanka. They drew up in military formation even though it was night. The full moon slowly rose up to display the huge army of monkeys who were camped on the mountain side.

Rama looked up at the city of Ravana with its turrets of gold and silver and thought of his beloved Janaki (Sita) who was a prisoner of love in that city of hate. He was lost in thought for a long time. At last he roused himself and talked to Sugriva and the commanders about their plan of action for the next day.

"You are the ever vigilant guard at the door of Sri Rama.
No one can enter without your consent."

— *Sri Hanuman Chalisa* by Tulsidas

ॐ *Sri Hanumathe Namaha!*

ॐ

Mahatejase Namaha!

CHAPTER NINETEEN

MAHATEJASVIN

The Siege of Lanka

"Dehadrishtya tu daasoham,
Jeevadrishtya twadamshakam,"

When I identify myself with my body, I am your servant,
When I identify myself with my ego, I am a part of you.

In the meantime, the spies sent by Ravana had returned and told him all the details about the enemies and how Hanuman had made it possible for them to pass over the bridge which had been broken by his missiles. He felt a bit dejected and decided to survey the enemy camp for himself and climbed up the turret of his palace which was as tall as ten coconut trees kept one on top of the other. He leant over the wall and saw to his amazement that the whole land beyond his citadel was filled with monkeys of all shapes and sizes. He brought the spies with him and asked them to point out the leaders of the army.

Pointing at one of the monkeys, they said, "That huge monkey with thick neck and golden hair, who is boisterous and facing us is Sugriva, son of Surya. The yellow-haired one, who is roaring like a lion and lashing his tail again and again, is the crown prince, Angada. The one who stands surrounded by a valiant army is Nila, the one who built the bridge. The white monkey in the forefront is Hanuman, son of Kesari who is also known as the son of the Wind God, Vayu. As you know he is the one who crossed the sea and set fire to Lanka. This prince among monkeys is able to change his form at will and is richly endowed with might and physical charm and cannot be swayed from his course just as the powerful wind cannot be forced to change its route. As a baby he saw the rising sun and thinking it to be a fruit, he jumped three thousand leagues towards it. He is totally devoted to Rama and the scourge of his enemies as you well know."

He then went on to point out the various other commanders of the *vanara* army, so that Ravana could have an idea of who they were.

"Now O King! Observe those black, ferocious bears that live on mountains. Their leader is that old, shaggy bear, Jambavan, who once helped Indra in his war with the demons. His troops are extremely ferocious and can scale huge mountains and are totally unafraid. All of them are valiant, powerful and daring and all are ready to lay down their lives for Rama!"

"Observe this valiant prince, O King with matted hair and dark blue in colour with lotus-like eyes, the scion of the race of Ikshvaku, foremost amongst those who know the Veda, expert in the use of the mystic missile of Brahma (*brahmastra*), whose wrath is like the wrath of Death and whose consort Sita, was abducted by you from Janasthana. His arrows can slice the earth and pierce the sky. Observe him closely for he is Rama, your arch enemy who is advancing towards you, determined to kill you at all cost!"

"The one who stands on his right, fair in colour, with broad chest, coppery eyes and dark curly locks is Lakshmana, Rama's younger brother who is totally devoted to him. He is foremost in the wielder of weapons and unforgiving towards the enemies of Rama. He is ever prepared to lay down his life for his brother's sake. Observe closely O King! Your brother Vibhishana who stands on Rama's right side and who has already been installed as King of Lanka by Rama! He is furious with you and is longing to come to grips with your army."

Ravana was furious with his servitors who spoke so highly of the enemy army.

"How dare you speak to me like this? You are my dependents and I can kill you for singing the praises of my enemies like this. Leave my presence immediately and never let me see you again!" So saying, Ravana dismissed them and sent some other spies to find out Rama's plans for the day. However, they were also spotted by Vibhishana and would have been tortured by the monkeys had not Rama intervened and allowed them to go free. They returned singing Rama's praises.

Ravana decided to try a final trick to make Sita succumb to his charms! He called the court magician and asked him to make a replica of Rama's head as well as a replica of Rama's famous bow – the Kodanda. The magician carried these two objects and accompanied the king to the Ashoka grove where Sita was sitting, the very picture of dejection.

Brandishing Rama's head before her, he said, "That good-for-nothing husband of yours was killed by my general while he was camping outside the gates of Lanka. Evidently your stock of spiritual merits was not enough to save him. Lakshmana as well as the foremost of the generals of their army have all been killed."

He shot a piercing look at her through his crystal green eyes and continued, "I see that you don't believe me. I anticipated this and have brought your husband's head to convince you!"

He ordered the magician to come forward. He arrived promptly with Rama's head stuck on a pole. This gruesome article was placed before Sita. Ravana took the bow and threw it in front of her and said, "Here is the famous bow of Rama. Surely you recognise it." Then leaning forward he whispered words meant for her ears alone, "Now will you agree to be mine?"

Sita gave one look at the head and shrieked, "O my beloved Lord! Have you deserted me? The astrologers had predicted a very long life for you. How did you meet this untimely death when you were well versed in the science of warfare? Why don't you look at me O prince? Why don't you answer me?"

Turning to Ravana, she said, "Kill me with the same weapon with which my husband was killed and lay my body over his on the battlefield. I shall follow him wherever he may be," so saying the poor lady fell to weeping and lamenting.

Just then one of Ravana's generals came and demanded his immediate presence at the council hall for a matter of great importance had to be discussed. As soon as Ravana left, both the magic head and the bow vanished much to Sita's astonishment.

Just then Vibhishana's wife came and told Sita not to worry since it was a trick of Ravana's and her husband was alive and preparing to attack Lanka. She revived Sita and told her to listen to the sounds made by the approaching army. Sita was most grateful to her and asked her to go and find out what plans Ravana was making and whether he would release her now that he realised that her husband was already camped outside the city. Vibhishana's wife returned soon after and appraised Sita of the situation.

"O princess of Mithila! Ravana is not prepared to let you go until he dies. He will certainly not release you through fear. So deep rooted is his infatuation for you. However fear not, your husband will come soon enough and kill the ten-headed monster and rescue you!"

In the meantime, Rama accompanied by Lakshmana and the other chieftains decided to climb to the top of the Suvela mountain in order to have a closer view of the city of Lanka which had been built on top of the Trikuta mountain. Suddenly he saw Ravana standing on the ramparts clad in all his finery, adorned in scarlet robes and fanned on both sides by beautiful females, surveying the camp of the *vanaras.*

Seeing this Sugriva could not control himself and suddenly sprang from one peak to the other and landed next to the astonished Ravana.

"I am Sugriva, the friend and servant of Rama. You shall not be spared by me this day!" With these words, he leapt on him and snatched his crown and threw it on the ground.

Ravana was taken by surprise and said, "I will deprive you of your beautiful neck in a moment. So saying, he caught hold of him and threw him on the ground. Sugriva bounced up like a ball and there was a small skirmish. However, Sugriva realised his mistake and hurriedly jumped back to the Suvela peak. The monkeys cheered their leader but Rama chided him gently for his brash act and told him never to repeat such a thing again. Had he been killed or caught, the results would have been disastrous for them.

He then told him to send Angada as a messenger of good will in order to give Ravana a last chance to save his people. Such an act was in accordance with the laws of a righteous combat. Hanuman said that in his opinion nothing on earth would make Ravana change his mind. However, Rama insisted that on his part there should be no deviation from the path of *dharma* and he should by all means give the demon a chance to change his mind even at this last minute, if he so wished.

Angada was longing to have a close look at Ravana and hardly had he got his orders than he leapt to the assembly hall where Ravana was confabbing with his ministers.

In the sunlight he looked like a fiery golden ball when he landed lightly in front of the Demon King.

"Who are you?" he asked.

"I am Angada, the son of Vaali and the messenger of Rama, prince of Ayodhya." As soon as he heard these words, Ravana rose up and welcomed Angada warmly.

"My dear child! You are the son of my good friend. You are like a son to me. But I don't understand why you should be befriending a person who killed your father in an unfair manner. Stay with me and I'll treat you like my son, Indrajit and give you all comforts. You are the son of a noble father and should not consort with such riff raff!"

"O King of *rakshasas*! Who are you to give advice to me when you yourself are steeped in sin! I have merely come to give you Rama's message. He has given you an ultimatum. Either you should return the princess of Videha to him and beg his pardon or else go out of the palace gates and confront him in a battle to the finish. The choice is yours – to live honourably or die dishonourably!"

Ravana was furious at this message and ordered the messenger, to whom he had proclaimed eternal love a few minutes ago, to be caught and put to death immediately!

"I will not blow out like a light with these windy words!" He said. He bent down and thrust his snarling face close to Angada. His eyes were aflame and his brows knit into a huge frown. He reached out for Angada who was quivering with fear but at the last moment, he merely brushed him with his hands and ordered his guards to catch him.

Angada caught hold of the four guards who rushed forward to seize him and leapt with them on to the wall of the palace and threw them down on the ground. He then took a flying leap on to the turret of the palace and broke it in two. He stood there and roared like an infuriated bull and then nimbly landed back in front of Rama and the other monkeys who were highly delighted at his antics. He then gave an account of all that had happened in the court.

"So Hanuman was right," thought Rama, "Ravana will neither relinquish Sita nor will he come for an honourable combat until he is forced to do so."

Hanuman ordered the monkeys and bears to howl and growl menacingly and challenge the *rakshasas* to a fight. The thunderous noise made by them filled the air and frightened the residents of Lanka who were used to a life of voluptuous debauchery and were not happy at having been asked to fight. They started raising their voices asking Ravana to give up Sita and allow them to live in peace.

"Our civilisation is doomed," they said, "unless the king complies with our wishes."

Ravana was furious when he heard this. "They are only a pack of monkeys and bears," he shouted. We will hang their heads as trophies on our walls. Their skins will provide clothing for your wives and their flesh will provide food for your children. Mount your chariots, let loose our dogs and let us drive off Rama's rabble!"

Rama asked Sugriva to choose the generals who were to attack from various gates.

Very soon the entire space between the walls and the moat was filled with monkeys. In fact they seemed to have formed a solid wall round Lanka. This news was forthwith taken to Ravana who immediately told his forces to stop them from entering the gates. He himself climbed up on the ramparts and was astonished to find the whole grounds outside the gates, swarming with monkeys all eager to fight. The green fields had changed to brown. He suddenly spied Rama seated on Hanuman's back urging the monkeys to destroy the barricades and invade the town. He had never expected that a puny human being helped by a pack of simians would ever be able to come close to his precious city and now it looked as if they would soon get inside the gates. At that instant Lakshmana pointed his bow at Lanka and Ravana raised his mace above his head and the commander of his armies waved his sword. He ordered the gates to be opened and let loose hundreds of wild hunting dogs followed by fierce *rakshasas* mounted on war chariots. He was sure that his well-trained army would easily rout a pack of unruly monkeys. The big north gate of Lanka opened and the youngest third of the *rakshasa* army rushed out.

The monkeys fell back in fear but Hanuman led the attack and threw a huge stone at the *rakshasa* who was in the forefront and knocked him down senseless. Thus emboldened the monkeys rushed forward, armed with sticks and stones, determined to overcome the army of the night wanderers. The bears frightened away the dogs and startled the horses. The monkeys leapt into the chariots, kicking, punching and biting the *rakshasas* who were ill-prepared for this type of warfare.

The monkeys now started filling up the moat with stones and branches so that their troops could cross easily. Then they started scaling the walls in various places. They grabbed trees and logs and stones for weapons and jumped on to the streets of Lanka shouting, "Victory to Rama! Death to the demons!" And so on. Very soon the whole place was alive with a mass of leaping, screaming *vanaras* bent on destruction.

The army of the night rangers now tried to stop the monkeys from advancing. All of them were decked in golden armour and carried swords and bows and arrows. They rushed forward with blood-curdling roars and swooped on the *vanaras*. They attacked them with flaming brands, javelins, spikes and axes while the monkeys retaliated with trees, rocks as well as their nails and teeth!

The young generals of Ravana's army now sallied forth, mounted on huge horses, elephants and chariots. All the horses and elephants had golden trappings and the heroes were dazzling in gold and silver coats of mail while the monkeys had nothing but their fur to protect them!

Since they did not have chariots, Rama rode into battle on Hanuman's shoulders and Lakshmana on Angada's. Soon the battlefield was covered with dust. Blood of the *vanaras,* bears and *rakshasas* flowed in streams on the ground. The air was filled with the din of drums, bugles and war cries. Banners were torn, chariots were smashed and weapons cast here and there. Bones were broken, flesh was torn and eyes gouged out as the monkeys clawed and scratched and jumped on the backs of *rakshasas.*

Ravana stood on the highest tower in Lanka and surveyed the devastating scene. His troops were being driven back into the citadel and he feared that the ancient prophecy made by Nandi would come true and he would have to face defeat at the hands of the monkeys. Hanuman saw Ravana and took a flying leap and landed on his head. He then danced on all his heads and kicked his ten crowns to the ground. The monkeys roared their approval while the *rakshasas* hung their heads in shame. Before Ravana could catch him, he had leapt back into the fray.

The first day's battle went on into the night which was the time when the night rangers were most powerful. The night was lit up by the brilliance of the gold-tipped arrows which were shooting across the sky. The night prowlers were jubilant at the advent of night.

Ravana said, "Let the young warriors take rest. Arm the veterans."

Demon soldiers knelt before fires praying for victory. They strung their bows and donned their armour and put garlands over them blessed by the priests with *mantras* for safety. Ravana gave his general Prahasta a few drops of *soma* juice and blessed him. Little flames started to come out of Prahasta's eyes. He bowed before Ravana and said, "I'll drive away the monkeys and isolate Rama and feast on his flesh."

He bowed to Ravana and got his blessings and mounted his chariot, which had wheels of gold which shone like twin suns. Sixty-four horned serpents drew the chariot which bristled with swords and harpoons. His flag had a snake of emeralds and a lion of topaz sewn on to blood red silk. Prahasta flexed his muscles and rolled his blood-shot eyes. The north gate opened and he led out the veterans, the grand army of the *rakshasas.* The soldiers followed with bells tied on their arms and legs. They charged at the animals who fled in terror. Nala alone faced Prahasta's chariot. He dodged thousands of arrows which were flung at him and threw a boulder which overturned his chariot. The demon broke free from his chariot and lunged at Nala with his mace. He dodged the blow and pulled out one of the wheels of the chariot and struck Prahasta on the heart. The mace fell from his hand and Prahasta fell down dead. The time was midnight. The *rakshasas* tore their hair in shame and returned leaderless to Lanka.

The monkeys and bears carried their dead and laid them in the forest. Many of the demons had died but since Ravana did not want anyone to know how many had fallen, he ordered that their bodies should be thrown into the sea.

Ravana immediately ordered his son, Indrajit as well as his foremost generals to go out and tackle the simian army. They challenged Lakshmana and the others to duels. Indrajit fought with Angada, Lakshmana with Virupaksha and Hanuman with Jambumali. They were two of the most trusted generals of Ravana's army.

Angada was determined to come to grips with Indrajit, the son of Ravana who had been named Meghanatha but had got the name Indrajit after he defeated Indra, king of gods. He was a master magician and prince of illusions. He was Ravana's golden boy who could take on any form at will. It was said that only Mandodari, his mother, knew his actual form. Angada wounded Indrajit and killed his charioteer and horses. Rama and the others applauded Angada for his feat for they all knew the might of Indrajit. In the meantime the wily son of Ravana leapt into the air and disappeared into the clouds. From this vantage point he sent the deadly *naga pasha* or noose of the serpents by which he bound the two brothers. The serpent ropes coiled round the necks of the brothers choking them till they became unconscious. Enmeshed by these magic cords, lacerated all over their bodies with Indrajit's deadly arrows, Rama and Lakshmana lay on the ground drenched in blood, with hardly a sign of life except for an occasional, feeble twitch. There was panic in the *vanara* army. They fell into a mood of dreadful despondency when they saw their heroes in this pitiable state. They jumped to the sky searching in vain for a glimpse of Indrajit but he remained invisible. All they could hear was his mocking laughter. Only Vibhishana could see him and he was also helpless against the snake arrows. Indrajit was jubilant for he was sure he had killed the brothers. Having created havoc in the rest of the army, he returned to his father and gave him the happy news of the death of the Kosala brothers.

The monkeys crowded round the fallen princes and gave vent to their grief. They felt that the fact that the very first day of war went so badly was a bad sign for them. However, Vibhishana approached them and told them not to grieve for he did not think that they were dead. He told them to protect the princes for he was sure they were only unconscious. Jambavan told them that Rama was Vishnu incarnate and could certainly never be killed by anyone.

"You took a colossal form and killed the demons.
Thus you fulfilled the mission of Sri Rama."

— *Sri Hanuman Chalisa* by Tulsidas

ॐ *Sri Hanumathe Namaha!*

ॐ

Ravana-maradanaaya Namaha!

CHAPTER TWENTY

VATAMAJA

War Continues

"Na mukhe netrayovapi
Lalade cha bruvosthata,
Anyeshwapi cha gaatreshu,
Dosha samvitita kwachit."

I can see no fault of expression anywhere on his face or even his eyes, Forehead, eyebrows or in any one of his limbs.

— *Valmiki Ramayana*

Ravana was elated at the thought of the death of Rama and immediately ordered that Sita be taken in an aerial car and shown this scene so that she would believe. "Tell Sita to forget her husband and come to me since she has no other recourse open to her but to accept my love and become my wife!"

Sita could not believe what the *rakshasis* told her so they forced her to enter the aerial car and took her to the battlefield. She wept at seeing the devastation on the battlefield and the scores of monkeys who lay dead. In the midst of this sea of corpses of the dead and dying monkeys, she saw her beloved husband and his brother lying on a bed of arrows, their bodies bleeding and inert. She could no longer see clearly due to the tears which were flowing in torrents from her eyes.

She started to moan and curse her fate.

"How is it that my Rama, who killed all the *rakshasas* at Janasthana single-handed was unable to counteract the deadly arrows of the evil-minded son of Ravana? Our *guru* Vasishta prophesied that Rama would perform many *Ashwamedha yagas* and win great fame as a king. He also said that I would never be a widow and would be the mother of heroic sons. How is it that all these sayings have proved false? Of what use are the lotus marks on my feet, which proclaim that I will be a queen. I have all the twelve auspicious signs of a noble woman on me. My body is symmetrical, my teeth even, my navel set deep in my stomach. My breasts are full and skin and hair soft. My complexion is pearly and soles touch the ground when I walk yet this calamity has overtaken me!"

One of the *rakshasis* who was kinder than the rest and had befriended her before, now comforted her with these words, "My lady, please do not weep. Your Lord is certainly not dead. In fact neither of them is dead. See how the *vanaras* are guarding their bodies. They appear to be waiting for them to recover. There is a glow about their faces which would not have been there if they were dead. Take this opportunity to have a good look at the face of your beloved from whom you have been parted for such a long time. Forget your sorrow and take heart!"

Sita was thrilled to hear this. She observed the two of them carefully and confirmed what the kindly *rakshasi* had said. She raised her palms and saluted Rama and then returned.

"Only the divine eagle, Garuda, can break these ropes and release the brothers," said Jambavan.

Hanuman had been standing quietly all the while for he was convinced that Rama and Lakshmana were not dead. He sat down facing the east and started chanting the Garuda *mantra.* Garuda was Lord Vishnu's eagle vehicle and the avowed enemy of snakes. Hardly had he finished chanting when a tempestuous wind arose in the sky and whipped the waves and made them rise to the sky. Trees were snapped like sticks and flung far off to the sea and animals ran hither and thither. Suddenly they saw Garuda, the king of birds who resembled a blazing fire cleaving his way through the storm-tossed sky. The storm had been caused by his enormous wings. Seeing him all the snakes which had bound Rama and Lakshmana released their deadly hold on them and slithered off in terror. Both of them now stirred and sat up as if from a deep sleep. Garuda came close to them and stroked their faces lovingly with his wings and instantly their wounds vanished and lustre returned to their faces. Their splendour and majesty were redoubled. Garuda embraced them warmly and Rama said,

"When you touched me with your wings I felt as if my father was caressing me. Because of you we have been saved from this deadly snake noose. Pray tell me who you are?"

The eagle said, "I am Garuda, the son of Vinata and I am the vehicle of Lord Vishnu. I am your constant companion and will always be hovering about you even though you are not aware of it. These snakes were converted into arrows by the magic *mantras* of Indrajit. I am the only one who could have saved you from this noose of snakes. I am their ancient enemy and that is why they vanished as soon as they saw me. Fear not O Rama! You and your brother are destined to destroy your enemies and have a glorious future. Your strength lies in your adherence to *dharma* and you will be victorious even though your enemies are treacherous. Now please give me leave to go. Whenever you need me, just think of me and I'll be there."

The monkeys chattered and shouted with delight when they saw this miraculous recovery. They thrashed their tails and thumped their kettledrums, beat their clay tom-toms and whooped with joy. Ravana heard these sounds and was quite puzzled. "How can they be so joyous when Rama lies dead?" he thought. He ordered his spies to go and find out the truth and was amazed when they returned with the news of the miraculous escape of the two brothers.

Ravana now ordered one of his best generals called Dhumraksha – the fiery-eyed one, to take a huge contingent and destroy the opposing army. He had the voice of a braying donkey and was mounted on a wonderful chariot driven by donkeys with harnesses of gold and heads resembling those of a wolf and a lion. He sallied forth through the western gate which was being guarded by Hanuman, accompanied by a host of *rakshasas* armed to the teeth and all wearing coats of mail. The monkeys were itching for a good fight and charged at the army as soon as it appeared through the gate. Dhumraksha who was in the forefront dispersed the monkeys in all directions with a shower of arrows. Infuriated at this

Hanuman took up a huge rock and flung it at Dhumraksha's chariot. He leapt out of the chariot in the nick of time and the chariot and the donkeys were smashed by the rock. Hanuman now started hurling trees and rocks at the *rakshasas* and then charged at their leader. Dhumraksha took up his huge mace studded with sharp spikes and hit Hanuman on the head with it. Hanuman brushed off the blow and retaliated by hurling a huge rock at his opponent. This was the end of the *rakshasa*. He fell senseless to the ground and the others ran back to report the matter to Ravana.

Ravana now sent his next champion, Vajradanta or the one with teeth like diamonds. His diamond-like fangs were long and sharp and hung over his lower lips. He was accompanied by a number of soldiers on elephants, horses, donkeys and camels. He was decked in lovely armlets and a diadem and had a coat of mail. His forces now came out of the southern gate which was being guarded by Prince Angada who immediately came forward to battle with the demon. There followed a terrific fight between the monkeys and Vajradanta's army. He sent a thousand arrows at the prince who retaliated by hurling a tree at his opponent. He then charged forward and shattered Vajradanta's chariot and forced him to jump out and face him on an equal footing. The demon held a huge shield and sword while Angada had only a tree. They wheeled round each other waiting for an opportunity to close in. When the ogre collapsed, Angada jumped and grabbed his fallen sword and lopped off his huge head. The panic-stricken army now ran back to their fortress and reported the whole matter to Ravana.

The next general to be sent by Ravana was Akampana. Mounting his huge golden chariot decked with jewels, he sallied forth accompanied by a huge army of soldiers. He caused great carnage to the monkey host till at last all the great leaders ran off in terror. Seeing this Hanuman entered the fray. The monkeys were gladdened when they saw his mighty form and untroubled demeanour and all of them rallied back around him. Akampana greeted him with a volley of arrows. Unperturbed by this Hanuman tore up a huge crag and hurled it at the *rakshasa* who split it into smithereens with his arrows. This enraged Hanuman who tore up a huge tree and rushed at Akampana who kept raining arrows at him.

Undeterred by this Hanuman brought the tree down with all force on Akampana's head and killed him instantly. The rest of the *rakshasa* army were in total disarray. With loosened hair and shrieking with fear at seeing the gigantic figure of Hanuman, they took to their heels in panic while the gleeful monkeys chased them with sticks and stones.

Ravana was slowly beginning to realise that he was not facing an ordinary foe. One by one all his great generals seemed to be dying. Now he called his commander-in-chief, who had advised him to wage war against Rama and told him that he was depending on him to defeat the foes. He set out with a thunderous roll of kettle-drums and a blast from scores of trumpets, in his enormous chariot decked with jewels and accompanied by thousands of soldiers all armed to the teeth. They rushed at the monkeys and fought with swords, javelins, double-edged swords, spikes, arrows, mallets, maces, iron bars, spears, axes and bows and arrows while the poor monkeys defended themselves with only trees and rocks.

They were met by Nila, the commander-in-chief of Sugriva's army. The two commanders met in a grim combat. Nila met the volley of arrows with closed eyes. He then grabbed a huge tree and shattered the demon's bow and chariot with it. The demon jumped down with his mallet and rushed at Nila and gave him a mighty blow on his head. Even though he was bleeding badly, Nila took a huge rock and hurled it at his head which broke into pieces. The army was sadly demoralised at the death of their commander-in-chief and fled to Lanka.

Ravana decided that he would have to enter the battlefield himself. His wife Mandodari approached him and begged him to reconsider his decision and to make peace with Rama. Ravana was outraged at this suggestion.

"Ravana has never bowed his head before anyone and will not do so now. But have no fear O Mandodari! By this evening I will have killed the Kosala brothers and avenged the death of my commanders."

Ravana sallied forth accompanied by a huge army of invincible warriors all of whom looked like huge mountains. Seeing the approach of this army Rama asked Vibhishana to point out the leaders to him. Vibhishana pointed out the various commanders to him and said, "There comes Ravana, king of the night rangers in the chariot with the white umbrella! He is accompanied by ghosts and ghouls with hideous forms having rolling eyes and heads of tigers, camels, elephants and horses. He is decked with a diadem and his ears have huge swinging earrings. He is the one who humbled the pride of Indra himself."

Rama gazed at him for a long moment and said, "Indeed he is a glorious figure. Such radiance! Like the sun at noon! He seems to be endowed with all the qualities of a great hero. Yet I cannot help but pity him for he is coming closer to his death!"

Ravana was discharging his deadly arrows at the monkeys who charged at him. Seeing this Sugriva could not help himself and tore a rock and sent it hurtling at Ravana who saw it coming and splintered it with his arrows. He then hurled his javelin at Sugriva who fell to the ground. Seeing this, the monkeys fled towards Rama who picked up his bow and decided to face Ravana himself. Lakshmana stopped him and begged him to allow him to go. Rama agreed for he felt the time had not yet come for him to come into close combat with Ravana.

In the meantime, Hanuman rushed at Ravana's chariot and said, "You have been granted many boons but none which will protect you from monkeys. Now allow my right hand to teach you a well deserved lesson."

Ravana replied, "Strike once and earn everlasting fame for having hit the great Ravana and after that I will destroy you."

Hanuman raised his fist and smote him on the chest. Ravana reeled under the blow and retaliated with a similar punch on Hanuman's chest.

Ravana said, "Well done O monkey! You are an adversary worthy of my praise."

Hanuman retorted, "Woe to my valour since you are still alive. Why don't you strike again and then I will send you to the abode of Yama!"

His eyes inflamed with anger, Ravana brought his right fist down with all his might on Hanuman's chest. Seeing Hanuman reeling under the blow, the *rakshasa* king did not wait to see more and drove his horses forward to confront Nila, the commander-in-chief of Rama's army. He discharged scores of arrows at him. Nila was the son of Agni, the god of fire. With great agility he reduced his size and leapt to the top of Ravana's chariot and then to the top of his crown and then kept hopping from place to place so that Ravana's arrows could never pierce him. Rama and Lakshmana were astonished to see the antics of this monkey. At last Ravana invoked the fire missile and flung it at Nila who fell to the ground. But since he was the son of the fire god, the missile could not kill him. Ravana thought him to be dead and turned towards Lakshmana. There ensued a formidable battle between the two. At last Ravana hurled a javelin at him, strengthened with a powerful *mantra.* It pierced Lakshmana's chest and made him swoon.

Filled with rage, Hanuman darted at him and gave him a mighty blow on his chest with his fist which made him fall to the floor of his chariot and lose consciousness. Hanuman immediately lifted up Lakshmana and brought him to Rama. Very soon both Lakshmana and Ravana recovered from their swoon. Rama decided to face Ravana himself and Hanuman begged him to sit on his shoulders like Vishnu sitting on Garuda.

Thus seated on the huge monkey, Rama charged at Ravana and said, "You shall not escape me wherever you may go and hide."

Ravana retaliated with a shower of gold-tipped arrows which covered Hanuman as well as Rama. The latter was furious at seeing Hanuman in this state and let fly a most potent arrow at Ravana's chest which made him reel so that his bow fell from his nerveless grasp. With another arrow, Rama tore off Ravana's crown and made him fall from his chariot. Seeing him dazed and without any weapons, Rama took pity on him and told him to go back to Lanka and return in another chariot when he was a bit refreshed.

Ravana returned to Lanka with his pride crushed, his bow broken in two, his horses and charioteer killed, his crown shattered and his body pierced all over with Rama's deadly arrows.

"You alone can contain your glory,
The three worlds tremble at your roar."

— *Sri Hanuman Chalisa* by Tulsidas

ॐ *Sri Hanumathe Namaha!*

ॐ

Daityakulanthakaaya Namaha!

CHAPTER TWENTY-ONE

DAITYAKULANTAKA

Kumbhakarna

"Life's alarms dispelling, all disasters quelling,
Comfort of the faithful,
Be our succour now."

— *Ramacharitamanas* by Tulsidas

Ravana was completely demoralised by the scene he had just gone through. Far from appreciating Rama's generosity in letting him go, he was filled with humiliation and thoughts of revenge. He sat and brooded on his golden throne and recalled all those painful incidents in his life when he had insulted so many people and had been cursed by them. He remembered Brahma's warning to beware of humans for he had not asked for immunity from them! He also remembered the curse of Punchikasthala and Nandi, the vehicle of Shiva and many others. His ministers crowded round him to find out his commands. At last he roused himself from these mournful thoughts and told them that the only way open to them was to rouse his brother Kumbhakarna from his sleep. He had been summoned to the council nine days ago and had gone back to sleep.

The *rakshasas* were terrified of calling Kumbhakarna before the stipulated time. However, the king's orders had to be obeyed. As they neared Kumbhakarna's subterranean abode they were blown back by the breath coming out of his nostrils! His mouth was like a yawning cave and his snores shook the rafters and made them rattle. His breath reeked of alcohol and blood for he had drunk and eaten his fill, nine days ago before falling into a deep stupor. The *rakshasas* who went to wake him carried wagon loads of buffalo and boar meat and buckets of blood and marrow and barrels of strong wine. They plastered his uncouth body with sandal paste and perfume and garlands. They made thunderous noises calculated to waken the dead, while others blew loudly on conchs, bugles and trumpets. Some used sticks and rods to prod him awake but he slept on, blissfully unaware of the tortures being done to his body! Then they fell to biting his ears and tearing his hair and jumping up and down on his stomach. At last the monster showed some signs of animation and gave a great yawn. Those who had been pulling his beard fell into his cavernous mouth and had to be fished out before he closed it. Furious at having been interrupted in his slumber of only nine days, he gave a mighty shout which made all of them flee in terror before he caught and started eating them. However, when he saw the mountains of food heaped before him he was a bit appeased and started greedily chomping his way through it. The *rakshasas* slowly crept back and informed him that his brother wanted him urgently. Having licked the pots and eaten the buffaloes which drew the carts containing the food, Kumbhakarna proceeded to dress himself with great care before going to the council hall to meet the king. The earth shuddered with every step he took. His gargantuan body occupied the whole width of the street.

Ravana was delighted to see him and informed him of the critical events which had taken place in Lanka while he was in the throes of blissful slumber. Kumbhakarna laughed heartily at Ravana's description of the *vanara* army and said, "My dear brother, I warned you of the consequences of your infatuation for that woman, just ten days ago in the council hall but you would not listen to me. The king, who follows the rules of *dharma* and listens to the words of the wise will reap the rewards of his good deeds, but the one who discards these words and acts according to his own perverted understanding will have to bear the consequences of his actions. Both Vibhishana and I advised you once but you would not listen. It is still not too late. Try to avert this crazy war and make friends with Rama. I hear that you have already lost your best generals and have been publicly humiliated. Will you not stop till your head is cut off from its shoulders?"

Ravana's lips quivered with rage and his eyes became like hot coals shooting sparks of fire. He shouted at Kumbhakarna, "An elder brother should be honoured like a father. How dare you try to advise me? What has happened has happened. I am not prepared to go back on anything I have done. If you have ever held me in esteem or love, then tell me what to do, now. Try to correct the results of my past indiscretions instead of harping on them!"

Kumbhakarna realised that his words were like a red rag to a bull so he pacified him with sweet words.

"Don't worry, brother, I will pulverise the whole lot of them just by walking in their midst. I will make mince meat of those puny princes. Just let me get my hands on them. I will tear them apart with my bare hands. I need no weapons. Cast off your worries and go into your harem and make merry with your wives. Once Rama is dead, Sita will be yours."

Ravana was delighted to hear this and placed many precious necklaces round his monstrous neck and sent him off with his blessings.

That night Rama could see the shadow of Kumbhakarna, dark and menacing striding behind the walls like walking death. Kumbhakarna's eyes were like cartwheels and his teeth like elephant tusks. He donned his bronze armour and golden helmet. His belt was as large as the chain on the drawbridge. He came to battle after having quaffed two thousand barrels of wine and a few thousand barrels of hot buffalo blood to give him strength. He entered the battlefield with great enthusiasm, flourishing his iron spear which was spitting flames from its tip. In front of him walked the person carrying his black banner with the wheel of death on it. He was followed by a mob of excited, shouting *rakshasas*, brandishing tridents, javelins and clubs. He looked like a colossal, black, thunder-cloud as he stepped over the walls instead of coming through the gate and the monkeys fled in terror.

Seeing him coming Rama questioned Vibhishana, "Who is this colossus who is now approaching us?"

Vibhishana replied, "He is the son of Sage Vishravas and the younger brother of Ravana. His appetite is so enormous that even while he was still an infant, he was in the habit of devouring thousands of creatures of all types for his breakfast and an equal amount for lunch and dinner with a few snacks thrown in at odd times. At last all the creatures of the world appealed to Brahma. The grandsire (Brahma) cursed him that he would sleep for the rest of his life. Ravana intervened for the sake of his brother and Brahma modified his curse and said that he would sleep for six months at a time and then wake up for a day so that his insatiable appetite could be appeased and then go back to sleep for another six months! Had he not been cursed in this fashion he would have eaten up all the life on this earth a long time ago. He can easily make one mouthful of our entire army!"

Brahma had promised that on the day when he woke up after six months of sleep, even the gods would not be able to defeat him in battle. However, if he was aroused from sleep on any other day, he would surely be killed.

In his eagerness to have his brother fight for him, Ravana forgot the warning and ordered his brother to be called.

Kumbhakarna stepped over the wall and advanced like a mountain on the move, his eyeballs rolling like chariot wheels. When he saw Vibhishana fighting in Rama's army, he was furious and shouted at him.

"Whatever Ravana's faults may be, he is still our brother. By fighting for his enemies you have turned against your family. Your treachery disgusts me!"

So saying he rushed at Vibhishana who immediately took refuge behind Rama. The monkeys fled in terror on seeing his advancing form which resembled a thundercloud.

Angada tried to rally the fleeing monkeys by telling them that he was only a war machine which had been trained to fight and they could easily conquer him. They started to rain rocks and boulders and trees on him but they glanced off him like feathers from a rock. The monkeys tried to jump on him and bite him but he brushed them off like flies. In fact he hardly noticed them and walked on crushing those who happened to get under his enormous feet. Angada rallied all those who were turning tail and encouraged them to return and face the monster but they were so terrified that they did not stop in their tracks. From the air Hanuman rained mountain peaks, rocks and trees of every kind on Kumbhakarna's head, but he intercepted them easily with his spike. Hanuman now came to the ground and struck him hard on the chest. This made the giant reel a bit and he retaliated by striking Hanuman on the breast with his spike. Such was the force of this blow that Hanuman burst into a loud cry of anguish much to the delight of the *rakshasas* and the dismay of the monkeys.

However, he quickly rallied himself and gave a mighty leap and jumped on to his shoulder and bit off his ear which made Kumbhakarna howl in pain.

All the other *vanara* leaders now surrounded Kumbhakarna and battered him but the colossus hit them viciously right and left and all of them fell to the ground. The other monkeys were now filled with rage and jumped on him from all sides and started to bite him and tear him with their nails. They scrambled up his trunk-like legs like locusts, scratching and biting. He simply lifted them from the ground and stuffed them into his mouth. Some of them escaped through his nostrils and some through his ears. Now Angada accosted him but the monster gave him one blow with the back of his hand, which made him fall down senseless.

Then Sugriva came forward and challenged him. Kumbhakarna was enraged and hurled his spike at him. Had it hit him, he would surely have died but Hanuman bounded forward and caught it in mid air and broke it in two even though it weighed as much as a mountain. The monkeys rejoiced to see this sight and rushed forward. However, Kumbhakarna picked off the top of a rock and flung it at Sugriva who became senseless. He caught hold of him in his arms and kept him under his armpit and walked on. Hanuman wondered if he should grow to his enormous size and rescue him but thought it better to wait till Sugriva came to his senses and rescued himself or else he would feel very despondent at having been defeated by the ogre. Very soon Sugriva came out of his swoon and clawed viciously at the ogre's massive ears and bit off his nose and ripped his thighs with his nails. Kumbhakarna swore and dashed him on the ground.

Sugriva got up painfully and loped off to Rama before the monster could catch him again. Kumbhakarna was by now famished and started to devour, monkeys, *rakshasas,* fiends and bears alike. Seizing huge handfuls of monkeys, bears and ogres he simply stuffed them all into his cavernous mouth.

Seeing the panic in the *vanara* army, Lakshmana came forward to try and stop this terrible destruction but his arrows could not penetrate the stiff, curly hair which covered the mammoth's body wherever his armour did not. Kumbhakarna brushed him aside and said "I will deal with you after having finished off your brother," and strode on. Lakshmana refused to let him pass and rained arrows at him till his mace fell from his hands but he continued to move forward like a huge road roller crushing everything in his path. Though he was without any weapon he played havoc amongst the monkeys with his fists and hands. At last he came face to face with Rama and gave a bloodcurdling roar which made all the monkeys fall down senseless.

Rama shot an arrow with bent knots which struck Kumbhakarna on the chest and penetrated through his armour so that blood started to pour out of the wound. He was so furious that flames shot out of his mouth. Even though the wound was fatal, his hatred for Rama kept him alive and he advanced towards Rama, bellowing with pain and rage. Lakshmana now spoke to Rama.

"This fellow is totally out of his senses now and doesn't know if he's killing his own people or ours. It is best if our monkeys climb on him and pester him so that he doesn't annihilate those on the earth."

The monkeys were delighted to get this order and jumped on him from all sides and got him thoroughly crazy with their antics. In the meantime Vibhishana, carrying his mace darted in front of his elder brother. When Kumbhakarna saw him he said, "Get out of my way before I kill you. I am so confused with lack of sleep and food as well as thousands of wounds that I no longer know who is friend and who, foe. But you I know are my younger brother. You are the only fortunate one amongst us who had the temerity to stand up to Ravana in order to vindicate your desire for truth and righteousness. You alone will be responsible for perpetuating our race. By the grace of Rama you will become sovereign over our people and uphold our traditions."

Hearing this Vibhishana retired to a corner of the battlefield, his eyes bathed in tears.

Again he turned round to see Rama standing in front of him and took a huge boulder and hurled it at him. Rama splintered it with five arrows and said, "Brave *rakshasa*! I am Rama, son of Dasaratha. Take a good look at me for soon your eyes will not be able to see!"

Kumbhakarna laughed and said, "I'm not one of your puny *rakshasas* who can be killed by you. I am Kumbhakarna – destroyer of the gods." So saying he wielded his mace and killed thousands of monkeys. Rama invoked the Wind God and sent an arrow with a broad razor head which severed the arm carrying the mace and made it fall along with the mace with a monstrous sound crushing many monkeys in the process. Undeterred by this the monster tore up a tree with his other arm and lunged at Rama, who cut off that arm also with another well aimed arrow. It fell to the ground carrying with it many trees and crushing both monkeys and *rakshasas.* But still the colossus kept advancing and shouting, "No one can slay me. No one can stop me!" He kicked and stamped and killed hundreds of monkeys with his enormous feet. Rama now cut off both his feet with two crescent-shaped arrows.

He was not put off even by this and stomped forward on the stumps of his legs with enlarged mouth belching fire. Rama now filled his mouth with gold encrusted arrows so that he could not speak or close it. Finally he sawed off his gigantic head with an arrow, shaped like a razor. His diademed head, brilliant with lovely earrings fell to the ground with a horrendous noise bringing down with it some of the buildings on the causeway and even parts of the defensive wall.

Far off in Lanka, Ravana heard this horrifying sound and a shaft of pure terror shot through him. He could not imagine that his monstrous brother could have been killed. The mountainous head rolled down the hillside and dropped into the ocean in a whirlpool of blood making the waves rise up in huge gory billows and killing the whales. It was nearing dawn and Rama stood silhouetted against the eastern sky. Kumbhakarna, the terror of the world, the sole hope of Ravana lay dead in a lake of blood and fat on the gory battlefield strewn with heads and arms and dead monkeys and *rakshasas.*

"You are the protector of sages and saints,
The destroyer of demons and the darling of Rama."

— *Sri Hanuman Chalisa* by Tulsidas

ॐ *Sri Hanumathe Namaha!*

ॐ

Lakshmanaprana-dataaya Namaha!

CHAPTER TWENTY-TWO

LAKSHMANA PRANADATA

Saviour of Lakshmana

"With Rama's lotus feet impressed upon his heart,
The son of wind started in confident assurance."

— *Ramacharitamanas* by Tulsidas

The *rakshasas* ran back and reported the news to Ravana.

"O king!" They said, "Your brother who vied with Yama, the god of death, in destroying people is now reduced to a headless and limbless mass with his trunk half submerged in the ocean and the rest of the body blocking the main gate of Lanka!"

Ravana fainted when he heard about his beloved brother's death. When he recovered he ran to the wall and saw his brother's body and limbs blocking the gate. He sat with his head in his hands and bemoaned his loss. He couldn't believe that a mere mortal could have killed his gargantuan brother.

"This is entirely my fault. I banished Vibhishana who was like my conscience and now my other brother who loved me so much lies dead."

Ravana hung his head and wept. Hearing him wail like this, three of his younger sons came forward and cheered him up.

"O father! Why should you be overpowered by grief like this? The creator Brahma himself has bestowed on you an invincible coat of mail, an arrow and bow as well as a chariot drawn by a thousand donkey-faced fiends. What need is there for you to fear? We will go to the battlefield today and slay your enemy for you."

All his four sons were capable of flying through the air and adepts in conjuring tricks. They entered the arena, vying with each other to exhibit their prowess.

Flaunting their flaming lances they dashed into the midst of the monkeys, creating havoc. Though the princes were all valiant, one by one they were crushed to death by Angada and Hanuman. Angada killed Narantaka and Hanuman smashed Devantaka and Trisira, and Lakshmana had a gruelling battle with Atikaya and eventually killed him.

The heroes who had set out so enthusiastically in the morning now lay like felled trees on the battlefield. Ravana could not bear it. He started to wonder if there was any truth in what he had heard about Rama – that he was Narayana incarnate who had taken on a human birth in order to kill him. He began to feel anxious about the safety of the city and gave orders that all precautions should be taken to avoid any infiltration by the simians.

As he sat sunk in gloom with his head in his hands, his golden boy, Indrajit, son of his favourite wife, Mandodari now came to him and tried to cheer him up. Ravana looked into Indrajit's quiet eyes and felt a great relief.

"My beloved father!" He said, "Why should you worry when I am here to help you? Today the sun and the moon and all the gods shall witness my immeasurable powers. I will go this very minute and punish your opponents. Before the end of this day, victory will be yours!"

Ravana cheered up considerably on hearing this. He looked with loving eyes at his golden boy. His skin and hair were the colour of gold and there were golden flecks in his eyes. His armour and helmet were of gold as well as his shoes and belt. He was as beautiful as his mother and Ravana was delighted to hear his promise.

"There is no one on earth who can defeat you my son. My blessings are upon you."

Indrajit bowed low before his father and went to his enchanted garden where he kindled a fire and poured oblations into it and worshipped Agni, his favourite deity. Soon enough there rose out of the fire, a golden chariot drawn by four tigers. The fiery chariot was decorated with the golden faces of demons and deer. His flag was that of a lion with sapphire eyes. Indrajit wrapped himself in his invisible coat of mail and got into his chariot of illusions and set out immediately, followed by a mighty army riding on elephants, horses and donkeys, bristling with weapons of every type.

Vibhishana shaded his eyes and looked at the blue sky but even he could not see Indrajit. Through the clouds, Rama and the monkeys could hear the creaking of chariot wheels and the flash of gold weapons. They could hear flag bells ringing and tigers growling, but of the warrior there was no sign.

Indrajit began raining arrows over the *vanara* host who began to fall in thousands. The whole field was strewn with dead and dying monkeys. Though all the monkey leaders did their best they were hampered by the fact that they could not see him since he was an expert in the art of illusory warfare. How could they fight against an invisible enemy? Through the dark clouds of illusion they could hear the sound of his chariot and the twang of his bow. Sometimes they could see the flash of his golden armour and the streak of his golden spear but of him they could see nothing. One by one all the great *vanara* heroes except for Hanuman and Jambavan fell to Indrajit's deadly arrows. A flaming axe flew through the sky and killed Sugriva. Thirty-three crescent-shaped arrows killed Angada and an iron hook crushed Nala's chest. Ten diamond-shaped arrows pierced the king of bears and a barbed spear tore Vibhishana's shoulder. Hanuman flew into the clouds. He couldn't see his opponent but he saw a flaming sword flying towards him like lightning. He grabbed the sword but it changed into a young woman who cried for mercy so he let it go and it changed back into a sword and cut him down to the ground. The whole field was covered with the dead and dying.

Rama stood amongst his dead friends and tried to aim his arrows at his unseen enemy but it was to no avail. At last only Rama and Lakshmana were left standing. Indrajit's arrows continued to rain down on them so that no space was left on their bodies which were not covered with wounds.

Rama turned to Lakshmana and told him to be careful. Hardly had he said this than Indrajit shot a poison-tipped arrow at Lakshmana that pierced his shoulder. Instantly his skin turned blue and he fell down senseless. Another arrow made Rama also fall unconscious. Exulting in his day's work, Indrajit withdrew all at once to his city and filled his father's heart with delight by his report of the day's work. He then went to his grove of trees outside Lanka and got out of his chariot. It disappeared along with the tigers in a ball of flame. Indrajit remained under the banyan tree closed his eyes and went into *samadhi.*

With the advent of night, Vibhishana stirred. He grasped the spear in both hands and pulled it out. He was trembling with the effort and the pain. Slowly he drew himself up and surveyed the ground strewn with dead monkeys. He knew that Hanuman could never be killed and scrutinised the field for him. At last he saw a blur of white. He went towards it and found Hanuman sitting up covered with sword cuts. Together they searched the field and found Jambavan who appeared to be close to death but was still breathing. Vibhishana knelt down and gave him some water and asked him, "O king of bears! Are you still alive?"

"I'm alive but I can't see. Tell me is Hanuman alive?"

Vibhishana growled in anger and retorted, "You don't show any regard for Rama but only for that white monkey!"

Jambavan said, "If Hanuman lives, the army lives. If he is dead we are all dead."

The three of them now painfully walked through the field and came upon the inert forms of Rama and Lakshmana. All of them were totally bereft at this sight. After some time Rama slowly came to consciousness. However, Lakshmana still appeared inert and lifeless. Seeing this Rama was filled with sorrow.

"If Lakshmana dies I have no desire to live. It is possible that I might find another wife like Sita but I will never find another brother like Lakshmana. I cannot return to Ayodhya without him. What will I tell his mother, Sumitra? I too shall follow him to the abode of death. Life has no meaning for me without my beloved brother."

Vibhishana told him not to despair and said that Ravana's court physician should be brought immediately for he had many mystic herbs and *mantras* at his command. Night had already fallen and without a word Hanuman flew into Lanka and woke up the physician who was fast asleep in his house. Vibhishana had already told him that even though he was a *rakshasa*, he was first and foremost a physician who was true to his vocation and would do his best to revive whoever went to him whether friend or foe. Hanuman explained the matter to him.

Without giving him time to think over the matter, he carried him in his arms and deposited him in front of Vibhishana who asked him to revive Lakshmana. He looked at him carefully and said, "The only thing that can help him is the miracle herb known as *mritasanjivani.* This is capable of awakening the dead. However, poison has already pervaded his entire body and unless he gets the proper treatment before sunrise he will surely die."

Rama and the others were delighted to hear that he knew of a remedy and asked him to apply it immediately.

He said, "I'm afraid I don't have it. It can only be found on the peak called Dronagiri which lies between Kailasa and Manasarovar, high in the Himalayas. This peak is covered with medicinal herbs and casts a matchless splendour on all sides. Right on top of that peak there are four flaming herbs illuminating all the directions. *Mritasanjivani* is capable of restoring the dead to life, *vishalyakarani* is capable healing all wounds inflicted by weapons, *suvarnakarani* restores the body to its original complexion and the great herb called *sandhani* is capable of joining severed limbs and healing fractured bones. If someone amongst you can get these four, I can revive all those who have fallen here but it has to be brought immediately, before the setting of the moon and the rising of the sun, then only will I be able to revive them. Every minute is precious. If anyone is capable of getting it, then the prince and the others can be saved."

Hearing this everyone looked expectantly at Hanuman and Jambavan prompted him and said, "O son of Anjana! You are the only one who can save Lakshmana's life as well as the lives of your countless friends who have fallen today. Go immediately to that golden peak which is filled with medicinal herbs and bring back the four mystic herbs."

Jambavan had the great quality of reminding people of their true worth. His words led them to realise that they were capable of anything. Very few people have this ability. Most of us try to criticise and ridicule another person's capacity and thus make him out to be less than he is!

Without losing a moment Hanuman grew in size till they could no longer see his head. Chanting the name of Rama, he sprang to the Trikuta peak and then kicked off and went like a huge cloud towards the Himalayas. As he was travelling with the speed of lightning, he crossed the sea and travelled over Kishkinda, Dandaka and the Vindhya mountains to enter Aryavarta. As he flew over Kosala, the residents of Ayodhya mistook him for a flying monster. They begged Bharata to save them. He shot an arrow and forced Hanuman to descend to the ground.

"Who are you?" asked Bharata sternly. When Maruti identified himself and spoke of his mission, Bharata's eyes filled with tears and he embraced him and said,

"I'm Bharata, Rama's unfortunate brother. I'm happy to get some news of him but filled with sorrow at Lakshmana's plight. I wish I could help you in some way but I'm afraid I can't leave Ayodhya."

"If you can help me to reach Dronagiri very fast and make up for my lost time that would be more than enough," said Hanuman.

Bharata meditated on Rama and mounted an arrow on his bow. He asked Maruti to sit on the arrowhead. Chanting a *mantra* he shot the arrow with such speed that it ripped through the clouds and reached the foot of the mountain known as Dronagiri.

The news of Hanuman's rescue operation was brought to Ravana by his spies. He immediately called his great friend Kalanemi who was an expert conjurer and told him to go to the mount called Dronagiri and stop Hanuman by fair means or foul from getting the required herbs.

Kalanemi reached the mount before Hanuman. He created a hermitage and changed himself into an old ascetic and pretended to be meditating. Hanuman felt very thirsty and when he looked down he saw the hermitage next to a lake and decided to go down and drink some water. He was surprised to see a *yogi* there and asked him politely if he could give him some water. The ascetic welcomed him and predicted that he would be successful in his attempt. He offered him water from his own water pot in which he had mixed poison. Hanuman refused the offer and asked permission to drink from the lake where he could also take a bath. The sage agreed and said he would give him a *mantra* which would enable him to recognise the herbs. Hanuman was surprised at the ascetic's knowledge of his mission and went to the lake as he was bidden. As he entered the water in the pitch darkness, he found that his foot had been caught by a crocodile which was slowly dragging him down. He realised that the creature was really big and strong. Time was running short so he exerted all his strength and shook his leg free. He then caught the crocodile's mouth and priced it open and split it in two and threw it far off. Immediately a beautiful damsel appeared out of its body and said, "Salutations to you O son of wind! I am actually an *apsara* from the celestial regions who had been cursed by a sage to take on the form of a crocodile. He told me that I would be released from my curse when the son of the Wind God came and killed me. I am deeply grateful to you for rescuing me but I have to warn you that you are in grave danger. That man who is posing as an ascetic is actually the great conjurer called Kalanemi who has been sent by Ravana to thwart you in your attempt to get the herbs so please be on your guard and never accept water from his water pot." With these words the damsel disappeared.

Hanuman returned to the hut of the ascetic and bowed before him. He took the lighted lamp which was in front of him and suddenly hurled it at the man's head and dashed it to the ground and killed him. Immediately the hut and all the other things which had been an illusion created by the demon, vanished and Hanuman was left alone in the pitch darkness of the night on the mountain top.

In the meantime Ravana feared that Hanuman would return in time and ordered the sun to rise and the moon to set before their appointed time. Maruti was horrified to see the moon slipping rapidly towards the horizon and the first light of dawn appearing beyond the hills. He realised that this was just another plot by Ravana. He rushed to the horizon, caught the moon between his jaws and trapped the sun in his armpit!

Time was running short and without wasting another moment Hanuman jumped to the peak called Dronagiri. As he was flying over he saw the whole peak aglow with a divine radiance. He realised that this was the place where the herbs grew but as he came down the radiance disappeared and he couldn't find what he was looking for since the only clue he had been given by the physician was that these herbs would glow in the dark. But it seemed as if the herbs did not want to be picked and had hidden themselves. Hanuman was angry at their behaviour and decided to break off the whole peak since dawn was fast approaching and his beloved Lakshmana's life was ebbing fast. There was no time to speculate, so without a moment's hesitation he grew in size till his head brushed against the sky. He then plucked the entire peak as easily as breaking off a flower from its stem and flew with it to Lanka where everyone was expectantly awaiting his arrival. All the gods, birds, beasts, reptiles and fish that saw Hanuman flying across Jambudwipa and crossing the sea to Lanka with the hill in his hand were wonder struck by this spectacular sight.

He circled the battlefield like a huge eagle and slowly started to come down. Such was the potency of the herbs that when the heady perfume of the *mritasanjivani* penetrated Lakshmana's nostrils, he stirred and turned round as if from sleep. All the other monkeys also recovered. Hanuman was still circling round the field not knowing where to land and place his precious burden. The royal physician, Sushena told him where to keep it. He scoured the slopes of the hill and found the life giving herbs.

"Now all I need is the divine pestle and mortar that Ravana keeps in his inner chambers," he said.

Hanuman immediately made his way into Ravana's apartments. However, Ravana had foreseen Sushena's need for a pestle and had hidden it next to his bed-side table, determined not to let it out of his sight. Maruti noticed that Mandodari was sleeping soundly next to the king and thought of a plan to distract Ravana. He slipped under his bed and tied Ravana's hair to the bedpost. He then grabbed the pestle and mortar and ran towards the door. Ravana woke up in an instant and tried to run after Hanuman but was yanked back to his bed by his hair. He tried to untie the knot but failed because Hanuman had cast a spell. The knot would not be undone until Mandodari had kicked Ravana on the head with her foot!

Hanuman chuckled as he watched the mighty king of the *rakshasas* shaking his wife awake. He bowed his crowned head before her and begged her to kick him. Hanuman had a hearty laugh and then sped back to Sushena and gave him the pestle and mortar.

Sushena immediately made a paste of the magic herbs and smeared it all over Lakshmana's body. The juice seeped through his skin and entered his blood stream and counteracted Indrajit's poison. He woke up as if from a long sleep and jumped to his feet looking more radiant than ever.

Suddenly Rama noticed that neither the sun nor the moon could be seen in the sky.

"What happened to these celestial orbs?" He questioned.

Hanuman looked a bit sheepish and opened his mouth to let out the moon and released the sun from his armpit. As the sun and moon returned to their celestial orbits, Rama and Lakshmana embraced Hanuman. They were totally bereft of words and did not know how to express their gratitude.

Jambavan then told Maruti to take the mountain back to its original position since, if it was kept on the battlefield, the *rakshasas* would also make use of it. So Hanuman once again returned to the Himalayas and kept the mountain back in its place and came back before dawn broke over the ocean. Actually this whole episode was known only to Rama, Vibhishana, Jambavan, Hanuman and the physician who was taken back to his home in Lanka.

Rama was so happy that he hugged Hanuman close and blessed him and said,

"Without you there will be neither Rama, nor Sita nor the *Ramayana*. May you be blessed and live forever!"

One might wonder how it was that none of the fallen *rakshasas* revived. This was because Ravana had commanded that all the dead in the demon army should be thrown into the sea so that no one could count their number and thus taint his reputation.

The monkeys were jubilant at their recovery. That whole day none of the *rakshasas* appeared for a fight since Ravana was sure that their leaders were lying dead. By nightfall the monkeys were determined to stake their claim as victors. Urged by Sugriva the whole hoard pushed their way into the fortress carrying flaming brands and torches and started on their journey of destruction. Once again Lanka went up in flames as the excited monkeys jumped from house to house and palace to palace setting fire to everything. Ravana was woken up by the wailing of the citizens and the acrid smell of smoke. He could not believe that the monkeys were carrying on the war without Rama. Surely his cousin Kalanemi must have stopped Hanuman from bringing the famous herb, so what made the monkeys rejoice and how could they dare to come within the walls of Lanka without their master? His ministers came and gave him the happy news that Rama and Lakshmana were very much alive and all of them were ready to fight. When he heard this he immediately summoned Kumbhakarna's sons, Kumbha and Nikumbha and asked them to go and avenge the death of their father.

The night stalkers issued forth once again, determined to slay their father's killer. They were both powerful warriors and the *vanara* host started falling like autumn leaves. Three of their leaders including Angada had fallen in a faint. Hearing this Sugriva went to the front and accosted Kumbha.

"I am full of admiration for the way in which you handle your weapons. I see in you a combination of your father and uncle – the solidity of one with the dexterity of the other. I don't feel like killing you since you are surely a jewel among your race but I have no option, since we are on opposite sides, so let us fight to the finish."

Though Kumbha was pleased by Sugriva's praise, he didn't like the insinuation that he was superior to himself. He rushed at him with a bellow and the two of them started wrestling with each other till the earth shook and the leaves fell off the trees. At last with a powerful blow, Sugriva felled him to the ground and killed him.

Seeing the death of his valiant brother, Nikumbha rushed at the monkeys and slew them by the hundreds. Seeing their plight Hanuman came to their rescue and punched him forcibly on his chest. Nikumbha flung a huge iron pestle at Hanuman. Everyone expected him to fall but to their astonishment the pestle shattered into a million fragments on his adamantine chest. Hanuman now rushed at him and after grappling for a while, threw him on the ground and sat on his chest till he suffocated to death. The *vanaras* set up a roar of jubilation.

When he heard the news, Ravana was at a loss to know what he should do. He couldn't believe that the enormous strength and modern weapons of his army counted for nothing in the face of these long-tailed tree folk, armed with only sticks and stones. Not one of them was capable of wielding a sword or using a bow and yet they seemed to be gaining the upper hand.

At last he went to his beloved son Meghanatha and exhorted him once again to go and try his hand at killing the two brothers.

Indrajit said, "O Father! For your sake I killed him once, but it appears as if the whole of Nature is supporting him or else how could he be still alive? Remember father, that in your youth, you ruled the world supported by *dharma*, but now you rule through *adharma* alone. The very gods tremble at the mention of your name and the curses of the saints whom you have killed have taken on the form of this battle which will be the end of you. You have made the whole of creation suffer through your inequities. It is the collection of your wrongs that is devouring us. The fear and anger of the helpless has taken on the form of this army of animals. The day you abducted Sita, you took death on your lap. *Dharma* is on the side of Rama. *Dharma* alone rules this world. Those who go against it will have to perish at some time or other. However, I am your son and will do your bidding. I shall kill the Kosala brothers as I promised to do."

Ravana said, "You are my beloved son who once conquered the gods. Now fight for me on earth as you fought in heaven."

"You brought the nectarine herb and revived the life of Lakshmana. Rama embraced you with deep joy."

— *Sri Hanuman Chalisa* by Tulsidas

ॐ *Sri Hanumathe Namaha!*

ॐ

Parajitaaya Namaha!

CHAPTER TWENTY-THREE

KAPINDRA

End of Indrajit

"The ground will be your couch, the bark of trees your raiment,
And your food – bulbs, wild fruits and roots,
Nor think that even they will be forthcoming everyday,
But only when they are in season."
— Rama to Sita, in the *Ramacharitamanas* by Tulsidas

Indrajit now thought of an ingenious plan to dupe Rama. Using his magical powers he made an identical living image of Sita and placed it in his chariot and drove to the battlefield surrounded by his army. The monkeys rallied around and forged forward to meet him. They were led by Hanuman who was carrying a huge boulder. Suddenly he stopped short for he recognised the pitiable and miserable figure of the princess of Videha. She was wearing the same soiled, yellow garment which she had on when he saw her last but it could not dim the radiance of her ethereal beauty. She was sitting forlorn and unhappy as if she did not care what was happening to her. Hanuman could not tear his gaze away from her grief-stricken face. He had no idea why Indrajit had brought her in his chariot to the battlefield. He did not dare to attack Indrajit in case he did some harm to her. Seeing him Indrajit grabbed hold of Sita's long braid and started to berate her with his sword. She called out loudly, "Rama! Rama," and burst into heart-rending sobs.

Tears of blood dropped from Hanuman's eyes to see the princess of Videha being treated so cruelly. "O ruthless one! What has the princess of Mithila done to you that you should treat her so cruelly? Such an act is not worthy of even a barbarian and you claim to be the grandson of the sage Vishravas!"

Indrajit laughed scornfully when he heard this tirade and drove towards Rama and shouted to him to watch carefully while he made an end of the woman who was the prime cause of the destruction of the *rakshasas* and who was the cause of his father's infatuation. Taking hold of her hair he lifted her up and decapitated her. He gave a gruesome laugh and said, "Behold O Rama! Your darling wife has been killed by me. Vain is your exertion now to get her back. The war is over. Go back to your country!" Seeing this gruesome scene Rama totally lost all will to live. He collapsed on the ground and bewailed the loss of his beloved wife.

Hanuman could not bear to see this. Taking up an enormous boulder he rushed at Indrajit followed by all the monkeys. There followed a sharp and furious encounter in which Indrajit disappeared from the field. Hanuman immediately realised that this whole thing was a trick of Indrajit's to subdue Rama. He immediately took the form of a bee and went to the Ashoka grove where Sita was sitting with her head in her hands and convinced himself that she was indeed alive. He instantly returned to Rama and gave him the happy news.

As he was saying this Vibhishana came forward and wanted to know what the commotion was about and why Rama looked so sad. When he heard the story, he laughed and said,

"How can you possibly believe such a thing? Don't you know the extent of Ravana's infatuation for Sita? He is prepared to sacrifice his country, his sons and his people for her sake. How can you believe even for a moment that his son would dare to kill a woman who is so dear to his father? This whole thing was planned by Indrajit, the master magician. He enacted this drama so that he could go and complete his *yaga* which will make him invincible. If he is allowed to finish this ritual, there will be no holding him back. No one will be able to kill him. There is not a moment to be lost. Let Lakshmana come with me and I'll take him to the spot where that misguided son of my brother is conducting his *yaga.* Brahma has told him that by performing this sacrifice he will become invisible and invulnerable. That is why he thought of this master plan to delude you into believing that Sita was dead!"

Rama immediately told Lakshmana to go with Vibhishana and intercept the *yaga*. He armed himself and took Rama's blessings before leaving. He was accompanied by Vibhishana, Hanuman and a host of other monkeys.

Vibhishana told Lakshmana that he would repeat some *mantras* by which the invisible grove would become visible. Suddenly the whole mountainside became dark as if it was shielded by some huge black umbrella. In and through this gloom, Lakshmana saw a grove of ancient, gnarled trees, plunged in darkness and shadow. Vibhishana proceeded towards this sacred grove where Indrajit was conducting his black magic rituals in order to invoke the great cosmic powers. His army was stationed between his hideout and the approaching army of the monkeys. Hanuman immediately sprang to the forefront and confronted the enemy host and engaged them in a fierce combat while Vibhishana took Lakshmana to the secret grove which none but the *rakshasas* could see. "The god of fire will give him a magic chariot yoked to tigers, which will make him invulnerable. Hurry! We have to disrupt this ritual."

Vibhishana touched Lakshmana who was then able to see Indrajit kneeling before an altar in the grove, invoking the aid of his favourite god. He was pouring ghee into the fire with a double ladle of black iron and muttering incantations. His back was turned to them. The black sacrificial goat was tied to a stake and was bleating piteously. Wearing a crimson robe with his hair all dishevelled, Indrajit beat the earth with his javelin and out came thousands of serpents and coiled themselves round his arrows which were piled near the altar. His axe fell with deadly accuracy on the neck of the goat and severed it neatly so that it fell in a pool of blood. He held the ladle filled with goat's blood above his head, ready for the final invocation. As the flames leapt higher and higher, the tawny figures of the tigers could be seen, snarling and growling, waiting for their cue to leap out of the flames, drawing the invincible chariot. Vibhishana nudged Lakshmana who sent an arrow straight at the upraised ladle and split it in two just as it was descending for the final offering.

His arrow screamed like an eagle, who was the deadly enemy of snakes and the *Nagas* hissed and slithered back to the nether world from which they had come. Agni, the Lord of Fire, rose from the sacred *kund* and seven tongues of flame shot out of his mouth. His eyes roved round the scene and he gave a secret smile and his form faded from the altar and the fire sank back into the hearth. There were no signs of either tigers or chariot.

Indrajit swirled round with a terrible imprecation and snarled at Vibhishana. "You traitor! You have betrayed me. You call yourself my uncle yet you have disclosed all my secrets to the enemy. Without you he would never have found out this place. You have eaten the salt of my father's table and yet you have defected to the enemy's side! You are a disgrace to our race! It's better to be a slave in one's own country than a Lord in the enemy's side by licking his boots. One who abandons his own people and adopts the ways of his enemy is a traitor and I should kill you first before killing Lakshmana! May your new friends forsake you when your old ones have died!"

Vibhishana retorted, "You are the wicked son of my wicked brother and I will have nothing to do with either of you. All these years my brother has revelled in sinful acts. His anger and arrogance are proverbial. All these years I have borne up with it because I was helpless. Though I was born in the clan of the *rakshasas,* my instincts were always those of a human being. If I have abandoned you all now it is because I am fed up of living a life of unrighteousness and wish to take up a noble path. You are a foolish, impulsive boy, bursting with pride, but beware! Both you and your father are doomed and so is this fabulous city of Lanka!"

By now Jambavan and his army of bears had joined Hanuman and they began to harass Indrajit's army. The commotion was so great that he was forced to put an end to his verbal combat with his uncle and come out through the secret tunnel into the open forest. The demon prince was furious at having to end his ritual. He came out looking like the god of death. He was wearing silver armour and carried a silver sword. Light glinted from his sliver helmet and silver bow. A quiver of silver arrows and a silver dagger hung at his side. He climbed on his huge chariot which was most artistically decorated and drawn by silver white horses. His hair was flowing behind him and his huge bow was kept taut and ready. He saw Lakshmana who was seated on Hanuman's shoulder facing him with his own bow drawn and ready. Indrajit hurled insults at him and swore to make an end of him before the day was over.

Lakshmana replied scornfully, "O son of Ravana! Make good your boast in a noble fashion. So far you have fought a secret battle remaining invisible all the time. This is the way adopted by thieves and cowards and not heroes! Make good your boasts now in the open when I'm facing you and let us see who is stronger."

Indrajit said, "Today you shall see my power. All I ask is for a single combat!"

"So be it," said Lakshmana.

Indrajit immediately let fly his arrows at Lakshmana. The deadly arrows went and buried themselves on Lakshmana's body making him bleed profusely.

"O son of Sumitra! Today jackals and vultures will have a grand feast. So prepare for the end."

"Give up your empty words and enforce it with action O devourer of human flesh!"

With these words both of them started shooting long, painful arrows tipped with golden feathers at each other, each more deadly than the other. Indrajit jumped out of his chariot and shot one thousand arrows at Lakshmana who cut them down as they flew at him. He then shot seven arrows and slit Indrajit's silver armour so that his coat of mail fell down like a cluster of stars. Both the warriors were well matched and so swift were their hands that none could see them take an arrow or draw their bows. Arrows flew so rapidly that the sky became dark. Indrajit seized a poisoned javelin and hurled it at Lakshmana who cut it down before it reached him. The silver boy now raised his bow again. Swift as a thought, Lakshmana cut it down before the arrow was shot. Ravana's son then threw a demon dart which separated into splinters and pierced Lakshmana all over his body. However, Indrajit was not capable of an open combat like this. He had always fought invisibly and soon he showed signs of flagging under Lakshmana's determined onslaught. Vibhishana advised Lakshmana to press forward since the mighty warrior appeared to be losing ground.

Lakshmana charged forward but Indrajit rallied himself and taunted him, "Have you forgotten our last encounter when I made you and your brother lie flat on the ground? This time I will not let you go as easily but will despatch you fast to Yama's city!"

With these words he discharged seven shafts at Lakshmana and ten at Hanuman. Then he turned towards his uncle and let fly a hundred arrows at him. Thus, they started another formidable battle which went on for hours with others looking on in amazement. Vibhishana now incited the other monkey chiefs not to lose time watching but to try and drive off Indrajit's army.

The two protagonists were set for a fight to the finish. Their brilliant arrows charged with incantations flew across the sky like meteors and collided in mid-air with earth-shattering explosions, each negating the other. Beasts and birds flew hither and thither and the very air seemed to hold its breath in fear. Lakshmana sent four silver-tipped arrows that instantly felled the four beautiful, caparisoned white horses. As the chariot started to swerve violently, another crescent-shaped arrow neatly severed the charioteer's head from his shoulders. For a second Indrajit faltered but undaunted, he took up his bow again and shot thousands of arrows at Lakshmana's forces. The monkeys quickly took shelter behind Lakshmana. Under cover of the darkness, Indrajit went back to the city and returned with another chariot. Lakshmana was wonderstruck at the swiftness with which he returned. Within minutes Lakshmana smashed this chariot also. Lifting his javelin high above his head, the night stalker whirled it round and round so that the blade seemed to become a blazing wheel. Lakshmana did not wait for him to release it but shattered it with a hundred arrows. Night was falling fast and Vibhishana advised Lakshmana to put an end to Indrajit since he would grow stronger with the advent of the darkness.

At last Lakshmana took out the arrow given to him by the sage Agastya which was charged with the power of Indra and prayed to the weapon, "If it be true that Rama, the son of Dasaratha has never swerved from the path of *dharma,* if it is true that he has ever been truthful, has ever been loyal and is absolutely unrivalled, then let this arrow kill Indrajit, the son of Ravana!"

So saying he let fly the *mantra*-charged arrow at Indrajit. It flew like a streak of lightning, straight to its target and before he could counter it with one of his own, it neatly severed his handsome head so that it fell on the ground looking like a silver lotus. Like the bright sun setting behind the hills lay the head of Mandodari's glorious son. The vanquisher of Indra was killed with the missile of Indra himself. For a moment his body seemed to stand against the light. Then it fell with a thud. In death his corpse reverted to its original *rakshasic* form. There was nothing beautiful about it. His face was set in a snarl with long protruding fangs. The gods rejoiced at his death for he had been a terrible scourge to them. The *vanara* army set up a roar of victory which could be heard by both Rama and Ravana. The *rakshasa* army fled in dismay leaving their weapons behind.

Monkeys and bears hugged each other. Vibhishana, Hanuman and Jambavan returned to Rama and gave him the news of the glorious combat which had ended in the death of the famous son of Ravana. Rama hugged his brother and praised him for his amazing feat. He immediately ordered the physician to come and administer to his numerous wounds.

Indrajit's body was covered and carried to the king's palace but no one dared to tell Ravana. At last his minister Suka went to him and said, "Your son has been killed by Lakshmana."

Ravana sank to the floor in a swoon. Then he roused himself and wept and said, "My son! My beloved son! There was no one like you in the whole world. You could defeat every enemy you encountered, yet you have been killed by that puny human being. How is it possible? Without you this entire earth seems to be an empty place. Life has lost its charm for me. Where have you gone leaving me and your mother and your beloved wife?"

Indrajit's wife was called Sulochana. She was the daughter of the celestial snake known as Ananta, on whom Vishnu reclines. As we know Rama was the *avatara* of Vishnu and Lakshmana of Ananta. So when she came to know that her beloved husband had been killed by the *avatara* of her father, Sulochana was grief stricken. She rushed to Ravana's assembly hall and accused him of having caused the death of her husband. Ravana was still in a state of shock. He refused to believe that his invincible son had died and continued to talk to the corpse as if it was alive. Indrajit who had once captured Indra and brought him in chains to his father, now lay dead, killed by an arrow which had been charged with the might of Indra himself.

"Indrajit's mother – Mandodari and his wife Sulochana threw themselves over the body and started weeping. When the time came to cremate his body, Sulochana threw herself on the blazing pyre like a chaste wife and immolated herself.

Ravana, in the meantime, started ranting and raving. He forgot that he was the sole cause for the destruction of all his sons. His sorrow turned to anger as it normally did with him and he decided to kill Sita in truth and not as a trick for she was the cause of it all. He forgot that he had no one to blame but himself. It was his cruel and unjust act which had brought calamity on his whole race as prophesied by Vibhishana. Tears like liquid fire rolled down his cheeks. Picking up his sword, he rushed to the Ashoka grove determined to kill Sita who was still devoted to Rama. His ministers and wives rushed after him. They had seen him angry before but that was nothing compared to what they saw now. Like a malefic comet approaching Venus, he flew at Sita with upraised sword. She saw him coming and realised that this time he was not approaching with words of love but with the sword of hate and meant to kill her as easily as he had professed to love her. How easily swayed are the minds of the wicked! One day they profess to love and the next day they begin to hate. Sita was ready to die since she was convinced that Rama had died. Luckily for her one of Ravana's ministers who was saner than the rest approached him and said,

"My Lord! How can you contemplate such a sinful deed! It was bad enough that you abducted her. How can you think of killing her now when she is helpless and at your mercy? Leave this poor, defenceless woman alone and turn your fury against the one who killed your son. Today is the fourteenth day of the dark lunar fortnight. Tomorrow is the night of the new moon, the most auspicious night for night rangers like us. That is the time for you to march against Rama and after having killed both of them you can return victoriously and claim Sita as your own!"

Luckily for Sita, Ravana seemed to find this advice palatable. He checked his stride and stood for a moment lost in thought. Then without another word to anyone, he whirled round and marched back to his assembly hall.

"May Sheshnag, the thousand-headed divine serpent sing your praises. Saying thus, the Lord of Lakshmi embraced you!"

— *Sri Hanuman Chalisa* by Tulsidas

ॐ *Sri Hanumathe Namaha!*

ॐ

Banda-mokshadaaya Namaha!

CHAPTER TWENTY-FOUR

MAHABALA

Journey to Patala

"Think of Vaidehi as your mother and Rama as your father,
Where Rama dwells there is Ayodhya,
As wherever there is the light of the sun, there is day."
— Sumitra to Lakshmana in the *Ramacharitamanas* of Tulsidas

Ravana was totally demoralised by his favourite son's death. He was at a loss to know what to do. Then he suddenly remembered his other sons – Mahiravana and Ahiravana, who were ruling in Patala, the lowest of all the seven worlds. They were born to Mandodari but their serpentine appearance was so terrible that it frightened even Ravana so he cast them into the ocean. There they were adopted by the snake demoness, Simhika and taken to the serpent world. They performed intense *tapas* to Mahakaali and acquired supernatural powers. She also gave them the boon that one day their father, Ravana who had insulted and abandoned them would call on them for help. They had married the daughter of the king of Patala and became kings in turn. Ravana suddenly thought of them and went to Patala, the nether world and asked them to help him.

They both said, "Don't underestimate your enemy. He is Vishnu incarnate. It would be better for you to make truce with him."

The brothers were great devotees of the goddess Kaali and Ravana slyly told them that they were missing a golden opportunity to please the goddess by offering the heads of the two handsome and virile princes!

"Think of the powers she will grant you if you make this sacrifice?" he asked.

Hearing this they decided to help their father.

In the meantime the ever watchful Vibhishana heard of Ravana's visit to Patala. He called Hanuman and told him to be on his guard for these two night wanderers were great practitioners of black magic and sorcery, and were capable of taking on many forms in order to fool people. Hanuman told him to have no fears and he would see to it that no danger came to Rama and Lakshmana. Hanuman lengthened his tail to enormous proportions and wound it round and round the camp so that the site became a fortress and sat in front so that no one could enter without his permission. The sorcerers came there and didn't know how to get in and kidnap the brothers. They cast a spell by which all the monkeys who were guarding the fortress went to sleep. However, Hanuman remained awake so they did not know how to get in since he was guarding the entrance. Then they thought of a brilliant idea. Mahiravana disguised himself as Vibhishana and went to Hanuman and told him to lift his tail a little and let him in. Naturally Hanuman wanted to know where Vibhishana had gone at that time of night; He was under the impression that he was inside. The false Vibhishana said that he had gone to the sea shore for his ablutions. Hanuman thought it a bit strange that Vibhishana wanted to take a bath at that time of the night however he allowed him to go in. Mahiravana went to the place where Rama and Lakshmana were sleeping and threw a spell over the whole camp so that everyone fell unconscious. His brother had slipped in invisibly when Hanuman lifted his tail. So the two of them easily lifted the brothers on their shoulders and made a tunnel to the nether world and transported them to Patala.

When the monkeys roused themselves from the spell, they discovered that Rama and Lakshmana were missing. There was uproar in the camp and they ran to give this news to Hanuman.

"Did any stranger enter the fortress made by your tail in the night?" Asked Sugriva.

"Only Vibhishana came at night," said Hanuman.

Hearing this Vibhishana came forward and exclaimed, "I certainly did not go out of the fortress at night. I was inside the camp all the time.

It must have been the Ahi-Mahiravanas about whom I warned you. They must have taken the princes to Patala. You are the only one who can get them back O Hanuman! Don't delay. Go immediately."

"Fear not! Wherever he might have hidden them I will discover their whereabouts and bring them back," said Hanuman.

Just then they saw the tunnel which the Ahi-Mahiravanas had made. Hanuman jumped into it without a second thought. The tunnel ended in a forest. There he heard a conversation between two birds. The female bird was sulking and the male was trying to cajole her with these words.

"My Dearest!" He said, "Please don't be angry with me. Tomorrow night Ahiravana and Mahiravana will be making a human sacrifice of two brothers in their Kaali temple in Patala. After it is over I promise to bring some tasty morsels of human flesh for you."

Hearing this, Hanuman immediately concluded that the two brothers were incarcerated in Ahi-Mahiravanas' dungeon. With the proverbial speed of wind he reached the nether world known as Patala which was the residence of the *asuras.* There he saw a huge fortress. He was wondering how to enter. He decided to make himself small so that he could squeeze in through some small door. Just then some ladies came outside and he heard them talk about the two handsome humans who had been brought there to be given as a sacrifice to Kaali. Hanuman was determined to find out where his Lord had been incarcerated.

As he went round the fortress, he suddenly found a door guarded by a handsome young monkey. He went to him and asked him to allow him to enter.

"Who are you and why have you come here?" asked the young monkey.

"I have come to rescue my master Lord Rama and his brother who have been stolen by your masters, the Ahi-Mahiravanas."

"You'll have to fight with me before you can enter. But beware I am Makaradwaja, son of Hanuman and you won't find it easy to beat me!"

Hanuman burst out laughing when he heard this. "What a stupid monkey you are to tell such stories. I am Hanuman and I am an eternal celibate. I have neither wife nor child."

When he heard this, the young monkey threw himself at Hanuman's feet and asked him to bless him.

"Blessed is my life, now that I have seen you," he said.

Hanuman shook him off and said, "You must be a *rakshasa* kept by Ahiravana in order to hinder me. Now stand up and tell me where they have been hidden. If not I'll kill you."

Makaradwaja begged him to listen to the story of his birth which had been told to him by the sage Narada.

"At that time when you were returning through the air after having found Sita, a drop of your perspiration fell into the sea and was swallowed by a crocodile that became pregnant with your seed. The crocodile was caught in a fish net and brought to the court of my masters. They cut open its stomach and I came out of it. They decided to adopt me and made me the guardian of their gate. That is why my name is Makaradwaja" (part crocodile, part monkey).

"This is certainly a wondrous tale," Hanuman said. "I suppose if this was told to you by the celestial sage, Narada, it must be true. I am indeed very happy to meet you but I have no time to lose so tell me where your master has kept the two princes. Did you know that he has captured Rama and Lakshmana and brought them here?"

I didn't know who they were but I know that he brought two hermits who were unconscious and has kept them under custody to be taken to the temple. They will be offered as sacrifices to Kaali tomorrow morning."

"I must rescue them immediately," said Hanuman.

"Father forgive me but if you want to enter the fortress, you will have to fight me and tie me up so that my master will not suspect me of having betrayed him. I am as loyal to my master as you are to yours," said the monkey fearlessly.

Then followed a fight between father and son in which Hanuman defeated Makaradwaja and tied him up before proceeding to the temple where Rama and Lakshmana were to be sacrificed. The boy told him that before he could kill his masters, he would have to put out five lamps which were placed in five different directions in the temple. Apparently their life force was kept in these lamps and they could never be killed just by cutting off their heads.

Hanuman thanked him and took the form of a bee and got into the fortress through the key-hole. He then went to the Kaali temple and hid himself in a small monkey form inside the idol of Kaali.

The temple was slowly starting to fill with people coming with different types of offerings to the goddess. The brothers now came with the two unconscious princes and threw them at Kaali's feet. They were slowly starting to recover from their swoon. The demons beseeched the goddess to accept this final offering of two humans so that she would be pleased to grant all their wishes. Hanuman was furious when he saw this and started eating all the things which were kept in front of the idol much to the astonishment of all those present.

"She must be really liking us very much," they thought. We've never seen her eat all these sweets before. They ordered more sweets to be brought all of which were consumed by Hanuman as fast as they were brought.

The two demons then said in pious tones, "Now we will offer you the blood of these two humans." So saying one grabbed Rama by his top knot and the other Lakshmana and prepared to chop off their heads. At that moment Hanuman, pretending to be the goddess, spoke from inside the idol.

"Leave everything here and go out. Let the temple be cleared of all people. I will eat these humans by myself."

The brothers were amazed at Kaali's words. But they immediately cleared the temple and went out closing the door.

Hanuman directly came out of the idol and bowed to Rama and Lakshmana who had almost recovered from their swoon. Very soon they became fully conscious. They were astonished to see where they were. Hanuman bowed low to Rama and told him the whole story briefly since time was passing and the monkeys would be awaiting his return anxiously.

As he came out of the door of the temple, the *asuras* who were waiting, saw him and realised that they had been neatly tricked. They pounced on him. Hanuman kept the two princes down and started to fight with the demon brothers. But however much he tried he could not put them down. Rama and Lakshmana now came forward for they had fully recovered and started to help Hanuman. But the brothers seemed invincible. With every blow they appeared to grown stronger. They laughed in scorn to see the bewildered look on Hanuman's face. Then suddenly he remembered his son's words. He told Rama and Lakshmana to keep them at bay and ran back to the temple. He looked around and saw the five lamps as described by Makaradwaja. He immediately assumed his *panchamukha* (five-faced) form and put out all five lamps simultaneously. These five faces were the faces of the three incarnations of Vishnu – as Varaha (boar), Narasimha (half man, half lion), and Hayagriva (horse). The fourth face was that of Garuda, Vishnu's eagle vehicle and the fifth was his own face. Having extinguished these five lamps simultaneously he ran out and killed Ahiravana and his brother easily. He also killed all the other demons who tried to stop him.

Another story about the invulnerability of the brothers is described in a different way. Every time Rama and Lakshmana and Hanuman killed the brothers, they revived and start fighting again. Hanuman was puzzled and flew to the city determined to discover the reason for their apparent immortality. He found the Naga princess who was Mahiravana's queen who promised to tell him the secret of his invincibility on condition that Rama agreed to marry her. Hanuman agreed but placed a counter condition that Rama would be relieved of this obligation if the cot on which they sat collapsed beneath him. The princess revealed the secret of her husband's immortality and told him that he owed his existence to the seven large bees which were kept in a hive thirty leagues away and which produced nectar that kept the two demons alive. Hanuman flew to the spot and killed six of the bees. He spared the seventh on condition that it go to the princess' room and hollow out the leg of her bedstead. He then returned to help Rama and Lakshmana and killed the demons in no time. Hanuman told Rama the whole secret. Rama went to the princess' room but just as he sat down on her bed, the frame gave way. He then blessed her to become his wife in another age – the Dwapara Yuga.

Hanuman now took Rama and Lakshmana on his shoulders and started to fly back. When they passed the bound figure of Makaradwaja, Rama asked him who that was. Hanuman said that he was a monkey who professed to be his son. Rama insisted on going down and freeing him. He also anointed him as king of Patala and told him to reign it according to the law of righteousness so that the Vedic *dharma* which the demons had destroyed would once again be established.

Makaradwaja fell at Rama's feet and at his father's feet and got their blessings.

Hanuman now returned to Lanka with Rama and Lakshmana and revived the hopes of the monkeys who had been waiting anxiously for their return.

"O Hero! Ghosts and demons can never come near one,
Who utters your name!"

— *Sri Hanuman Chalisa* by Tulsidas

ॐ *Sri Hanumathe Namaha!*

ॐ

Satyasandaaya Namaha!

CHAPTER TWENTY-FIVE

RUDRASYA-SOONU

Fight to the Finish

"The birds and deer will be my attendants,
The forest my city and strips of bark my glistening robes.
With my Lord a hut of grass will be as the palace of the gods,
And all will be well."

— Sita to Rama in the *Ramacharitamanas* by Tulsidas

Ravana was rejoicing in the thought that the Kosala brothers must now have been given as a sacrifice to Kaali by his sons, when he heard the commotion outside the fortress. He climbed up the battlements to see what was happening and saw Rama and Lakshmana being feted in the midst of the *vanaras.* He just couldn't believe this. One by one fate was depriving him of all his friends and his hopes. But he revived himself and decided to send the last of his generals to the battlefield. The next day he sent his crack regiment of carefully chosen men famed for their valour to the battlefield. With them went his remaining commanders – Mahodara, Mahaparswa and Virupaksha. They were all supposed to be invincible warriors.

Armed with all the best weapons of their time, the ill-fated army gathered at the western gate at break of day. Their fires threw off dark smoke. Carrion birds hovered over the sky and jackals barked and howled. Clouds of ash floated over the city of Lanka. Outside the golden walls there was an explosion as Indrajit's enchanted grove went up in flames. The west gate opened and the drawbridge dropped with a thunderous sound. The sentinels on the walls beheld the bears and apes watching them but the *rakshasas* were not afraid and drew out their swords with a grating noise. The two armies met with a terrible clash and blood flowed like a river. Now Rama told the monkeys to stand aside and tackled them single-handed as he had done the army at Janasthana. The army could hardly be seen due to the shower of arrows which engulfed them. Then Rama took up the weapon called the *gandharva,* and created a kind of illusion by which many hundreds of Ramas could be seen on all sides. Within an hour he had totally reduced Ravana's crack regiment to nothing.

In the meantime, his three wonderful commanders were having a hand to hand battle with Sugriva and Angada. After some hard fighting, Virupaksha and Mahodara were killed by Sugriva and Mahaparswa by Angada.

There was a loud wail in the whole of Lanka, set up by the wives of the deceased. They blamed Surpanekha for being the sole cause of all their roubles. Every house in Lanka was sunk in sorrow. Those houses from which at one time, only the sound of music and revelry were heard, now reverberated with the shuddering sounds of moans and sobs.

Ravana was filled with gloom and foreboding when he heard this news. He consulted the court astrologers who studied his horoscope and decreed that the alignment of celestial bodies was not in his favour. Indian astrology is governed by nine planets, known as the *navagrahas.* Ravana thought that by changing the alignment of these heavenly bodies he would be able to alter his destiny. Mounting his flying chariot he rose to the skies, captured the nine planets, and herded them to his capital and bound them in chains. He then began a series of rituals which if successful would force the planets to re-align themselves in his favour.

Vibhishana who was always alert saw the fumes rising out of the *yajnashala* where the *Yaga* was being conducted and warned Hanuman to try and stop it. He led Hanuman and a band of monkeys through a secret passage to Ravana's sacrificial hall. They found the ten-headed one sitting beside the altar, with eyes shut, chanting *mantras.* The monkeys let out a piercing war cry and rushed into the hall, creating havoc. They stamped out the ceremonial fire and kicked the utensils around and wiped out the occult diagrams drawn on the ground. Ravana was in deep meditation and remained unperturbed by all this commotion.

"We must stop him at all costs," said Vibhishana, "or else he will succeed in changing the course of his destiny."

Hanuman now came up with a plan. He told the monkeys to go into the inner apartments and frighten Ravana's wives. Nothing loathe, the monkeys attacked his queens and concubines, pulling their hair, scratching their faces and tearing their clothes.

They ran to the *yajnashala* crying to Ravana to help them. Still Ravana did not open his eyes. The monkeys now gathered round Mandodari and bared their teeth, beat their chests and growled menacingly. Hearing her pitiful cries Ravana opened his eyes and rushed to her defense. With Ravana out of the way, Hanuman ran to the sacrificial hall and liberated the nine planets that had been held captive. For having successfully aborted Ravana's attempts to subvert fate, Hanuman won the eternal gratitude of the planets (*grihas*). Because of this Hanuman is believed to exercise considerable power over them. He is worshipped by those whose planets are placed in unfavourable positions. Some of his paintings show him to be trampling under his feet a woman who is said to represent Panavati, a personification of baneful astrological influences.

On the eve of his death, the desperate Ravana made one final attempt to gain victory. He went to his *guru* and asked him to prescribe some means by which he would be victorious in the battle that would follow on the night of the new moon. The *guru* advised him to do another *Yaga* to the goddess Kaali, which would make him invincible but he warned him not to antagonise her for she was capable of saving anyone who prayed to her. He assembled a large number of Brahmins who had been kept as prisoners and who were deeply learned in all forms of *tantric* rituals and commanded them to invoke the most violent form of the goddess as Kaali. If she was on his side, victory was assured. The Brahmins were to recite a certain hymn to the goddess a thousand times, bracketing each recitation with an appropriate offering in the fire, followed by a request to the goddess expressing Ravana's desire.

Vibhishana learnt of this scheme and informed Hanuman who instantly took the form of a Brahmin and went and started helping the others who were preparing various things for the ritual. The Brahmins were impressed by him, since they didn't normally get this type of service from the inhabitants of Lanka. In return for his services they offered him a boon. Hanuman pretended to be dismayed and professed that he wanted nothing except to serve them. But they were insistent that he be given something for his devotion so he innocently asked them to change one syllable in the final *mantra* they were reciting to get the favour of the goddess. The Brahmins instantly realised the grave implication since with the changing of that one syllable, the entire meaning of the *mantra* changed and instead of asking her to help them, they would be asking her to hinder them! They glanced meaningfully at each other but since they were bound by their oath, they decided to carry on as the little Brahmin wished.

The all-night ritual commenced but since they were saying the wrong *mantra,* the goddess refused to manifest herself as expected after the recitation of the thousand and first *mantra.* The priests looked around but found that the helpful young Brahmin had disappeared. Ravana lost his temper with them and wanted to know where they had failed. They replied that the goddess was angry with him for all his *adharmic* acts and had therefore refused to comply with his wishes.

Ravana was furious when he heard this unpalatable truth and rushed at them with sword upraised to kill all of them but his wife Mandodari caught his hand and stopped him from this heinous crime.

She begged him to make a truce. "What have the Brahmins done? They have only told the truth. All your brothers, our sons, our friends, ministers and commanders have died. Will you not stop this outrage until the last of your people have died? What have we left to live for? As for myself, I don't want to live after the death of my beloved sons! Will you not listen to reason at least now?"

She begged and pleaded but Ravana had gone too far to back out now and he simply waved her off and thought of another strategy by which he could still vanquish the Kosala brothers. "What Mandodari said is true. All my closest and dearest ones have left me. Tomorrow I will have to face my enemies alone. However, I have never bowed my head before anyone so far and I shall not do so now!"

Mandodari now asked all his wives to undertake a long vow of fasting and complete chastity and keep an all-night vigil so that the goddess would protect their husband. Jambavan heard of this and knew that any vow would come to naught if the women committed adultery even by thought if not by deed. So he told Hanuman to fly past their palace window in his most handsome form. Ravana's wives noticed him and admired his lithe limbs and graceful movements and a passing thought came to their mind that they would like to be clasped in his strong arms! This mental infidelity detracted from the power of their vow to protect Ravana and thus he became vulnerable to Rama's arrows.

After the disruption of his *Yaga* in which he had made a desperate attempt to change the positions of his ill-fated planets, Ravana began to realize that one cannot really change one's destiny. That night, as he sadly approached his bedroom, the fascinating Mandodari, daughter of Mayan, the maker of illusions, approached him and softly wound her arms round his neck.

"My Lord!" She said, "Do you have to go for battle tomorrow. Can you not change your mind?"

Gently he put her away from him and said, "My faithful one, you know I have to go, but please believe me, I will never let you down."

"You have never let me down, my Lord. From the day you married me, you have given me nothing but delight. How can I forget?"

"You must believe me," said Ravana. "Put your faith and hope in me once more – just once more. I will not let you down."

"You are my beloved husband. I know that you will never let me down."

Ravana held her in his arms once more and said, "Farewell my love."

She watched him sadly while he climbed up the ramparts of the castle for the last time. He sang the Sama hymns in which he was an expert and by singing which he had once pleased Shiva, the Lord of the world, so much that he gave him all his desires. The whole of nature seemed to be providing an accompaniment for his chants, with the sighing of the wind, the lashing of the waves and the eerie creaking of the trees as they swayed to and fro, in tune with the rhythm of his chant. He lifted up his foot and brought it down again and again and began to dance. His breath came fast but he felt calm. He threw back his head and waved his arms and spun around. The wind was rushing round him and even the gods came to watch. Blue flames shimmered round his form high above Lanka, and electricity crackled in his long loose hair. Rama and the animals saw him from down below and watched fascinated as Ravana's mighty figure, silhouetted against the sky, swayed and flowed with his own music.

At last with the approach of midnight, *amavasya*, the night of the new moon, the wind dropped, the waves calmed down and Ravana came down for his final battle.

For the first time, there was a tinge of fear in Ravana's voice as he ordered the last of his generals to get ready for battle, for he had decided to go himself and avenge the death of all his loved ones. He wore his night armour made of finely woven black steel and donned his dark helmet that hid his face. Over his chariot was raised the battle banner of Lanka made of golden cloth. Tied loosely on the flagstaff were ten golden arrows for the ten directions of his empire. The chariot was protected with shields and plates cut from brass. It was equipped with all the latest weaponry and gleaming with jewels. It was loaded with tough, horn-tipped arrows, a long straight sword and a heavy eight-sided mace. As it was driven to the gate Ravana leapt into it like a tiger and took the reins himself. He rode out into the streets and the demon warriors who lined the streets cheered and clapped as he thundered down. He chose to take the fifth gate, the gate of illusion and rose up like a huge black swan into the midnight sky.

The *vanaras* were watching all the four gates but Ravana came through the illusory gate in the sky and landed in their midst with a thud. As he emerged from the gate, it is said that the wind began to blow, the whole sky was pitch dark since it was the dark night of the moon, owls started to hoot and jackals to howl. Clouds rained drops of blood and horses tripped and fell. Ravana's face lost its customary glow and his voice became hoarse. His left arm and eye started to throb. All these omens were indicative of death.

Paying no heed to any of these he drove at a fast pace trough the ranks of the monkeys accompanied by the remains of his loyal ministers. In the distance, he could see the golden tips of Rama's bow. He was standing on the ground and totally unafraid. Ravana pushed through the ranks of the monkeys and fought like one possessed. None of the *vanaras* were able to face the onslaught of his fury. Like a lake drying up as summer advances, the simian forces were decreasing as more and more of them fell dead. Ravana hardly glance at them for he was bent on reaching Rama. As he saw him approach, Rama asked all the animals to go behind him for this was the moment he had been waiting for and he preferred to face his enemy alone.

Ravana ordered his charioteer to take him to Rama. He preferred to forget their first encounter when Rama had treated him so chivalrously. He saw Rama holding his famous bow, the Kodanda, with Lakshmana beside him and the thought crossed his mind that he looked like Narayana himself, with Indra by his side. Since Ravana was seated in his chariot, Hanuman offered to carry Rama since that would enable him to face him on an equal footing. In the battle that followed, Hanuman skilfully dodged every weapon sent by Ravana so that not even a scratch fell on Rama! Rama managed to shoot an arrow that severed Ravana's head but to his surprise another head grew back instantly. This happened several times and Ravana laughed mockingly at the puzzled look on Rama's face. Frustrated, Rama left the field to Lakshmana and sought Vibhishana's advice.

Vibhishana said, "I'm not sure but it is rumoured that there is a pond in Ravana's garden into which a drop of the nectar of immortality fell when Jayanta was carrying it away. The lotuses that grow there are imbued with the power to regenerate the body and heal even the most lethal of wounds. Ravana must be eating these lotuses every time he is injured and thus getting rejuvenated."

Hanuman immediately took the form of a bee and discovered the fabled lotus lake. He swallowed all the lotuses and drained the pool of water and returned as fast as he had gone.

In the meantime, Lakshmana had been longing to come to grips with Ravana and shot a number of shafts at him, resembling tongues of fire. Ravana intercepted them with ease and split them with his own. He then passed over Lakshmana and stood face to face with Rama and let fly a shower of arrows at him. Rama retaliated in kind and soon the sky was overcast with arrows of various kinds. The shafts were extremely sharp-pointed, adorned with plumes of vultures and flew with amazing speed. Both were well matched, equally skilled and both were adepts in the use of different missiles. Ravana's arrows had the heads of lions, tigers, geese and vultures as well as jackals and wolves. Rama countered all his arrows with ease much to the joy of the monkeys.

Now Lakshmana came to the fore and with a single arrow he felled Ravana's splendid banner which had been fluttering in the breeze. Lakshmana could still see his sister-in-law's piteous face when she had begged him to go after Rama, Outside their hut in Panchavati. Keeping this in mind, he severed the head of Ravana's charioteer with a single arrow. Then with five whetted shafts, Lakshmana split asunder Ravana's huge bow which resembled the trunk of an elephant. Vibhishana now rushed forward and struck his huge horses with his mace and killed them. Ravana was furious and sent his famous *Shakti* weapon at his brother. Lakshmana intervened and saved him. Ravana decided it was high time he put an end to this impudent brother of Rama's. His green eyes sparkling with copper fire and roaring like a lion, Ravana hurled a javelin made by Mayan endowed with magic powers. It sizzled through the air making a horrendous noise. It flew like an awesome meteor at its target. Rama saw it going towards his beloved brother and quickly made a *sankalpa*. "May you prove ineffectual! May your attempt to kill Lakshmana be frustrated." However, though the missile lost its power to kill, it was still potent enough to knock Lakshmana down senseless.

Seeing Lakshmana lying in a pool of blood, Rama was totally unnerved. He ran and took him to his bosom even though Ravana kept pelting him with his potent arrows. He then shouted to Hanuman and Sugriva to come and take care of Lakshmana since he would not leave till the ten-headed monster was killed. He had many scores to settle with him.

"It is obvious that the world cannot contain the two of us. Either he or I will have to die. You may all take vantage positions on the hill and watch, for this battle will be talked about as long as the world remains, as long as the earth stands above the sea and as long as living beings inhabit this earth!"

All the pent-up fury he had against Ravana which he had been bottling up for eleven months now rose to the surface and he fought like a mad tusker.

Then followed a tremendous battle between the two. However, the *rakshasas* were night stalkers and with the approach of day they became weaker and Ravana perceptibly started to lose his strength. This encounter with Rama was even fiercer than the previous one and the spectators could only hear the twang of the bowstrings and the clap of their palms as they released the arrows from the bows. At last stung and pierced by the numerous gold-tipped arrows sent from Rama's flaming bow, Ravana fled from the field. Rama gladly turned his attention to his brother who lay unconscious. He begged Sugriva's court physician to do something to save him.

"If my brother dies, I care not if I win or lose the war. I do not desire the kingdom or even my life. I seem to have lost the desire even to rescue Sita. A wife like her may perhaps be found, but I will never find another like Lakshmana, who was born with me and was like my shadow and who has been my sole support and comfort during these dark days." So saying Rama sobbed over the body of Lakshmana.

The physician said, "My Lord! Lakshmana's face has not lost its glow, which makes me believe that he is still alive. His skin does not have the darkness which is associated with death. His palms are still pink and soft. Moreover he has all the auspicious signs of a long-lived man. So please do not grieve."

Turning to Hanuman, he requested him to go once again to the Himalayas and bring back the herbs known as *mritasanjivani* and *vishalyakarani* which had the property of bringing a person back to consciousness. Before he could complete his sentence, Hanuman had winged his way to the north but as before he could not recognise the medicinal herb in question so once again he lifted the whole peak and carried it back so that the physician could choose what he wanted. When he breathed the healing fragrance of the herb, which the physician crushed and held to his nostrils, Lakshmana woke up as if from sleep with no loss of energy or signs of fatigue. Rama was overjoyed to see him totally recovered. Shedding tears of joy he clasped him to his bosom and exclaimed, "My dearest brother! My life would have been purposeless without you. Neither Sita nor kingdom would have meant anything."

Lakshmana was embarrassed at this and said, "O Rama you have taken a vow to kill Ravana today and rescue the gentle princess of Videha. That should be your aim now. Never mind about me. Challenge him to a fight. Before the sun sets you should kill him."

Then both of them embraced Hanuman and blessed him for having come to their rescue for the second time.

"Diseases vanish and pain removed,
O Great Hero, when your name is repeated constantly."

— *Hanuman Chalisa* by Tulsidas

ॐ *Sri Hanumathe Namaha!*

ॐ

Dhumraketave Namaha!

CHAPTER TWENTY-SIX

VIRUPA

End of Ravana

"All glorious shone forth Raghupati on the field of battle,
In his immeasurable might and manifold beauty,
With the drops of toil on his lotus face,
With his lovely eyes and body specked with blood,
While in both hands he brandished his bow and arrows,
With the bears and monkeys grouped round him."

— *Ramacharitamanas* by Tulsidas

Rama knew that his brother spoke the truth but he went into a reverie and for a moment felt that perhaps he might not be able to defeat Ravana. Seeing him looking utterly exhausted and sitting in deep thought, the sage Agastya came to him and gave him the great hymn known as the "Aditya Hridayam". It is a hymn to the Sun God, said to have the power to overcome all obstacles.

"O Prince of the solar race – mighty armed Rama!" he said, "Listen to this ancient *mantra*, by which you will be able to vanquish your foe in battle. The presiding deity of this hymn is the sun and if it is chanted fervently, it will result in the destruction of your enemies and bring you victory and unending bliss. It is guaranteed to destroy all sins and allay all anxiety. Worship the golden-orbed deity of the sun, therefore, with this hymn for he represents the totality of all celestial beings."

The all-knowing sage knew that Rama was Narayana incarnate but he also knew that he was unaware of his divinity and so he initiated him into the esoteric *mantra* as a *guru* would initiate an ordinary mortal. By the sincere chanting of this holy hymn, not only will material obstacles be removed but also all obstacles on the path of the seeker of eternal truth. He advised Rama to look at the sun and repeat it and he would surely be victorious in battle. Hearing this, Rama was thrilled and gazing intently at the rising sun; he repeated the hymn with all fervour and sincerity.

"O Lord of Victory! Lord of the East! Lord of the West! O thou immeasurable one! Thou resplendent one! Golden-limbed creator of the universe! Witness of all the actions of all created beings! Again and again I bow to you!"

Rama belonged to the solar race and as he repeated the hymn three times, the sun burst forth in all his glory as if he applauded Rama's decision and urged him to hurry up with the deed on hand!

At dawn Ravana also offered prayers to his favourite deity – Shiva – and prepared to ride to the battlefield.

After chanting the *Aditya Hridayam*, Rama was filled with enthusiasm and challenged Ravana to come out. He was clad in bark with matted hair and walked barefoot.

The demon king watched in scorn as he came forward looking like a hermit. Suddenly a star seemed to come down from heaven. As it approached him Rama saw that it was a brilliant aerial car, with weapons that shone like lamps drawn by ten silver grey horses. Its many fan blades were spinning and silver wheels flashing as it landed softly, close to Rama. The charioteer jumped out and bowed to him and said, "I am Matali, Indra's charioteer. These are Indra's rain steeds, the misty runners of the sky. O King of the Solar race, Indra as sent me here to take you to victory."

"Welcome to you," said Rama and sprang lightly on to the chariot.

Matali touched the horses and told them to advance. They rushed forward with flashing silver shoes.

Ravana's chariot leapt forward to intercept them. A fierce battle began between the two. The gods assembled in the sky to witness this final scene. The animals and demons took up safe positions to watch this concluding scene.

The charioteers drove their respective chariots in a series of skilful and bewildering manoeuvres. Both Rama and Ravana discharged a number of deadly arrows charged with various potent *mantras*. The snake arrows of Ravana, which flew with unerring precision at Rama, spitting poison from their wide open mouths, were foiled by the eagle arrows of Rama. Eagles are the avowed enemies of snakes. The sky became dark with arrows flying in the air, colliding and negating each other with horrendous noises resembling thunder claps. The world trembled to witness the wrath of Rama. The sun lost its brilliance and the sea came in huge waves to watch the terrifying spectacle. The terrible frown on Rama's face, which was so seldom seen, made even Ravana tremble in terror. Birds and beasts ran about in panic. Valmiki says that just as the ocean can only be compared with the ocean and the sky with the sky, so the battle between Rama and Ravana can only be compared to the battle between Rama and Ravana!

At last Ravana took hold of a javelin which was covered with spikes and had a sharp point which was sizzling and blazing like a huge fire, as if anxious to go and find its rest on Rama's chest and sent it flying at Rama.

He roared, "This will make short work of you and your brother, O scion of the race of Raghu!"

Rama immediately countered with a host of arrows but they were all burnt to ashes by the fury of Ravana's javelin. In a trice Rama took up the javelin sent by Indra, which had been kept in the chariot and hurled it with all force at the oncoming dart of Ravana's. The two weapons collided in mid-air and Ravana's javelin broke into a thousand splinters and fell on the ground, its power totally exhausted. Ravana immediately took another missile and shattered Rama's pennant. Rama turned to Hanuman and said,

"O Vayu Putra! Get me another flag-staff immediately and do thou be seated on my flag and terrify the enemy."

Hanuman immediately cut off a branch from a *sal* tree and hoisted it on top of the chariot and sat on it himself. From this vantage point he cast his eyes on all sides and gave the most ferocious and terrifying roars.

Now Rama spoke to Ravana, "You call yourself a hero after having abducted Sita when she was alone and unattended in the *ashrama*. What chance did she have against brute force? You are nothing but a thief and a molester of women and a coward. But beware! Your head will provide food for hungry vultures and your blood with be lapped by wolves before the day is over!" With these words, Rama harassed Ravana with hundreds of arrows.

Ravana was beginning to be unnerved by Rama's unflagging enthusiasm and barrage of arrows and fell into a faint. Seeing the condition of his master, his charioteer skilfully steered the chariot away from Rama. When Ravana came out of his swoon he swore at his charioteer and ordered him to drive fast to the midst of the fray.

"Ravana never turns his back on his enemies," he said. "He does not retreat till he has wiped out his foes!"

"My Lord," said the charioteer, "It is the duty of a charioteer to protect his master. Our horses were tired and you were also fatigued and in a faint. I saw nothing but ill omens and thought it best to bring you away from the situation."

Ravana was pleased with his devotion and presented him with his own bracelet. The charioteer whipped up the horses as commanded by his master and took him in front of Rama once again.

Rama requested Matali to manoeuvre the chariot to a good position. He raced his horses straight at Ravana's chariot and deflected them to the left just before they collided. As they passed, Rama shot an arrow deep into Ravana's shoulder. The demon king clutched desperately at the flagstaff to stop himself from falling. The chariots turned and faced each other once again. The rest of the army stood like painted figures, spellbound by the awesome scene. Ravana tried to bring down Indra's divine banner and failed while Rama's arrow found its mark and brought down Ravana's pennon. Ravana was biting his lips and darting sparks from his eyes when he found that none of his arrows were hurting Rama. The latter on the other hand was having a slight smile on his lips as his arrows seemed to be finding a sure mark. There ensued another terrific battle between the two heroes. Matali advised Rama to make an end of the ten-headed demon before the approach of night. Rama then fitted an arrow resembling a venomous snake and sliced off the resplendent head of his opponent adorned with huge earrings. But, to his astonishment, in front of his very eyes, there arose another head in the place of the previous one and then another and another as each was cut off.

Ravana's ten heads are meant to convey his enormous ego. With just one head all of us have egos which are impossible to control, think of the ego of a person with ten heads! When each ego head was chopped off, another reared its haughty hood. It is the same with us. When our ego is put down in one place, we immediately find another place or situation by which we can make ourselves feel important.

Rama was beginning to feel a bit worried, though his face remained calm and he kept sending a continuous stream of arrows from his bow. Then Vibhishana approached him and whispered to him that Ravana could be slain only with the *brahmastra*, which Brahma himself had given him. This was hidden in Mandodari's apartments and without it the fight could go on forever. Hanuman immediately leapt to Lanka and taking on the form of an aged Brahmin, he hobbled before Mandodari. She was delighted to see this venerable Brahmin and offered him all hospitality. The Brahmin then warned her that Vibhishana had told Rama of the existence of the only weapon which had the power to kill her husband and which was hidden by her. He advised her to remove it to a new hiding place.

Mandodari became panic stricken and ran to rescue the arrow from inside the crystal column in which she had carefully hidden it. Hanuman immediately reverted to his own form, grabbed the arrow and flew back leaving Mandodari in tears.

Hanuman gave the arrow to Rama and whispered in his ear, "My Lord! Remember who you are. Ravana's moment of death has come. Despatch the *brahmastra* and kill him. Do not aim at his head but at his chest!"

The time destined for Ravana's death had come. But when Rama looked at Ravana's heart it is said that he saw Sita enshrined within and inside Sita's heart, he saw himself. He was in a dilemma. What could he do? He waited for that split second when Ravana forgot Sita in his anger against Rama and at that precise moment, he whispered the incantation of Brahma and sent his golden-tipped arrow straight at Ravana's heart. It was the most powerful weapon known to man or god and very few human beings were initiated into its mysteries for its power for destruction was so great that no one who had not learnt to control himself could be trusted with it. Hence, in ancient India scientific knowledge was only given to those who had moral and ethical qualities and who could be depended to use it for the good of mankind!

The dart was made of the essences of all the elements. Flaming like the fire of universal destruction and as fatal as the power of Time, the dart fled from Rama's bow like a streak of lightning and found its mark on Ravana's chest. Piercing his body through and through, it sank into the earth and then swerved and returned to Rama's hand like a meek servant. The invincible bow of the king of demons dropped from his nerveless grasp and his body, full of splendour, fell like a thunderbolt from the chariot. Seeing him fall the night rangers fled in all directions shrieking with fear.

The watching gods rained flowers from the sky and the sun came out from behind the clouds. Ravana's life was fast ebbing away. The mighty king of the *rakshasas,* who had ruled the entire world with the might of his arms alone, now lay dead on the battlefield, a prey to every passing vulture and jackal. He, who had no equal in might and valour, he who had terrified the whole world and thus earned the name, "Ravana" (the terrifier), who had pleased Lord Shiva himself by his glorious chanting of the *Samaveda*, had been killed by a mere mortal as had been prophesied. His lust for another man's wife had killed him as well as the curses of all those women whom he had ravished. Even in death, he had not lost his splendour. He looked as dazzling as a fallen sun, glorious even in death.

Lakshmana, Sugriva and the others crowded round Rama and congratulated him. Vibhishana was suddenly struck with remorse and wept for his proud brother who had come to such an end. Rama comforted him by saying that Ravana had indeed died a hero's death.

"This is the path pursued by the heroes of old," he said. "For a Kshatriya, there is a right way of living and a right way of dying, and he has chosen the right way of dying if not of living, on the battlefield. Vibhishana! All enmity ends with death. Now go and do whatever rites are to be performed for him as per the rules, for there is no one else to do it for him but you."

Mandodari, foremost queen of Ravana, mother of the brave Indrajit, now came running to the battlefield, her hair dishevelled, her face streaming with tears and threw herself over the body of her dying husband.

"How could such a calamity have overtaken you, my noble Lord? How is it possible for a mere mortal to have killed you? This Rama must be divine. The fact that he defeated Khara and Dhushasana single-handed should have convinced you that he was not an ordinary human being. When I heard that he had built a bridge across the sea, I knew that he was not an ordinary mortal. I know now, who Rama is. He is the Lord Narayana himself – the Supreme Purusha. He has assumed the garb of an ordinary mortal for the purpose of saving the world and the gods themselves have assumed the forms of these monkeys. It is Narayana who has killed you my Lord, not a human being. How can you lie on the bare ground shrouded by dust when you are used to reposing on the softest and most sumptuous of couches? Why do you not speak to me, miserable creature that I am? Once upon a time, you performed a lot of austerities with your senses under perfect control and now those very senses, like untamed horses, have dragged you to your death. Sita is a noble lady, devoted to her husband. She should have been honoured by you but instead you chose to insult her. Her tears of shame and despair have killed you and not Rama's arrows. What does she have that I lack? In birth, I am her equal, in beauty she is in no way superior, yet blinded by lust, you chose to carve out your dreadful end. You brought death to Lanka, the day you brought her here. Now she will be reunited with her Lord and will live happily with him, while I will have to lie on my lonely bed, plunged in sorrow without you. Where has your smile gone my Lord, where is the look of love in your eyes when you gazed at me? How proud I was of my good fortune? I was the daughter of the architect of the *asuras* and my husband, the king of the *rakshasas* and my son, the most valiant warrior in the whole world. How could I believe that death would rob me of my dearest treasures in one fell stroke?"

So lamenting, Mandodari fainted over the dying body of her husband and the other women had to carry her away. Again and again she ran back to have a last look at her husband's beloved face which she would never see again. Refusing to go away she sat on the ground next to him and put his head on her lap whispering words of comfort to him.

Following close on her heels came the rest of his harem composed of thousands of ravishing women who had been picked from all over the world, famed for their beauty, whom not even the sun had seen for they had never been allowed to go out in the streets. They ran to the gory battlefield and threw themselves over his blood-stained body and wept piteously.

"Our Lord had been granted immunity from death by Brahma and now he has been killed by a mere mortal. Why did you never listen to us? You abducted Sita despite our advice. She has been the cause of the extermination of the entire race of *rakshasas.* Had she been restored to Rama, all this would never have happened. You spurned the words of Vibhishana. Fate is indeed all powerful. It was ordained that Ravana, the greatest of all monarchs would be defeated by a mere human being, helped by a pack of bears and monkeys!"

While the rest of the monkeys were celebrating, Hanuman came near Rama and said, "Ravana was a great scholar even though he was unrighteous. Let us take advantage of his enormous knowledge before he dies. Both Rama and Lakshmana went near Ravana. Lakshmana stood at his head and said, "I have heard that you have a lot of knowledge. We are the victors and therefore you should pass it on to us before you die!"

Ravana painfully turned his head away in silence, refusing to answer Lakshmana's request.

Now Rama came forward and knelt at the dying king's feet and said softly, "Ravana! I have killed you not out of malice but because it was my duty to save my wife. However, I have great respect for your vast knowledge and would deeply appreciate it if you would share it with me before you die so that it will not be lost to the world!"

Ravana slowly opened his eyes and said, "I accept you as my pupil, O Rama! For you sat at my feet and spoke with all humility as a student should. I'm willing to impart my knowledge to you."

Then to the astonishment of all those who had gathered there, the dying Ravana, with his head on Mandodari's lap revealed to his enemy Rama, the subtleties of philosophy, politics, economics, fine arts, dance, music, drama and statecraft. Thus, the villain became a teacher and the hero a student!

Ravana was fast losing his life breath and could do no more than whisper. At last the mighty hero could no longer speak and his lifeless head was held in a tight grasp by his faithful queen whose hot tears fell unheeded over his face.

Rama now told Vibhishana to set about the task of cremating Ravana. His body was placed on a pyre made of sandalwood and many other types of fragrant wood and herbs. It was draped with the skins of black antelopes. Curd and ghee were poured on his shoulders and a wooden mortar inserted between his thighs. The corpse was draped with different types of costly silks and garlands. Roasted grain was sprinkled over it. It was then carried in state by everyone and placed on the pyre of sweet-smelling wood. With great reverence Vibhishana touched the earthly remains of his brother with a flaming torch and set fire to it. He completed all the rites connected with the funeral and gave oblations to the departed soul. Then he went and saluted Rama and told him that everything had been done according to his wishes.

Rama prostrated to Indra's chariot and thanked Matali and sent him back. He then asked Lakshmana and Sugriva to take Vibhishana to the city and crown him as king. He did not go himself since his fourteen years were not over. Lakshmana took Vibhishana to the city of Lanka and placed him on the throne and gave him the ceremonial bath by pouring consecrated water over his head and thus pronounced him as King of Lanka. Only a few citizens were left to cheer the new king. The once populous and prosperous capital of Lanka now looked like a deserted ghost city. Even royal fortune fails at last and turns away from the greatest kingdom.

The great Rama/Ravana war ended on the morning of the fourth day, just past the first night of the new moon, close to the summer solstice when the sun turns in the sky to begin his journey to the north.

"The ascetic king Rama is the ruler of the universe,
And you are the one who carries out his tasks."

— *Sri Hanuman Chalisa* by Tulsidas

ॐ *Sri Hanumathe Namaha!*

ॐ

Uttamaaya Namaha1

CHAPTER TWENTY-SEVEN

UTTAMAN

Trial by Fire

"The flame was as cool as sandalwood, as Sita entered it,
Meditating on her Lord.
"Glory to the king of Kosala, for whose feet,
Ever worshipped by Shiva,
I cherish the purest devotion."

— *Ramacharitamanas* by Tulsidas

Though the thought of Sita must have been foremost in his mind, Rama sternly subdued it and saw to Ravana's cremation as well as the welfare of the citizens of Lanka by crowning Vibhishana before seeing to the matter which was closest to his heart.

Turning to Hanuman, he told him to go to Sita and give her the happy news and find out how she was faring. Hanuman was delighted to be given this most pleasant task.

He flew in a flash to the Ashoka grove, his white fur round his neck ruffled with happiness. He saw Sita surrounded by *rakshasis,* sitting in a forlorn mood for no one had told her the news so far.

With folded palms he bowed low to her and gave her the happy news. "Take heart, O divine lady! Rama and Lakshmana are well and happy and have sent me here to give you the glad tidings. The ten-headed one has been killed by your husband! Lanka has been placed under the rule of Vibhishana who will be coming here shortly to pay his respects to you. Sita couldn't say a word since she was overcome with joy.

At last in a trembling voice she said, "I really don't know how I am to repay you for the wonderful tidings which you have brought me, my dear monkey! Neither silver, gold, precious stones nor even the sovereignty of the three worlds can equal in value this message which you have given me."

"This speech of yours O Mother, so full of love is the most precious gift I can receive. I have received the blessings of all the gods by these words."

Out of the overflowing gratitude she felt, Sita told Hanuman, "O son of Vayu! You will always be the stronghold of valour, strength, knowledge of scriptures, vigour, and prowess, skill in action, forbearance, firmness, stability and humility. These and many other brilliant qualities will always exist in you!"

Standing meekly in front of Sita, Hanuman said, "My Lady! Believe me, I have spent sleepless nights thinking of your pathetic condition and now it is my luck that I have been chosen by our Lord to bring you this joyful news. Mother! If you will permit me I will kill these *rakshasis* who have been torturing you for such a long time."

Sweetly Sita said, "Why should servants be blamed for carrying out the orders of their master? Moreover, it is my fate that has ordained that I should be treated thus. Perhaps I have committed some crime in the past for which I am being punished now. Everyone reaps the fruit of his or her own actions of the past. So spare them dear monkey. No one is infallible. To err is human. The virtuous do not return evil for evil. It is my duty to condone their conduct which was forced upon them by a higher authority."

Hanuman bowed to Sita and desisted from killing the *rakshasis.* He then asked her for a message to be given to Rama. Sita told him to tell Rama that she was longing to see him. Hanuman once again bowed and said, "You will undoubtedly see the scion of the race of Raghu very soon."

He leapt into the air and returned to Rama and said, "The princess of Mithila has heard of your victory. At the very mention of your name she became wild with joy and her eyes filled with tears. She is thin and wan with grief and told me to tell you that she is longing to see you so please go to her."

Rama's eyes filled with tears when he heard this but he remained sunk in thought for a while. At last he sighed and told Vibhishana to bring Sita to him after she had been given an auspicious bath and clothed in beautiful apparel.

Vibhishana went to the Ashoka grove and conveyed this message to Sita.

She replied, "I want to see my husband now and not waste time in bathing and ornamenting myself."

Vibhishana said that it was his duty to obey Rama's commands implicitly and that he could not take her as she was. Sita contained her impatience to see her Lord and allowed Vibhishana's wife to bathe and anoint her with sandal paste and unguents and clothe her in costly apparel. She wore a silk yellow robe and a crown of fresh and fragrant wild flowers. She was even more beautiful than Lakshmi. She then got into the richly decorated palanquin which was kept ready for her and went before Rama. He was still lost in thought and sat with his eyes fixed on the ground.

The *vanaras* and *rakshasas* crowded round the palanquin eager to have a glimpse of the beauty for whose sake so much trouble had been taken and the whole race of demons annihilated! Vibhishana and the others pushed them back and ordered them to go away since Rama would want to see his wife alone and anyway it was not correct for the common populace to view a lady of the royal household.

Rama chided him and said, "A woman's protection should be her purity and chastity and not a wall or a veil. Let them stay where they are and see her if they wish. Let them gaze as much as they want on the beauty of the princess of Videha. Moreover, it is only right that she should be seen by those who fought and died for her sake. Ask her to step out of the palanquin and approach me all alone."

Lakshmana, Hanuman and Vibhishana were all puzzled by Rama's strange behaviour. Vibhishana led Sita who had covered her face with a veil, to her husband. Like the *chakora* bird drinking in the nectar which drops from the moon, she lifted up her veil and gazed adoringly at his beloved face. It was many months since she had seen his beloved face and as she gazed, she felt her strength return to her limbs and the glow to her face.

Rama averted his face and spoke in an unusually harsh tone, "I have accomplished what I have set out to do. I have vindicated my honour and kept up the reputation of the fair house of the Ikshvaku clan. I have wiped out the insult which was offered to me and killed the one who abducted you. Hanuman, who leapt across the ocean and destroyed Lanka, has been rewarded, so has Vibhishana who left his brother and took refuge in me. Sugriva and all the other monkey leaders have been applauded for the help they rendered to me."

Sita had been waiting for a year for this moment, when her beloved husband would come and rescue her and take her in his arms and comfort her and make her forget the trials which she had gone through. She could not understand why Rama who had never spoken harshly to her at any time was now using this tone of voice and why he was narrating all these incidents and avoiding her eyes. She looked at him with her fawn-like eyes which were slowly beginning to fill with tears and Rama's heart was torn with agony and love but he kept a stern check on his natural emotions and continued to speak harshly.

"Don't think that I have fought this war for your sake. I did it only to save my name and the honour of my race. Having lived for eleven months in the city of a notorious womaniser like Ravana, do you expect me to believe that he could refrain from ravishing you – you who are so lovely and alluring? That lecherous wretch has feasted his eyes on you and carried you in his arms. Rumours will be rife about you and I cannot take you back. You are now free to go where you wish, O Janaki! I can no longer bear to look at you. Your presence hurts my eyes like blinding sunlight for sore eyes. Now that I have done my duty and rescued you, I owe you nothing more. I belong to a noble house and it does not befit me to take you back. What man born in a noble family would take back a woman who has dwelt in another man's house for eleven months?"

Hearing this cruel speech coming from the mouth of her husband from whom she had heard nothing but words of love, Sita swayed like a creeper which has been torn from its prop. Tears streamed from her eyes and she looked like a wilting flower. To make matters worse, there was an interested and sympathetic audience to witness this painful scene. She had thought her heart had been broken when she had been abducted by Ravana but now she realised that it was nothing compared to this frightful ordeal.

At last she said in faltering tones, "Why do you speak such harsh words to me? This is the talk of a common man to a woman of the streets and you are not a common man, neither am I a woman of the streets. If you doubted me why did you come to search for me and why did you send Hanuman with your ring? Why didn't you tell him that you had no further use for me! Why did you take the trouble of crossing the sea and fighting and killing Ravana? You risked your life and the life of all your friends by coming here. You could have saved yourself a lot of trouble and I could have given up my life then and there and then I would not have had to hear these cruel words. If I had been touched by that sinner when I was being carried away, it was because I was too weak and helpless to protect myself. How can you blame me for that? Even after living with me for so many years, it looks as if you have never understood me. My thoughts and love have never strayed from you, even for a moment. I might be called Janaki, the daughter of Janaka but I am really Sita, the daughter of the earth. Did you never consider my exalted birth before passing judgement? Does my love and chastity mean nothing to you? If that was so, why did you come? You have given me leave to go where I want. There is only one place I want to go and that is into the heart of a fire."

Turning to Lakshmana she said, "Lakshmana make a pyre for me. It is the only cure for the grief which is burning me more than flames. I have been falsely accused and I don't want to live any more. My husband has repudiated me in front of this big crowd of people and asked me to go where I want. There is only one place for me and that is the world of Yama!" Her voice choked with emotion and she could no longer speak.

Lakshmana looked angrily at Rama who stood with his head cast down, like a statue. No one dared approach him or try to argue with him. Rama made a gesture with his hand and Lakshmana reluctantly went and made a pyre.

Sita circumambulated Rama three times as he stood with a stony face and a dreadful frown on his face and went slowly towards the blazing fire. She stood with folded palms before it and said,

"If it be true that my thoughts have never at any time wavered from my husband then let this fire which is the witness of all things, protect me. If I have never been unfaithful in thought, word or deed to Rama who is the repository of all virtues, let the god of fire afford protection to me. If the deities of the sun and the moon and my mother, the earth as well as the deities of the four quarters know me to be of unblemished character, then let the fire god protect me."

So saying she went three times round the fire and then flung herself into the heart of the conflagration before the horrified eyes of the spectators. All the *vanaras* and the *rakshasas* who had assembled there set up a loud wail of protest. Clad in yellow silk and adorned with gold ornaments, Sita glowed like molten gold in the heart of the fire. Rama turned his face away for he could not bear to see this pitiable scene. Though his heart was breaking and his eyes were streaming with tears, he did not do anything to save her, who was dearer to him than his own life.

At that moment there appeared two chariots in the air and the celestials showered fragrant flower petals from the air. Brahma came down and spoke to Rama, "How can you stand and watch unmoved while Sita immolates herself in the fire. Don't you know that you are Narayana, the primeval Being and Sita is Lakshmi, your eternal consort? You were born to destroy Ravana and establish peace on earth. Now your task is accomplished and *dharma* has been re-established."

As soon as Brahma had finished speaking, Agni, the god of fire, stepped forward from the blaze with Sita in his arms. She was dressed in red and looked as lustrous as the morning sun. Even her garland was not singed by the fire. He handed her over to Rama and said, "Here is your wife, the noble princess of Videha, who is totally without blemish. She was never unfaithful in thought, word or glance. Believe me and accept this jewel among women!"

Hardly had he finished speaking than Indra, king of gods appeared next to Sita. He wore a thin cloak of mist trimmed with stars and stood barefoot, just a finger's width above the ground. His body cast no shadow and his black eyes never blinked.

He bowed before Rama and said, "O Narayana! Thou art the primeval being. You were born on earth as Rama in order to save humanity from the inequities of Ravana. Sita is your divine consort – Lakshmi. Both of you can never be parted so take her back and return to your country and rule in peace."

He asked Rama to ask for a boon for he had done him a great service by killing Ravana who had been a thorn in his side for years. Rama immediately asked him to resurrect all those monkeys who had given up their lives to help him.

"May all these long-tailed monkeys and bears recover from their wounds and rise up once again filled with life and enthusiasm. Let fruits and flowers and roots abound wherever these monkeys live."

Indra was only too happy to grant this request and all the fallen monkeys and bears now rose up as if from sleep.

Tears flowed unchecked down Rama's eyes as he took his beloved wife's hands into his own.

"I know that my wife is pure and chaste as unsullied snow. I never doubted her even for a moment, but if she had not undergone this ordeal by fire, people would have spoken ill of her and of me. They would have said that Dasaratha's son blinded by love for his wife was willing to take her back even though she had lived so long in the house of another man. I knew fully well that Sita was totally protected by her purity. Ravana could never have sullied her. She is to me what splendour is to the sun. As a good man cannot abandon a good name so also I can never abandon Sita. If I spoke harshly to her and watched unmoved when she entered the fire, it was only to vindicate her name before the eyes of all."

So saying he lifted up her face to his and looked deep into her lovely eyes as he had been longing to do. When Sita turned her reproachful, tear-filled eyes at him, Rama chided her softly so that none could hear. "O daughter of the earth! My lovely Sita! How could you think even for a moment that I doubted you? Why do you think I trudged through the length and breadth of this country if not to catch a glimpse of your bewitching face? Why do you think I faced the wrath of the demon king and risked my life, if I did not crave for you? My dearest love, I repudiated you so that none could ever point an accusing finger at my darling."

Hearing this passionate declaration, Sita was slightly pacified and looked up at him with all her love pouring out of her eyes. Thus, for a long moment they were lost to the world and gazed long and deep into each other's eyes to the joy of all who were assembled there.

Then Lord Shiva came and extolled Rama and told him that the world owed him a great debt for having exterminated the scourge of Ravana. He blessed him with all success in his life as king of the land of Kosala.

As Sita, Rama and Lakshmana stood beside each other they were delighted to see their father, Dasaratha who had been brought in an aerial car so that there could be a happy re-union between all of them.

The celestials now reminded Rama to return immediately to Ayodhya for the fourteen years were drawing to a close and Bharata was waiting for his arrival with great anxiety.

In order to end the hostility between the *vanaras* and the *rakshasas*, Hanuman suggested that Sugriva's son should be given in marriage to Vibhishana's daughter. Everyone approved of the idea and the marriage was conducted in style and blessed by Rama and Sita.

"You are the dispenser of the eight supernatural powers
And the nine treasures.
Mother Janaki bestowed this blessing on you!"

— *Sri Hanuman Chalisa* by Tulsidas

ॐ *Sri Hanumathe Namaha!*

ॐ

Sahasravadanaaya Namaha!

CHAPTER TWENTY-EIGHT

SAHASRAVADANA

Return to Ayodhya

"Hearken O Sugriva!
This city is so holy and the country so charming,
That although men speak of Vaikunta as being most beautiful,
It is not as dear to me as Ayodhya."

— *Ramacharitamanas* by Tulsidas

Vibhishana now approached Rama with folded palms and humbly requested him to enter the city of Lanka where everything had been prepared for a royal welcome.

My Lord, I have prepared various types of baths and oils and unguents for you to refresh yourself. Garments of various kinds and garlands have all been laid out. Kindly refresh and adorn yourself before setting out on the return journey."

Rama smiled and said, "You may offer all these precious things to Sugriva, for my thoughts are all with my dear brother, Bharata. The way back to Ayodhya is long and hard; the fourteen years are coming to a close and Bharata has sworn that he will take his life if I do not reach by the end of the stipulated time."

Vibhishana said, "My Lord! I will help you to reach in a single day. My brother Ravana forcibly took the aerial vehicle called Pushpaka from his brother Kubera. It was his prized possession. Please accept my hospitality for a few more days and then you can return to Ayodhya in this vehicle."

Rama was touched by his devotion and said, "Vibhishana, I am well aware of your love for me but my heart yearns to return to Ayodhya and see my brothers and mothers and the people of Kosala, who must be anxiously awaiting my arrival. However, you may take Hanuman to Ravana's palace and show him the wonders inside while the rest of us take some rest after the battle." So saying he took Sita's hand in his and went towards the sea shore where they sat close together and she told him of all the sorrows she had gone through.

Hanuman was anxious to know the secrets of the city of Lanka so Vibhishana led him into Lanka along the empty brick streets to the royal palace. He took him via a secret door to the storeroom. It was locked with ten thousand and one locks all made with strange, ornate designs. Though the keyholes were of different shapes, Vibhishana opened them all with the same key! The door opened into a huge room which was lit with lamps placed inside glass domes. Hanuman gauged that the room had been dug into the heart of Trikuta Hill. Many shelves lined the wall on which were kept fine linens, patterned silks and skins of tigers, leopards, lions and wolves. There were many books made of stone and secret treasure maps. Exquisite vials of perfumes and piles of jewels, gold and silver filled the shelves.

Vibhishana spoke, "These are the ancient, timeless treasures of our race. In these vaults lie all the lore of old, gathered from the beginning of Time. This room was built by Vishvakarma, the architect of the gods. The *rakshasas* have a lot of knowledge which must not be allowed to perish. You are the only outsider who has ever seen or will ever see this room."

Hanuman looked curiously around the room and asked, "Why have you favoured me like this?"

"Because you are my first and only friend from another race," said Vibhishana. "Moreover you are wise and faithful. You put your whole heart into whatever you do and you never seek for any gain. I am really happy to have you as my friend. I know that your heart lies with Rama and you will go with him but remember that you are always welcome to come here any time you want."

Hanuman thanked him and they locked the room and retraced their steps to where Rama, Sita and Lakshmana were waiting along with the rest of the valiant army of monkeys and bears.

Rama told Vibhishana to go and get the aerial car which would transport them in a day to Ayodhya since he was keen to see his brothers and mothers and the citizens who were waiting so anxiously for him. Vibhishana returned to Lanka and came back with the Pushpaka.

It was a fantastic, flower-bedecked chariot, drawn by white swans. It was like a small city, glittering with gold and silver and adorned with blossoms of every kind and season. Rainbows were made into coloured knots over its frame. Inside there were summer houses and ponds and pools and dining halls. It had benches and beds and a kitchen which supplied every type of food. It was a mind driven chariot taken forcibly by Ravana from his brother, Kubera. It came rolling out on its thousand wheels with all flags flying and wind-bells chiming. Vibhishana walked in front of it and bowed before Rama and requested him to climb into it.

Rama, Lakshmana and Sita got in without further ado. Even though the Pushpaka was as big as a palace, Rama sat with Sita on his lap, much to her delight. He looked at Hanuman, Vibhishana, Sugriva and all the other *vanaras* and said with tears in his eyes, "I don't know in what way I can repay you all for the love and devotion you have shown to me. Sugriva, please return to Kishkinda with your army. My blessings will always be with you. Angada, my dear child, I can never forget your prowess and as for you O Hanuman, what can I say. Both of us owe our lives to you. Now please give me leave to return to my own city. I have been in exile for so long that my heart yearns to return."

Sugriva bowed low and said, "Lord, please give us leave to come with you to Ayodhya. We promise not to indulge in any act of destruction, as we monkeys are wont to do. We are most anxious to witness your coronation."

Rama laughed at their eagerness to accompany him and their promise to behave themselves and said, "I am delighted at the thought that I will enter my ancestral city, accompanied by those who have helped me most. Sugriva, ask your people to get in."

Vibhishana and the other ogres also expressed the same desire. Rama gladly gave his consent and the whole party got into the Pushpaka and still there was enough place in it for another army!

One of the most endearing things about Rama was his great love for all animals and birds. Monkeys, bears and birds wander in and out of the pages of the narrative of his life, as if it was the most natural thing in the world. His love and regard for his animal and feathered friends shows a unique facet of his character.

He then turned to Hanuman and asked him what reward he wanted for his invaluable services. Hanuman replied, "My Lord! Give me leave to spend the rest of my life in your service!" Rama smilingly agreed.

The divine chariot now rose into the air effortlessly, carried by the four white swans. Celestial flowers rained from the sky as it rose up. The *vanaras* shouted and whooped with joy, peering over the edge at the ground below, which fell with alarming rapidity.

Sita's face glowed with happiness and beauty as Rama pointed out the various sites which would interest her, through which they had wandered during their long and painful search. First of all he showed her the battleground and the spot where Ravana had fallen and then he pointed out to her the amazing bridge built by Nala, over which they had crossed. He kept reiterating the fact that everything he had done was for her sake alone as if trying to make up for all the harsh words he had spoken to her previously.

"O Princess of Videha! Observe this roaring, swelling ocean, teeming with all sorts of reptiles and fish that is Varuna's domain. Now we will land on the shore so that you can pray at the temple to Shiva which I had installed."

The plane gently landed on the other side of the bridge so that Rama could worship at the shrine of Shiva which he and Hanuman had consecrated before they set out. At that time he had made a vow to the three-eyed Lord that he would return and pay his homage to him along with his wife, Sita.

"Here on this spot, Shiva, the supreme deity, bestowed his grace on me and accepted my worship in the form of Rameshwara (Rama's Lord). This place where the bridge was constructed will be known as Sethubanda and will be adored in all the worlds. This spot will be held as supremely sacred and will be capable of washing away all major sins. This is the place where Vibhishana made his first appearance."

Once again they got into the plane and he pointed out to Sita, Sugriva's fortress – Kishkinda. Sita immediately asked for the car to be brought down so that they could take Tara and Rumi, Sugriva's wives as well as the wives of the other monkey leaders.

So the chariot landed and the ladies joyfully joined the group. Later Rama pointed out Rishyamukha, where he had met Hanuman for the first time.

"There is Lake Pampa, filled with lotuses where I was reminded of you so painfully and where we met the old lady ascetic, Shabari."

"O look Sita! He said, "There is our *ashrama* at Panchavati where you were so cruelly captured. There is the enchanting hut of leaves made for us by Lakshmana close to the holy river, Godavari. We abandoned it immediately after you were abducted for I could not bear to stay there without you." He remained silent for a few minutes reliving the painful scenes of that time and Sita buried her face on his shoulder and wept.

"Here is the delightful forest of Chitrakuta where we spent so many happy days together and where Bharata came to meet us. Now we come to Bharadvaja's *ashrama* which is at the most holy confluence of the divine Ganga with Yamuna and Saraswati."

Rama requested the Pushpaka to land. The sage was delighted to see them and Rama, who was starved for news of his people, was relieved to hear that all was well in Ayodhya. The sage also went over all the hardships he had undergone including Sita's capture and his killing of Ravana, for he had known everything by his divine powers. Bharadwaja requested Rama to stay for the day and proceed the next morning, so Rama told Hanuman.

"I cannot refuse the request of the sage so please proceed to Nandigrama and give Bharata all the news and that I am coming tomorrow. If his face shows the slightest disappointment at my return and any desire to keep the kingdom, please return and tell me. I will not stand in his way. Even the best of men may be tempted by riches at some time or other."

On his way to Ayodhya Hanuman stopped at the homestead of Guha, chief of the tribe who had helped Rama to cross the Ganga on his way to the forest and gave him the happy news. He then flew to Nandigrama and observed Bharata from the air. His hair was bound in matted locks on top of his head and he had a long, black beard; he was clad only in bark and the skin of a black antelope and was totally emaciated, for he had been subsisting on fruits and roots alone for fourteen years as his brother must have also done. He had undertaken to guard the kingdom till his brother returned and that he had done to the best of his ability. He ruled the country from the little village of Nandigrama outside Ayodhya. He kept Rama's wooden sandals on the throne and took his orders from them. He considered himself to be merely a regent. He seemed to be keeping alive, only for that purpose. In fact he looked like a *brahmarishi,* sitting with eyes half closed, absorbed in deep meditation. His lips were constantly murmuring "Rama, Rama!" Seeing his condition Maruti was overjoyed. Assuming the guise of a Brahmin, he approached in all humility, for he realised that he was in the presence of a truly superior human being, the very personification of *dharma*, one who had conquered his senses and who had no desire for worldly possessions and whose only thought was for Rama!

Hanuman repeated the name of Rama loudly in order to catch Bharata's attention. He immediately opened his eyes and looked at him in surprise.

Hanuman said, "O Prince! I bring you tidings of your brother, Rama, for whose sake you have donned this garb and for whose dear sake you have given up all thoughts of a happy, normal life which you could have well enjoyed. He for whose loss you sorrow night and day, the catalogue of whose virtues you are incessantly reciting, the glory of the line of Raghu, the benefactor of the pious, the deliverer of the saints, has arrived safely. After conquering his foes in battle, with the gods to hymn his praises, the Lord is now on his way with Sita and Lakshmana. He has sent me in advance to tell you that he will be arriving here very soon."

Now in order to test him, Hanuman said, "However, it is my duty to advice you. Why have you deprived yourself of the kingship, which your mother got for you with such difficulty? Why do you feel guilty about accepting the throne? This type of renunciation is only for weaklings!"

Bharata was horrified to hear the Brahmin's advice.

"Go away, you wicked Brahmin! Like my brother I too am an upholder of *dharma.* I would rather die than sacrifice it on the altar of ambition!"

Hanuman was very happy to hear this and revealed his true form to him and gave him the happy news of Rama's approach.

For fourteen years Bharata had been waiting for this moment and now when he heard the news he swooned with happiness. He recovered himself and embraced Hanuman and said, "I don't know who you are but you have brought me the happiest news of my life and thus you are my best friend. Many, many years ago my beloved brother went away to the forest and all these years I have been waiting only for his return. Tell me how I should reward you?"

Hanuman's eyes filled with tears to see such devotion. He had thought that he loved Rama more than any one else, but now it appeared that there were many who had the same adoration for Rama. "I am the son of the Wind God, a monkey, Hanuman by name, a servant of the glorious Raghupati."

On hearing this, Bharata rose up and embraced him. Tears were flowing unchecked down his cheeks and he could not contain his delight.

"O monkey! Now I remember you are the one who halted here when you were going on your way to get the magic herb to revive Lakshmana. Your very sight has dispelled my sorrows for today I have embraced a friend of Rama's. Now tell me of my Lord's adventures. Did my brother make mention of this poor servant?"

Hanuman was amazed at Bharata's humility.

"My Lord, you are as dear to Rama as his own life. Believe me this is the truth!" Hanuman now seated himself beside Bharata on the grass mat and told him all the details of Rama's life after leaving him. At last he told him that he had reached the *ashrama* of sage Bharadwaja and would be reaching Ayodhya shortly.

Bharata called Shatrugna and all the others and all of them made haste to prepare the city for Rama's arrival. The city of Ayodhya, which had been like a dead city all these years, suddenly blossomed to life. Once again banners and streamers flew from the battlements of the palace. Musicians re-strung their silent *vinas*. The trees burst into bloom and the streets were sprinkled with rose water and fried rice and decorated with auspicious signs. Once more the fountains started to play and the streams to run and the sound of laughter and rejoicing floated in the air. The citizens donned their best clothes, which had been locked away in their chests for fourteen years and thronged the streets. The ladies formed a procession singing and bearing golden salvers laden with curds, *dhruva* grass, turmeric paste, fruits, flowers and springs of the holy *tulsi* plant, and many other auspicious articles. The whole city waited in anticipation for the arrival of her rightful Lord. The king's highway leading from Nandigrama to the city was decorated with auspicious patterns, traced with coloured powder and sprinkled with rose water. Rama's sandals were kept on top of a caparisoned, white elephant, with the white umbrella of sovereignty held above it. Bharata and Shatrugna shaved their beards, cut their hair and dressed themselves in princely attire.

The dowager queens rose up in haste and eagerly questioned Bharata about Rama's welfare. He assured them that he was arriving soon.

Everything was ready and everyone was eagerly waiting when the *Pushpaka* reached the sacred village of Nandigrama in which the flame of devotion had been kept alight for fourteen years by Bharata. Many of the ladies crowded on the roof tops of houses in order to see the chariot as it descended. The chariot hovered for some time in the air so that Rama could point out the various familiar landmarks to the excited monkeys and *rakshasas*.

"There is Ayodhya, the city of my fathers and the citadel of the kings of the solar dynasty. This city is even more precious to me than Vaikunta, the abode of Vishnu. The dwellers here are indeed very dear to me. There is the river Sarayu which holds the land of Kosala in its embrace and there are my dear brothers, Bharata and Shatrugna, saluting me from below. Those are my mothers, Kausalya, Kaikeyi and Sumitra, who are standing on the palace ramparts."

At the very first sight of the aerial chariot, Hanuman shouted, "Here comes Sri Ramachandra!" The citizens took up the cry and soon the whole air was reverberating to the shouts of "Jai Sri Rama!"

As soon as the car landed, Rama got out and dropped his bow and arrows and went and fell at the feet of his preceptors, Vasishta and Vamadeva as well as the other Brahmins.

Bharata now rushed forward and fell full length at Rama's feet. Bharata could hardly speak when Rama asked about his welfare.

"I was sinking in an ocean of sorrow but now that I have seen you, all is well with me."

The brothers had a tender reunion, which brought tears to the eyes of the watching monkeys. Bharata took the sandals which were the virtual rulers of the state and placed them lovingly on his brother's holy feet and said,

"I give you back the kingdom which was given to me to look after. It was a great burden on me but I have guarded it carefully. Today my mother's name has been cleared and I have atoned for her sins. Please allow us to conduct the coronation which should have taken place fourteen years ago."

Sugriva and Vibhishana were touched to see this brotherly affection and pained by the thought of their own brothers, Vaali and Ravana, who had treated them so harshly.

Rama agreed to this and then sent the Pushpaka back to Kubera who was its rightful owner. The flower bedecked chariot slowly rose up into the air and circled Rama thrice and then floated away in a northerly direction. Rama turned to the citizens and personally greeted each and everyone of them, much to their delight. He then proceeded to the palace where the mothers were eagerly awaiting him. They embraced him in turn with eyes filled with tears of joy.

Urmila was Lakshmana's wife. The goddess of sleep had given her a boon that she would sleep for fourteen years while her husband was away. It is said that during this period Lakshmana did not sleep at all so that he could serve his brother night and day! As soon as Rama and Lakshmana reached the outskirts of Ayodhya, Urmila woke up from her long slumber and bedecked herself in order to meet her husband.

Rama and Lakshmana shaved off their matted locks and discarded their clothes of bark. The three mothers now gave them a ceremonial bath.

They washed away every trace of forest life on their bodies and anointed Rama with oil, sandal and turmeric paste. They bathed him in milk, curd, butter and perfumed water and bedecked him in yellow silk and adorned him with fragrant garlands and gem-studded ornaments of gold. Janaki was also lovingly bathed and dressed by Kausalya, Sumitra and Kaikeyi. She was clad in heavenly attire and every part of her body was adorned with jewels. Kausalya condescended to dress the hair of the wives of the *vanaras,* much to their delight.

Sumantra, the charioteer, now brought the royal chariot and Rama, and Sita ascended it and were taken in state to the main palace. Bharata asked Sumantra's permission and took over the reins of the chariot. Shatrugna held the white umbrella of royalty over Rama's head while Lakshmana and Vibhishana stood on either side and fanned him with the white-tailed *yak* fans. Hanuman knelt at his feet. Sugriva came at the back, riding on an elephant. The citizens who were lining the streets went mad with joy and shouted, "Jai Sri Rama! Jai Sita! Jai Lakshmana!" Thus, they arrived in state to the palace which had been occupied by the kings of the Ikshvaku dynasty for centuries. For the first time in fourteen years Rama entered a city. He had deliberately declined from entering any city all these years. He had not seen either Kishkinda or Lanka from the inside.

Rama then asked Bharata to prepare the best rooms in his own palace for Sugriva and Vibhishana to reside along with their wives. Bharata in turn requested Sugriva to send his people to bring waters from all the holy rivers and oceans of the land for the coronation. Five hundred monkeys sprang to do his bidding and brought water from five hundred different sources! Sage Vasishta was the *guru* of the solar dynasty and he was the one in charge of the whole function.

He made Rama sit on the jewelled throne of the Ikshvakus with Sita beside him. All the great sages poured the consecrated waters brought from all the sacred rivers and seas of the land, in golden pitchers, over Rama's head, to the accompaniment of sacred Vedic chants. Shatrugna held the white umbrella of sovereignty over his head. Lakshmana and Bharata stood on both sides and Sugriva and Vibhishana waved the royal yak-tail fans.

Hanuman sat at his feet and offered his paws as a footstool. Vasishta now crowned him with a crown studded with precious stones and fashioned by Brahma himself.

The Wind God came and presented Rama with a golden garland with hundred golden lotuses as well as a beautiful necklace of pearls. The gods and celestials stood in the sky watching the wonderful scene.

Rama now gifted a hundred thousand cows and horses to deserving Brahmins. To Sugriva he presented a golden garland studded with jewels and to Angada, the son of Vaali, a pair of lovely armlets made of diamonds, and other precious stones. He then gave Sita the pearl necklace given to him by Varuna, the god of the ocean, which had the lustre of moon-beams as well as many splendid garments and jewels. All the *vanaras* and *rakshasas* were also given many exotic gifts. However, he didn't give anything to Hanuman.

Sita now looked at Hanuman with great love and glanced enquiringly at her husband. Rama knew what was passing through her mind and told her, "O Janaki you are free to bestow the pearl necklace on the one whom you are most pleased with. Gift it to one who has all the qualities which you think a great hero should have – like fidelity, truth, skill, courtesy, foresight, prowess and good intellect."

Sita took out the precious necklace of pearls which Rama had given her and without a moment's hesitation she put it round the neck of the son of the Wind God. Hanuman bowed respectfully and returned to his seat.

He took out the necklace and started to examine it carefully. He smelt it and scratched it and put it to his nose and his ears as if listening to something. He then took each precious bead and cracked it with his teeth and peered into the shiny fragments before throwing it off as being worthless! Everyone was horrified at this terrible behaviour. "What an insult to the queen," said some. "What can you expect from a monkey?" asked another.

Sita couldn't bear to see such monkey-like behaviour on the part of one, whom she loved so much and who had done so much for her. She asked him to explain himself.

Hanuman looked surprised and replied, "To me the only thing worthy of respect is the name of Rama. Anything which does not have it, is worthless. I examined the beads to see if they had his name written anywhere, then I smelt it to see if his perfume was there and bit it to see if it contained anything of Rama inside, but there was nothing. This is only an ordinary pearl necklace and what use is such a thing for a monkey like me? My Lady! I am of course proud that you have chosen me as a fitting recipient for this signal honour but please forgive me for not wearing it."

The spectators were astonished by this statement and Sita asked him, "O Hanuman! What about your body? Is it not made up of the five elements? What does it have of Rama?"

Hanuman now asked Sugriva to keep his ears to his chest and to his amazement, Sugriva heard the continuous chanting of "Rama, Rama" coming from his heart.

Then, as if to put an end to further dispute, it is said that this great devotee of Rama split his chest open with his nails and to the astonishment of all, there was Rama enshrined within with Sita beside him! A great gasp of wonder rose up in the assembly and everyone shouted, "Jai Sri Rama! Jai Hanuman!"

Rama came down from his throne and embraced him warmly and placed his blessed hands on the wound, which healed miraculously at his touch. He then asked him to choose whatever gift he would like.

Hanuman replied, "My Lord! May my supreme affection for you live forever. May my devotion to you be constant. Let my love not be diverted to anything else. May life remain in my body as long as your story remains on the face of the earth. Let me imbibe the nectar of your stories so that I shall be able to ally my longing to see you in front of me. Let me be present whenever and wherever your name is chanted and your songs are sung. This is the only gift that I want." Rama placed his hands on Anjaneya's head and blessed him with all the boons he had requested.

"So shall it be, O prince of monkeys! There is no doubt that your fame will endure and life too will continue in your body as long as this story remains current in this world. My stories will abide as long as the world lasts. When I think of all the services you have rendered to me, Sita and Lakshmana, I should be prepared to give up my life for you here and now. But I prefer to remain in your debt forever O monkey! I pray that I will never get an occasion to repay you for all that you have done since normally one wants to be repaid only when one is in trouble!"

Rama then hugged Hanuman and blessed him over and over again.

He then presented each and everyone with some precious gift. No one was left out, not even the hunchback Mandara who was the sole cause of his having been banished from Ayodhya by poisoning the mind of Kaikeyi. The whole day long the citizens and the monkeys ate and drank to their heart's content. That night for the first time in fourteen years Lakshmana slept in the arms of his wife Urmila.

Rama wanted to confer the title of prince regent on Lakshmana but he steadfastly refused to play this role and insisted that the post belonged to Bharata alone.

The monkeys were in a state of bliss. They had quite forgotten their forest homes and continued to stay on with the Lord of their hearts. At last Rama called them to him and told them all to return to their homes and take up their allotted duties and maintain their devotion to him. Rama gave a jewelled robe to Sugriva and one to Vibhishana. Sorrowfully Sugriva and his brood of monkeys returned to Kishkinda and Vibhishana and his people to Lanka. Hanuman, however, opted to stay with Rama for he could not bear to be parted from him.

Rama *rajya* or the rule of Rama is famed over the whole world up to the present day as being a glorious one. There was no danger from beasts or snakes or fear of diseases. There were no robbers for everyone had enough. There were no untimely deaths and there were no widows. Every creature was happy and devoted to righteousness. People lived to a ripe old age without suffering from any decrepitude. The rod was never seen except in the hand of a *sannyasin,* the word "beat" had no meaning except to mark the time for a dancer and the only victory was over one's own self. The land flourished and the people were supremely happy for their worshipped Rama as god incarnate.

Nature gave lavishly of her bounty. The forests abounded with fruit trees and flowers. The elephant and tiger lived amicably together. Bees laden with honey droned and made pleasant sounds. The earth was clothed with crops and every river flowed with pellucid water.

"All affliction cease, all pain is erased,
When one recalls the mighty hero, Hanuman."

— *Hanuman Chalisa* by Tulsidas

ॐ *Sri Hanumathe Namaha!*

ॐ

Shubhangaaya Namaha!

CHAPTER TWENTY-NINE

SHUBANGANA

Dharma Triumphs

"Glory to Rama, the home of beauty,
The merciful, the refuge of the suppliant.
Equipped with quiver and bow and arrows,
Triumphing in his mighty strength of arms."

— *Ramacharitamanas* by Tulsidas

Soon after their return to Ayodhya, Hanuman requested Rama to accompany him to the Himalayas to meet his mother who was living an ascetic life absorbed in meditation and prayer. Rama agreed and they went to Anjana's hermitage. She was delighted to see them and welcomed Rama with all love and seated him on a special mat. Now she asked her son to tell her the whole episode of the war with Ravana, and the part he had played in it. Hanuman narrated the whole sequence of events. Strangely enough, the story didn't seem to impress her. As he kept describing his own part in it, her brow knitted and her face darkened. At last, she gave vent to her feelings and burst out.

"You are not worthy of being my son. You have disgraced your mother's milk. It looks as if my giving birth to you and feeding you with my milk has been of no use. Could you not have prevented the whole war by destroying the city of Lanka and killing Ravana by yourself? You could then have rescued the princess and brought her back to Rama and thus saved him the trouble of going there after undergoing so many hardships! I see that the milk you drank from my breasts has proved unfruitful. I am quite ashamed of you!"

Hanuman was amused by his mother's tirade and told her lovingly that he had only obeyed the orders given to him both by Rama and Sita.

"I would have been overstepping my limits as a servant had I rescued the princess of Videha. She was also of the opinion that her husband should come himself and rescue her after killing the ten-headed monster and thus saving his honour as a king!"

Anjana was a little mollified by this and said, "Ah! Then I'm happy that my milk did not go waste."

All those who were assembled there, especially Lakshmana was wondering what the potency of her milk was, upon which she kept harping. Understanding his unspoken question she said, "I will prove to you that my milk is indeed very special."

So saying she squeezed her breast so that a thin stream of milk arched through the air and fell on the summit of the hill opposite. There was a deafening crash as of thunder and to the amazement of the onlookers, the summit split in two!

She laughed and said, "Now, do you believe me? Maruti was brought up on this potent milk. Can you doubt his strength?"

The entire entourage returned after having spent some time with Anjana. Many years passed while Rama reigned in Ayodhya with Sita by his side, ably helped by his brothers and ministers and ever served by the faithful Hanuman. There are many stories connected with Maruti during this period which highlight other aspects of his unique personality. He was always seated at the feet of the royal couple, listening intently to every word they spoke. Pleased with his devotion, the divine pair revealed to him the secret of their incarnation.

Rama told Sita that Hanuman was now a worthy spiritual aspirant and deserved to be told the esoteric secrets of their incarnation.

Rama said, "Listen O monkey, carefully to what I have to tell you for you have proved yourself to be a fitting recipient to hear this abstruse truth. Know me to be the Supreme Purusha, the eternal, unchanging, infinite spirit. I am that one Supreme Consciousness, totally indivisible. Everything is in fact nothing but that Consciousness."

Sita then continued. "Know me to be Prakriti, cosmic matter, the supreme embodiment of all manifestation. I am the cradle of Time and Space and all things exist in me. Rama is the transcendent Absolute and I am his manifest power. I am that principle which performs all these apparent acts of creation, preservation and destruction. Actually all the events which have taken place till now are only the sport (*lila*) of the divine. They should not be confused with Rama's transcendent state which is changeless, eternal and imperishable."

Rama continued, "Together we constitute the universe. We validate each other's existence and delight in each other's company. I am the *Paramatman*, soul of the universe and Sita is the *jivatman,* the embodied soul. Ravana is the ego that separates these two entities. What unites them is *bhakti* or devotion. You are the embodiment of *bhakti* and hence this esoteric secret has been revealed to you."

Hanuman listened intently to this discourse. Next morning when he appeared in court, Rama asked him.

"Who are you?"

Maruti realised that the question was meant to test him and replied.

"From the point of view of the body I am your servant,

From the point of view of the mind and intellect I am a portion of you,

But from the point of view of the *atman* I am yourself!"

Rama and Sita were highly pleased with his beautiful explanation.

Sometimes Bharata and Shatrugna would take Hanuman to their own palaces and make him relate again and again all Rama's wonderful doings for they were never tired of listening to his amazing tales. But Hanuman would never stay long with anyone else. He would always contrive to return and sit at Rama's feet. He anticipated his every need and would do it before anyone else could.

This behaviour of his began to irritate Sita and his brothers who found that there was nothing left for them to do. At last Rama's brothers went to Sita and complained about the fact that due to Hanuman's amazing attentiveness there was nothing left for anyone else to do and they all wanted to serve Rama in some way. Sita had to agree that this was indeed true so they drew up a daily schedule of all the services to be performed for Rama. Each of them was given some task and nothing was left for Hanuman. This schedule was presented to Rama for his approval and seal. He was a bit suspicious since he noticed that Hanuman's name was not included. However, he didn't say anything. Next day, when the court assembled, Hanuman started to press Rama's feet as usual. Immediately Lakshmana pointed out to him that this task had been assigned to someone else. He then flourished the time schedule in front of his face. Hanuman was sadly disappointed to see that his name was nowhere in the picture. Lakshmana cheerfully told him that if any service had been omitted he could do it. Maruti inspected the document carefully and realised that every single thing from the time Rama got up till the time he went to bed had been allotted. At last he thought of a brilliant idea.

"I don't see yawning service," he said.

"What on earth is yawning service?" asked Lakshmana.

"You know when anyone yawns they normally snap their fingers in front of their open mouth in order to ward off evil spirits from entering, so I can take up that service and spare my Lord from the exertion of snapping his fingers!"

"Indeed why not?" asked Lakshmana.

"Well, then I want it in writing too with my Lord's seal on it."

Lakshmana promptly had this done but little did he realise the consequences of such a demand!

A yawn might come at any moment; therefore Maruti had to be with Rama all the time! He had to sit near him with his eyes fixed on his face so that he would never miss an opportunity to snap his fingers in the advent of a yawn! On that day he even ate with his left hand so as to leave the right free for a yawn! At night he went with Sita and Rama and tried to enter their bedroom but Sita was firm on this point and told him that he could go and rest. Hanuman was a bit sad since night is the time when most people yawn and he wanted to be sure to fulfil his part of the bargain. But what could he do? He went and sat on the balcony just above their bedroom and closed his eyes and started to repeat Rama's name so that he wouldn't sleep. In the meantime, he kept snapping his right hand fingers constantly so as to forestall any yawn that Rama might have. Inside the bedroom Rama found that he was hit by a mighty yawning fit which didn't seem to stop. Yawn after great yawn split his face into two. Soon he couldn't even close his mouth since the yawns kept coming one after the other. He collapsed on the bed in sheer exhaustion. Sita was terrified and called the physician, ministers and Vasishta, the royal *guru*. Nobody was able to do anything. Suddenly Vasishta noticed that one person was missing. He immediately set about searching for Hanuman. He was sure he couldn't be far off and sure enough he found him on the balcony intently repeating his *mantra* and snapping his fingers continuously. He shook him awake and brought him to Rama's presence. Maruti was devastated to see the condition of his master and inadvertently stopped snapping his fingers. The effect was immediate. Rama stopped yawning. Now, the whole story came out and Sita and the brothers were most contrite for they realised that they had done an injustice to this great devotee. All of them fell at Rama's feet and promised that henceforth the zealous monkey would be allowed to perform whatever service he wanted.

Hanuman was as attached to Sita as he was to Rama and would watch all her actions with great attention. Every morning he would observe Sita put a red mark on her forehead and smear the parting of her hair with vermilion powder, enacting a ritual which is the exclusive prerogative of married women in India. He was very curious to know the reason for this and asked her the reason behind this daily ritual.

"I do this for the well-being of my husband, as indeed all married women do," she said with a gentle smile. Hanuman, ever the humble well-wisher of his chosen lord wondered: "If a virtuous woman like Sita has to apply vermilion in this manner for the good of Lord Rama, I, a mere monkey, need to do more." Thinking thus he bounded off to the market in haste and bought a big sackful of vermilion powder. He mixed some oil and made a paste out of it and smeared his whole body with it. He entered the court and took his usual place at Rama's feet. Everyone was most amused to see his strange looks. Rama also glanced at him in some amusement and asked him why he had done this. Hanuman looked at him with tears in his eyes and said, "My Lord! May you live for as many years as there are hairs on this servant's body!" Sita immediately guessed the reason for his strange behaviour and whispered in her husband's ear. Needless to say, both Rama and Sita were moved by the purity of his heart. Rama got up from his throne and hugged him and said, "Today is Tuesday and anyone who offers oil and vermilion to my beloved servant on this day will be blessed by me and have his wishes granted." Since then, idols of Hanuman are coloured a rich vermilion red.

Since Sita had no children of her own she used to shower all her maternal affection on Hanuman. Normally he used to eat only Rama's leftovers. One day she decided to prepare something special for him. She made him sit and started feeding him with all the choice dishes she had prepared with her own hands. Hanuman was ravenous and the more she fed him the hungrier he became. Sita was a bit dismayed since all the food she had cooked was over. It was then that she realized that her "son" was actually the great Lord Maheswara who was capable of consuming the whole creation at the time of cosmic dissolution! She quietly went behind him and wrote the five-syllabled *mantra* of Lord Shiva at the back of his head (*Aum Namashivaaya*), thus acknowledging his true identity! Immediately Hanuman belched and thus showed that he was satiated and went and rinsed his mouth.

One day Hanuman was strolling through the market place when a foolish merchant called out to him. "Hey Maruti! Tell me what Lanka looked like when you burnt it?"

Hanuman replied that he couldn't describe it but was willing to demonstrate. He asked the merchant to wrap his tail in cloth, dip it in oil and set fire to it. As soon as he had done this Hanuman immediately set fire to the merchant's shop which burnt to the ground. He then went to a pool and put out his lighted tail.

The next day the merchant went to court and complained to Rama. "Your monkey destroyed my business!"

Rama asked Hanuman to explain his behaviour and he gave him a true account of the affair. When Rama asked the merchant if this was correct, he admitted it but added. "But I never expected him to burn my shop!"

"O! So you would have been happy to watch another person's shop burn?"

The man hung his head in shame and Rama dismissed the case.

Sometimes Hanuman would take the form of an ordinary monkey and raid the fruit gardens of Ayodhya. No one dared to do anything to him since they never knew if he was an ordinary monkey or Rama's favourite, Hanuman. He used to regularly raid one particular garden with luscious fruits, which some men had been tending carefully so that they could pluck the fruit when it was ripe. They were quite exasperated by the antics of this monkey and decided to catch and take him to court. If it happened to be Hanuman they knew that Rama would recompense them and if not they would be free to berate it as they thought fit. So, one day they set a trap and caught him and took him to court. Rama recognised him but pretended not to. He told the boys to take it back and give it whatever punishment they thought fit. Hanuman used his strength and broke out of the trap but before entering Rama's presence he caused huge welts to appear all over his body and hobbled into court with a doleful expression. Rama was filled with remorse when he saw him and hugged him. Hanuman then laughed and said,

"Well you played a joke on me by pretending you didn't recognise me so I also played a trick on you!"

One day in court, Rama decided to tease Hanuman. He wanted to know who his most devoted servant was. Naturally everyone raised their hands but Hanuman raised three by including his upraised tail which is actually another hand for a monkey. The other couriers were always a bit jealous of Hanuman so they devised a scheme of bringing up a proposal of marriage for Hanuman who they knew to be a lifelong celibate. What started as a joke turned out to be a serious test of obedience.

"O Maruti! Now that the war is over, isn't it time you gave up your celibate life and married and settled down?" Rama asked teasingly.

Hanuman knew that Rama was joking so he decided to play along with him and said, "My Lord! Which good looking woman would even look at me much less marry me?"

Rama promptly said, "If I find someone who is ready to marry you would you agree?"

Hanuman was in a dilemma. He was faced with an ethical crisis – his vow of celibacy as against his obedience to his Lord. "If the woman is perfectly agreeable well I suppose I will have to agree since it's your wish."

Someone said, "Since the boy is ill-formed the girl can be a hunchback and so I propose the hunchback Mandara, queen Kaikeyi's maid as a fitting bride!"

Hanuman was stunned and said, "My Lord! That woman sent you to the forest for fourteen years! Think of what she might do to me?"

Rama laughed and said, "Don't worry. She's a reformed woman now. We will summon her to court tomorrow and see if she agrees!"

Late in the night Hanuman went to Mandara's room and told her of the discussion which had taken place at court that morning. Surprisingly she seemed rather pleased at the idea and said that she would like to get married. If she couldn't get a man, a monkey was the next best bet. Maruti tried to talk her out of this but she was adamant. At last Hanuman lost his temper and grew to an enormous size and started choking her with his tail, to give her a taste of what marriage to him would be like! She was terrified and promised not to agree to the proposal when summoned to court. The next morning she appeared before the court and Rama put the suggestion to her. There was an expectant silence. Hanuman glared at her and she quickly turned down the offer. Hanuman breathed a sigh of relief and looked at Rama who was regarding him with a twinkle in his eye and he realised that the whole thing was a joke on his part.

One day Rama and Sita had an amicable argument as to which of them got greater devotion from Hanuman. They asked him outright but the wily monkey managed to get out of it by saying that he was devoted to both of them jointly – Sita-Rama. Sita promptly asked him to get her a pitcher of water since she was dying of thirst. Rama immediately countered by feigning a swoon due to the heat and begged Hanuman to fan him. They both waited expectantly to find out which request would be attended to first. The clever monkey expanded both his arms and fetched water with one hand while fanning Rama with the other. This placated both his divine masters.

Once the divine sage Narada, who was noted for his great devotion to Vishnu, visited Ayodhya and asked Hanuman if Rama kept a record of his greatest *bhaktas*. Hanuman wasn't too sure of this so the sage went and asked Rama himself. The Lord showed him a huge ledger in which Narada's name appeared on the top of the very first page. He was very pleased but after going through the pages he was puzzled at not finding Hanuman's name anywhere. He went and reported the matter to Hanuman who said, "Ask him to show you his little diary."

Narada returned and asked the Lord to show him this little book. In this he found that Hanuman was listed first and his own name was not to be found at all. Naturally he asked Rama about the difference between the two. The Lord replied that the large book was a record of all those worthy souls who remembered him all the time whereas the second book was a record of all those whom he remembered all the time! Narada's pride was duly humbled for he had always thought he was the greatest of all devotees.

Narada now enacted another drama to show the glory of the Lord's name. Once the king of Kashi was going to Ayodhya with his full retinue when he was stopped by the sage, who always loved to create some situations for the further play of the Lord. Narada told the king that when he reached the court, he should pay his respects to all the sages except Viswamitra. The king was not at all happy about this but was bound by his promise. Vishwamitra was noted for his volatile temper and was furious at the king's behaviour and complained to Rama. The Lord took out three arrows from his quiver and vowed to kill the king of Kashi before the end of the day. This news reached the king who was terrified and ran to Narada and told him to save him since the whole fault was his. Narada cheerfully replied that he could not hope for a better death than at the hands of Rama. The king was not impressed by this and ran to the river to hide himself from Rama's wrath. Narada followed him and told him not to worry and he would save him. He told him to sit on his lute and he would carry him to the Kanchana Mountain.

"Who is there in that mountain that will be able to save me from Rama's wrath?"

"Hanuman's mother, Anjana, is doing *tapas* there. Throw yourself at her feet and beg her to save you. Don't get up till she gives her word."

As instructed the king threw himself at the feet of Anjana and begged her to save him from imminent death. She promised him asylum and told him that no one could harm him in her presence. Then she asked him to name the person from whom he was running.

At last the king whispered, "Rama is the one who has sworn to kill me before the day is over!"

"Rama!" Exclaimed Anjana, "He is the soul of compassion! What crime have you committed to make him take such an oath?"

The poor king related the whole incident. Anjana then decided to invoke her son since she had given her word to the king to protect him. Just at this time Hanuman also arrived to meet his mother.

She was really happy to see him and told him that she was in a great dilemma and begged him to rescue her. Hanuman immediately agreed to take care of it whatever it might be but she made him give his word three times before she disclosed the secret. Naturally Hanuman was astounded to hear the whole story but having promised his mother he had no other go but to do so. He immediately transported the King of Kashi to the banks of the Sarayu River which encircled the city of Ayodhya. He told him to stand waist deep in the water and continuously chant the name of Rama.

"Remember, you must never get out of the water till I tell you and you must never stop chanting "Rama, Rama."

The unhappy king had no other recourse but to give his promise. Hanuman now went post haste to Rama and prostrated before him humbly.

Rama looked at him enquiringly and asked, "Is there something you want?"

Hanuman said, "My Lord, please give me your word that I will always be able to protect those who are chanting your name."

"My dearest Maruti! I have already given you this boon. Why are you asking for it again?"

Hanuman insisted that he give his word once again and Rama laughingly obliged. Anjaneya now returned to the river and stood with upraised mace, ready to protect the king of Kashi who was devotedly chanting Rama's name loudly and clearly. Very soon the news spread that the one whom Rama had sworn to kill before nightfall was being guarded by no less a personage than Hanuman himself!!

Rama soon learnt of the whereabouts of the king and went to the river accompanied by the sage, Vishwamitra. Hanuman saw him coming and warned the king to keep chanting relentlessly whatever happened. Rama fixed his arrow on the bow and shot it at the king. The arrow however went round the king and returned to his quiver. Rama was astonished to hear a voice from the arrow, "My Lord! I can't kill someone who is chanting your name while Hanuman is around."

Rama refused to listen to this and sent another arrow which also returned and said, "O King! You have given your word to your devotee that anyone that chants your name will be protected by him. We are only helping you to keep to your word."

Vishwamitra was getting angry by this time so Rama fitted his third arrow to the bow. Hanuman warned the king of Kashi to repeat the sacred *mantra* without even pausing for breath. The king's teeth were chattering with cold but he repeated the *mantra* continuously.

Just as Rama fitted his third arrow, his family *guru,* Vasishta arrived on the scene and begged Hanuman to stand aside and allow Rama to redeem his pledge.

"The king will attain heaven if he dies at the hands of Rama, so don't try to thwart him."

Hanuman said, "But I am indeed redeeming Rama's pledge to me that I can save anyone who chants his name!"

Vasishta was puzzled as to how this dilemma could be solved. He decided that the only one who could do it was Vishwamitra. So he went to him and begged him to forgive the king of Kashi and let Rama off his pledge. Vishwamitra said that he was prepared to do so if the king fell at his feet and promised never to insult anyone in future especially a sage.

Hanuman told his protégé to get out of the river and throw himself at the sage's feet. The king was shivering so much that he could hardly get out of the river. Still repeating the name of Rama he went and prostrated full length at the feet of Vishwamitra. He clutched his feet and begged him to forgive him since the whole thing was a drama planned by the sage, Narada who had a curious sense of humour and who was even now watching the whole scene with great amusement.

Vasishta now told Rama to keep his third arrow back in its quiver. Rama did so just as the sun slipped below the western horizon. Hanuman fell at the feet of his master and begged him to forgive him. All he wanted to do was to prove to the world the glory of the Lord's name.

There is another story with the same theme which is well worth mentioning here.

The king of Kashi was called Yayati. He was a great *bhakta* of Rama. Once when he had gone hunting, he met the great sage, Vishwamitra and failed to do reverence to him in his eagerness of the chase. The sage as is to be expected cursed him, "I'll see to it that your head falls at my feet!"

Yayati ran after the sage and begged his pardon and told him that he was quite innocent of the whole affair and had been too engrossed in the chase and had not seen him. Vishwamitra was not to be appeased and went straight to Ayodhya and told Rama.

"O Rama! If you are my true disciple you should see to it that the head of the one who insulted me is brought to my feet!"

"My Lord who is it that has dared to insult you. Name him and I shall do your bidding immediately."

When Rama heard the name of Yayati, he was shocked for he knew that he was his true devotee but after considering the matter carefully he decided that it was his duty to obey his *guru's* commands. He sent his minister to Kashi and commanded the king to be ready to have a duel with him. The king did not know what to do but he decided that it was his duty to obey his Lord so he started off towards Ayodhya so as to spare Rama the trouble of coming to him. En route he was met by the divine sage, Narada who was always on the look out to see more of the Lord's *lilas.* The sage knew that the whole of life was indeed a game of the Supreme and he always did his bit to give interesting twists to the drama of life.

"O King!" He said, "I see that you are proceeding towards Ayodhya in order to spare the Lord the trouble of coming to you. But why do you give in so easily? Don't you want to save your life?"

The poor king nodded his head miserably and said that he didn't know what he should do in this predicament and was hoping to persuade Rama that he was innocent.

Narada said, "Rama knows that but he has sworn to do as his *guru* commands so I advise you strongly not to go to Ayodhya."

"What should I do then?" Asked the desperate king.

"You should go to the mountain of Kanchana and take refuge at the feet of Anjana, the mother of Anjaneya. She is the only one who will be able to help you."

"Now we will see some fun," thought Narada as he proceeded towards Anjana's *ashrama.*

Yayati also went as fast as he could to Anjana's *ashrama* and fell at her feet and begged her to give him sanctuary. She told him not to be frightened and that no one would be able to hurt him in that place. She then thought of her son and asked him to come to her aid.

Hanuman was disturbed by these mental vibrations of his mother and immediately came to her hermitage.

He bowed to her and to the king of Kashi whom he recognised as a great devotee of Rama and asked his mother why she had summoned him. She explained the whole matter to him. Hanuman also promised to protect the king. It was only then that they thought of asking him who his adversary was. When he heard the name of "Rama," both Hanuman and Anjana got a shock. They didn't know what to do but Anjana begged her son to back her word even if it meant fighting with his beloved Rama. Narada also arrived on the scene, strumming his lute and looking quite delighted.

Both Rama and Vishwamitra arrived soon after on the scene. Hanuman kept the king behind him and told Rama that his mother had afforded him protection and he was bound to keep his mother's word.

God and devotee stood looking at each other. At last Rama took up his fire missiles and flung it at Hanuman. However, Anjaneya simply absorbed it as well as all the other missiles. Nothing seemed to affect him. At last Rama took up his famous arrow and said, "I have no recourse but to use this. Prove that you are my devotee and deliver king Yayati to me for I have to keep my word to my *guru*."

Hanuman replied, "My Lord! I am indeed your true devotee and disciple, so I have to keep my promise to my mother. Here is my breast. Please shoot your arrow at me."

So saying he bared his breast and stood with closed eyes repeating the Rama *mantra.*

The arrow flew unerringly and split Maruti's breast and disappeared into his heart. To everyone's amazement within his throbbing heart, they saw Rama and Sita enshrined.

Narada now went to the king and told him to run and lay his head at Vishwamitra's feet. This was the right moment to save himself. Even though he was frightened to show himself, the king obeyed the sage and ran and put his head on Vishwamitra's feet and begged him to forgive him for whatever sin he might have unknowingly committed.

Rama turned round ready to take Yayati's head but Narada stopped him and said,

"My Lord, please desist from killing Yayati. Your *guru's* curse has been fulfilled. All he told you was to lay the king's head at his feet and this has been done. So you are not guilty of going against your *guru's* command."

Rama looked enquiringly at Vishwamitra who was already regretting his hasty action and had forgiven the king long ago. The sage said, "Narada is right, O Rama. The king's head is at my feet so please consider that you have obeyed my command."

Rama put his arrow back into the quiver and turned to Hanuman and said, "O Anjaneya! You have conquered me. You are indeed my true devotee. In order to keep your word you were even prepared to fight with me. In future you will be known as "Veera Hanuman".

Hanuman bowed at Rama's feet and said, "It is you who have conquered me, my Lord from the day you first cast your gracious glance over me. You are ever in my heart and it is you yourself who intercepted the arrow sent by you and saved me. I had nothing to do in this matter."

There is another story about Hanuman proving the superiority of the Lord's name.

Once it is said that Rama picked up his bow to kill a person called Kuvachana who had insulted his ancestors. He immediately sought Hanuman's protection. Without going into the nature of his crime Hanuman promised to defend him at any cost.

When he saw Rama approaching, bow in hand, he realised he had been tricked. Since he had given his word, he placed himself, arms akimbo between Rama and Kuvachana.

Chanting the name of Rama, Hanuman created an enclosure round Kuvachana with his tail. The enclosure reverberated with the sound of the Rama *mantra*. Try as he might, Rama himself could not breach this fortress.

"More powerful than Rama is the name of Rama," murmured Hanuman.

The gods intervened to end the stalemate. Rama was allowed to kill Kuvachana to avenge the insult to his ancestors. Hanuman was allowed to bring Kuvachana back to life with the power of Rama's name!

"Whoever brings any yearning to you,
Obtains the fruit of immortal life."

— *Sri Hanuman Chalisa* by Tulsidas

ॐ *Sri Hanumathe Namaha!*

ॐ

Samsara-bhayanashanaaya Namaha!

CHAPTER THIRTY

VEERA

Sita Abandoned

"Again and again I beg of thee a boon,
Be gracious and grant it – an unwavering faith in thy lotus feet,
And constant communion with the saints,"

— *Ramacharitamanas* by Tulsidas

It is in the last book known as "Uttara Kanda" that Valmiki recounts the previous history of Ravana, the king of the night wanderers. It is also in this book that the painful episode of Rama's repudiation of Sita is told. We may well wonder at the intention of the sage in doing this. Maybe he wanted to compare the polaric differences in the towering personalities of the two men, both of whom loved Sita so passionately. One was the lusty, powerful, *rakshasa* – Ravana who was prepared to exterminate his entire race, his brothers, his friends and even his own sons, in order to quench his infatuation for another man's wife! The other was the divine personality of Rama, who made the heart-rending decision to subdue his passion for his lawfully wedded wife and place his duty to his subjects first – who was prepared to sacrifice the one he loved most, on the altar of the cosmic law of *dharma*, which proclaims that a king should put god first, his country next and his own personal desire last. Ravana perished along with the rest of his tribe while the land of Kosala flourished under the rule of its saintly king!

Sages from all over the land used to come to Ayodhya in order to bless Rama and Sita. He seated them on golden thrones and gave all hospitality to them. Once he questioned them on Ravana's history. How had he become so powerful and what was the story behind his son, Meghanatha and so on.

Agastya now gave the whole story of Ravana. He had been a great devotee of Shiva. He had done great *tapas* to Brahma and got many boons from him. He had asked for invincibility from all types of gods, demons, animals and celestials but he had forgotten to add humans and monkeys in his list. Having got all these boons, he became very arrogant and fought with everyone including the gods. In his pride he even tried to lift up Mount Kailasa but Shiva pressed the mountain down with his big toe so that Ravana's hand was smashed under it. It was then that he composed the famous hymn to Shiva known as *Shiva Thandava Stotra*, which pleased Shiva so much that he released his hand and gave him many other boons.

When he was returning he saw a very beautiful lady anchorite staying in an *ashrama.* She had no ornaments and was clad in bark with matted hair and was doing intense *tapas.* Despite her lack of embellishments, she was very beautiful and Ravana was not one who could resist a woman's beauty. He approached her and asked her who she was and why she was doing *tapas.*

She replied, "My name is Vedavati and I am the grand-daughter of Brihaspati, the preceptor of the gods. My father refused all other offers of marriage for me and insisted that I should do *tapasya* in order to get Vishnu as my husband. My parents were killed by a demon and ever since then I have been practising austerities in order to get Vishnu as my husband."

Ravana laughed in scorn and said, "How stupid your father was and how stupid you are to follow his foolish advice and waste your youth. I am as great as or even greater than Vishnu and you would do well to become my wife." So saying he made a lunge at her. She ran for her life but he followed her and grabbed her by her hair. She managed to free herself and said,

"O you monster! I will give up this body which has been defiled by you. But I will take another body which will eventually bring you to ruin." So saying she gave up her life in front of his eyes.

The sages told Rama, "That Vedavati was born as Sita and you are the *avatara* of Vishnu."

Agastya then told Rama another story about Ravana which was the reason why he abducted Sita. Ravana had done a number of good things in his life and was a fitting recipient to go to heaven but due to his atrocities, all the good he had done was negated. Once during the *Yuga* known as Satya, Ravana had asked the great sage, Sanat Kumara to tell him which of the trinity was capable of giving liberation. The sage told him that Vishnu was certainly the one who could liberate. Anyone who was killed by Vishnu would attain instant emancipation. Ravana's eyes gleamed with interest when he heard this. He asked Sanat Kumara to tell him which was the next incarnation of Vishnu so that he could somehow see to it that he was killed by him. The sage told him that in the *Yuga* known as Treta, Vishnu would be incarnated as Rama, scion of the race of Ikshvaku and Lakshmi would take birth as the daughter of the king of Videha and marry him.

Ravana pondered over this matter and decided that the only way he could get liberation through Vishnu in his form as Rama was to make him so angry that he would be forced to kill him. The best way of making him angry was to abduct his wife. Agastya told Rama that this was the secret behind Ravana's abduction of Sita! He also gave him all the other details about the past lives of his son Meghanatha and his wife Mandodari. Thus, all the intricate threads which were woven by destiny to make up the tapestry of their lives, were revealed to Rama.

Many years passed while Rama reigned with Sita by his side, helped by his able ministers and beloved brothers. Once when he was sitting with his three brothers and Hanuman, Bharata wanted to put a question to him but he asked Hanuman to speak for him since he was known to be Rama's favourite.

"My Lord!" said Maruti, "Bharata wants to ask you to dilate on the difference in behaviour of the noble and the wicked."

Rama replied, "The difference in the conduct of the good and the wicked is like the difference between sandal wood and the axe. The fragrant wood imparts its perfume even to the very axe that fells it! For this reason the sandal wood is desired by all and has the honour of being put on the head of the gods. The axe, on the other hand, has its edge heated in the fire and then hammered till it becomes flat!"

"O brother! There is no religion like charity and no sin like hatred. There are many types of sinful and noble acts which people might do but the truly noble look on everything with an equal and loving eye."

His brothers and Hanuman were thrilled to hear his words.

There was an *ashoka* grove next to the palace, which was even more beautiful than the one in Lanka. Flowering trees like the *champaka*, *kadamba*, *ashoka* and *sandal* were there and fruit trees like mango and pomegranate. After finishing his day's work, Rama would often walk in these fragrant gardens with his adorable queen. One day while they were thus sitting in the grove and talking to each other, Rama noticed that his wife showed all signs of pregnancy. She was wearing a glistening red robe and her skin glowed with an ethereal beauty. Rama was delighted to see this and taking both her hands in his, he led her gently to an arbour in the grove and seated her tenderly on a jewelled seat. He offered her a golden goblet with the nectar of many flowers, untouched by bees. With his own hands he raised the glass to her lips and made her sip the delightful concoction. He embraced his alluring wife with great love and asked her.

"My darling one! How radiant you look. I see that you are with child. A son is the only thing that we lack in our lives. I have no doubt that the child will be a wonderful infant. Tell me, my dearest love, how can I make you happier? Is there some wish of yours which is still to be fulfilled? Ask for anything and it shall be yours."

Sita raised her lotus face to his and whispered, "My Lord, I consider myself to be the luckiest woman alive. What further wish can your wife have, than to be beside you always?"

But Rama insisted, "My lovely one, I want to make you even happier than you are now, if that were possible. Tell me something I can do for you. I am longing to shower you with everything, for it is said that a pregnant woman should have all her whims humoured."

Sita smiled and looked at him with her fawn-like eyes, "Do you remember the forest near Chitrakuta where we used to wander hand in hand? Do you remember the sages and their wives and the peace of their hermitages? I have a great desire to go and visit them once again and eat the wild fruits and roots and drink the pure water of the Ganga and perhaps even stay there for a day or two."

Rama looked adoringly at his beloved wife. There was nothing he could deny her. If anything his love for her had increased with the passing years. He had never felt the desire to take another consort, as the rest of the kings used to do. In fact the very idea was abhorrent to him. Sita was the most charming woman he had ever known and he desired none other.

Holding her hands in his, he gazed at her doe-like eyes and said, "O Vaidehi! My beloved wife, you shall certainly go there if that is what you wish. In fact, I will see that you are taken there tomorrow."

Having given his promise to his queen, Rama left her and went to the outer courtyard to talk with his friends and Sita went to her own apartments where she was surprised to see her new hand maiden waiting for her. Actually this woman was none other than Ravana's sister, Surpanekha, who had slipped into the palace under the guise of a maid and was plotting to avenge her brother's death.

She had endeared herself to Sita and now when she saw her, she playfully asked her to describe what Ravana looked like.

Sita said, "I've no idea what Ravana looked like since I never saw his face. I once saw his shadow as it was cast on the sea on the way to Lanka."

The woman now begged Sita to draw this shadow on the wall and Sita innocently did so. As soon as Sita left the room, Surpanekha completed the drawing and slipped out of the palace. She took good care to spread the news of the painting of Ravana on the wall of Sita's private apartment. Of course people are ever ready to see evil in their rulers so the gossip mongers lapped up the tale and embellished it with their own data!

After leaving Sita in the garden, Rama had gone to the outer courtyard to speak to his close friends. In the course of their light banter, he turned to his friend Bhadra and asked, "Tell me Bhadra, what do the citizens of Ayodhya say about me and Sita and my brothers? Kings are always a butt of criticism for the common folk and it's always wise to know what they think."

Bhadra folded his palms and said, "Sire, people speak only well about you. Sometimes they discuss the events of the past years, when you achieved the impossible by killing the ten-headed demon and rescuing the princess of Videha. Your exploits are recounted with great enthusiasm by everyone."

"What else do they say, Bhadra? Tell me all. Why do you avert your face? Is there something which you feel should not be reported to me? Have no fear. I want to know the good and the bad. No king can afford to ignore what people say of him, so tell me everything frankly."

In a low, faltering tone, Bhadra said, "They also remark that though your action in having killed the *rakshasa* was laudable, your conduct with regard to your wife is shameful. 'How could the king have accepted a woman who had been kept on Ravana's lap and who had lived in his palace for so many months? How can the queen forget the indignities she must have suffered? We will have to put up with a similar conduct from our wives. They will be able to go from one man to another as they please and we will be forced to condone them. As the king so the subjects!' This is what the people say, in their ignorance."

Rama's whole face changed when he heard this slanderous accusation against him and his immaculate wife. He could not utter a word. His friends tried to comfort him and said, "Your Majesty! It is the nature of the common people to speak ill of the nobility. A king need not pay heed to such vile accusations."

Rama hardly heard what they were saying. Taking leave of them in his usual, courteous manner, he went to the garden and sat immersed in thought. He decided that it was his duty to check on this matter before coming to a decision. That evening he wore the clothes of an ordinary citizen of Ayodhya and went incognito on a tour of the city. As luck would have it, as he passed the house of a washer man, in one of the back streets of the city, he heard the sound of a man's voice raised in anger. He went close to the door and stood outside listening. The husband was berating his wife.

"I have heard reports of your indecent behaviour. You have been seen talking to the nobleman who comes for a walk down this street. You may go back to your own home. I will not keep you here any longer. I belong to a respectable family and will not keep a loose woman as my wife. You are free to go where you please."

The poor woman pleaded that she was totally innocent and had only answered some questions the man had put to her. The washerman replied sternly, "Do you think I am Rama to tolerate such behaviour? He is the king and can do as he pleases. As for me, I will never keep a wife who has been seen talking with another man."

Rama stood riveted to the spot for a few seconds. He felt like a tree which had been struck by lightning. The tender buds and leaves of hope which had sprouted in his heart after their return from Lanka were scorched and the naked, charred and blackened branches raised their arms, in mute appeal to the heavens. He felt as if his whole body was on fire. He managed somehow to stagger back to the palace. He went to his private chamber and requested his brothers to come to him at once. They came immediately and were surprised to see his demeanour. He stood with his back to the door, gazing out on a wintry garden. His face was pale and his eyes had a glazed look as he turned round to face his brothers. His hands trembled slightly.

Lakshmana knelt before him and said, "Brother, what is it? Tell me. Where is the enemy? You know that you have but to command and I shall obey."

Rama spoke in a voice which was drained of all emotion, "Do you know what the citizens are saying about Sita and me?"

All of them hung their heads and Rama continued, "I see that all of you know and have hidden the truth from me all these years. O Lakshmana! You were a witness to the fact that I refused to take her back after the war until her purity was proved by the ordeal in the fire. Yet, these people now talk as if I have done a heinous crime. My heart is breaking and I am drowning in sorrow, yet my duty as a king is clear to me. The first duty of a king is to his subjects and not to himself. Sita is dearer to me than life itself but I have no choice but to abandon her for the sake of my subjects.

Lakshmana, take her away in the chariot with Sumantra, and leave her on the other side of the Ganga near the Tamasa River, where we stayed a long time ago. Just yesterday morning she requested me to take her there. Let her have her wish. She will suspect nothing."

Lakshmana jumped to his feet and said, "Brother, you cannot do this to her! She is burnished gold, purified by fire. Please do not ask me to do this. I will do anything else you ask but not this. Don't you know that she is carrying your child in her womb? How can you bear to do this? Can you not wait at least till the child is born?"

His face carved out of stone, Rama said in a stern voice, "After the child is born you will say, let her stay while she suckles the infant and then you'll say, let her stay till he is five years old and thus it will go on indefinitely and eventually Rama would have betrayed his country for the sake of his own felicity."

Bharata and Shatrugna also added their pleas.

Rama continued in a hard, loud voice, "I do not want to hear another word from any of you. I want none of your advice, I am your king and I demand implicit obedience."

For a few stunned moments there was absolute silence, except for Rama's heavy breathing due to his effort to suppress an emotion which threatened to overpower him.

At last, ashen in hue and a mask-like face he said, "Go Lakshmana! Leave her in a secluded spot on the banks of the Tamasa River, near the holy Ganga close to some hermitage and return immediately. Don't wait to talk to her. Don't try to explain anything. Let her think the worst of me or else she will die of a broken heart. Don't look at me so accusingly. Anyone who objects to my decision is my enemy. Take her away this very instant, O Lakshmana! If I see her even once, I am doomed. I will be unable to carry out my own command. If I see her fawn-like gaze fixed on me with a beseeching look, I will be lost and not all the slander in the world will enable me to let her go. So go now, before my heart fails me, before emotion weakens my adamantine resolve. Why do you hesitate? It is I, the king of the country who is commanding you."

His brothers could not speak a word. Lakshmana cursed his luck for having been chosen to carry out this terrible command.

His eyes brimming with tears, Rama stumbled out of the room and went to an enclosed spot in the garden where he would not be able to see Sita.

He spent the night in the garden, keeping a lonely vigil with the stars. If he went to his room and took his beloved in his arms, he knew that he would never be able to let her go.

Who knew what bitter thoughts passed through his mind but he was firm in his resolve. *Dharma* was his god and to *dharma* he was prepared to sacrifice his beloved queen and his unborn child. Sita slept alone that night. She wondered at her Lord's absence but then she thought it must have been because he was held up with some official matters. Like a child, she was excited at the thought of the treat in store for her on the morrow. Some of the happiest moments of her life had been spent in the forest with her loving husband and she was eagerly looking forward to spending at least another night in the hermitage with the loving wives of the sages. She had already tied up a small bundle of gifts for the *ashramites* and their wives, and she was ready to go when Lakshmana arrived and knocked at the door.

Without looking at her, he said in a voice which was totally drained of emotion, "The king, your husband, has commanded me to fulfil your desire to visit the Ganga and the hermitages of the sages. Are you ready to leave?"

Sita was delighted and happily accompanied him to the waiting chariot. It was a grim twosome which set out in the pearly mist of the morn. Neither Sumantra nor Lakshmana could speak a word or even look at her. Sita alone was full of cheer. She turned around for a last look at the sleeping town, not realising that it was indeed, her last look. Suddenly her heart had misgivings.

Everywhere she saw ill omens. Her right side and eye were witching and she felt weak all of a sudden.

In an agitated voice, she asked, "O son of Sumitra! Tell me, is all well with your brother? I have not seen him this morning or in the night. Where was he? I fear something inauspicious has happened."

In a choking voice Lakshmana answered, "The king, your husband, is quite well. He gave orders that you should have an undisturbed night since you had to undertake a strenuous journey in the morning. He told me to wish you well." More than that he could not say.

By afternoon they reached the banks of the river Gomati and camped at one of the *ashrams*. Next morning they went forward in the chariot and reached the banks of the holy river. Here Lakshmana could contain himself no longer and broke down and wept like a child.

"Why are you crying Lakshmana?" asked Sita. "You are making me nervous. I have been longing to come here and now that you have brought me here, you make me sad, by your weeping. Is it because you have been parted from Rama for two days? Then what about me? How much should I cry? I cannot endure life without him. Come, let us hurry and go to the *ashrams* and distribute our gifts and then we will return. I too am beginning to feel uneasy. I fear something is wrong with my Lord."

Wiping his eyes, Lakshmana brought a boat and escorted Sita to the opposite bank. He then fell at her feet and sobbed his heart out. Sumantra stood on the side, shedding silent tears. Sita was really disturbed at the sight.

"Tell me Lakshmana, what is the matter? Has something happened to my dear husband? Why didn't he come with us? I was hoping he would also come." Till the end, her one thought was for him, who was her all. She never dreamt that the misfortune which the omens foretold was meant for her.

Eyes blinded with tears, Lakshmana looked pleadingly at her. "My noble queen! Forgive me for what I have to do. Rama has entrusted me with the ignoble task of abandoning you here. Better for me to have died rather than carry out this command." So saying he prostrated himself before her.

Sita bent down and gently lifted him up, "What is it Lakshmana? What are you trying to tell me? What is the reason for my husband's sudden decision?" She could not believe that she was hearing rightly.

"Rumours are afloat everywhere, dear lady, about you and about him. I cannot tell you all. He forbade me to tell you anything. All I can say is that his heart broke when he heard the vile accusations against you. But he is the king. He is *dharma* incarnate. The king's duty is always to safeguard the interests of his subjects. Forgive him and forgive me also, O gracious queen of Ayodhya! I can say no more. Night is fast approaching. How can I bear to leave you here, all alone, with none to protect you? Rama never left you even for a minute, without asking me to guard you. The only time we both left you, was when the wicked king of the *rakshasas* came and abducted you. Now who is there to look after you? May your mother, the earth, give you all protection. May the sky be your canopy. May this holy river look after all your wants. Remember, My Lady, you are carrying the seed of the Ikshvaku line in your womb. It is your duty to safeguard it at all times."

Lakshmana feared that in her agony, Sita might put an end to her life.

Sita looked like a frightened deer, listening to Lakshmana's words and then said in a bewildered tone, "What sin have I committed, that for no reason of mine, my husband should repudiate me, twice? Surely I was born for sorrow. Grief alone seems to be my constant companion. Patiently I have to look at his forlorn face. Leaving my all, I followed my husband to the forest, inhabited by wild animals and demons. No woman would have done as I did; and now he has abandoned me. Was it my fault, that the *rakshasa* abducted me? When the sages ask me what crime I have committed, that my husband should abandon me, what should I tell them, O Lakshmana? What wrong have I done? I cannot even take the easy path of ending my life in this holy river, for I will be guilty of breaking the noble line of the Ikshvaku race. Lakshmana, do not grieve. Leave me here and return to the king, my husband, and tell him that his wife wishes him well. A husband is a woman's god and I have always considered him as such. May he find eternal fame by following the *dharma* of a king. More important than my suffering is that his honour should remain intact. Never will Sita be guilty of bringing dishonour to Rama. Farewell Lakshmana. You have been more than a brother to me. I have deep regard for you. I hold nothing against you. The shades of night are falling fast and you must go, lest my Lord becomes agitated."

Lakshmana fell at her feet once more. He could not speak a word. Slowly he backed his way to the boat and was ferried to the other shore. He turned back to look at her once again and saw her lying on the ground, on the bosom of her mother, weeping as if her heart would break.

Sita looked up and saw the chariot receding into the distance. The plaintive cry of the peacock calling to its mate, jarred on her delicate nerves.

The Ganga flowed smoothly on, as if to comfort her in her agony. She gazed mesmerised, by the glistening water and wondered what it would feel like to have it close over her head like a balm, but then she felt the life within her move and she knew that she could not take the easy way out.

"Victory, victory, victory to Lord Hanuman,
Be merciful even as is the master,"

— *Sri Hanuman Chalisa* by Tulsidas

ॐ *Sri Hanumathe Namaha!*

ॐ

Ramayana-priyaaya Namaha!

CHAPTER THIRTY-ONE

RAMAPRIYAN

The Ramayana

"As a word and its meaning are inseparable,
And a wave cannot be distinguished from the water,
So Rama and Sita, the refuge of the distressed,
Whom I adore."

— *Ramacharitamanas* by Tulsidas

The hermitage of the sage Valmiki was very close to where Sita had been abandoned. That morning when he had gone to the river for his morning ablutions, he happened to see two cranes mating. He gazed with joy at their spontaneous love for each other. Just then a fowler aimed a fatal arrow at the male bird and shot him, contrary to all the rules of *dharma.* Pierced by that cruel arrow, in the midst of the act of love, the bird fell to the ground with a hear-rending cry. Wrenched from her lover, the female bird screamed piteously. Beating her breast with her wings, she fluttered around, terrified and bewildered. Her piteous cries brought a gush of compassion in the heart of the sage and he cursed the fowler. As soon as the curse left his lips, he felt great remorse. He was horrified that his compassion for the bird had made him break his vow of non-violence. The fowler was after all only a helpless victim of his own *karma.* He felt very unhappy about the whole episode. Then he realised that that curse had flowed from his lips in a spontaneous verse of four lines with eight syllables. He was struck by the beauty of the verse and told his disciple to memorise it. The sage then continued with his interrupted ablutions and retuned to his *ashrama.* That evening two young *brahmacharis* ran to him and told him that a beautiful woman had been abandoned near the river and appeared to be contemplating jumping into it and ending her life. Valmiki ran to the river and knew that this was Sita, the wife of Rama, as told by Narada. He escorted her home and told the wives of the sages to look after her for she was carrying the heir to the throne of the Ikshvakus.

Later, when he sat for meditation, he was still filled with remorse over the episode of the two cranes and his involuntary curse of the hunter. Brahma, the creator appeared to him and told him not to brood over the strange event because from this incident would arise the inspiration to narrate the story of Rama and Sita.

Brahma spoke, "You will be inspired O sage, to compose a most memorable poem on the exploits of Rama. His whole life will be revealed to you. Everything that you say in your poem will be based on facts which you have witnessed. You will be able to see each and every one of the glorious episodes in the life of this great *avatara* of Vishnu. You will become famous as the *adi kavi* – the first of all poets. The story of Rama will endure as long as these mountains and rivers stay on the face of this earth. Your fame will resound in the heavens above and the kingdoms below."

Having blessed Valmiki thus, Brahma departed to his own abode. Valmiki then sat down and meditated on the Lord and out of his mouth gushed forth the immortal poem, called the *Ramayana – The Way of Rama.*

This is how the *Ramayana* came to be written, from the depths of Valmiki's sorrow, at the fate of the two birds who were so much in love with each other and who were parted so cruelly. It does not need much imagination to see the parallel between this story and the fate of the two lovers, Rama and Sita who were parted time and time again, despite their intense love for each other.

The poem took twelve long years to complete and by then Sita's babies had become twelve years of age. She had been looked after by the women of Valmiki's *ashrama* and had given birth to twins, nine months after her arrival. They had been named Lava and Kusha by the sage himself and had grown up as *ashramites.* They had no idea of their parentage.

Having composed this remarkable poem consisting of twenty-four thousand verses on the life of Rama and Sita, the seer was on the look-out for a person with a prodigious memory who could memorise the entire poem. Just then Lava and Kusha appeared before him, clad in hermit's garb. Knowing them to be endowed with great intelligence and mastery of music, the sage decided to teach them the entire poem which they mastered with ease. At an august assembly of sages, the twins sang the whole poem, exquisitely, in one voice. The sages were charmed and gave them many boons.

After Sita's banishment, Rama became withdrawn and disconsolate and when not engaged in official business he spent most of his time alone. He performed his stately duties by placing a golden idol of Sita on the throne meant for the queen. When his subjects asked him to remarry he totally refused.

"I have abandoned the woman I love due to your whims but I will forever remain faithful to her who is my very life."

He denied himself the privileges of a royal life and lived in his palace like a hermit. Though deprived of personal joy, he made sure that there was peace in the country and plenty in the houses of his citizens.

Seeing Rama in this mood, Hanuman decided to go to the Himalayas and reside there, chanting his name. Somehow the life of a hermitage suited his temperament more than the intricacies of a life at court even though it meant that he would have to be parted from his beloved Rama. He imposed this penance on himself for he wanted to experience the anguish which Sita must be going through at this cruel parting from her beloved. Immersed in his *tapas* he did not know what was happening in the world and that Sita had delivered twin boys in Valmiki's *ashrama.*

It was at this time, twelve years after the birth of his sons, that the great sage Agastya visited Ayodhya. Rama asked his advice on how to expiate from the sin of having killed so many people during the war and especially of killing Ravana who was a Brahmin. Agastya advised him to perform the *Ashwamedha yaga* or horse sacrifice, which is the biggest of the *yagas* of the Vedic civilization. His *guru* Vasishta approved of this idea and consecrated an auspiciously marked stallion and fastened a golden crown on its brow with the royal proclamation that any ruler who supposed himself to be mightier than the owner of the horse could attempt to halt its progress. But those who were prepared to accept the suzerainty of the king would allow the horse to pass. The royal stallion would be let loose to wander for one year all over the country, followed by the king's army. The question of which of his brothers should follow the horse was solved by Rama. He said Bharata had suffered a lot during his exile and Lakshmana had the unique privilege of accompanying him so he ordered his youngest brother, Shatrugna and his son Pushkala to follow the horse accompanied by an army of four divisions, including many of the monkey champions who had helped him during the war.

The royal stallion was allowed to wander all over the country. Every piece of land the horse traversed unchallenged came under Rama's sovereignty. Anyone who dared to stop the horse had to stand up to the might of Rama's army. The *Yaga* could begin only if the horse returned unmolested and unhampered.

At this time Rama thought to himself that the presence of Anjaneya would no doubt add to the glory of the *Yaga.* Since Hanuman was ever immersed in the thought of Rama, he knew immediately that he was wanted and arrived at the court and asked Rama to command him. Rama asked him to accompany Shatrugna and see to his welfare. News of the *Yaga* spread like wildfire over the whole land. It finally reached the hermitage of Valmiki and was told to Sita as well.

The horse made its way through many lands where it was honoured by all the kings. The army followed it and paused at various *ashrams* and paid obeisance to all the sages. At last it arrived at the *ashrama* of the famous sage Chyavana. Shatrugna begged him to bless them and the sage started to praise Rama as Vishnu incarnate. He then announced his intention of going to Ayodhya with his family to have Rama's *darshan.* Hanuman asked Shatrugna's permission to transport the sage and thus save him from the tedious journey on foot. Shatrugna agreed to this and Hanuman expanded his body and carried the whole party through the air and placed them in Rama's presence in an instant. The sage was delighted and blessed him.

The horse and army now approached the city of Chakranka ruled by King Subahu who was a great devotee of Vishnu. His son Damana had gone hunting and when he saw the magnificent horse, he captured it without knowing anything about the matter. The army charged forward and attacked him but they could not subdue him. He then engaged in a single combat with Shatrugnan's son – Pushkala. The prince was a remarkable warrior and soon knocked down Damana. The king heard about this and rode out of the fortress accompanied by his brother and his nephew, Chitranga. A fierce battle ensued with heavy losses on either side. At last Pushkala slew Chitranga. The king started to rain arrows at Hanuman. He responded by binding the king in his tail and throwing him to the ground. Undeterred by this the king struggled to come to his feet. Immediately Hanuman jumped on to his chest and made him unconscious. In his unconscious state Subahu saw a wondrous dream in which Rama was seated in his heavenly state surrounded by celestials. When he regained consciousness he called Hanuman and praised him and called off his forces. He recalled that once he had been cursed by a sage for doubting that Vishnu could take on the *avatara* of a man. The sage predicted that his ignorance would be removed when the Lord's servant struck him with his foot. Subahu invited Shatrugna to his palace and paid him homage. He then paid great reverence to Hanuman for having removed his ignorance and given him *darshan* of the Lord.

The horse then approached the magnificent city of Devapura, whose king Viramani had once propitiated Shiva and received his protection. His son Rukmangada captured the horse and tied him up. Hanuman and Shatrugna ordered the boy to release the horse. When he refused they were forced to fight with him. His father soon came with a huge army to help the boy. Hanuman now came forward and challenged the king and his brothers. He had a unique method of fighting. He would wrap warriors round his tail, including their chariots and horses and dash them to the ground. When he saw his army being slaughtered, Veeramani prayed to Shiva who immediately arrived with his brood of ravenous familiars, to help his devotee. His servant Veerabhadra now seized Pushkala by the feet and hurled him to the ground where he fell dead. Uttering a maniacal laugh he took his trident and decapitated the head of the prince. Anguished by the death of his son, Shatrugna challenged Shiva. Though he fought bravely, he was no match for the divine opponent and fell with an arrow in his heart. Hanuman was furious and attacked Shiva, abusing him for having killed the brother and son of Vishnu in his *avatara* as Rama. Shiva told him that he had to defend his own votaries and uphold their *bhakti.* Each of them now started to fight with re-redoubled vigour. Hanuman started to rain mountain peaks and trees on Shiva, who retaliated by hurling fiery darts at his breast. At last Hanuman encircled him in his tail and thrashed him on the ground again and again. Even Nandi, Shiva's bull, was terrified to see this. Shiva released himself and told Hanuman that he was satisfied with his special *puja* and offered him a boon. Hanuman smiled and said that he had received everything he could ever want by Rama's grace but he begged Shiva to look after Shatrugna and his son while he went to the Drona Mountain and got the life reviving herb which had saved Lakshmana.

He reached the Drona peak on the heights of the Himalayas and was just about to uproot the peak when the *yakshas* appealed to him to stop from uprooting the peak which belonged to them and by the power of which they kept up their immortality. Hanuman graciously agreed and took only a portion of the herbs. He returned to the battlefield and placed the herbs on the breasts of the dead and dying soldiers and reconnected Pushkala's head to his body. He then said, "If my devotion to Rama is unwavering, let the prince revive."

The prince immediately sat up as if from sleep. He then revived Shatrugna also. Father and son now resumed their fight with Shiva and Virabhadra. Seeing them weakening, Hanuman advised Shatrugna to meditate on Rama who alone could save them. Rama instantly appeared on the scene dressed for a sacrifice, holding an antelope's horn in his hand. All of them bowed at his feet and praised him as the Supreme Being. Rama replied that there was no difference between him and Shiva. "He is in my heart and I in his. Only a person of tainted intelligence would see a difference between us." Shiva passed his hand over the dead and wounded and revived them and all of them joined in praising Rama. King Veeramani returned the sacrificial horse to Shatrugna and the party resumed its journey.

The royal army followed the horse and reached a meadow on Mount Hemakuta or the Golden Peak. The horse suddenly became paralysed and fell to the ground. Every effort to make it rise up failed. Shatrugna went to a nearby *ashrama* where he met a sage and asked him the reason for this. The sage declared that the horse was possessed by a spirit who was once a Brahmin and had been cursed by some sages. When he begged for reprieve, they told him that he would be released from the curse when he heard the story of Rama and this would take place when he took possession of the sacrificial horse which Rama would let loose. Hanuman sat next to the horse and lovingly recited the whole of the story of Rama in the horse's ear. When he finished, he called on the long suffering spirit to depart to its proper destination. A divine being now appeared and thanked Hanuman for having released him from the spell. Immediately the horse got up and started grazing contentedly on the meadow.

The next person to attack them and steal the horse was a relative of Ravana known as Vidyunmali. He created a haze through which he spirited away the horse. Then he started attacking Shatrugna and the rest from between the fumes which he had created. Hanuman advised Shatrugna to repeat the *mantra* of Rama and he would undoubtedly be able to overcome the *rakshasa.* Shatrugna now sent the missile known as the *mohastra* which completely cleared the illusion which had been created by the ogre, after which he was able to kill him easily and retrieve the horse.

The horse next approached the city of Kundalapura ruled by the great king called Suratha, who was a great devotee of Rama. He had received a boon from Yama, the god of death, that he would never die till he had had *darshan* of Rama. When the king learnt of the identity of the horse grazing outside his city, he decided to capture it so that he could obtain an audience with Rama. When he heard of this, Shatrugna immediately sent Angada to the king demanding the release of the horse. The king frankly told Angada of his intentions and that he would keep the horse captive till Rama came and gave him *darshan.* Though Angada sympathised with the king, he told him in no uncertain terms that it was his duty to safeguard the horse at all times and if he didn't release it, he would have to face the wrath of Rama's army. Suratha cheerfully told him that in that case he would take all of them as prisoners and never release them till Rama came! Angada returned with this message and preparations for battle began.

The king rode out accompanied by his ten sons and a huge army. Prince Pushkala was captured by Suratha's son, Champaka. Hanuman challenged the latter and after a severe fight he managed to knock him unconscious. He then turned to face Suratha whom he recognised as a great devotee of Rama. The king vowed to take him prisoner and Hanuman smilingly told him to do so since Rama would definitely come to release him. However he continued to resist the king, warding off all his supernatural weapons with ease. The king was amazed when Hanuman proved to be impervious even to the *brahmastra.* He then devised a ruse to capture this great devotee. He sent a weapon with the name of Rama written all over it. Hanuman refused to retaliate to this weapon and bowed low before it and allowed himself to be captured. Once Hanuman was captured, Suratha was able to overcome the rest of the army with ease. All the heroes including Hanuman were taken to his throne room as prisoners. The king then asked Hanuman to invoke Rama and ask him to come to their aid. Hanuman now composed a long paean of praise to Rama describing his adventures and begging him to come and release them. Rama immediately appeared in Kundalapura in the king's throne room. Overcome with joy, Suratha fell at his feet and begged him to pardon him for having captured his men. The Lord smiled and displayed his form as Vishnu and clasped the king in his arms. When he glanced at Hanuman and the other fallen heroes, all their bonds fell off. The king along with his citizens now worshipped both Rama and Hanuman and thanked the latter for having fulfilled his heart's desire.

The horse then roamed into an *ashrama* on the banks of the Narmada. There in a leaf hut resided the great sage, Aranyaka, who was constant in his worship of Rama. When the members of the royal party paid their respects to him, he was overjoyed and delivered a sermon on Rama's glories, including the teachings he had learnt from the sage Lomasha.

"There is but one god – Rama; one discipline which is his worship; one *mantra* – his name; one scripture – his praise!"

All of them were delighted to hear this but Hanuman felt a thrill go through him. The sage recognised him as a kindred spirit and embraced him with great joy. Both of them were drowned in bliss.

All of a sudden the horse made straight for Valmiki's *ashrama.* When Lava went to the forest with some of the other children he saw the horse and after reading the proclamation, he was determined to show his prowess and tied the horse to a tree. The army followed and ordered him to release it but Lava refused. The army started to advance but Lava reached for his bow and cut off their arms. Shatrugna was informed about this and sent his general with another consignment. The general tried to reason with the boy but Lava said that what intrigued him was the proclamation on the horse's head which he took as a challenge. Battle ensued in which Lava killed the general and most of his troops. Pushkala and Hanuman arrived on the scene and Lava felled Pushkala and made him lose consciousness. As soon as he saw the boy Hanuman thought that this must indeed be his Lord's son but since his orders were to protect the horse at all cost, he took up a tree and a boulder and hurled them at the boy but the child shattered them to pieces. Then Hanuman wrapped his tail round him and whipped him into the air but Lava meditated on his mother and freed himself. He then struck Hanuman so forcefully that he fell to the ground stunned. Shatrugna now came to the front and with great difficulty he managed to wound and bind the boy and put him in his chariot.

The rest of the children who had accompanied Lava were watching all this in great astonishment. When they saw him taken, they ran and told Sita about it. She was quite distraught at the news but her other son Kusha told her not to worry and he would go and free his brother. By the time he reached the battle ground Lava had recovered consciousness. When he saw his brother he managed to free himself, jumped out of the chariot and both of them took up positions and started to ravage the army. When the troops identified themselves as the king's army, the boys merely laughed and very soon they decimated the army. Even Hanuman finally succumbed. However, they desisted from killing him and tied him with the *naga pasha* and dragged him before their mother to be kept as a pet!

Sita was overjoyed to see her sons return but horrified when she saw their prisoner whom she recognised at once. She ordered them to release him and tell her the whole story. They gleefully described the whole episode to her of how they had caught and tethered a stallion which belonged to a king called Rama and how they had killed many people including some persons called Shatrugna and Pushkala! Hearing this Sita began to weep and said, "My children! Do you know who they were? They are your uncle and his son and as for this monkey which you have brought, do you know who he is? He is the great Hanuman who is the greatest devotee of Rama. He has immense strength."

Lava and Kusha said, "Mother do you know what message was hung round the horse's neck? "If anyone with Kshatriya blood dares to capture this horse he will have to pay the penalty." O Mother! We know we are Kshatriyas and we thought it our duty to tie the horse and prove our point."

She ordered them to release the horse immediately since it belonged to their father. The boys were surprised to hear this since they didn't think much of a father who had abandoned their mother. However, they went to do her bidding. In the meantime, Sita conversed with Hanuman who told her the whole story of why they were there.

"How did two young boys manage to put down a hero like you?" she asked.

Hanuman replied, "O Mother! A son is the very soul of his father. The bright and brilliant faces of these two precious boys are exactly like my beloved Lord's. So when they bound and harassed me, I felt that my Lord was having some fun at my expense. Forgetting everything else, I dissolved myself in that sweet thought and knew nothing else." In this incident, Valmiki portrays beautifully the great humility and devotion of this great *bhakta.*

Sita now used the power of her chastity and prayed to god to revive the fallen warriors. All of them rose up and Hanuman and the rest of the army returned to Naimisharanya where the *Yaga* was being conducted.

"Pay no heed to any other deity,
Serving Hanuman, one obtains all delights."

— *Sri Hanuman Chalisa* by Tulsidas

ॐ *Sri Hanumathe Namaha!*

ॐ

Shashwathaaya Namaha!

CHAPTER THIRTY-TWO

LOKABANDHU

Ashwamedha Yaga

"Devotion to Rama is for the faithful Tulsi Das,
Like the rainy season for the rice fields."

— *Ramacharitamanas* by Tulsidas

The *Yaga* was conducted on a gigantic scale for one full year after the return of the victorious stallion accompanied by Shatrugna and Hanuman.

In the meantime, a hundred-headed *rakshasa* called Sahasramukha Ravana was causing havoc in the country. He was actually a son of Ravana who had been a baby when his father was killed. When he came of age he did *tapas* and got a boon from Brahma that only a woman who was completely chaste in thought, word and deed would be able to kill him. After having got this boon, he started harassing his uncle Vibhishana in Lanka and Sugriva in Kishkinda. His next target was Ayodhya and with this in view he entered Kosala. Rama was forced to send his army to defeat the *rakshasa.* However, the army found itself helpless against this foe. When they heard of his boon, the women of Ayodhya volunteered to enter the battle and stop the demon from advancing. However, there was not even one woman who came up to the high expectations of the boon and thus none of them could stop the progress of the demon. Rama knew that Sita was the only one who could save his city and his people but he doubted if she would agree to enter the city which had rejected her. So he sent Hanuman and told him to tell her that he was very ill. Naturally she rushed to Ayodhya where she was stopped by the demon that was standing outside the gates. When he refused to let her enter, she was furious and picked up a blade of grass, charged it with the power of her chastity and hurled it at the *rakshasa* who was killed instantly. The citizens now acclaimed her as their saviour. She cared not for their acclaim and asked after her husband's health. When she heard that he was hale and hearty, she realised that she had been tricked.

Turning to Hanuman she said, "Because of you I have experienced the horror of thinking my husband dead. You will outlive Rama and will also experience the pain of separation." So saying she returned to the *ashrama.*

Having witnessed the amazing power of her chastity which none of their own wives seemed to possess, the citizens of Ayodhya were anxious to welcome her back as their queen and requested Rama to bring her back. He was only too willing but did not know how to go about it. In the meantime the *yaga* was still going on.

Valmiki decided that this was a good opportunity for the boys to meet their father and sent the two boys to the *yaga* and made them sing the whole *Ramayana* in front of Rama and the others. The children did as they were told and sang twenty cantos in a melodious voice before the noble audience. People were spellbound by the sight of these two hermit boys, who sang so sweetly. They also remarked on their uncanny resemblance to Rama, who had looked exactly like them, when he went to the forest, so many years ago, wearing bark, with hair in matted locks. Rama was enchanted with the boys and told Lakshmana to give them twenty thousand gold coins and expensive clothes but the boys refused and said that hermit boys who lived on fruits and roots had no necessity for such things.

Rama was astonished and asked them, "Who composed this poem and how many cantos does it have?"

The boys replied, "The venerable sage Valmiki is the composer of this wonderful poem which recounts the doings of your Majesty. It has twenty-four thousand verses and six *kandas*. The seventh is the *Uttara Kanda* which is now going on. With your leave we will recite the whole poem in its entirety to you, between the functions of the horse sacrifice."

"So be it," said the king.

For many days, Rama and his brothers as well as the collection of sages, kings and monkeys heard the whole story of Rama. All were enthralled by the recital. By the end of it, Rama realised that these boys were indeed his own sons, the children of Sita. All the pent-up emotions which he had bottled up for so many years, now surged forward and he was filled with an intense desire to see her once again. He could no longer suppress his feelings. The day that he had banished her, he had enshrined her in his heart and thrown away the key. But these young boys, who looked like him and smiled like her, had broken open the door of his heart and let loose a flood of emotion which threatened to overwhelm him with its intensity. Their smiles brought to his mind only too vividly Sita's charming face. The desire to see her again was too strong to be subdued. Surely the fates would not deny him this final bid for happiness. The citizens had already informed him of their decision to have her back. He sent messengers to the hut of the sage with this request.

"If the Queen of Ayodhya is prepared to take an oath in front of this assembly and thus give proof of her innocence, I am prepared to take her back."

Valmiki assented to this.

The next day everybody from all over the realm as well as the guests who had been invited for the sacrifice, assembled in the *yajnashala* in the forest of Naimisha to watch the final scene, in the drama of the lives of their king and queen. Into that motionless crowd of expectant citizens, Valmiki arrived with Sita, the daughter of the earth. Her head was bent to the ground, her palms folded in devotion, her eyes filled with tears and her heart with Rama. At the sight of their queen dressed in bark as befitting an anchorite, yet looking divinely beautiful, the fickle crowd set up a spontaneous cheer of welcome. They, who had not made any demur when Rama banished her, now appeared eager to take her back.

Valmiki entered the *yajnashala* accompanied by Sita and her two sons who were the split images of their father and said,

"O son of Dasaratha! This pious lady was abandoned by you near my hermitage out of fear of the censure of the citizens. For the good of your people you were prepared to sacrifice your noble wife whom you loved dearly. However, she is purer than Agni. Fire itself will cool at her approach. If Sita is tainted then let my austerities be in vain. These twins are indeed your sons as their valour will prove. I assure you that Sita is as pure as gold and totally devoted to you. You may now take her back and no one will say a word against this decision of yours, O noble king!"

Then Rama spoke, "With the gods as witness, the queen proved her innocence once before in Lanka and I accepted her, but still the people whispered and maligned and I was forced to send her away to uphold my *dharma* as a king. I hereby acknowledge Lava and Kusha as my own sons and will accept Sita too as my wife, if she proves her innocence once more in front of the people of Ayodhya as she did long ago before the *vanaras* and *rakshasas* at Lanka."

As he said this, Rama allowed himself the luxury of gazing at his beloved wife once more. Bereft of jewels and adornment, dressed in bark, with matted hair tied in a knot on top of her head, stood his queen, the queen of Ayodhya and the queen of his heart. His own heart smote him as he looked at her. Involuntarily he stretched out his hands to her. Without thinking, she put her delicate, pink tipped palms into his. Despite her lack of adornment, she was still incredibly lovely and he could not tear his gaze away from her. Sita gazed back at him and as their hands and eyes locked in a mutual embrace, they felt as if they were drowning in an ocean of love, mirrored in their eyes. They held infinity in their hands and eternity in their eyes.

A ring of interested spectators had formed a circle round them but Sita and Rama stood alone within that circle, gazing at each other as if they could not bear to look apart. For twelve long years they had been starved of this pleasure. Time stopped as they beheld heaven in their eyes, and their whole life passed like a dream in front of their interlocked gaze and still they could not bear to look away.

At last Sita broke the spell and whispered, "My Lord, do I have your permission to make a public avowal of my purity?"

Rama nodded. Wearing the ochre robes of the ascetics, yet looking as beautiful as a bride, Sita, the daughter of the earth, stepped into the centre of the circle and with folded palms she bowed before her mother earth and said,

"O Madhavi! Goddess of the earth, beloved mother! If you know that I have never loved any man other than my husband, even for a moment, then please open your arms wide and accept me, your daughter, for I can no longer bear to live in this vale of tears. Grief alone has been my lot in this life and now I long for the comfort of your arms O mother! Take me to your bosom, as you brought me once out of your womb to the field of my father, Janaka!"

Hardly had she finished speaking when the earth split open with a shudder and out of the chasm there arose a beautiful flower-bedecked throne on which was seated the goddess of the earth in all her bounty, covered with flowers and carrying the nine types of grains in sheaves in her hands.

She opened her arms wide and Sita ran into them and was made to sit beside her on the throne of flowers. In front of the astonished gaze of the spellbound audience, the earth gaped open once more and the throne carrying Sita and her mother slowly descended into the bowels of the earth as the gods rained flowers from above. The earth shuddered and the wind moaned as the gap closed over their heads. The crowd came out of their mesmerised state and a great sigh broke from every mouth.

As she disappeared from sight, Rama woke up from the grip of terror which had paralysed him and ran to the spot where she had disappeared and called to her piteously.

Holding a staff, picked from the sacrificial ground, he leant on it as if his body was too weak to stand alone. Bending his head over it, he cried out loud, "O Janaki! O Vaidehi! O Sita! My beloved wife! Why have you deserted me, just when I thought I could have you back? Once you were stolen by the wicked Ravana but I brought you back and then I was forced to send you away again. At that time, I was able to bear the parting only because I knew that you were alive and being looked after somewhere, but now, I cannot bear to live, when I know that I cannot see you any more. I fear I am being punished for my cruel act in having banished you."

His sorrow turned to anger and he smote the earth with the staff and said, "O goddess of the earth, return my beloved to me at once. I have suffered enough. I cannot live without her. Or else open your arms once again and accept me also. I would rather live with her in the bowels of the earth, than here as a king. Remember I am your son-in-law and have pity on me. You know my valour. If you refuse my reasonable request, I will destroy you, burn your forests and crush your mountains and reduce everything to liquid!"

All the worlds trembled with fear at the anger and agony in Rama's voice. None dared to approach him.

At last Brahma, the creator came to him and said, "Rama! Remember who you are. Let me remind you of your divinity. Immaculate Sita will be reunited with you in heaven for she is none other than your consort, Lakshmi. Do not grieve. Take delight in your children and listen to the rest of the tale of your life which your sons will recite at dawn tomorrow. It is an exquisitely beautiful poem of a life that was ruled by *dharma* alone. You should be the first to hear it. For it is about you. O Rama! You are not just the foremost of all kings but of all *rishis*." With these words, Brahma vanished.

Rama and his sons spent a night of anguish in the hut of Sage Valmiki grieving for Sita. Valmiki had the unhappy task of comforting all three of them. It is only to be expected that a poem which began with the bereavement of the female bird should end with the bereavement of the human couple. At that time when he had watched the male bird being shot down by the cruel arrow, Valmiki had felt as if he had been pierced by the same fatal arrow. How much more did he feel it now, when he saw the tortured king bemoaning his loss over and over again, throughout the long and lonely hours of an endless night?

The next day, in front of the assembled crowd, Rama asked the children to chant the last portion of the epic. He then distributed wealth to all those assembled there, the Brahmins, the citizens, the tree-dwellers, the cave-dwellers and the night wanderers who had come from Lanka. The *yaga* was over, the people dispersed and the jungle once more crept over the space which had been cleared for the function.

Rama returned to Ayodhya and spent the rest of his life, a lonely ascetic. Without Sita, life had no meaning for him. He never married again but kept the golden effigy of his lovely wife beside him and performed ten thousand *Ashwamedha yagas* in order to please his *guru* and the people. His rule was noted for its exemplary nature. The kingdom prospered and thrived and the citizens rejoiced. Rama and Sita had paid for this glory with their unceasing tears. They suffered so that the rest of the country could rejoice, blossom and flourish. Never once did the citizens think that the price of their prosperity was the sacrifice of their queen – their land was watered with her tears, their happiness bought with her sorrow. She was the sacrificial offering, tied to the stake of their malice, banished to the forest of their poisonous tongues and eventually swallowed in the chasm of their doubts! They rejoiced and sported with their wives, while their king retired to his lonely chamber every night, with only his memories for company. Rama carried on his duties for the rest of his life with his usual charm and adherence to *dharma* and showed a pleasant and happy face to all. Only Lakshmana knew that this was just a façade and inside he was burning with regret at what he had done to his queen and waiting for the day when he could join her in their celestial abode.

After reigning for several years, Rama chose to leave this world. The gods with Brahma at their head came to him and said, "O Rama! You have fulfilled your destiny on earth. It is time for you to return to your divine abode."

"So be it," said Rama. He was only too happy to leave this world which offered no joys to him without Sita.

Brahma continued, "Kaala, the spirit of Time, cannot enter your portals which is guarded by Hanuman so send him away."

Rama bowed his head. He then dropped his signet ring in a hole in the ground and requested Hanuman to bring it back. Maruti immediately dived into the hole to search for the ring. The search led him to the land of the serpents (*Naga Loka*). There he found a huge platter of rings each exactly like the one worn by Rama.

The Naga king told him, "The wheel of time keeps turning and each time it comes to the *Yuga* known as Treta, Vishnu takes an *avatara* as Rama. Whenever his time on earth comes to an end his ring falls here and he sends you to retrieve it. This is done to help you to accept the fact that your master's time on earth is coming to an end." Hanuman was filled with sorrow at the thought of his master's approaching end but he had to bow to the decree of the eternal law.

In the meantime when Hanuman was away, Kaala, the Time spirit, came to the palace in the guise of an old Brahmin. Rama was waiting for him. He had been waiting for a long, long time. He seated him on a golden seat and politely asked him what he wanted.

"If you want to honour me and the gods, you will have to promise me that our meeting shall be private. Anyone who dares to interrupt us should be put to instant death."

"So be it," said Rama. "Since Hanuman is not here, I'll ask Lakshmana to guard the door so that we can be sure that no one will interrupt us."

He asked Lakshmana to take up the position of the door keeper for anyone who dared to enter would be put to death. Then he returned to the ascetic and asked him to freely say whatever he wished to say without fear of interruption.

"Listen O king" said the spirit of Time, "I have been sent by Brahma to recall you to your heavenly abode. Your time on earth is over. You have accomplished all that you have set out to do. You are Vishnu! The Eternal, the Immutable – the all pervading, protector of the universe. Your stay among the mortals is over. It is time now for you to return to your heavenly abode."

Rama smiled and said, "I am honoured by your visit and happy with your message. I will do as you say."

Just as they were talking, Durvasa, the short-tempered sage arrived and demanded an immediate audience. Lakshmana politely barred the way and declared that he had strict orders that no one should be allowed to enter since Rama was giving a private audience to someone. Hearing this, the sage lost his temper and shouted, "Announce my presence immediately or else I shall curse you and your brothers and your whole race, as well as the land of Kosala, so that nothing and no one remains to tell the tale!"

Lakshmana thought for a minute and decided that it was better to sacrifice his own life for the sake of the country and so he went in and announced the arrival of the sage. Rama was horrified to see him but went out immediately to attend to the needs of the sage.

He asked the sage politely what he wanted and was told that since he had just ended a fast which had lasted for a hundred-years, he wanted to be fed sumptuously. Rama saw to it that he was fed lavishly. Durvasa was immensely pleased and showered his blessings on the land instead of his curses and returned to his *ashrama.* Now Rama remembered the promise he had made to Kaala and went inside with bowed head, lost in thought. Was this going to be the last sacrifice? Was he being asked to sacrifice his beloved brother, his alter ego at the altar of *dharma*?

Lakshmana knew what was passing through his mind and said cheerfully, "Brother! Do not hesitate. Kill me this minute. I am prepared for it. I thought it better for me to die rather than that the whole country be cursed by the sage as he threatened to do. If you wish to abide by *dharma*, then kill me, O King! One who does not keep his word will go to hell. In order to keep our father's word, you were prepared to forgo a kingdom. What am I compared to that!"

Rama spoke not a word but summoned his priests and ministers and asked them to advice him, for he had promised the ascetic that anyone who interrupted him would be executed, little realising that this was going to be his final test.

The priests and ministers were silent since they knew the agony that was passing through the king's mind. At last Vasishta spoke, "If a king does not keep his word, *dharma* will be corrupted and the morals of the country will decline. But banishment can be given in lieu of death, so it is your duty to banish Lakshmana!"

Lakshmana stood with his head thrown back, his eyes gazing fearlessly into Rama's. Rama looked into those adoring eyes which had always regarded him with such love, looked at that beloved form which he had known since childhood and which had followed him faithfully like a shadow, which can ever be parted. He knew that one need not die when parted from a shadow but what about the shadow? Would it not come to an end, when parted from the body? Pain flowed out of his eyes while love flowed from Lakshmana's.

"It does not matter brother," he whispered. "Command me to leave, as sternly as you once ordered me to leave Sita in the forest."

Rama was in anguish. Over and over again he murmured, "Everything passes, everything perishes, nothing will remain. Time is all powerful. Everything will be swept away in the powerful river of time. I have to abide by my promise; I have to be true to the only thing to which I have clung to all my life – *dharma,* the cosmic law. I have been tested time and time again and I have not failed. Let me not fail now."

He was facing Lakshmana but could not look into his eyes. Instead, he fixed his gaze at a spot just above his head and said in an expressionless voice, drained of all emotion. "In honour of truth, in honour of *dharma,* in honour of the law which I have always upheld, I banish you, O Lakshmana, forever. You shall never return to this land of Kosala again on pain of death!"

Lakshmana looked lovingly at his brother whom he had implicitly obeyed all his life and said, "My dearest brother, do not grieve. I have loved you all my life and obeyed you without a murmur. It shall be as you wish. Farewell! And once again fare thee well. We will never meet again in this life. Perhaps we will meet in heaven."

So saying he went thrice round Rama and prostrated to him and went without a backward glance out of the gates of the palace. He proceeded to the banks of the swiftly flowing river, Sarayu, which encircled Ayodhya like a girdle. The thought of a life apart from Rama was unthinkable. Death was preferable to such a life. He did not even consider it. Going to the Sarayu River he sat in *yogic* contemplation on the banks. He gathered in his vital breaths and withdrew into his *atman*, and merged into the Brahman, the cosmic whole. Thus he sat in deep *samadhi*. Indra, the king of gods, sent his chariot and took Lakshmana, the fourth part of Vishnu, to heaven, where he became one with that essence.

Back in Ayodhya, Rama knew that Lakshmana would never be able to live without him and he himself no longer cared to carry on a life which had ceased to have any meaning for him. He realised that firm as he had been in his vows of *dharmic* discipline, he had been forced to part, one by one, from all those whom he held most dear. He had always known that life was only a dream, a drama in which he had been called upon to play a part. He had come to the end of his lines. The curtain was going up for the final scene and he had already been given his cue to quit the stage. He called his priests and ministers and announced his decision to them.

"I hereby appoint Bharata, as Lord of Ayodhya. The southern portion of this fair land of Kosala will be given to Kusha and the northern to Lava. I myself shall follow Lakshmana."

Both Bharata and Shatrugna refused to live without Rama and decided to follow him. Many of the citizens for whose sake he had sacrificed his all, decided that they could not live in a land without their beloved king. Hearing of his decision to leave this world, the monkeys and the bears and Vibhishana from across the sea, arrived and begged to accompany him. Hanuman also arrived from the nether world where he had gone to get the ring.

Rama said to Vibhishana, "O Lord of the *rakshasas*! Stay on in Lanka and continue to perform your duty. Rule with *dharma* as your guide. Your kingdom will endure as long as I am remembered on earth."

Turning to the bear Jambavan, he said, "O wise one! You shall continue to live on this earth till my advent as Krishna, scion of the race of Yadu. Until then you shall suffer no defeat. When you meet one who is able to defeat you, then you will know that I have returned."

To the others, he said, "All those who wish to follow me, may do so. This very day you will enter heaven along with me."

"What about me?" asked Hanuman with tears streaming out of his eyes.

"Live long, O Noble Hanuman! Wherever my story is told, wherever the name of Rama is mentioned, you will be there to hear it. This story will be told as long as the sun and the moon shine, as long as people remain on this earth and as long as you are there to hear it!"

Most of the people of Ayodhya followed Rama with love and devotion. Even the animals followed him, the cows and goats and elephants, not to mention the monkeys and bears. The very stones on the streets of Ayodhya wept, for they could not follow him and the trees bent low and brushed his head while he passed. Every creature that could walk or roll or dance or totter, followed him. The whole procession wound its way to the pellucid waters of the river, Sarayu, which circled the land of Kosala like a silver girdle. Sumantra was waiting at the banks of the river with the four red horses, which he had freed from the chariot. Guha, the hunter king was also there. Rama walked into the icy waters of the river accompanied by all the rest. The waters closed over their heads like a benediction.

Hanuman stood on the banks with closed eyes, rapt in ecstasy while the heavens opened and the celestials rained flowers.

"Brahma spoke, "O gracious Vishnu! Be pleased to return to your celestial abode. Thou art the soul of all – indestructible, immutable and eternal. Be pleased to give up this form of *maya* and resume your *swarupa*."

As he finished speaking, out of the waters rose the incredibly beautiful form of Lord Vishnu, holding the discus, conch, mace and play lotus in his hands. All those who had decided to join him also came out of the waters, endowed with celestial forms and all rose up to the heavens as the music of the spheres floated down in the velvet twilight.

With the ascension of Rama to his heavenly abode, the twenty-four thousand verses were complete. Back in the deserted city of Ayodhya, Lava and Kusha sang the final verses of the song, to an invisible audience –

the song known as the *Ramayana – The Way of Rama*, the first poem ever to be composed by the first of all poets, Valmiki.

"At death one goes to Rama's realm,
Or is born on earth as his devotee."

— *Sri Hanuman Chalisa* by Tulsidas

ॐ *Sri Hanumathe Namaha!*

ॐ

Sathyavachaaya Namaha!

CHAPTER THIRTY-THREE

TAPASWIN

Dwapara Yuga

Sri Raama Raama Raamethi, Reme Raame manorame,
Sahasranama tat tuliam Raama nama varanane

Repetition of the name of Rama is equivalent to the chanting of the Thousand and one names of Lord Vishnu.

As foretold by Sita, Hanuman witnessed the departure of Rama from this earth and experienced the heartbreak that followed. He returned to his habitat in the wild on the Himalayan Mountain. As the years passed he heard of the deaths of all his friends and loved ones – his mother, Sugriva, Angada, Vibhishana, Lava and Kusha. This was the price he had to pay for being a *chiranjeevi* (long-lived). All alone on the slopes of the Himalayas he meditated in order to experience the ultimate truth. He remembered the advice given by Sita.

"Rama is the Supreme Purusha, the eternal spirit, Sita is Prakriti, cosmic matter, the embodiment of all manifestation. Together they constitute the entire universe." He witnessed the unending transformations of matter – birth and death, joy and sorrow, aspiration and frustration, union and separation. Amidst all this change he remained in the stillness of the *atman,* the serenity of the soul.

It was at this time that he felt the need to record the glorious doings of his master to which he had been an eye witness. The summit of the mountain beneath which he had a cave was composed of sparkling crystalline slabs and with his diamond-like nails he began to inscribe Rama's story. He recorded his own version of the glories deeds of his Lord and master,

Rama in the divine language of Sanskrit. He scratched it laboriously with his nails on the rocks. The work continued for a long time and Hanuman, lost in the intricacies of the story, became oblivious to the passage of time.

One day Valmiki came to know that the great Hanuman too had penned the adventures of Rama, engraving the story with his nails on rocks. His curiosity was aroused and he travelled to the Himalayas where Hanuman was residing, in order to see this version. The monkey warrior was no doubt an eye witness to much of the incidents but was he a poet? He questioned Hanuman about the rumour that he had composed his own Ramayana. Hanuman carried him and placed him on a ledge from which he could read the narration. Valmiki kept reading and reading, scanning the cliffs from top to bottom, climbing and descending now and again in order to see well. Sometimes he laughed loudly and at times his eyes brimmed with tears. Valmiki was overwhelmed by the sheer power and depth of devotion of the amazing narrative. It was truly a lofty work inspired by great love. After finishing the story Valmiki gazed for a long time into the distance. Joy and sorrow flitted over his face. He was joyous at having had the chance to read such an exquisite work of art and sad because it obviously overshadowed his own work.

Hanuman politely asked him the reason for his sorrow. "O best of sages! Is something wrong? Does the poetry have many faults?"

Valmiki turned to him and said, "It is indeed a marvellous bit of work. Every image, every word is alive and pregnant with devotion. There is not and never can be an equal to it. My version, which I created with such pains over a period of twelve years is no match for the magnificence of your work and will therefore, be despised."

For a moment Hanuman was dumbstruck. Then he said, "Is that all that is bothering you?" He promptly tore the slabs on which he had scribbled the poem on the mountain and piled them on one shoulder. He placed the aged saint on another shoulder and flew to the ocean. When they reached the middle Hanuman called loudly, "May these be an offering to my Lord." With these words he threw his own version into the sea where they raised huge waves before disappearing into the depths of the sea. Valmiki watched speechless, overcome with shame and guilt. "It would have been better," he thought, "if he had thrown me into the sea and saved that wonderful story."

But Hanuman seemed unperturbed and cheerful. He returned the sage to his own hermitage in a trice. "Please don't worry about this," he said, "It was just something I did to while away the time!"

The *Ramayana* is a story of *tyaga* or renunciation and this aspect of Hanuman's personality is considered to be far more important than his rhetorical skills. Selfless and compassionate, his loyalty was always to his master and not to any particular telling of the tale and he willingly drowned his own masterpiece in order to spare a poet's wounded pride. This was the first and greatest *Ramayana*, called the *Hanumad Ramayana*, which like the original Veda, was lost and preserved only in fragments.

Hanuman bowed to Valmiki who blessed him and said prophetically, "O Son of Vayu, in another age I will take birth again and devote myself to your service. I will sing your praises and teach others to do so. I will retell the story you have told, using the language of the common man so that everyone may understand it."

Hanuman smiled and said, "Victory to Lord Rama!"

It is said that Saint Tulsidas who composed the *Ramacharitamanas* was none other than the Maharishi Valmiki, reborn to fulfil his own desire.

Later, one tablet is said to have been washed ashore during the time of the great poet Kalidasa when it was exhibited at a public place. It was in an extinct script and Kalidasa is said to have deciphered it and recognized that it was from the *Hanumad Ramayana* as recorded by Hanuman, and considered that he was very fortunate to see at least one stanza of this immortal work.

Hanuman's heart was so full of Rama that it was bound to pour out of him in the form of music. He composed verses and set them to music in praise of his Lord. He sang these in his powerful voice and they reverberated across the hills and valleys of the Himalayas. Birds paused in their flight and animals gathered round to listen to Hanuman sing and chant the name of Rama unceasingly, without even pausing for breath.

By this time the *Yuga* known as Treta in which Rama had lived was long over. It fact it was almost the end of the next *Yuga*, known as Dwapara in which Vishnu had taken another incarnation on earth, as Krishna. Hanuman was the instrument that Krishna chose to curb the pride of many of his attendants. He had many wives but Sathyabhama thought that she was his favourite, little realising that he was equally affectionate to all. None was specially dear or hateful to him. She considered herself to be very beautiful and had once asked him whether she was not more beautiful than Sita to whom he had been so attached in his previous incarnation. Krishna's vehicle was Garuda and his weapon was the discus, called Sudarshana. All of them became very proud of themselves and Krishna decided that it was time to teach them all a lesson. Along with them he also wanted to teach a lesson to the sage Narada and his disciple Tumburu who thought themselves to be the greatest of all musicians.

Once the two celestial sages came to the court of Krishna and asked him which of them he considered to be the best musician. Krishna smiled and asked them to go to the Himalayas and listen to Hanuman. The two agreed condescendingly and went to the icy slopes where they found Hanuman and asked him to sing. With his usual modesty Maruti said that he was no singer but only wanted to pour out the glories of Rama. But since they insisted, he picked up his lute and started to sing. Narada and Tumburu were enchanted by the music. Such was the power of his voice that the snow began to melt and when he stopped the melted snow became ice. Narada and Tumburu found that they were truly stuck to the ice. They begged Hanuman to release them.

"Why don't you both sing so that the snow melts and then you can free yourselves?" asked Hanuman.

But try as they might neither of their voices could melt the ice. They realised that their voices were filled with ego while Hanuman sang out of pure devotion. Now they understood why Krishna had sent them to Hanuman.

Another time Narada went to Dwaraka, strumming his lute in order to pay his respects to Krishna. Narada was a great *bhakta,* so Krishna paid him homage and made him sit and then asked him if there was anything he wanted to tell him.

Narada said, "Well actually I came to tell you of how I was insulted by your vehicle, Garuda. I had gone to Indra's assembly hall and there everyone paid homage to me except this eagle who said that he saw no reason to respect a person like me who was noted for creating troublesome situations! I didn't curse him since I knew he spoke out of his ignorance but I thought I might as well mention this to you since I think it is time he was taught a lesson."

Krishna smiled in his usual mysterious fashion for he knew that his three favourites were filled with pride and he was waiting for an occasion to curb them a little. This was a good opportunity to teach all three of them a lesson. He told Narada to go and call his wife Satyabhama. Narada was bewildered and wondered how Satyabhama, who was herself noted for her arrogance, could help in this matter. However, he did as he was bidden and went to Satyabhama's apartment. He asked someone to announce his arrival but was told that she was busy with her toilette and would not be able to see him. Naturally he was quite annoyed at this and returned and gave the news to Krishna.

"Don't worry, O Narada!" said Krishna with his usual smile, "if she won't come then you should go to the Himalayas and ask Hanuman to come. As you know he has been meditating there since Treta Yuga, from the time of my advent as Rama.

Again Narada was puzzled as to why he should be sent off to Hanuman whom he had already met once and who had humbled his pride. However, he was always ready to play along with the Lord so off he went to the icy mountains where Hanuman was meditating. He went close to him and said loudly.

"I have been sent by Lord Krishna to call you to Dwaraka!"

Hanuman was in deep meditation and did not even open his eyes. Narada repeated the message in a louder voice. At this Maruti opened his eyes and asked.

"Who is Krishna? I know no one by that name." He then closed his eyes and lapsed into *samadhi* once again.

Narada was perplexed and thought for a while. Then he realised that Hanuman was Rama's devotee. He probably didn't even know that the present epoch was Dwapara Yuga. He had no contact with the world and probably didn't know about the advent of Krishna. Then he had a brilliant idea. He went close to him and taking out his lute he started to chant the name of Rama. Even though he was immersed in a super conscious state, Hanuman started to come closer to Narada without realising what he was doing. Narada now started to sing the glories of Rama and began to walk off. Again Maruti started to follow him with closed eyes. Narada went all the way to Dwaraka and there he stopped his singing. He went to give the news to Krishna. When the singing stopped abruptly, Hanuman opened his eyes and was surprised to find himself in a beautiful garden. He realised that he had been tricked somehow and started destroying the trees in his anger. He mowed down the guards who came to drive him off. The news of a monkey destroying the garden was reported immediately to Krishna. The Lord summoned the eagle, Garuda and ordered him to go and chase the monkey from his garden.

Garuda went and saw a monkey sitting with his back to him, munching fruit.

"Vile one!" the eagle screeched. "Who are you and why have you destroyed Lord Krishna's garden?"

Without even turning around, the monkey replied, "As you see I am a monkey and I'm doing the normal thing that all monkeys do!" Saying this he resumed his feast of the fruits. Garuda was enraged at this treatment and attacked Hanuman who quickly wrapped him in his tail and began to choke the life out of him.

With his remaining breath, Garuda gasped, "Lord Krishna has sent me."

"Who is he?" asked Hanuman loosening his grip a little, "I know only Lord Rama."

"They are the same you fool!" said Garuda in a choking voice.

"Maybe you are right," said Hanuman "but I only answer Rama's call."

Hanuman had no intention of killing the bird so he tossed him head first into the ocean and bounded off to the southern mountains.

After swallowing a lot of sea water, Garuda revived and made his way back to the court where with downcast face and dripping plumage he presented himself before Krishna.

"I see you have been having a dip in the sea!" said Krishna with an innocent look.

Garuda fell at his feet and said, "My Lord! That is not an ordinary monkey. He bound me with his tail and threw me into the ocean."

Krishna comforted him and said, "That monkey is Hanuman, the great *bhakta* of Rama. Go to the Malaya Mountains in the south and call him again but this time tell him 'Sri Rama is calling you.'

Still proud of his speed Garuda streaked across the sky to the southern mountains to find Hanuman. He was a bit wary about approaching him and respectfully gave Krishna's message to him. Hanuman of course was delighted and told him to go and he would follow him. Garuda thought to himself, "This monkey may be strong but he certainly won't be able to match my speed! Wonder when, if ever he'll reach Dwaraka!" He grinned to himself and took off in a trice and flew at full speed towards Dwaraka.

Krishna decided to welcome Hanuman by taking on the form of Rama.

Turning to his wife Satyabhama, he asked her to take on Sita's form and accompany him since that would give greater pleasure to Maruti. She saw to her amazement that Krishna had already taken on the form of Rama, complete with bow and arrows. Then Krishna summoned his discus, Sudarshana and told him to stand guard outside his door for he was going to meet an important guest. Bristling with his own importance, Sudarshana stood guard at the door. It took a long time for Satyabhama to finish her toilette and dress like Sita.

After his conversation with Garuda, Hanuman meditated on Rama and reached Dwaraka in a trice. He was just about to enter the throne room when Sudarshana stopped him. Not wanting to waste time in pointless arguments, Maruti simply grabbed the discus and stuffed it into his mouth and entered without any further delay. He couldn't believe his eyes when he saw Rama and Sita awaiting him. When Hanuman saw them, he was totally bewildered. He ran forward and prostrated to them.

"My Lord!" He said, "I see now why my meditation was interrupted and I was brought to this strange place. I have been longing for this blissful vision for a long, long time." Glancing at Satyabhama standing on Krishna's left he said, "My Lord! Where is my revered mother? Who is this woman standing beside you? She has no resemblance to the princess of Videha."

Satyabhama was truly mortified to hear this. She had always thought herself to be superior to Sita. She hung her head in shame.

Krishna gave his side-long glance at Satyabhama and turned to embrace Hanuman and said,

"My dearest devotee! Do you realise that this is already the *Yuga* known as Dwapara. Your Rama has incarnated himself in the form of Krishna in this epoch."

With these words, the Lord showed himself to Hanuman as Krishna. Maruti was overjoyed to see this and once again fell at his feet and begged his pardon for having devastated his garden. Narada was, of course, an interested spectator to the whole drama. Just at this moment there was a flurry of wings and Garuda flew in, huffing and panting. Seeing Hanuman standing before Krishna, he was totally bewildered and hung his head in shame.

Krishna looked askance at him then turning to Hanuman he asked, "By the way did someone try to stop you from entering this room?"

Hanuman looked a bit sheepish and said, "Actually there was some sort of metallic thing which kept buzzing and trying to stop me but since I was in a hurry to reach you, I didn't wait to exchange blows but simply popped him into my mouth."

With these words he spat out Sudarshana who naturally looked very crestfallen. Krishna pointedly looked the other way so as not to give further embarrassment to the three who had set themselves up as his favourites and who were in great need of a set down.

Turning to Hanuman, Krishna said, "O Hanuman I have incarnated myself in order to establish the rule of *dharma* once again in the world. For this my chosen instruments are the Pandavas who belong to the Kuru dynasty. They are five in number and the second brother, Bhima is your brother since he was born of the Wind God, Vayu. They have been banished from the court and will be coming to the Himalayas soon. You will have a chance of meeting both Bhima and Arjuna. You will also be called upon to help them in their war of righteousness. We will meet again on the battlefield of Kurukshetra."

Hanuman took his leave and returned to his solitary mountain fastness.

Krishna now turned to Garuda and placed his hands over him and made him get up. He gave a quizzical look at Narada who was standing close by.

Garuda hung his head in shame and begged Narada's pardon for having slighted him.

"My Lord," he said to Krishna, "I know this is all your game and you wanted to teach me a lesson never to be rude to your devotees. Indeed now I realise that Narada is one of your greatest devotees."

Sudarshana, in the meanwhile, had also realised that this was all a game of his Lord to put down his pride and had slunk away in shame. Krishna now glanced at Sathyabhama who refused to meet his eyes and looked fixedly at her toes. She realised that her beauty of which she was so proud and by which she thought she could enslave Krishna was nothing compared to Sita's. She was slowly beginning to realise the greatness of her Lord who was supreme in himself and a slave to none!

There is another story connected with these three in which Krishna employed Hanuman to destroy their pride. In this story, Sathyabhama, Krishna's proud consort, demanded to get some flowers from Rama's sacred grove in the Himalayas which was guarded by Hanuman. Krishna sent Garuda to get the flowers but he was challenged by Hanuman who stopped him from entering.

"These flowers are meant only for Rama and Sita," he said.

Garuda did not bother to answer him but charged into the grove to pick the flowers. Hanuman simply picked him up and crushed him under his armpit and flew to Dwaraka so fast that he created quite a tempest which terrified the citizens. Seeing Hanuman in the sky they thought he was some demon and ran to Krishna to ask him to protect them. Though he knew who it was, Krishna threw his discus – Sudarshana – to stop him. Hanuman calmly tucked it into his other arm-pit and landed on the roof of the palace, terrifying the people. Krishna explained to them that this was Hanuman, a great devotee of Rama and if he wasn't pacified he would destroy Dwaraka as he had destroyed Lanka. He told Sathyabhama to dress like Sita, but she took so long that he called Rugmani and asked her to take on Sita's form. She immediately closed her eyes and begged Krishna to allow her to take on the correct form of his beloved in another age and thus prove that she was a true replica of Sita.

Krishna himself donned Rama's garb and the two of them approached Hanuman who immediately bowed and placed the flowers at their feet.

Krishna welcomed Maruti and hugged him, then with a twinkle in his eye, he asked Hanuman what he was hiding beneath his armpits.

Maruti replied, "A bird came to my Lord's garden and tried to pick flowers and then when I reached here some sort of metal wheel tried to stop me so I took both of them under my arm-pits."

So saying he produced the bird and the wheel and placed them before Krishna. Both of them looked very crestfallen with their pride duly humbled. Sathyabhama found to her chagrin that Rugmani had already masqueraded as Sita with no difficulty at all. She also realised that the whole drama had been arranged by her Lord to destroy her pride.

"Whoever recites this a hundred times,
Is released from bondage and gains bliss."

— *Hanuman Chalisa* by Tulsidas

ॐ *Sri Hanumathe Namaha!*

ॐ

Veeraaya Namaha!

CHAPTER THIRTY-FOUR

BHIMA

Mahabharata

"Tava maya bas firaum bhulaana,
Ta te me nahi prabhu pahichata."

Overpowered by your maya,
I as a jiva forgot my real nature.
Hence I could not recognise thee O Lord, appearing in human form.
— *Ramacharitamanas* by Tulsidas

Since he was a *chiranjeevi*, Hanuman lived through many eons. The Treta Yuga in which he was born gave place to the Dwapara Yuga and Vishnu who had incarnated himself as Rama, in Treta now became Krishna in Dwapara. As predicted by Krishna, Hanuman made many appearances in the *Yuga* known as Dwapara and was given a chance to help the Pandavas.

In the *Bhagavad-Gita*, Krishna proclaimed that every time the law of cosmic righteousness declined in the world, he would incarnate himself to uplift *dharma* and punish those who did not uphold it. In this fight against *adharma*, Krishna's chosen instruments were the Pandavas, who belonged to the Kuru dynasty which was the ruling dynasty of that time. They were five in number and had extremely noble qualities. The eldest was called Yudhistira and he was actually the heir to the throne of the Kurus. Bhima was the second and Arjuna the third, while Nakula and Sahadeva were the fourth and fifth. However, their cousins who numbered hundred and were the sons of their uncle, Dritarashtra, were bent on destroying them and denying their rightful heritage to the throne. The *Mahabharata*, written by the sage Vyasa, is mainly the story of the events leading up to the battle between these two set of cousins known as the Pandavas and the Kauravas. In this battle Krishna sided with the Pandavas and thus they were able to overcome the Kauravas even though the latter were superior in numbers. Krishna became the charioteer of Arjuna and helped him to win the war. The *Bhagavad-Gita* is the discourse given by Krishna to Arjuna at the beginning of the war and is one of the greatest scriptures in Hinduism.

Each of the five Pandavas are said to have been fathered by a celestial. Bhima, who was the strongest, claimed Vayu as his father. In this way Hanuman was Bhima's brother since he was also "Vayu-putra."

The five brothers had been cheated at a dice game and had been banished by the Kauravas to the forest where they had to spend fourteen years. Arjuna had gone into the deep recesses of the upper Himalayan ranges in order to do *tapas* to Lord Shiva to get the boon of his divine weapons. The other four brothers accompanied by their wife, Draupadi followed him and came to these remote regions. The sage Lomasha was the one who led them on along this dangerous path where the cruel winds howl and storms constantly ravage the slopes. Draupadi fainted during one of these storms. Yudhistira was anxious to return but Bhima insisted that they should go forward and summoned his *rakshasa* son, Gatotkacha who took the exhausted Pandavas through the air to Badarikashrama, the abode of the great sages, Nara and Narayana. Here they rested for six days. It was here that Draupadi saw a thousand-petalled lotus that was drifting in the wind. The divine perfume made her reel and she begged Bhima to get more for her.

Bhima was ever ready to do her bidding and departed, roaring and beating a path for himself with his mace through the jungle and destroying much of the flora. He blew his conch loudly and slapped his thighs like a wrestler. Hanuman was living in this forest. When heard this commotion he decided to curb his brother's pride.

After walking a long way Bhima climbed a high ridge and discovered a beautiful orchard of banana trees that seemed to stretch on forever. He plunged through this like a maddened elephant, shattering and uprooting trees and terrifying the animals and birds. Suddenly in the middle of his path he saw a huge, golden-coloured monkey with amber eyes, languidly feeding on the bananas. He heard the commotion made by Bhima's passage and thumped his tail on the ground, producing a sound like thunder. Bhima also heard the sound and considered it as a challenge. He charged forward and soon came face to face with the monkey who was lying right across his path.

"His short, thick neck lay on the cross of his arms, his waist over his hips looked slender below his towering shoulder and he shone as with a flag with his erect, long-haired tail that was slightly bent at the end. His face like the beaming moon showed red lips, a mouth with copper red tongue, pink ears, darting brows and round-tipped protruding tusks. The brilliant white teeth inside his mouth shed luster on it and a massive mane crowned it like a mass of *ashoka* blossoms. Thus he sat, resplendent amidst the golden banana trees, ablaze with his beauty like a blazing fire, staring fearlessly from honey-yellow eyes." This is the description of Hanuman as given by Vyasa in the *Mahabharata.*

The monkey chided Bhima for his lack of consideration for the creatures of the forest but the arrogant Bhima merely ordered him to get out of the way or else he would be the next to suffer from the effects of his wrath. The monkey protested weakly that he was too old and tired to move and told him that he could jump over him if he wished.

Bhima protested, "I believe the divine to be present in all creatures, even an old and prostrate monkey like you, so I will not commit such an act. Otherwise I would have leapt over you as easily as Hanuman once leapt over the sea."

The old monkey's eyes gleamed momentarily and he asked in a weak voice, "Hanuman! Who might that be?"

Bhima replied scornfully, "Everyone knows that Hanuman was the great *bhakta* of Lord Rama and the son of Vayu, and therefore my own half brother! As for me I am Bhima, second of the great Pandavas. Demons tremble at the mention of my name and poets write odes to my strength. Now get up before I kick you aside!"

The monkey seemed unimpressed by all this and languidly continued to peel another banana. He said in a weak voice, "I'm too tired to move but if you like you can remove my tail from your path. If you feel you can't do this, then have a banana since it's sure to give you strength!"

Bhima was enraged by this but he did not like to step over the tail nor did he want to touch it so he decided to lift it a little with his mace and toss it and the monkey high into the air! When he tried to shove his mace beneath the tail, he found to his surprise that it was hard as iron and when he tried to lift it he nearly fell. He strained until sweat poured down his face and veins bulged on his forehead. It was only then that he realized that this was no puny monkey as he had thought but some powerful being, much more powerful than him. His pride was duly humbled and he stood before the monkey with folded palms and begged him to reveal his identity.

"Surely you are no ordinary monkey but some god in monkey form. Kindly deign to tell me your name."

Hanuman got up and said, "I am Hanuman, son of Vayu and you are my brother. I have been lying here waiting for you since I wanted to meet you."

Bhima was overjoyed to hear this and the two brothers hugged each other with great affection. Bhima told Hanuman that he had been his hero since childhood and that he had always wanted to see him. The brothers embraced each other once again and Hanuman asked Bhima why he was wandering around that lonely forest. Bhima told him that he had come to get the mysterious flower with an intoxicating perfume for his wife Draupadi.

Hanuman said, "The golden lotuses bloom in the lake of Kubera, king of *yakshas*. It is closely guarded by them. You'll have to fight with them if you want to get the flowers."

Bhima replied, "I'm willing to fight anyone to get the flower for Draupadi. With your blessings I'm sure I'll be successful." Hanuman then blessed him and told him to go to the pond and mention his name to the *yakshas* and they would gladly give him as many flowers as he wanted.

Bhima now had another request. "I have always pictured you in your youthful form when you crossed the ocean to find Sita. Please bless me with this vision."

Hanuman said, "That form belonged to the age known as Treta. Now it is the Dwapara Yuga. Even though I'm immortal I have to conform to the standards of the current age. Moreover, if I were to assume that form by which I crossed the ocean, you will not be able to endure it."

However, Bhima continued to plead for this vision and finally Hanuman relented and before he had finished speaking, he changed from an old, grey-bearded monkey to a young and handsome simian. He then started to grow in size before Bhima's astonished gaze until it appeared as if his head would touch the skies. Bhima could hardly see the top of his head which was as radiant as another sun so that he had to close his eyes since he couldn't bear to gaze at that effulgence. He fell at his feet and begged him to return to his former size. Hanuman resumed his usual form and blessed Bhima and warned him against wanton acts of violence. He told him the secrets of Kubera's lake and offered him a boon. He said that he would destroy the Kauravas and return the kingdom to the brothers if he so wished. Bhima replied that just by meeting him, he was assured of success. Hanuman promised to be present on Arjuna's standard and in Bhima's battle cry. With these words he disappeared. A wiser and more chastened Bhima found his way to the lake and was able to get the flowers and return to Draupadi without any further mishap.

There is another interesting story of how Hanuman met Arjuna who was the middle brother amongst the Pandavas. He was the one to whom Lord Krishna gave the advice of the *Bhagavad-Gita* on the battlefield of Kurukshetra. During the battle Arjuna's pennon had Hanuman sitting on it. There is an interesting story connected with this incident.

During their fourteen years of exile Arjuna went to the Himalayas in order to do *tapas* and propitiate Lord Shiva so that he could get a divine weapon from him, for he knew that a battle between his brothers and his cousins was inevitable. Once while roaming in the forest he came across a most distinguished looking monkey meditating under a tree. He was struck by his looks and sat close to him, waiting for him to open his eyes. At last the monkey opened his eyes and Arjuna asked him who he was and why he was meditating here.

The monkey answered, "A monkey's natural habitat is the jungle. I am Hanuman, the servant of Lord Rama. Now would you care to introduce yourself?"

Arjuna went and touched Hanuman's feet and said, "I am indeed fortunate to have met you. I'm Arjuna, the middle one amongst the Pandavas. I have come here to meditate and propitiate Lord Shiva and gain some weapons from him. I am glad to have met you for I have one doubt about Rama. I have heard that he was a great archer and I'm wondering how he could not have constructed a bridge of arrows across the straits instead of having to take the help of monkeys to bring stones and rocks."

Hanuman could hear the arrogance underlying Arjuna's question. It was as if he wanted to prove his superiority as an archer. Hanuman replied, "Making a bridge of arrows would have been a simple task for my Lord, but remember hundreds of gigantic monkeys would have had to cross the bridge and it's very doubtful whether a bridge of arrows could have supported their weight."

Arjuna replied proudly, "I'm sure I could easily make a bridge which would hold the weight of any number of monkeys."

Hanuman said with a smile, "Here is a pond. Why don't you go ahead and make a bridge of arrows over it. If it can take just my weight I'll be satisfied and acknowledge your claim. If however it doesn't stand my weight, what will you do?"

Arjuna said scornfully, "I'm quite sure the bridge won't break with your weight but if it does, I promise to immolate myself in the fire. Now tell me what you will do if the bridge holds your weight?"

Hanuman said, "If you prove successful I promise to sit on your flag in the coming war and lead you to victory."

Without wasting time in more words, Arjuna lifted his legendary bow, the Gandiva and reached into his inexhaustible quiver and started shooting arrows with lightning speed. He linked them and thus created within moments, a marvellous span across the lake. Mighty pleased with his feat he stepped aside and invited Hanuman to walk over it. Hanuman said he would prefer to test the bridge with one foot rather than walk on it and fall into the cold water. Arjuna was furious when he heard this but contained his anger and watched while Hanuman advanced and put one foot gingerly on the bridge. To Arjuna's utter astonishment, the bridge immediately shuddered, cracked and disintegrated and the arrows fell one after the other into the pool! He couldn't believe that just one monkey's foot was enough to make his splendid bridge collapse.

"Now Arjuna," Hanuman asked, "If your bridge can't stand the weight of my one little paw, how do you think it could have withstood the weight of hundreds of monkeys?"

Arjuna was totally demoralised. However, he was determined to keep his word. Silently he collected firewood and made a pyre. Just as he was about to jump in, he was stopped by a *yogi* with matted hair, carrying a staff and water pot.

"You are young and intelligent as I can see by looking at you. Tell me why you have decided to immolate yourself?"

Arjuna told him the whole story and the celibate turned to Hanuman and asked, "Did you have a third person to witness this pledge? In such cases of life and death, it's always normal to have a witness."

Hanuman shook his head and said that in this case there was no need for a witness since he quite believed that Arjuna was an honourable man who would keep his word. The *yogi* insisted that a witness was always necessary in these dire cases and suggested that Arjuna should be allowed to make another bridge and the whole experiment repeated with him as witness. Both of them agreed and once again Arjuna took up his bow but before starting he made a silent prayer to Krishna to help him. He then made another bridge even stronger than the previous one. Hanuman put his right foot forcibly down on the bridge at one side but found to his astonishment that the bridge hardly quivered. He then started to walk over it with no problem at all. He turned round and came to the middle and jumped up and down on it with all his force and still the bridge did not stir. He expanded his size and brought his full force down with a crash. The bridge did not stir. He was really puzzled. He thought for a while and knelt down and peered under the bridge but was amazed to find a huge tortoise upholding it. He then turned round to look at the *sannyasin* and saw instead Lord Krishna looking teasingly at him.

Hanuman ran and prostrated to him and realised that his Rama was standing before him in the form of Krishna and that he had taken on his incarnation as the tortoise in order to uphold Arjuna's bridge and stop him from immolating himself. The same love that Rama had for Hanuman, Krishna had for Arjuna.

Seeing the beloved form of his friend before him, Arjuna ran forward and prostrated to him. He realised that once again, Krishna had come to his aid as he had done many times before. Krishna raised him up and looked lovingly at him and said, "Remember Arjuna that pride should always be curbed. You would have had to pay a heavy price for your arrogance had I not come in time."

Arjuna hung his head in shame and promised to curb his pride in future. He turned to Hanuman and begged his pardon for having questioned his Lord's ability.

Now Krishna asked Hanuman, "O son of Vayu! I hope you will keep your oath and help Arjuna in the war which is soon to come. You should sit on his pennon and help him in all possible ways without actively participating in the war." Hanuman promised to abide by his promise. Arjuna thanked him and went off to complete his *tapasya* to Shiva, and Hanuman returned to his own cave to perform his evening worship.

The Pandavas finished their exile successfully but the Kauravas still refused to give them their rightful portion of the kingdom. Yudhistira did his best to avert war but Duryodana refused to part with even the smallest bit of land. Krishna went as ambassador to the court of the Kurus and tried to prevail upon the elders to reason with Duryodana and make him see reason but it was all to no avail. At last the two factions met on the field of Kurukshetra, prepared for battle. Krishna went as Arjuna's charioteer and Hanuman as promised sat on his pennon and made terrible grimaces and contortions which sent chills down the spines of those who faced him. Some accounts say that Krishna asked Arjuna to repeat the Hanuman *mantra* a hundred thousand times in order to ensure victory. Thus, Arjuna was the first person to worship Hanuman as a god. Krishna then told Hanuman to accept such worship in the ensuing Yuga known as Kali.

At the very commencement of the war, Arjuna told Krishna in his role as charioteer to place the chariot in the middle of the two armies so that he could survey the enemy formation. However, when he saw the opposing army to be filled with his teachers and grandsire and cousins, his heart failed him and his bow fell from his nerveless grasp and he refused to fight. The great advice given by Lord Krishna to Arjuna is known as the *Srimad Bhagavad-Gita.* It is a scripture which gives a practical approach to spirituality and tells us how to deal with any situation however horrific it might be.

"This is not a war for a kingdom but a war of righteousness in which you should fight without hatred for the enemy is within yourself. Only the person who conquers his own base nature can be called a hero. Be equal in success and failure, happiness and sorrow, honour or dishonour and you will incur no sin. Therefore, O Arjuna! Arise and fight as a divine instrument."

This advice of Krishna to Arjuna was meant for all posterity and it holds equally good today as it did five thousand years ago on the battlefield of the Kurus.

From his perch on Arjuna's flag Hanuman enjoyed the unique privilege of being the first one to hear the complete discourse between Krishna and Arjuna known as the *Bhagavad-Gita* on the battlefield of Kurukshetra. He was also the sole witness of Krishna's revelation of his cosmic form. Krishna also told Arjuna that the only reason his chariot did not burn with Karna's arrows was because Hanuman was sitting in it. In fact at the end of the war, when Hanuman descended from his perch, the chariot burst into flames.

"One who reads this Hanuman Chalisa,
Gains success – Gouri's Lord is witness."

— *Hanuman Chalisa* by Tulsidas

ॐ *Sri Hanumathe Namaha!*

ॐ

Shubakaraaya Namaha!

CHAPTER THIRTY-FIVE

SHUBHAM

Kali Yuga

"So sab tava pratapa Raghurai!
Natha na kachu mori prabhutai."

"Everything is due to your might O Lord!
No credit is due to me for the same."

— *Ramacharitamanas* by Tulsidas

The Dwapara gave place to the Iron Age of Kali and Hanuman continued his contemplation of his Lord in the Himalayas.

At this time Shani, son of the Sun God and ruler of the planet Saturn, approached him. Hanuman recognised him since he had once released him from Ravana's dungeon. Shani was black, ill-figured, and had a crooked neck that kept his head bent downward. If ever his glance fell on anyone he was bound to be doomed. Shani informed him that the age of Dwapara was over and that Lord Krishna had left the earth along with the other celestials that had incarnated with him. Shani had been granted enhanced powers to torment earthly beings in the dismal age of Kali. He did this by invading their zodiacal sign for a ruinous seven-and-a-half year cycle. He specially loved to prey on the elderly by afflicting them with lingering and painful bodily afflictions. Exulting in his new powers, Shani announced to Hanuman that now that he was old and his strength greatly reduced, he was going to afflict his body straightaway.

Hanuman did not fear Shani any more than he feared his death dealing brother – Yama. "There is no room in my body for anyone but Rama," he said, "so I advice you to go somewhere else."

Shani laughed and said, "We'll see about that!" Then he outlined his normal plan. Which was to start with two-and-a-half years on the head to weaken the mind and an equal period in the stomach to destroy the digestion and overall health and finally another two-and-a-half years of crippling the knees and legs, by which time the victim was usually ready to welcome his elder brother – Yama!

"Well, better get started," said Hanuman pointing to his head. "We can see about the stomach and legs later."

Shani gleefully clambered on top of Hanuman's head and very soon his scalp began to itch. Hanuman was annoyed and breaking off a large boulder he clapped it on his head.

"Hey! What are you doing?" Shani shouted.

"This is how I generally deal with itches and headaches," said Hanuman.

When the itching persisted he selected a second and larger boulder and slapped it on top of the first. Shani writhed in agony and managed to gasp. "Perhaps we could negotiate. Maybe I'll make an exemption in your case and make it seven and-a-half weeks or perhaps even days!"

"O that's all right," said Hanuman, "you should get on with your work while I get on with mine!" So saying he picked up a third and even heavier boulder and piled it on top of the other two.

Shani shrieked and started to vomit blood. "Let me go! Please let me go and I'll never bother you again," he pleaded.

"I know you!" said Hanuman, "you'll just go and bother someone else!" So saying he delicately placed another boulder on top of the last.

Shani screamed for mercy and said, "Save me O Son of Vayu! Release me, O Messenger of Rama! I promise henceforth never to afflict anyone who remembers you!"

Hanuman was pleased especially by the invocation to his Lord and removed the boulders. Shani descended and swore to keep his word.

There is another version to this story which is worth mentioning here.

One evening Hanuman was meditating at the seaside in one of his favourite haunts, which happened to be the bridge made by the monkeys to Lanka so many eons ago. The inauspicious Shani came ambling along and noticed him. He was feeling particularly good since his powers had become stronger and people everywhere went in terror of him. He was well aware of Hanuman's reputation and thought that if he could get the better of him, his own reputation would go up by leaps and bounds. So he went up to Maruti and shouted, "O Monkey! I am Shani, most powerful of all the planets. Stand up and fight with me instead of pretending to be a great *yogi*!"

Hanuman greeted Shani respectfully and suggested him to go elsewhere to find a more worthy opponent since he had become very old and was not interested in anything but the remembrance of Rama. Shani replied that once he had selected a victim he would never let him go until his full cycle of devastation was complete. He stepped closer and seized Hanuman's paw. Hanuman stood up and enlarged his, and wound it round Shani and bound him from head to toe. Shani did his best to free himself but could hardly get his breath to talk.

Hanuman ignored him and looked at the sinking sun and said, "I have to do my daily circumambulation of the Lord's bridge!"

So saying he sprang on to the rough causeway and set out at a brisk trot – two hundred leagues to Lanka and back. Periodically he punctuated his strides by slapping his tail down hard on the jagged rocks. The tail was like adamant and did not suffer from this treatment but the same could not be said of its unwilling passenger. By the time the journey was complete Shani was beaten to a pulp and was babbling for mercy. Hanuman stretched himself out leisurely on the sand and said, "If you promise to stay out of the horoscopes of my worshippers, I will let you off."

Shani could hardly talk but he nodded his head weakly and was freed. He hobbled away and begged for some *til* oil to rub on his wounds. To this day his worshippers offer him this oil on Saturdays which happen to be Shani's day.

During the time of Rama, in the Treta Yuga, a woman called Vaishnavi wanted to marry Rama but he turned her down because he was already married. However, he promised to marry her in Kali Yuga so Vaishnavi decided to do *tapasya* in the Himalayas till the advent of Kali.

One day a sorcerer called Bhairo visited her *ashrama.* As was customary, Vaishnavi offered him food. However, Bhairo was not interested in vegetarian fare and asked for wine, meat and sex so that he could perform an occult rite.

Vaishnavi who had sworn herself to Rama refused to comply with his request and when he tried to use force she ran away. Of course he ran after her. Vaishnavi ran over hills and dales for days until she was totally exhausted and thirsty. She begged Rama to help her. At that moment Hanuman appeared before her. He kicked a rock and out sprang a stream of water. He also punched a cave into the hillside. She drank the water and rested in the cave for nine months performing severe austerities while Hanuman fought with Bhairo. At the end of this period she shed her human form and emerged as Adi Shakti, the Divine Mother armed with all the eighteen weapons. She raised her trident and beheaded Bhairo.

She thanked Hanuman for his timely assistance and accepted him as the attendant guardian of her shrine. The shrine of Vaishno Devi in the Himalayas has an idol of Hanuman at the gateway.

The great *yogi* known as Matsyendranath once wished to enter the shrine of the goddess and learn occult secrets from her. Hanuman stopped him at the gate and fought with him. He found the *yogi* to be a worthy opponent and let him in. Matsyendranath was so pleased with him that he offered to do whatever he wished. Hanuman decided to test the worth of this *yogi* so he told him to go to the land peopled only by women – *stree rajya* and offer them the pleasure of his company! The gods had decreed that any man who entered *stree rajya* would die an instant death.

Matsyendranath was surprised to hear this strange request so Hanuman told him the story of this place and why he had undertaken to help the women. The event had taken place long ago when he was serving Rama in Ayodhya. Hanuman would take care of Rama's every need, much to Sita's annoyance. To keep him away for a while she told him. "It's my wish that you father a child. Leave Ayodhya and return only after you have done so. Naturally her request horrified Hanuman since he had taken a vow of celibacy. Thus, he feared he would never be able to father a child and never be able to return to Ayodhya! In despair he wandered over the whole earth singing Rama's glories.

The women of *stree rajya* heard him sing and such was the potency of his voice that it made them all pregnant. In due course they produced children whom they presented to Hanuman who returned them to their mothers since he said he was not a *grihastashrami* (householder).

They said, "Now you can return to Ayodhya since you have produced children without breaking your vow of celibacy!"

Hanuman was so pleased with them that he offered them a boon. They promptly asked him to send a man to their land so that they could enjoy the pleasure of male company. Hanuman had promised to do so and Matsyendranath was the chosen man since Hanuman knew that he was the only one who had the power to overcome the curse of the gods! Such was the *yogic* power of this great sage that he was able to go into this strange land and stay in the company of the women for some years and thus keep Hanuman's word to them. The curse of the gods had no power over the sage!

The Tulsidas *Ramayana*, known as the *Ramacharitamanas* is the best known *Ramayana* after that of Valmiki's. In fact the popular theory is that Valmiki himself was born as Tulsidas since he felt that he hadn't done enough justice to Hanuman in his own *Ramayana.* The story of how he saw Hanuman's *Ramayana*, inscribed on rocks has been narrated earlier.

During the time of the Moguls, when Akbar, the Great, was emperor, he had a very good Hindu minister called Atmarama. His son was called Tulsiram and he was extremely fond of the child. When the boy came of age, he got him married to a very pious girl called Mamta Devi. He then left his wife in the care of his son and taking the emperor's permission he went to Kashi (Varanasi), in order to mediate on God. Due to his love for Atmarama, Akbar appointed Tulsiram in his father's post. Unfortunately the young man got into some wild company and his whole character changed. He was always seen drinking and gambling and moving with women of low morals. Hearing this Atmarama came back and tried his best to advice his son who turned a deaf ear to his father's exhortations.

Atmarama then shifted his whole family from the Mogul capital at Delhi to a small village on the banks of the river Yamuna near the town of Mathura.

Tulsiram now turned his passion towards his own wife and spent his whole time in her company, totally neglecting his work as well as his spiritual duties. His wife kept advising him to return to a normal state of affairs but the man was so bemused by her beauty that he could think of nothing else but consorting with her. Akbar now sent word asking him to return to the capital since he had some work for him. Tulsiram refused to see the officers who had come to get him. At Mamta's insistence he decided to go. When he reached Delhi, he was in a fever of impatience to get back since he was craving for his wife. At last he asked the emperor to give him leave since he had not bid farewell to his mother and wife when he left. He promised to return very soon.

As soon as he got permission he took a one horse bogey and started off with all speed to his village even though it was already evening. Very soon the sky darkened and it started to rain. The driver begged him to stop somewhere for the night but Tulsiram refused to listen to reason and urged him to whip the horse and make it go faster. The storm did not abate and the poor horse carried on in the face of the bitter wind and rain. At last it just could not go any more and collapsed at the outskirts of the village. Tulsiram cursed the driver and the horse and jumped out of the carriage and ran all the way to his house. His mother was astounded to see him standing at the door all wet and bedraggled at two in the morning.

"What's the matter?" She asked. "Why have you come at this time of the night?"

Tulsiram did not even bother to reply to his mother. "Where is my wife?" He demanded. "I must see her immediately."

"She has gone to her own house across the river," said his mother.

Without wasting a moment, Tulsiram ran to the river which was swollen and rough due to the storm. There was not a boat or boatman in sight. He was afire with the desire to see his wife and without even thinking of how he was risking his life, he jumped into the swirling waters of the Yamuna and started swimming against the strong current. He found that he was not progressing very well. At that moment as if in answer to a prayer he saw a log floating down. He caught hold of it thankfully and was taken across the river. He jumped on to the banks and when he turned round to look at the river, there was a sudden burst of lightning and he saw to his horror that the thing which he had thought was a log was actually a corpse!

Without wasting time on unnecessary speculations, he dashed to his wife's house and found the gate locked. The walls were quite high and it was impossible for him to get a foothold to jump over it. He shouted and shouted to her to come and open the gate, but the noise of the thunder and the storm drowned his voice. By this time he was crazed with lust and totally devoid of reason. He went round and round the walls like a crazy man and suddenly spied a thick rope hanging down the wall. He grabbed it and somehow managed to scrabble to the top of the wall and jump into the compound. He then went and pounded at the door till he woke the whole household. They were all aghast to see his wild condition and wondered how he had managed to cross the river and climb over the wall. He told them that he had hung on to a log and found a rope on the wall. When they went to inspect the rope they found that it was actually a python!

As soon as they reached their bedroom he could contain his lust no longer and grabbed his wife in his arms. She pushed him off in all fury and burst into a tirade of rage and sorrow.

"How can you behave like this? Have you lost all sense of decency and decorum? This body for whose sake you have dared to cross this raging river and climb a wall with the help of a snake is only made of flesh, blood and bones, and will decay and become old in no time. If you have half the love for God as you have for me, you would have become a realised saint! If you longed for the vision of Rama as much as you craved for my vision, you would have seen him by now. Actually it is not love that you have for me but lust for this flesh! You are born in a noble family and you have the possibility to become enlightened in this life. Don't waste this precious life in sexual pleasures. Repeat the name of Rama and get liberation!"

Tulsiram was stunned when he heard this. Her words made a deep impression on him. It was as if she had given him a blow on his head and something had burst inside. As the dawn appeared in the sky, a light flamed in his head. Without another word, he left the house and went to the city of Kashi and started intense austerities. As much as he had yearned for the sight of his wife, now he yearned to have a sight of his beloved deity – Rama. He could not eat or sleep. He went around as one possessed enquiring for Rama. At last he met someone who told him that the only one who could fulfil his desire was Hanuman.

"Where can I meet Hanuman?" He asked.

"He is always present wherever the story of Rama is told. The *Ramayana* is being sung at a certain place right now. You will surely find him there. But remember he will not be in his own form. But I have often noticed that a Brahmin dressed in tatters, is always present at the discourse. He is the first to come and the last to leave. No one knows who he is or where he lives. I suspect that he is indeed Hanuman. Catch hold of him. Never leave him and he will be able to give you the vision of the Lord."

Tulsiram went daily to the discourse and observed the old Brahmin carefully. However, every time he tried to follow him, he found that the old man disappeared instantly. Yet, nothing could deter his urgency to meet Rama. The same determination which compelled him to risk his life in order to reach the side of his beloved on that stormy night was now directed to meeting the divine beloved! One day he jumped and caught hold of the Brahmin's *dhoti* which was around his waist and tied his hand to it. The old man ran very fast into the dense forest and very soon Tulsiram could not keep up with his speed. But he hung on to the cloth and was dragged over the rough ground until he was torn and bleeding. All the while he kept repeating the *mantra* of Rama. He was determined never to let him go until his wish was fulfilled. At last the Brahmin stopped. Tulsiram grabbed hold of his feet and said,

"My Lord I know who you are. I will not let you go till you give me a vision of Rama!"

Anjaneya now took his own form and raised him up and said, "Indeed I am pleased with your devotion. You shall have a vision of the Lord tomorrow!"

Thus saying, he vanished. Tulsiram returned to his abode and spent the night in ecstasy thinking of the joy in store for him in the morning.

The next day he cleaned his whole hut and compound and waited anxiously for his Lord to come. However, the only ones who came were two hunters dressed in green and mounted on horseback. That evening he went to the Brahmin and cried loud and long for he had not got the vision that had been promised.

Hanuman replied, "He did come but you did not recognise him for he was dressed as a common hunter! But fear not tomorrow evening he will give you the *darshan* you are longing for."

The local people heard about this and many were present in Tulsiram's courtyard. The shades of night were falling and the yard was filled with people all chanting, "Rama! Rama! Suddenly all of them were thrilled to see Rama approaching with Lakshmana and Sita on either side. Tulsiram fell at Rama's feet and was unable to get up. Rama lifted him up tenderly and told him.

"My son, your love alone has brought me here. You are truly blessed. From now on you shall be known as Tulsidas. It is your duty to write the story of the *Ramayana* in simple language which the common people can understand."

Tulsidas was astounded, "My Lord! He said, "I am totally incapable of writing on such a great subject. All I know is to chant your name. How can I fulfil your command?"

Rama looked tenderly at him and said, "Fear not. You will be given guidance by Hanuman, who is not only erudite but also filled with devotion. He has been a living witness to the story of my life. He is the best person to guide you."

Thus, it happened that Tulsidas started writing the *Ramayana* in the common man's language – Awadhi which was a dialect of Hindi. It was written in the year AD 1575. When Valmiki wrote his *Ramayana*, India was at the peak of its cultural refinement, while Tulsidas produced his work at a time when there was a widespread degradation in moral values. There was rivalry between different faiths and sects. Through the story of Rama, Tulsidas sought to acquaint the masses with all that was best in the Hindu scriptures and to bring about a synthesis and concord among the various schools of religious thought. In North India, it gained instant popularity amongst labourers, peasants and householders alike. It came to be known as the *Ramacharitamanas*.

Many miracles were attributed to Tulsidas. Hearing about these, the Mogul emperor Akbar sent for him and asked him to perform some miracle for him. Tulsidas replied, "I am only a humble servant of Rama. He alone is the worker of miracles."

"Show me your Rama then", said the emperor.

Tulsidas remained silent. The emperor became angry at his silence and ordered him to be put in jail. It is said that Tulsidas composed the *Hanuman Chalisa* when he was in prison at Fatehpur Sikri, which was Akbar's fortress at the time. During those forty days when he was composing the verses, he prayed to Hanuman to save him from this predicament. At the end of the forty days the whole of the emperor's fort was swarming with monkeys. They clawed people, tore their clothes, entered houses and destroyed gardens. At last the emperor realised that this must be the work of the man he had thrown into jail. He ran to him, fell at his feet and begged him to order the monkeys to go away. Tulsidas prayed to Hanuman and immediately the monkeys vanished but he told the emperor, "You should leave this spot and take up your residence at some other place, for this is Rama's abode and no one should stay here except the monkeys."

Hearing this, the emperor is said to have changed the location of his fortress. Tulsidas died in the year 1624. Two copies of his *Ramayana* written in his own handwriting are said to be existent. One is preserved at Rajpur and the other in the temple of Sita-Rama, which he himself had constructed, at Kashi. Although many of the Sanskrit pundits of his time attacked him for having lowered the dignity of his subject by clothing it in vulgar vernacular, the fact remains that his book is found everywhere, from the court to the cottage and is read or heard and appreciated by every class of the Hindu community, high and low, rich and poor, young and old.

"Says Tulsidas, 'Hari's constant servant,
Lord! Make your abode in my heart.'"

— *Hanuman Chalisa* by Tulsidas

ॐ *Sri Hanumathe Namaha!*

ॐ

Mangalaaya Namaha!

CHAPTER THIRTY-SIX

MANGALA MURTI

The Auspicious Form

"Then Sita spoke, greatly pleased,
'Son of the Wind, wherever you reside, by my decree,
You will receive abundant offerings.
In villages, fields, cities and cowsheds,
By roadsides, in hamlets and homes.
Forests and forts, on hilltops and in temples,
By rivers and pilgrim places,
By tanks and towns.
In gardens and groves, under fig and banyan trees,
And in sacred sites.
Men will worship your image to assuage their afflictions,
When you are remembered, ghosts, goblins and ghouls will flee.'"

— *Ananda Ramayana*

Sita's blessing to Hanuman proved to be prophetic since all the blessings she gave him have come to pass over the years. Hanuman's shrines are in keeping with his personality and are rarely elaborate. They are humble structures built by ordinary people, without the help of priests. He is often seen in the open, under trees or on the walls of temples, forts and palaces. His idols are mainly carved out of stone or sometimes out of roots of trees with stubs that vaguely resemble simian features. They are often covered with vermilion or saffron paste and sometimes decorated with silver foil. Images normally show him carrying the mountain of herbs or standing guard in front of a Rama temple holding his mace. It is rare to see him in a meditative posture like a *yogi.*

His images are also seen at the gateways to settlements and villages to keep out malevolent forest spirits or at cross roads where ghosts lurk, or at the entrance to forts, palaces, temples, monasteries and gymnasiums. In the famous Krishna shrine of Nathdwara, in Rajasthan, Hanuman stands guard before the four gates to the temple. In both Jaipur and Vrindavan, there are many Hanuman shrines. During the early twentieth century, many of the little known shrines to Hanuman which claimed to be ancient and self-formed suddenly sprang into prominence. Varanasi claims many such shrines. The small road-side shrines of Nichi Bagh and Kabir Choura are so crowded on Tuesdays and Saturdays that all traffic comes to a grinding halt. A small shrine in a lane behind Assi Ghat in the midst of a *dalit* settlement sprang into prominence when the great nationalist leader, Madan Mohan Malaviya began stopping there for prayers after his morning ablutions in the *ghat.* He kept a forty-day vigil to get Hanuman's blessing for establishing the Benaras Hindu University and of course with Maruti's blessings, the world famous university was established in 1916.

Of course the most well known shrine in Varanasi is the huge *murti* in the Sankata Mochana temple. The story of this is closely connected with Tulsidas. He used to pray to a small Hanuman under the twisted roots of a peepul tree after his ablutions in the Ganga. This tree was the abode of a tormented spirit who was grateful for the water which Tulsidas used to pour over it daily. In return he offered Tulsidas a boon. The saint asked for *darshan* of Rama but of course the poor ghost could not arrange this. However, he told him that the only one who could help him was Hanuman himself. He told him that Maruti used to come daily to the *ghat* in the form of an old leper, to listen to the narration of the *Ramayana.* He sat at the back and was always the last to leave. Tulsidas followed the leper who led him deep into the forest. He fell at his feet and hailed him as "Vayu putra!" The leper denied vehemently that he was nothing but an old, sick man but Tulsidas persisted and eventually Hanuman revealed his own glorious form. Raising one hand over his shoulder he pointed south-west and said, "Go to Chitrakut," and placing the other hand over his heart he added, "I promise that you will see Rama." This is supposed to have taken place at the very spot where the Sankata Mochana temple now stands and the posture of the idol there has the same gestures which are mentioned here:

It is said that Tulsidas entreated Hanuman to stay in that spot for the benefit of his devotees. Maruti agreed but dived into the ground and disappeared. Tulsidas dug frantically into the sand throughout the night and finally as dawn was breaking, he unearthed a *swayambhu murti* (self-formed) with the same posture in which Hanuman had addressed him. He established this *murti* and thus created the first temple to Hanuman. This miracle is supposed to have occurred on the eighth day of the dark fortnight of the month of Margashirsha (November/December) in 1550. The Bara Hanuman or the Great Hanuman is seen in the Hanuman *ghat* of the city.

The very popular temple at Mehndipur is situated in a small valley, five kilometres from the Agra-Jaipur highway. It is identified as the place where Bala (baby) Hanuman was returned to the lap of his mother by the Wind God after he had been chastised by Indra for daring to swallow the sun. Hence, he is known as Balaji. There are many stories connected with this place. It is said that one of the priests had a dream in which he saw the idol of Balaji. Suddenly he saw thousands of flickering lamps approaching from afar. When they came near he discovered that the lights were being carried by a huge army of men accompanied by horses and elephants. They circumambulated Balaji and the commander came and prostrated to him. After this striking performance all of them disappeared the way they had come. At that very spot the priest saw three *murtis* and heard a voice saying, "Rise up and attend to my *pujas,* I intend to perform many miracles here. When he woke up the Brahmin started to search and eventually located the site he had seen in his dream. He discovered the three idols and started offering ritualistic worship to them. Very soon miracles started to occur in the temple and many people started to come. During the time of the Muslim rule the temple went into a decline and one king even tried to uproot the idol of Balaji but he could never find its base. He soon realised that the whole mountain was its body! With the passing of time the temple rose to its present state of fame and glory.

Actually there are three main deities here. The first is Balaji himself. This idol is carved out of the boulder and covered with *sindoor* (vermilion) and silver foil. In the hall upstairs, there is the idol to Pretaraj or the king of ghosts. He is sometimes referred to as Yamaraj or the king of death. Balaji is supposed to be a most powerful deity for exorcising people from evil spirits. Petitions are offered to Balaji by those who are possessed of spirits and healing occurs in many ways. The person starts speaking in the voice of the spirit and is exhorted by Balaji and Pretaraj to leave the sufferer in peace.

In Ayodhya it is said that Rama turned over the city to Hanuman when he left the earth and thus Hanuman is the present day king of Ayodhya. His most important temples here are in Hanuman Garhi and Nagesvarnath.

Lucknow is noted for two temples in the Aliganj area. The Hanuman temple here is the most renowned and the Mahavir Mela is said to attract all the different religious communities. During this festival many male devotees circumambulate the temple with full body prostrations or by rolling in the dust while clad only in a red loincloth.

The famous recumbent Hanuman lies near the Triveni Sangam or triple confluence where the visible rivers of Ganga and Yamuna meet the invisible Saraswati in the place known as Prayaga, near modern Allahabad. The huge figure, half buried in the sandy riverbank, is approached by descending a flight of steps. It is said that two hundred years ago when the idol was being transported down the river by a wealthy merchant, the boat ran aground and the figure tipped over into the sand. All attempts to dislodge it failed and Hanuman revealed in a dream that he wished to remain at this spiritually potent confluence.

Seventy miles south of Allahabad, near the pilgrim site of Chitrakut stands another temple perched on the summit of a wooded hill and approached by three hundred and fifty stone steps. This is known as Hanuman Dhara and commands a sweeping view of the region where Rama, Sita and Lakshmana are supposed to have resided for twelve years. The idol is carved into the back wall of the cliff and over it a stream of water emerges and constantly bathes the *murti.*

In the temple of Lord Jagannath in Puri, Orissa, Hanuman guards all the four gates of the temple in order to prevent the sound of the sea from entering the shrine and disturbing his master. There are many other famous shrines to Maruti in Puri apart from the four which guard the gates. The Dariya Hanuman was installed near the sea so that he would protect the city from onslaughts by the ocean. However, Maruti abandoned his post to go and have *darshan* of his Lord. When the citizens complained to Lord Jagannath, he told them to chain him to his post. Since no ordinary chains could bind him, he was secured with a stout chain of gold links on which were inscribed Rama's name.

However, the most famous Hanuman in Orissa is in the village of Siruli on the Puri-Bhuvaneswar road and is known as Mahavir. It is a black stone idol believed to have emerged from the earth. Its left eye gazes through a small window towards Puri and the right eye stares balefully towards Lanka in the south.

In the very heart of modern Delhi, just behind the bustling circle known as Connaught Place, stands a most vibrant Hanuman temple known as Sri Hanumanji Maharaj. The main statue is fairly recent and is of white marble but the actual *murti* is on one side and placed at the right side of the statues of Rama and Sita. Normally the features are hidden by a heavy coating of *sindoor* but now and again this falls off to reveal the original idol. It is a small bas relief of a simian profile with head facing south and bared teeth. One raised fist brandishes a tiny club and the other rests on his heart. He wears a tapering crown, sacred thread over his right shoulder and has a loincloth hanging between his short legs. The *murti* is said to have been established by the Pandavas when their capital was in Indraprastha – modern Delhi.

Another important Hanuman temple in Delhi is found in Old Delhi, in the place known as Yamuna bazaar near the river next to the burning *ghats*. It is known as the Marghat Baba Hanuman. The small complex set among huge peepul trees is barely noticeable from the street. The shrine is tiny, with a low doorway, approached by a narrow flight of steps which descend to the sanctorum in which the small figure stands with eyes gazing straight ahead. The descent to this subterranean sanctuary creates a mysterious atmosphere. During the monsoons, the waters of the Yamuna seep into the sanctum and at times Hanuman stands neck deep in water but the temple never closes. This is known as a seat of power and was founded by Bhima, the strong man amongst the Pandavas. These two Hanuman temples provide a great contrast. They denote the two aspects of Hanuman – *bhakti* and *shakti.*

Maharashtra abounds in Hanuman shrines and they are even said to exceed the Ganesha shrines. In South India, the medieval city of Vijayanagara is supposed to have been the place of the ancient monkey kingdom of Kishkinda. The small hill known as Ajanadri (hill of Anjana) is supposed to mark the birth place of Hanuman.

One of the most important shrines to Hanuman is found in Suchindram in Tamil Nadu. It has a twenty-foot statue which is said to be growing. *Abhishekam* or the ritual bath has to be done by priests who have to climb up ladders. This is supposed to be the form that he took to reassure Sita. There is another shrine to him in Kanyakumari, close to Suchindram, at the tip of the Indian sub-continent. Another important Hanuman shrine in South India is located at the place known as Namakkal near Salem. The huge idol is plastered with butter on Saturdays and even on hot days the butter remains without melting till the next morning. The priests make a fascinating design on the butter with leaves and flowers. Hanuman stands facing a temple to Narasimha Murti, who is the fourth *avatara* of Vishnu. Since Narasimha has no roof over his head, Hanuman also refused to have a cover above him and stands exposed to the elements.

In the famous Krishna temple of Udupi, devotees always have *darshan* of Anjaneya before proceeding to the main temple of Krishna.

In some of the temples in Gujarat, Hanuman is depicted as a stout figure with a handlebar moustache. In Sourashtra several figures of Maruti are found alongside the one thousand and five hundred steps going up the sacred Girnar Mountain.

Many books contain a list of famous Anjaneya shrines. The list above is far from being complete. It is doubtful if anyone can take an account of the number of shrines and idols which have been dedicated to this amazing being, many of which are said to have miraculous properties. There are speaking and shaking Hanumans and subterranean and submerged Hanumans and those that emerge from boulders and farm furrows like Sita. For those who want to make a pilgrimage to the Hanuman shrines, one safe way is to follow Rama's path in the *Ramayana* from Ayodhya to Lanka. All along this route are found many of Anjaneya's most important shrines.

Power and devotion or *shakti* and *bhakti* are his dual characteristics. As such Hanuman *murtis* are divided into these two types. Those which denote *bhakti* are known as having *dasa bhava* and those with a virile mood are known as having *vira bhava.* The former *murtis* should be worshipped with *sattvika* or pure types of offerings like fruits and nuts while the other types can be worshipped with *rajasic* offerings which might even include alcohol. The latter figures are supposed to denote his form as Rudra or the incarnation of the 11th Rudra and are often just a stone smeared with *sindoor.* It is commonly noticed that if the right foot is placed to the front, it depicts his mild devotional aspect while the demon-slaying aspect is stressed if the left foot is kept forward. As an embodiment of *shakti,* Hanuman is closely associated with control of the elements and the destructive aspects of creation which are the characteristics of Shiva and his consort Shakti. As an example of *bhakti,* or self-effacing love, he drowns himself in the river of Rama's love.

Hanuman is supposed to be the *pratyaksha devata* or most efficient deity of the present age of Kali since he is still alive. He alone is supposed to be capable of bestowing all the four aims of life (*dharma, artha, kama* and *moksha*) and that is the reason that in this Kali Yuga more and more temples are being built for him.

On the way to Badrinath, which is the famous shrine to Lord Vishnu, one has to pass a small village called Pandukeshwara. Above it is the mountain known as Hemakuta. This is the place where Lakshmana is supposed to have done *tapasya,* to atone for the sin of having killed Indrajit. The Sikhs have built a huge temple here which is supposed to be the highest temple in the world and is known as Hemkunt Sahib. Above that in the towering heights of the "golden mountain" (Hemakuta), is the abode of the Kimpurushas or mystic beings that are half human and half animal. Here Hanuman still resides and many *yogis* claim to have seen him there.

"Son of the Wind, banisher of affliction,
Embodiment of auspiciousness,
Dwell in my heart, king of gods,
Together with Rama, Lakshmana and Sita."

— *Sri Hanuman Chalisa* by Tulsidas

ॐ *Sri Hanumathe Namaha!*

POEMS

Hail to Thee O Son of Wind!
Messenger of Rama!
Harbinger of light and life!
Light to Sita,
Life to Lakshmana,
You flew into my heart,
Like a tender bud,
And made it blossom into a full blown lotus.

ॐ ॐ ॐ ॐ ॐ ॐ

What did I know about bhakti,
Till you came and took residence in my heart.
What did I know of shakti,
Till you empowered my limbs,
Ah! precious harbinger of hope and love,
Show me your form when you crept into Lanka,
Sweet and small like a little cat,
The form which enticed Sita,
As you parted the leaves and gazed at her.
As you chanted the tales of her beloved,
Filling her with rapture.
I shudder to think of your enormous frame,
Reducing Lanka to cinders.
O gentle one!
People say you are mighty and impossible to control,

But I see thee kneeling at Rama's feet,
Vanamali's feet that I cherish in my heart.

ॐ ॐ ॐ ॐ ॐ ॐ

O Lordly One!
Terrify me not with thy brooding looks,
And horrific grimace scattering the demons in fear,
Let me drown in thy amber eyes,
Piercing me to the depths of my soul,
Filled with compassion,
For this hapless soul,
Floundering in the sea of samsara.

ॐ ॐ ॐ ॐ ॐ ॐ

Give me the eyes to perceive thee,
Take me to thy abode.
In the heart of the golden peak,
To the land of the kimpurushas
Half wild, half human,
Waft me away in thy arms to the mystic mountain,
Surrounded by celestial beings,
I shall turn my face to thy father,
And feel his caressing tendrils on my face,
I shall lie near thee on the lap of nature,
And gaze upon the face of god,
For you will be where Rama is,
And Rama is none but my beloved,
Vanamali!
Therefore O Vanara!
Take me to Vanamali!
I have searched for Him far and wide,
In thee I have found the perfect vehicle,
My sweet Maruti,
Deny me not this request,
For I am thy eternal servant,
Sent by Him to me,

For now I know that thou and He,
Are never two but always one.
Who came first god or bhakta,
None can tell for they are united in eternity.

ॐ ॐ ॐ ॐ ॐ ॐ

I gaze at the monkeys that flock in my garden,
And wonder if you could be amongst them,
They destroy the garden like you did,
They eat up the fruits and despoil the pools,
Am I to tolerate their inequities?
They belong to your race?
Tell me O Divine Vanara!
Why the violence and the worry?
Can you not protect me from this?
Am I your servant for nothing?
Teach them to curb their nature,
As indeed you did.
And then I shall love you even more,

ॐ ॐ ॐ ॐ ॐ ॐ

My noble Hanuman, help me to understand,
The vagaries of the monkey mind,
Help me to control mine,
Direct me to the source divine,
From which alone your inspiration comes.
Hold me aloft in your hand like the herb mountain,
Waft me to Vaikunda, the abode of Vanamali,
O Vanara! Be my messenger to Vanamali!
Whisper in his ear as you did to Rama,
Of the love of Sita for Rama,
Of the love of Devi for Vanamali!

ॐ ॐ ॐ ॐ ॐ ॐ

ॐ *Sri Hanumathe Namaha!*

GLOSSARY OF SANSKRIT TERMS

abhijit	a favourable star
abhishekam	ceremonial bath for gods and kings
adharma	unrighteousness
adi kavi	the first poet (Valmiki)
ahamkara	ego
amavasya	new moon
amsa	a part
anga	limb
apana	the outgoing breath
apsara	heavenly nymph
artha	wealth
arya	noble
ashoka	a tree; without sorrow
ashrama	spiritual sanctuary
ashramite	one who lives in an *ashrama*
ashwamedha yaga	horse sacrifice; conducted by kings to establish supremacy
astra	weapon
asura	demon
atma(n)	the divine spirit embodied in the human being; the soul
aum Namashivaaya	*mantra* for Shiva
avatara	incarnation
bandar	monkey
bhajan	religious song

bhakta	devotee
bhakti	devotion
bhakti yoga	the yoga of devotion
brahmachari	a celibate
brahmacharya	celibacy
brahmajnana	integral knowledge of the Supreme Brahman
brahmarishi	a sage who has *brahmajnana*
brahmastra	the weapon of Brahma
chakora	bird who is supposed to drink moon beams
champaka	tree with sweet-smelling flowers
chandala	an outcaste
chiranjeevi	long-lived person
chourie	yak tail fan
chudamani	a jewel for the hair
daitya	demon
dakshinayana	six months of the year from July to December
dalit	a low caste
darshan	auspicious sight of god or a noble being
darshanas	the different schools of Hindu philosophy (six in number)
dasa bhava	attitude of a servant (male)
dasya bhava	attitude of a servant (female)
deva; devi	god; goddess; shining one
dharma	righteousness
dhoti	cloth worn round the waist by men
dhruva	type of grass
dwarapalas	guardians of the gate, especially in temples and palaces

gada	mace
gandharva	celestial singer
gayatri mantra	famous hymn to the Sun God
ghat	bathing place on the river
griha	house
grihastashrami	one who leads a householder's life
guna	one of the three strands of nature
guru	spiritual preceptor
guru-dakshina	fee given to the guru
han	to destroy
hanan	to annihilate
hanu	jaw
hatha yoga	special branch of yoga in which physical postures are taught
hatha yogi	one who practises this type of yoga
japa	repetition of the names of god
jivatma	the embodied spirit
jnana	wisdom
kadamba	a type of flower
kaala	time
kama	love
kanda	one portion of a book
kapha	phlegm
karma	action
karma sakshi	the witness of all action (god)
karma yogi	one who practises the yoga of action
kirtan	spiritual song
kshetrapalas	guardians of the temple
kund	a lake or pool
kunjara südana	killer of elephants
kusa	type of grass used in rituals

lakh	a hundred thousand
langur	black-faced monkey
laya yogi	one who practises the yoga of immolation
lila	play; game of God
lingam	a stone symbol of Shiva
loka	an astral world
madari	trainer of monkeys
man	mind
manduka	frog
mantra	mystic sound
maya	illusion
mohastra	weapon of illusion
moksha	liberation from mortality
mritasanjivani	herb which brings the dead to life
munja	type of coarse grass
murti	idol
naga	snake
naga pasha	rope made of snakes
navagrahas	nine planets
navami	ninth day of the lunar calendar
navaratri	nine days of worship of the goddess
panchamukha	five-faced
Paramatma	the Supreme spirit
pitta	bile
prana	life current
pranava mantra	Aum
pranayama	science of breath control
pratyaksha devata	that god which can be seen by our physical eyes; the Sun God
puja	ritual worship of god
puranic	pertaining to the Puranas or epics

putrakamesti yaga	fire sacrifice for getting a son
rajas	one of the three strands of nature; passion
rajasic	pertaining to rajas; passionate
rakshasas	cannibals
rakshasi	female *rakshasa*
rakshasic	having the nature of a *rakshasa*
rigvedic	pertaining to the *Rigveda* which is one of the oldest of the Hindu scriptures
rishi	great sage
sadhaka	one who does spiritual practices
sadhana	spiritual practice
sal	type of tree
saligrama	stone symbol of Vishnu
samadhi	super conscious state
samana	equilibrium
samkhya yoga	yoga of wisdom
sandal	sandalwood tree
sandhani	herb capable of joining fractured bones
sandhya	twilight
sankalpa	intention
sannyasi(n)	one who has renounced the world
sapta rishis	the seven original sages
sari	a 5 metre piece of cloth worn by Indian women
sattva	one of the three stands of nature standing for balance and harmony
sattvika	harmonious; peaceful
shakti	power
Shakti	the divine feminine force
Shani	the malefic planet Saturn
shastras	scriptures
siddhis	supernormal powers

sindoor	red powder used to put a dot on forehead of married women
sita	furrow
soma	medicinal plant used in Vedic sacrifices
sthitha prajna	one of steady intellect (enlightened one)
stree rajya	land of women
surya namaskara	a yogic exercise in praise of the Sun God
suvarnakarani	herb which restores the colour of a dying person
swarupa	actual form
swayambhu murti	self-formed idol
tamas	one of the three strands of Nature, standing for inertia, dullness
tantras	scriptures giving certain esoteric rites
tantric	pertaining to *tantra*
tapas; tapasya	askesis; austerity
til	sesame
tulsi	the holy basil
tyaga	renunciation
udana	one of the five breaths
uttarayanam	six months of the year from January to June
vaal	tail
vadas	savoury doughnuts
vajra	thunderbolt
vanara	monkey
vata	wind
vayu	air
vedic	pertaining to the Vedas
vina	stringed instrument like a lute
vira bhava	hero's pose

vishalyakarani	magic herb
Vishnu Sahasranama	thousand names of Vishnu
vyakarana	text which explains the meaning of the Vedas
vyana	one of the five vital breaths
yaga; yajna	fire sacrifice
yajna kund	hollow in the ground in which fire is kindled for the sacrifice
yajnashala	the place where the (*yajna*) or sacrifice is conducted
yak	an animal found in Tibet
yaksha	celestial being; guardian of wealth
yantra	mystic geometric diagram
yoga	any activity which leads to union with the divine
yogasanas	physical postures which purify the body and mind
yogi	one who practises yoga; one who is in union with the divine
yogic	pertaining to yoga
yojana	measurement of distance
yogini	a female yogi
yuga	epoch

Mantra heenum, kriya heenum,
Bhakti heenum sureshwara,
Yad poojitam maya Deva,
Paripoornam tadastu me

"O Lord! I beg of you to accept and make perfect
This puja of mine, which is,
Devoid of proper chants, actions or devotion."

ॐ *Sri Hanumathe Namaha!*

NAMES OF HANUMAN

Hanuman	one who has controlled the mind one with a broken jaw
Mahavira	the great hero
Anjaneya	son of Anjana
Kesari Putra	son of Kesari
Vayu Putra	son of Vayu (Wind God)
Maruti	son of Marut (Wind God)
Kesari Nandana	Kesari's pet
Jitendriya	one who has controlled his senses
Sugriva Mitram	Sugriva's friend
Ramadasa	Rama's servant
Pranadeva	giver of breath (life)
Ramaduta	messenger of Rama
Sundara	beautiful
Pavana Putra	son of the Wind God
Sankata Mochana	dispeller of sorrow
Bajarangabali	strong as a thunderbolt
Shoora	the courageous one
Mahatman	the noble one
Bhaktavatsala	one who is kind to devotees
Mahatejasvin	one who is filled with spiritual lustre
Vatamaja	born of wind
Daityakulantaka	destroyer of the *rakshasa* clan
Lakshmana Pranadata	giver of life to Lakshmana
Kapindra	king of monkeys
Mahabala	one with extraordinary might

Rudrasya-soonu	son of Rudra (Shiva)
Virupa	strange-faced one
Uttaman	the noblest one
Sahasravadana	possessing thousand faces
Shubangana	having auspicious features
Veera	heroic one
Ramapriyan	beloved of Rama
Lokabandhu	relation of the world
Tapaswin	one who practises austerities
Bhima	one with a huge form
Shubham	auspicious one
Mangala Murti	the form of auspiciousness

ॐ *Sri Hanumathe Namaha!*

NAMES OF OTHER CHARACTERS

Agastya	great sage with divine powers
Agni	god of fire
Ahalya	wife of Sage Gautama
Ahiravana	sorceror son of Ravana
Akampana	name of a *rakshasa*
Aksha Kumara	Ravana's youngest son
Amabalika	celestial nymph
Anasuya	wife of Sage Atri
Angada	son of monkey king Vaali
Anjana	Hanuman's mother
Ananta	celestial serpent on which Vishnu sleeps
Arjuna	the middle one amongst the Pandavas
Aruna	charioteer of the sun god – Surya
Atikaya	one of Kumbhakarna's sons
Atri	great sage
Ayyappa	incarnation of Dharma Shasta
Bhadra	Rama's friend
Bharadwaja	great sage who lived in Prayaga
Bharata	Rama's brother
Brahma	the creator in the trinity
Brihaspati	preceptor of the gods
Bhima	the strong man of the Pandavas
Dasaratha	Rama's father
Devi	goddess

Devantaka	one of Kumbhakarna's sons
Dharmashasta	son of Shiva and Vishnu
Dhumraksha	Ravana's general
Dhushana	Ravana's general
Dundubhi	buffalo demon
Durvasa	sage noted for his bad temper
Ganesha	elephant-headed son of Shiva
Ganga	the holy river
Garuda	eagle vehicle of Lord Vishnu
Gautama	great sage; husband of Ahalya
Hanuman	son of the Wind God
Hayagriva	horse-faced incarnation of Vishnu
Hema	Mandodari's mother
Himavan	king of the Himalayas
Indra	king of the gods
Indrajit	Ravana's eldest son
Jambavan	king of the bears
Jambumali	son of Ravana's general
Janaka	Sita's father
Janaki	Janaka's daughter – Sita
Jatayu	eagle who was Rama's friend
Jayanta	Indra's son who came in the form of a crow
Kaikeyi	Dasaratha's wife; Bharata's mother
Kaala	the spirit of Time
Kaali	horrific aspect of the goddess
Kalanemi	*rakshasa* who tried to obstruct Hanuman
Kampan	author of the *Ramayana* in Tamil

Kartikeya	Shiva's son; general of the gods
Kausalya	wife of Dasaratha; Rama's mother
Kesari	Hanuman's monkey father
Khara	*rakshasa*
Kunjara	Anjana's father
Krishna	supreme incarnation of Vishnu
Kubera	god of wealth; Ravana's step-brother
Kumbhakarna	Ravana's brother known for his enormous body and appetite
Kusha	one of the twin sons of Rama
Kuvachana	a man who had insulted his ancestors
Lakshmana	Rama's brother
Lakshmi	goddess of wealth and auspiciousness
Lankini	guardian of Lanka
Lava	twin son of Rama
Madhavi	goddess of the earth
Madhvacharya	founder of the Dwaita school of Vedanta
Mahakaala	the great god of death, Shiva
Mahakaali	the great Kaali; horrific form of the Devi
Mahaparshava	Ravana's trusted general
Maheswara	the great god; name of Shiva
Mahiravana	sorcerer son of Ravana; king of the nether world
Maithili	Sita – princess of Mithila
Makaradwaja	Hanuman's son born of a crocodile
Mandavya	great sage
Mandodari	chief wife of Ravana
Manthara	hunch-back maid of Kaikeyi
Manu Swayambhu	progenitor of the world

Maricha	*rakshasa* who enticed Sita in the form of a golden deer
Matali	Indra's charioteer
Matanga	great sage
Mayan	architect of the demons
Mayavi	*rakshasa* who fought with Vaali
Meghanatha	eldest son of Ravana, later known as Indrajit
Mohini	alluring form of Vishnu as a woman
Muruga	another name of Kartikeya
Nala	monkey who designed the bridge to Lanka
Nandi	bull vehicle of Shiva
Narada	celestial sage noted for his mischief making ways
Narantaka	one of Kumbhakarna's sons
Narayana	the primeval being who slumbers on the waters
Narasimha	fourth incarnation of Vishnu
Nila	another monkey who helped to design the bridge
Parashurama	sixth incarnation of Vishnu
Panavati	embodiment of baneful astrological influences
Parvati	wife of Shiva; daughter of Himavan
Prahastha	commander-in-chief of Ravana's army
Prahlada	demon boy who was a great devotee of Vishnu
Punchikasthala	celestial nymph who became Hanuman's mother Anjana

Raghava	another name of Rama
Raghu	an ancestor of Rama
Rahu	malignant planet which eclipses the sun
Rama	seventh incarnation of Vishnu
Ramachandra	another name for Rama
Ravana	king of Lanka and of the *rakshasas*
Riksha	the very first *vanara* (monkey)
Rudra	fierce aspect of Shiva
Rumi	wife of Sugriva
Sagara	name of the monarch of the ocean
Sampati	eagle brother of Jatayu
Sanat Kumara	one of the four boy sages
Saraswati	goddess of the arts
Satabali	white-furred bear
Shabari	old female ascetic
Shambasaadan	*rakshasa* who tried to entice Anjana
Shani	Saturn – the malefic planet
Shatrugna	Rama's brother and Lakshmana's twin
Shilada	a sage
Shilavati	a very chaste woman
Shiva	the destroying aspect of the trinity
Shurpaneka	Ravana's sister
Sita	Rama's wife; princess of Videha
Skanda	Kartikeya; general of the gods
Suka	Ravana's minister
Sugriva	monkey king; brother of Vaali
Sulochana	Indrajit's wife
Sumantra	charioteer of Dasaratha
Sumitra	mother of Lakshmana and Shatrugna
Surya	Sun God
Sushena	1. father-in-law of Sugriva 2. Ravana's court physician

Swaminathan	another name for Kartikeya
Swayamprabha	nymph who was guarding the cave
Tara	Vaali's wife
Trijata	*rakshasi* who helped Sita
Trisira	one of Kumbhakarna's sons
Tulsidas	author of *Ramacharitamanas*
Tulsiram	previous name of Tulsidas
Ugratapas	leper husband of Shilavati
Vaali	monkey king; Sugriva's brother
Vaidehi	Sita; princess of Videha
Vaishravas	Ravana's father
Vajradamshtra	name of *rakshasa*
Valmiki	author of the *Ramayana*
Varaha	the second avatara of Vishnu as a boar
Varuna	Lord of the waters
Vasishta	great sage; guru of clan of Ikshvaku
Vayu	Wind God; Hanuman's father
Vedavati	name of Sita in a previous incarnation
Vibhishana	noble *rakshasa*; half brother of Ravana
Vinata	Sugriva's general
Virupaksha	one of Ravana's generals
Vishnu	the preserver in the Trinity
Vishwakarma	architect of the gods
Vishwamitra	the royal sage
Vrishakapi	monkey god mentioned in the Vedas
Vyasa	author of the *Mahabharata*
Yama	god of Death
Yayati	king of Kashi
Yudhistira	eldest of the Pandavas

'Karacharanakritam vakkayajam karmajam va,
Shravana nayanajam va manasam vaaparatam,
Vihitam-avihitam va sarvametad kshamaswa,
Jaya jaya karunambde Sri Mahadeva Shambho"

Hail to Thee O thou Great Lord,
Pray forgive all the mistakes I have made,
Through my hands, feet, words or actions,
Through my ears, eyes, mind or anything else,
By right means or wrong,
For thou art the Ocean of Compassion.

ॐ *Sri Hanumathe Namaha!*

BIBLIOGRAPHY

Gita Press Gorakhpur translation of the *Valmiki Ramayana*
Growse, F.S., *Eternal Ramayana*; *Ramayana* of Tulsidas.
Parvathy Bai, *Hanuman Purana* (Malayalam)
Philip, Lutgendorf, *Hanuman's Tale*

ॐ *Sri Hanumathe Namaha!*